TROUT
TACKLE
Part Two

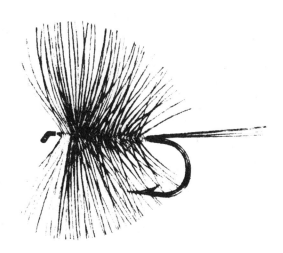

BOOKS BY ERNEST SCHWIEBERT

Matching the Hatch
Salmon of the World
Remembrances of Rivers Past
Nymphs
Trout
Death of a Riverkeeper

TROUT PAPERBACK EDITIONS

Trout Strategies
Trout Tackle • Part One

"Ernest Schwiebert's *Trout* is a masterpiece, the most useful and inclusive study ever written on a timeless subject noted for classical and scholarly works. Worldwide in scope, brilliantly researched, beautifully written, illustrated by the author with hundreds of drawings and color paintings, Schwiebert's *Trout* is destined to remain *the* great reference work for generations of trout fishermen to come." —A. J. McClane

"A stupendous achievement ... unparalleled and unapproached by any writer." —Arnold Gingrich

"For several weeks I have been sampling and savoring it the way one samples and savors the contents of the pastry cart at a great French restaurant. One cannot consume every calorific delicacy at a single sitting. One cannot digest the contents of Ernest Schwiebert's 1,745-page masterpiece in a month of sittings. I suspect, indeed, that every fact known to man about trout and trout fishing can be found therein.... Ernest Schwiebert's *Trout* will remain a classic so long as a single trout survives in the last clear-running stream." —Les Line

"Cold numbers aside, *Trout* is a prodigious landmark in the literature of angling. It is more than a book about fishing. It is *the* book about fishing for *trout*, which means it is about insects and rocks, about rivers and fine bamboo. It is about good fellowship, sturdy adventures, and a hundred other experiences that make time worth wasting. It is about how life evolves, sustains, and ends—and it is about how life may be craftsman-copied through delicate creations of marabou, mallard, and hare. *Trout* does not mark the arrival of Ernest Schwiebert; it seals his place in the fisherman's pantheon. It retires his fly rod. For it is hard to imagine a more rigorous and loving examination of why something happens—or doesn't—when a man throws a calculation of feathers at a fish." —Lee Eisenberg

"Certain to stand as a landmark book in the history of angling literature, *Trout* is Schwiebert's crowning achievement and firmly establishes his place in the firmament of the immortals of angling." —William Kaufmann

Ernest Schwiebert has travelled the trout fishing world with his flies and paint boxes and tackle for nearly forty years. Fishing and collecting fly hatches evolved into his first book, *Matching the Hatch*, in 1955. It has been printed and reprinted more than a dozen times. His portfolio of 30 paintings titled *Salmon of the World* was published in a limited edition of 750 sets in 1970. His collection of streamside stories, *Remembrances of Rivers Past*, was published in 1972, and his major book on stream entomology, *Nymphs*, was published in 1973. Schwiebert's magnum opus is his two-volume *Trout*, from which this work is drawn. Published in 1978, fifteen years in its planning, writing, and preparation of extensive illustrations, *Trout* is nearly 1,800 pages in length, including fifteen color plates of flies and trout species and more than 1,000 black-and-white drawings and diagrams. Its first edition was sold out shortly after publication, and a second edition is planned for Fall 1984. Schwiebert's most recent book is *Death of a Riverkeeper*, which appeared in 1980. Like his earlier *Remembrances of Rivers Past*, it is a gathering of fishing stories from several countries.

Ernest Schwiebert (pronounced Schwee-bert) is an architect and planner who has played a major role in several famous projects around the world. He holds degrees from Ohio State and Princeton, where he completed both the master's program and doctoral studies in art history, as well as architecture and planning. Schwiebert practiced architecture and planning for many years with a major firm in New York. Twelve years ago, he founded the design and planning group called Ecosystemics, and has provided consulting services to the national park systems of Chile, Argentina, and the United States.

Profiles of his several careers have appeared in *The New York Times*, *The Washington Post*, and *The Philadelphia Inquirer*, and in *Life*, *Esquire*, and *Town & Country*. His two-volume *Trout* was recently honored by the White House, when it was chosen as a gift-of-state to the Prime Minister of Australia.

When not fishing or working in some remote corner of the world, Schwiebert lives and works in Princeton, New Jersey.

TROUT

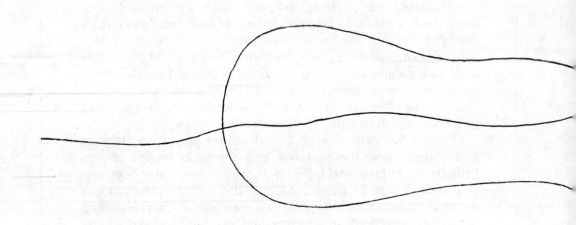

ERNEST SCHWIEBERT

Illustrated by the author

TACKLE
Part Two

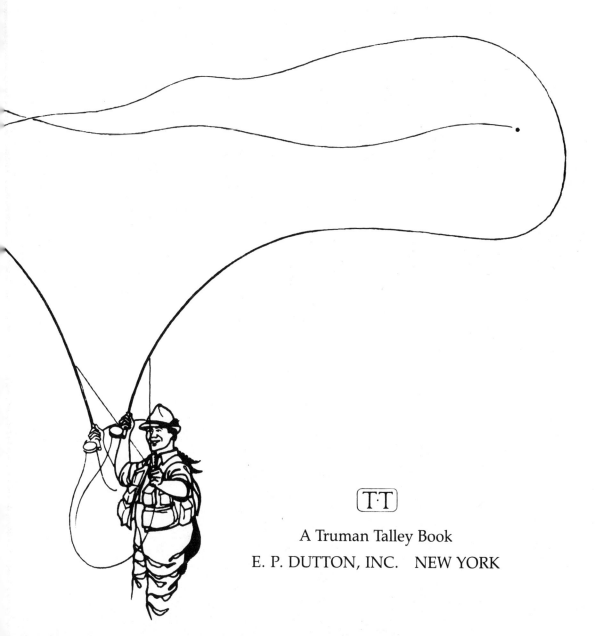

T·T

A Truman Talley Book

E. P. DUTTON, INC.   NEW YORK

Front cover illustrations, left to right: 1874, Hiram Leonard rod, in the collection of Gary Howells; 1935, James Payne rod, in the collection of the late Harry Darbee; 1945, Lew Stoner Winston, in the collection of Doug Merrick; 1955, Everett Garrison rod, in the collection of the late Sparse Grey Hackle; 1970, Wes Jordan Orvis rod, in the collection of Leigh Perkins; 1980, Thomas & Thomas Sans Pareil rod, in the collection of John Malcolm Fraser, presented to the prime minister of Australia by the White House.

Published by Truman Talley Books • E. P. Dutton, Inc., 2 Park Avenue, New York, N.Y. 10016

Published simultaneously in Canada by Fitzhenry & Whiteside, Limited, Toronto

Copyright © 1978, 1984 by Ernest Schwiebert

Library of Congress Cataloging in Publication Data
(Revised for vol. 2)

Schwiebert, Ernest George.
Trout tackle.

"A Truman Talley book."
Drawn from Ernest Schwiebert's
two-volume Trout, published by E. P. Dutton, Inc., in 1978.
Includes indexes.
1. Trout fishing—Collected works. 2. Fishing tackle—
Collected works. I. Title.
SH687.S253   1983   799.1'755   83-14190
ISBN 0-525-48082-X (pbk. : v. 1)
ISBN 0-525-48107-9 (pbk. : v. 2)

Manufactured in the United States of America

10 9 8 7 6 5 4 3 2 1

CONTENTS

TROUT
TACKLE
Part Two

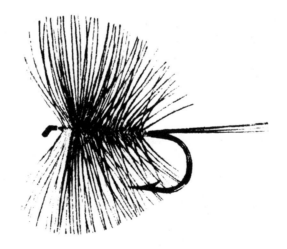

1. The Iconography of the Split-Cane Rod

The first really fine fly rod that I ever saw was an eight-foot Payne owned by a physician in Chicago. It had been built by Edward Payne, one of the original apprentice disciples of Hiram Leonard in Bangor, and had been refinished by James Payne many years later. Their names meant nothing to an eight-year-old who was still more interested in catching fish than in the subtle rituals and liturgies of fishing. However, the craftsmanship and beauty of the rod were obvious, although I found it strange that the doctor loved his gleaming four-ounce Payne so much that he utterly refused to fish with it. The old man laid it reverently on his red felt desktop in the lamplight and looked at the exquisite rod for hours. It obviously had the overtones of some religious relic.

It would be many years later before I fully understood that a skilled fisherman did have almost religious feelings about his tackle. It had great beauty and fished with elegance, and had the votive powers to reawaken memories of rivers past. It was my first exposure to the iconography of the split-cane rod.

The Payne was kept in a saddle-leather case, its heavy stitching frayed and pale against the tube and cap. There was a leather strap attached to the case that slipped through two loops on the cap and fastened with a small leather-covered buckle. Both the case and its cap were scuffed and worn, smelling faintly like a fine saddle or a favorite pair of English riding boots, but their patina was only a prelude to the sensory riches they contained.

The first impression was the faintly musty smell of the original poplin bag that held the rod, plus the rich perfume of the tung-oil varnish, its gleaming mirror flawlessly smooth and perfect. The delicate silk wrappings

1

were a pale brown that almost matched the color of the bamboo itself, and they were embellished with ornamental wraps of yellow. It was a three-piece rod with a classic medium Payne action. The German silver ferrules were beautiful, and each female socket was protected with a perfectly fitted German silver plug. There were no silk wrappings except at the guides, ferrules, grip check, and tip tops. The guides were exquisite English tungsten steel in a bronzed finish, while the stripping guide and tip tops were entirely tungsten. The grip was beautifully shaped of handcut specie cork, remarkably solid and free of checks and markings. It was the classic Payne-style grip, slightly flared at the butt to conceal a reel cap inside the cork. The reel-seat filler was darkly grained American walnut, and its reversed fittings gleamed like fine jewelry. The locking threads were perfectly machined and specially designed to inhibit binding or jamming. Although the heavy locking hood was made of high-quality aluminum alloy, its weight and elegant knurling and richness seemed more like fine sterling—as beautifully conceived and executed as a silver piece displayed on velvet in the windows at Cartier or Tiffany.

The doctor assembled the rod in his library, hovering protectively while I flexed it hesitantly. Its action was delicate and smooth, with a sweetness and elusive poetry impossible to describe, like the subtle quality of a fine Burgundy or a seasoned full-bodied Bordeaux.

Such perfection is rare, and it is easy to understand the half-religious feelings of a fisherman for his trout rods. Although salmon tackle has similar overtones, it is unquestionably the light split-bamboo instruments designed for trout that evoke the most reverence. Fly rods from the skilled hands of artisans like Garrison, Payne, Halstead, Gillum, Orvis, Leonard, Winston, Young, Edwards, Thomas, or Howells are probably more cherished than the equipment used in any other sport.

Fine guns are perhaps their only rival. Certainly an elegantly stocked big-game rifle, with its raised comb and cheekpiece and gleaming engine-turned bolt, is beautifully designed and made. The simple beauty of a fine double shotgun is probably a better comparison, particularly the traditional English-style with its slender stock and sleekly tapered forepiece, elegant and totally devoid of decorations or embellishments. Such guns were first conceived in the shop of Joseph Manton, who set the classic imagery that has governed double shotguns ever since, just as Hiram Leonard first worked out the technology and esthetics that evolved into the modern fly rod more than a century ago.

Shotguns and split-cane rods have much in common. Both achieve their functional purpose afield, perfectly attuned to the grouse covers and bright gravel riffles of the Catskills. Both are almost living extensions of the body and the senses when they are skillfully used. Yet the split-cane rod is alive, flexing gracefully in its response to the touch and will of its owner. It has its own singular character, yet it fully accommodates itself to the character and moods of anyone who fishes it. The favorite trout rod is a constant friend. Trout seasons are longer than bird seasons, and a woodcock

DANIEL BREMAN ROD IN THE COLLECTION OF THE ANGLERS' CLUB OF NEW YORK

FARLOW   1845   FIVE-PIECE GREENHEART

JAMES HENSHALL ROD IN THE COLLECTION OF THE ANGLERS' CLUB OF NEW YORK

SAMUEL PHILLIPPE   1847   FOUR-PIECE BAMBOO

hunter will fire his precious Fox or Greener or Purdey only a few times compared with the thousands of casts delivered each day astream. Perhaps only an exquisite violin is equally alive, its fragile wood vibrating in concert with its strings. The violin is beautiful too, particularly the flawless instruments conceived by craftsmen like Antonio Stradivari and Giuseppe Guarnieri, who were the apogee of the legendary School of Cremona. Like a fine split-bamboo rod, their work probably represents the ultimate equilibrium of utility and craftsmanship and esthetic qualities.

Leonard Wright caught something of this subtle mixture between poetry and function in his essay on bamboo rods for the *American Sportsman Treasury*, adding his observations on the stream itself as a fitting place to fish a particularly beautiful rod:

> The trout stream is set apart from the other scenes of sport with its hemlock and rhododendron, willow and warbler, the play of sunlight on a riffle. Many fine authors have tried to capture this magic, but it simply beggars description. One great naturalist described a trout stream as the artery of the forest. It is that and more. It is also the life blood of the trout fisherman.
>
> In this setting and in this spirit, a rod becomes far more than just a tool for casting. And fortunately, this bond between rod and man is an especially happy one. The experienced angler seldom blames his rod. In fact, he is liable to consider it perfection.
>
> This happiness with things as they are can be observed in almost any fine tackle store. There are seldom requests for unconventional rod actions or special embellishments. If you examine a sampling of rods by the finest makers, you will see that they are almost uniformly modest in appearance. The cane glows warmly through the clear varnish. The reel seat is harmonious butternut or walnut. Windings will usually be some neutral hue. This is the quiet beauty of the partridge, not the gaudy beauty of the cock pheasant.

Yet a knowledgeable fisherman knows the fingerprints with which each maker signs his work. Silk wrappings are signatures in both color and character, and in their absence or embellishments. The windings on a Powell are typical, since those with semihollow construction were always identified by a distinguishing mark in the silk: narrow wraps of white and black just ahead of the cork grip, while the solid rods had a single color at the keeper ring. The grips are another hallmark. Even when the fittings and silk wrappings are identical, an expert can separate a rod built by old Edward Payne from the work of his son, since James Payne preferred a slightly more slender grip. Cane construction is often a clue, particularly in the placement of the nodes. The nodes of an artist like Everett Garrison is unique, since the graining of the same node in the same face of each tip clearly reveals its origins in adjacent strips of the original cane.

The color of the cane is another fingerprint of its original maker.

ROBERT WHITMAN ROD IN THE COLLECTION OF THE MUSEUM OF AMERICAN FLY FISHING

DOROTHY TEMPLE FULLER ROD IN THE COLLECTION OF THE ANGLERS' CLUB OF NEW YORK

DOROTHY TEMPLE FULLER ROD IN THE COLLECTION OF THE ANGLERS' CLUB OF NEW YORK

FARLOW   1851   THREE-PIECE BETHABARA

THADDEUS NORRIS   1853   THREE-PIECE SNAKEWOOD

THADDEUS NORRIS   1859   THREE-PIECE LANCEWOOD

Garrison and Leonard and Winston pride themselves on the pale natural color of their bamboo. Gillum cane is darker, a rich medium brown, like the work of Payne and Howells. Gillum and Garrison both used dark modern adhesives which make their glue lines clearly visible. Orvis and Halstead rods are often darker still, while Thomas chose to work in both natural cane and a rich chocolate color. Paul Young was a fanatic about flame-tempering his bamboo, and his rods reveal that penchant in the contrast between their pale nodes and almost carbonized surfaces.

The number of split-cane strips is also revealing, since most split-cane rods employ the conventional six-strip hexagonal construction. Most other systems varied from three to twelve strips and were soon abandoned since they either failed to improve performance or radically multiplied the work involved in building rods. However, William Edwards continued to make his four-strip quadrate rods until his recent death, and a five-strip rod is usually the work of Robert Crompton, Nathaniel Uslan, or Frank Wire. These three remain the leading partisans of five-strip theory.

The perspective of history tells us that split-bamboo rods evolved slowly over thousands of years. Chinese fishermen used rods of thornwood and natural bamboo centuries before Christ, and *The Treatyse of Fysshynge wyth an Angle* tells us that Dame Juliana Berners preferred a rod with butt section of hazel, willow or aspen and a tip section fashioned of blackthorn, crabtree, medlar or juniper. Almost two centuries later, Charles Cotton recommended a Yorkshire rod between fifteen and eighteen feet. Cotton favored a butt section of fir with a tip section of thornwood, juniper, or yew. Across the next 150 years, English rodmakers dominated the art, and their Empire provided them with an astonishing spectrum of exotic woods for rod building.

Craftsmen experimented tirelessly with ash, basswood, hornbeam, barberry, cedar, blue mahoe, osage orange, degma, lancewood, bethabara, greenheart, lemonwood, yew and American bamboo. Hickory had briefly dominated the trade after its introduction into American rod building in 1660, although the nineteenth-century craftsmen in the United States soon experimented widely.

Thaddeus Norris published his *American Angler's Book* in 1864, and included both a discussion of contemporary rod building and a happy recommendation for carrying a wicker creel generous enough to hold his clothing, catch, and a bottle of fine claret. His favorite rod consisted of a white-ash butt section, a middle joint of ironwood, and tip section of four-strip bamboo derived from the inventive mind of Samuel Phillippe. Norris later manufactured Phillippe-type bamboo rods in Philadelphia, and his firm was one of the pioneers in American rodmaking.

Genio Scott added his *Fishing in American Waters* to the literature of the sport in 1873, providing his observations on the evolving technology of the fly rod. It is clear that split-cane construction had not yet triumphed. Scott recommends a rod butt of ash, lancewood for the middle joint, and a split-bamboo tip section. Other anglers of that period advocated rods of maple, ash, and lancewood. Spliced lancewood and bamboo hybrids were also popular, and Henry Wells strongly recommended rods of ash and lancewood for trout fishing. His book *Fly Rods and Fly Tackle* was published in 1885, and it was quickly acclaimed as the definitive work of its day. Wells argued that greenheart was still the premier wood for fly rods in his time, although he also liked bethabara, snakewood, Cuban mahoe, ironwood, hickory, beefwood, paddlewood, and shadblow. Other acceptable materials listed in *Fly Rods and Fly Tackle* were exotic woods like pyengadu, chow, pingow, ironbark, kranji, purpleheart, dagame, and jucaro prieto. It is interesting to observe that several American builders like Phillippe, Green, Norris, Murphy, and the celebrated Hiram Leonard had all been making split-cane rods for years when Wells published his book, and superb Murphy and Leonard designs were available to American fishermen as early as 1873.

However, the triumph of split bamboo came gradually. Spliced-cane rods had a minor place in the price lists of John Krider that were published at Philadelphia in 1878. Dame, Stoddard & Kendall of Boston still listed only lancewood and greenheart rods in their catalogue of the same period. Thomas Chubb was a major manufacturer of fishing tackle in 1882 with a surprisingly large plant in Vermont. Although his catalogue advertised bamboo fly rods, its principal emphasis still lay with ash and lancewood. The Orvis catalogue published in 1884 included rods of ash, lancewood, hornbeam, and split bamboo alike. Chubb published another catalogue in 1890. It still included rods of ash, lancewood, and greenheart, but it gave a place of growing prominence to bamboo construction.

William Mills & Son was clearly the watershed in American triumph of split cane. Mills had become sole agents for Hiram Leonard in 1877, three years after Leonard had perfected his six-strip rods, and he soon purchased an interest in the rod company. Mills took controlling interest in the Leonard concern a few years later and in 1881, moved its rodmaking subsidiary and Leonard himself to Central Valley, a few miles up the Hudson from New York. The Mills catalogue published in 1894 still offered rods of greenheart and lancewood, but its emphasis clearly lay with cane. There were four-piece cane rods with independent handles and three-piece models with cane-wound grips. The famous Catskill series of Leonard rods had already evolved, with nine-and-a-half-foot models weighing four and five-eighths to three and one-eighth ounces. These rods were awarded a special gold medal at London in 1883, leading Thomas Bate Mills to propose the still lighter Catskill Fairy. It was a slender three-piece rod of eight and a half feet, and it weighed a remarkable two ounces. The catalogue also illustrated the Leonard ferrule patents of 1875 and 1878. These introduced a waterproof cup inside the female socket and the split ferrule that eased the transfer of stress between the metal and the cane in casting. It is obvious that fishermen were first wary of split-cane construction on esthetic grounds, simply because they had learned to like the appearance of round fly rods, and found the hexagonal bamboo ugly. The Mills catalogue included these comments on such arguments:

> It had become evident to us that many parties, in considering this question of round rods, have in many cases quite overlooked the maker in considering the principle.
>
> It should be borne in mind that the great bulk of round rods [we think we can safely say nine-tenths] were made by Mr. Leonard, and it was on the merits of the rods made by him that the excellence of split bamboo was first established. But Mr. Leonard was the first to make a six-strip rod and leave the outside hexagonal; in his increased experience on this work, and after severely testing the hexagonal rod, he has been manufacturing them almost exclusively for the past twelve years, and recommends his hexagonal rod as being far superior to any round rod, which we most heartily endorse.

The Leonard waterproof ferrule was an important development in a time when split cane was assembled with fish or animal adhesives, because it protected the integrity of its laminations. The screw-locking reel seat was also a Leonard innovation, as was the split-type ferrule that permitted the smooth transfer of casting stress across the rim of the metal. But perhaps more important was the growing awareness that it was the power fibers in the outer layers of bamboo that provide its primary resiliency and strength. With rods of more than six strips, these power fibers are considerably reduced, while the glue surfaces and the deadening effects of the adhesive itself is greatly multiplied. Leonard was also aware that in delicate rod calibrations, the cane strips in the tip sections are reduced to fragile shavings. There was often more glue than cane. Once the importance of the power fibers was understood, making his hexagonal rods round in a lathe was also foolish, since it completely sacrificed them at the corners and left only a fraction of the original enamel in each face of the finished rod. His understanding of rod dynamics, his innovative fittings, and his understanding of the attributes of bamboo clearly establish Hiram Leonard as the true father of the modern split-cane rod.

However, its origins lie almost a half century earlier when rod building was dominated by lemonwood, lancewood, and greenheart. Lemonwood, the lovely *Pittosporum eugenioides* plant, is found in New Zealand, and has relatively light weight, good resiliency, fine resistance to moisture, and a straight, densely formed graining. Lancewood was largely harvested in British Guiana, coming from the graceful *Oxanda lanceolata* tree, and it boasts similar qualities. Short of split cane in its modern square, pentagonal and hexagonal construction, greenheart was probably the premier wood for rod building in the nineteenth century. Greenheart is finely textured, surprisingly heavy, and is remarkably resilient and strong, having about twice the bending strength of select white oak. It is classified as *Nectandra rodioei* and is also predominantly harvested in British Guiana. Greenheart

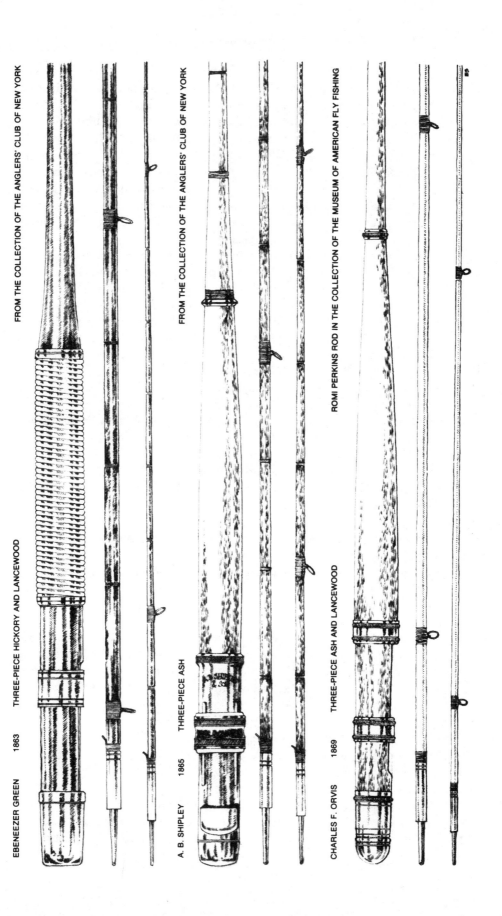

EBENEEZER GREEN   1863   THREE-PIECE HICKORY AND LANCEWOOD

FROM THE COLLECTION OF THE ANGLERS' CLUB OF NEW YORK

A. B. SHIPLEY   1865   THREE-PIECE ASH

FROM THE COLLECTION OF THE ANGLERS' CLUB OF NEW YORK

CHARLES F. ORVIS   1869   THREE-PIECE ASH AND LANCEWOOD

ROMI PERKINS ROD IN THE COLLECTION OF THE MUSEUM OF AMERICAN FLY FISHING

works easily under a semicircular rodmaking plane, but cross-grain work with a lathe is difficult. It can be dried to twelve percent moisture content, and weighs between sixty-five and sixty-eight pounds per cubic foot. It is dense and strongly resistant to water rot and fungus. The color of its heartwood varies from olive to almost black with pale, veinlike patterns. Although these dark heartwoods were once considered the best material for rods, the pale olive greenheart is equally suited. Rodmakers also used *Piptodena africana,* the golden brown African greenheart, in many antique rods. Jamaican greenheart was also popular, and the heartwood of *Ceanothus chlorozylon* is a strong yellowish green material.

Greenheart was popular with nineteenth-century rodmakers, particularly in the United Kingdom. It makes up into a heavy, relatively slow rod ideally suited to wet-fly work for both salmon and trout. Its rhythms are ponderous, making false casting relatively difficult, but its character is perfectly adapted to the classic Spey and switch-cast techniques. Some of the old greenhearts were truly fine wet-fly rods, but with the rise of the dry-fly method on the Hampshire chalkstreams, their popularity rapidly declined among skilled trout fishermen.

However, greenheart has not suffered total oblivion in modern times. Last year there were many slender greenhearts in evidence during the Irish mayfly season on Lough Derg, twenty miles above Galway, dapping live *Ephemera* flies downwind on delicate blow lines of silk. Some boats in the sheltered bays at Oughterard bristled with archaic greenheart and lancewood rods as long as seventeen and eighteen feet.

It's almost funny, Clare De Bergh laughed. *Some of the larger boats will look remarkably like hedgehogs!*

This year on the classic Balmoral water of the Dee, my friends Jock Ropner and Angela Farrar still fished beautiful spliced greenhearts made in the workrooms of Sharpe's at Aberdeen, partly from a sense of tradition and partly because of their Spey-casting qualities on several beats. Their rods would clearly perform feats impossible with cane, on famous pools like Punt and Laundry near Balmoral Castle, and on the famous Cairnton water downstream at Banchory.

Snakewood was also used in many American rods well into the nineteenth century, and there was a famous Samuel Phillippe rod built as late as 1876 which combined eight milled strips, four of snakewood and four of Calcutta in a handsome pattern of alternating woods. Snakewood is the *Moraceae piratinera* widely distributed along the northeast coast of South America. It can be air-dried to approximately twelve percent moisture content and is dense enough to weigh as much as eighty to ninety pounds per cubic foot. Its sapwood is pale and unsuitable for rods. The heartwood is a rich brown marked with darker graining, with a dense, relatively straight grain that works easily.

These materials were all available in lengths between four and six feet, that naturally evolved into rods between twelve and eighteen feet and weighed more than a pound. Such woods were hand-ripped into long

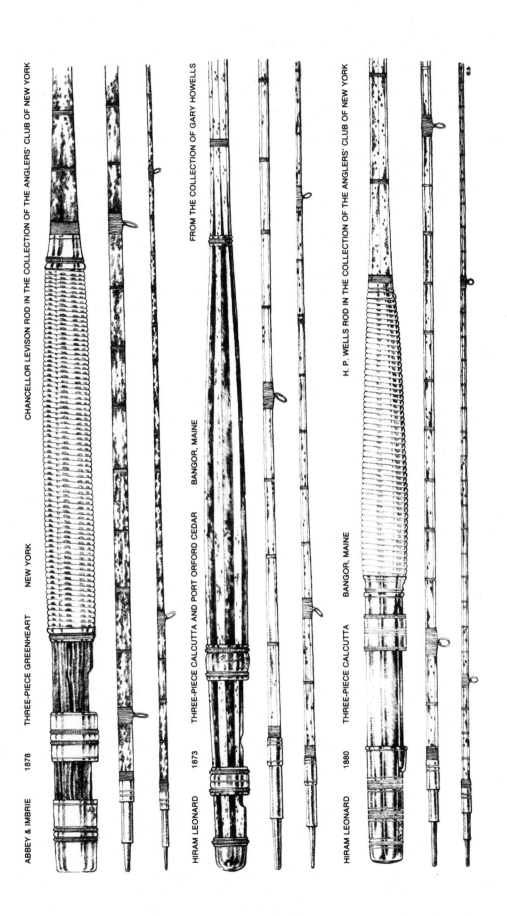

ABBEY & IMBRIE   1878   THREE-PIECE GREENHEART   NEW YORK

CHANCELLOR LEVISON ROD IN THE COLLECTION OF THE ANGLERS' CLUB OF NEW YORK

HIRAM LEONARD   1873   THREE-PIECE CALCUTTA AND PORT ORFORD CEDAR   BANGOR, MAINE

FROM THE COLLECTION OF GARY HOWELLS

HIRAM LEONARD   1880   THREE-PIECE CALCUTTA   BANGOR, MAINE

H. P. WELLS ROD IN THE COLLECTION OF THE ANGLERS' CLUB OF NEW YORK

splines ranging from one-quarter inch to one inch square. These roughcut sections were seldom straight and were hung either in a drying kiln or a warm, relatively dry place for several months.

The calibrations specified by Thaddeus Norris in his *American Angler's Book* are typical of American rod design in the period before the Civil War. His favorite rod measured an inch along its first eight inches, tapering to fifteen thirty-seconds of an inch eighteen inches above the butt. Two feet from the butt it calibrated twelve thirty-seconds of an inch, and eleven thirty-seconds at the first ferrule, forty-eight inches above the grip. The taper had dropped to nine thirty-seconds at the six-foot point, and at the second ferrule it measured seven thirty-seconds of an inch, eight feet above its butt. Ten feet out the rod had reached four thirty-seconds and tapered to a surprisingly delicate one-sixteenth of an inch at its tip guide. Such delicate tip calibrations made these solid wood rods extremely fragile, far more susceptible to breakage than laminated bamboo.

Henry Wells described the details of fabricating such rods in his *Fly Rods and Fly Tackle*, recommending a series of thin brass templates for monitoring rod diameters at each foot of its length. Each template was a semicircle cut in one-thirty-second-of-an-inch plate, placed over the partially tapered section and slipped carefully toward the butt. When a template failed to reach its checkpoint, more wood needed planing to hold a relatively straight taper between calibrations.

The semicircular planes were relatively simple to make. Cutters of the proper diameter were fashioned from steel of blade quality, and were fitted into planing blocks as a ninety-degree angle. These planing blocks, which fitted comfortably into the hands, were rectilinear and milled with a precise, semicircular groove on their working faces.

Greenheart, snakewood, lemonwood, and lancewood all worked easily once they were properly cured and straightened. The planing blocks readily achieved the proper tapers and were useful in making minor corrections. The splines were first planed to a rough approximation of their final tapers. Properly aged woods planed with surprising precision and ease, and amateurs flourished throughout the greenheart era, its techniques being better suited to handwork than machine tools. Yet however difficult it may have been to cast beyond thirty or forty feet with these rods, they clearly performed as superb tools for manipulating a three-fly cast.

Modern fishermen who attempt to fish a trout rod of greenheart or lancewood are invariably disappointed and surprised. Typical trout rods measured ten to twelve feet and weighed between ten and thirteen ounces. Such rods were so heavy that William Mills & Sons neglected to mention their weight in the catalogue of 1894 because their split-cane Leonards were so much lighter. Surprisingly, when such a rod is assembled and strung with a matching line of silk it can be bent into a perfect semicircle. Its tip will flex down smoothly until it reaches the level of the handle, although it will not bend back to touch the handle without fracture. It is almost impossible to flex the butt sections of ash or hickory or maple unless they are assembled into a whole rod. Yet with a relatively light casting load, these butt joints bend freely, accepting the loads from the middle and tip joints like a living part of the entire rod. Although they are rather heavy, and badly balanced by modern standards, these antique wood rods produce a casting action that is surprisingly whippy and soft.

Although casts longer than fifty feet were virtually beyond reach and popping off flies was a continual hazard, it was possible to propel remarkable roll casts with such rods. Controlling fly swing and mending line—both primary techniques of wet-fly tactics—were accomplished far more easily with these supple rods longer than ten feet. And the Spey cast, which lifts the flies from the bottom of its downstream swing to a fresh entry directly across the current in a single rolling twist, is completely impossible with our fashionably shorter modern tackle.

These antique rods of exotic woods were unquestionably more than the primitive tools of a handicraft culture. It is foolish to assume that their owners were merely marking time until the appearance and development of split bamboo. They fished the wet fly both downwind and downstream with virtually no false casting, and their rods performed beautifully.

The origins of split-cane construction are clouded in controversy, with British partisans arguing for its invention in the United Kingdom and Americans fiercely claiming credit for the United States. History tells us that both positions are based on considerable fact. The case clearly hinges on what is meant by the origins of the split-cane methods. Mere rending of the raw bamboo, without regard for the placement and role of the bamboo power fibers under stress, unquestionably evolved among the bowmakers of England. Both four-strip and six-strip construction, using Calcutta cane worked into round cross sections, and the later hexagonal sections that preserved the power fibers intact are clearly American inventions.

James Chetham mentions building rods by sawing and planing wood in *The Angler's Vade Mecum*, first published in London in 1681. Chetham actually recommends using a bowmaker for building laminated rods, although bamboo was clearly not the material being split and assembled into fishing rods, since tip sections of natural, unsplit bamboo were still in use early in the nineteenth century. Alfred Ronalds describes using a bamboo tip in his *Fly-Fisher's Entomology*, which appeared in 1836, but there is strong evidence that his tip sections were still unsplit cane. History also tells us that similar rods of raw bamboo were used in Chinese fishing thousands of years ago, during the Chou Dynasty.

R. B. Marston pointed to *Blaine's Encyclopaedia Of Rural Sports*, which mentioned split-bamboo construction in its section on fishing rods in 1840. That historical footnote seems to prove that the basic concept of rending and laminating cane first appeared in England. No details concerning the techniques of such split-bamboo work were included. Edward Fitzgibbon clarified this puzzle in his *Handbook of Angling*, written seven years later, when he described a three-strip rod fashioned of bamboo. Charles Bowness of Temple Bar in London was its maker, and Fitzgibbon clearly states that his rod had been made several years before his book was written. William Little was another London tacklemaker mentioned in the *Handbook of Angling*, and it described his similar techniques of handling bamboo. The butt sections of both the Bowness and Little rods were both made of kiln-dried ash, while their middle joints and tip sections were three-strip cane. Bowness placed the power fibers inside his rods, filling the core with fish glue, and turned the pith surfaces into a round rod joint. Little worked the slender Calcutta cane into three strips, cutting its pith core into 120-degree glue faces and placing the dense power fibers outside. The evidence clearly places the origins of split-bamboo rods, with their power fibers placed both inside and out, in the United Kingdom.

Samuel Phillippe was also building two-strip and three-strip bamboo rods in Pennsylvania as early as 1844. Phillippe was a famous gunsmith and violinmaker from Easton, a small canalboat town on the Delaware, and had received a silver medal for one of his stringed instruments at the Franklin Institute in Philadelphia. Phillippe was also a skilled trout fisherman who often travelled to the Brodheads with American angling notables like Thaddeus Norris, and local experts like Thomas Heckman, William Green, Colonel T. R. Sitgreaves, Judge James Madison Porter, and Phineus Kinsey. It is logical that a skilled craftsman like Phillippe should turn to rodmaking, and his parallel knowledge of metallurgy was soon applied to manufacturing the Kinsey hook pattern.

Since Phillippe was born in 1801, and his family history tells us that he was apprenticed as a gunsmith at sixteen in the shop of Peter Young, his skills were probably well developed before 1830. His shop unquestionably produced rods of ash, hickory, greenheart, snakewood, lancewood, and lemonwood before 1845. His close friendship with Thaddeus Norris indicates that rod specifications meticulously described in *The American Angler's Book* probably originated with Phillippe, and other sources tell us that his first cane rods appeared in 1846.

Dr. James Henshall is the angling historian who documented the developments attributed to Phillippe before the old rodmaker died in 1877, corresponding with many of Phillippe's disciples and fishing companions and customers before he published his *Book of the Black Bass* in 1881. Henshall knew Phillippe's family well, particularly young Solon Phillippe, who had joined his father in gunsmithing and rod building in 1849. Although many other rodmakers attempted to claim the invention of modern four-strip and six-strip construction for themselves and sought to discredit Phillippe and his work, the evidence of Henshall and his exchange of letters with many of Phillippe's contemporaries clearly vindicate the Pennsylvania craftsman and his claim to fame.

Phillippe first tried two-strip and three-strip rods, with their power fibers outside, and fitted with butts of ash and unsplit bamboo. Obviously, these experiments loaded eccentrically and refused to deliver a cast properly. Phillippe soon turned to four-strip construction with the power fibers outside, and found they cast much better, although such quadrate rods are still demanding under casting stress. Four-strip rods are slightly stronger and more resilient than other cane construction of equal weight, because they place more power fibers in the bending plane, slightly farther from the longitudinal axis of the section. However, four-strip rods are also unforgiving taskmasters, refusing to cast clearly if a fisherman has poor casting habits and works outside the casting plane. Such demanding temperament soon led Phillippe to experiment with other theories of split-cane construction, although he built many four-strip rods completely split from bamboo as early as 1846. His six-strip rods entirely built of cane were also perfected before he sold his first bamboo rod in 1848, although Phillippe earlier made a four-strip rod with an ash butt section for Colonel Sitgreaves.

Phillippe's account books clearly show that the first all-bamboo rod sold in 1848 was a four-strip design, featuring a cane tip, middle joint, and swelled butt section. Solon Phillippe was making his own six-strip rods as early as 1859, using twelve laminated strips of hardwood and bamboo in the grip. Similar rods were later made by famous makers like Ebenezer Green, Charles Murphy, and Hiram Leonard. Solon Phillippe and his father made both six-strip and eight-strip rods between 1865 and 1870, when ill health ultimately forced the retirement of the elder Phillippe, who died in 1877.

Doctor Henshall interviewed a number of Phillippe contemporaries to confirm the elder Phillippe's role in bamboo rod theory and construction. Thomas Heckman knew Phillippe across sixty-odd years, and fished with him often, sometimes camping for a week along the Bushkill or Brodheads. Heckman watched Phillippe building bamboo rods in 1846, and machining his own ferrules, reel fittings, and ring-and-keeper guides. Phillippe built two rods for Heckman, and another was built for Edward Innes, who often visited his rodmaking shop after 1840. Innes confirmed watching Phillippe make a bamboo fly rod in the winter of 1847, and George Stout reported seeing a Phillippe rod when he arrived at Easton in 1851. Stout later became an amateur rodmaker, building about a dozen in the Phillippe style, starting in 1860. Charles Imbrie also corresponded with Henshall concerning Phillippe and his rods. Abbey and Imbrie was a fine Manhattan tackle house that evolved from the older Andrew Clerk & Company in 1875, two years before Phillippe died at Easton. Andrew Clerk & Company had been founded in 1820, and Clerk had sold Phillippe rods well before the Civil War. The letter from Charles Imbrie to Henshall contains this revealing paragraph:

> Your account of the origin of the split-bamboo rod is perfectly correct. Our Mister Abbey was the active member of Andrew Clerk & Company at the time of the origination, by Mister Phillippe, of the split bamboo rod, and is therefore well acquainted with its history to the present time.

Doctor W. W. Bowlby of Manhattan also exchanged letters with

Henshall concerning Phillippe and his bamboo rods. Bowlby lived in New Jersey, just across the Delaware from Easton, and often saw Phillippe on rivers like the Musconetcong and Pequest. According to Bowlby, Phillippe was already fishing with a split-cane rod in 1852, and it was the first time he had seen such tackle.

Perhaps the most revealing evidence confirming the role that Phillippe played in development of the bamboo rod is a little-known letter from Charles Murphy to Doctor Henshall. Many angling historians argue that Phillippe did not originate the prototypes of modern split-cane construction, preferring to believe other rodmakers and angling writers. Some jealous contemporaries admitted that Phillippe had invented four-strip and six-strip construction, but attempted to downgrade his workmanship—yet the three Phillippe rods that I have examined demonstrate a technical skill superior to the first work of Hiram Leonard.

The Phillippe rod in the collection of the Anglers' Club of New York, and particularly the Phillippe in the Oldenwalder collection, unmistakably confirm his rodmaking skills. The Oldenwalder rod was calibrated by Vincent Marinaro, himself a skilled rodmaker and author of *A Modern Dry-Fly Code*, when it was exactly a century old. It measured eleven feet in three joints of six-strip bamboo. The rod featured a swelled handle of cane that calibrated an inch, tapering to seventeen thirty-seconds of an inch just above the grip. It tapered to twelve thirty-seconds at the midpoint of its butt joint, and eleven thirty-seconds at the first ferrule. The ferrule was rolled and soldered from German silver, measuring nineteen sixty-fourths of an inch. The middle section calibrated ten thirty-seconds at the first ferrule, tapering to nine thirty-seconds at its center and seven thirty-seconds at the upper ferrule. The second ferrule measured twelve sixty-fourths of an inch, while the tip section tapered from six thirty-seconds to a delicate three thirty-seconds at its tip ring. It is interesting to compare these tapers with the specifications recommended by Thaddeus Norris in lancewood, lemonwood, or greenheart. The swelled grip was finished with the precise checkering typical of a highly skilled gunsmith.

Several other critics of Phillippe argued that his butt joints were always shaped from ash, and that his rods were never fully made of bamboo. William Mitchell was a skilled British rodmaker who emigrated to the United States, and Mitchell was apparently the first rodmaker to appreciate the unique properties of Tonkin cane, and he used business contacts in London to acquire his supply of culms from China. His articles in *The American Angler* promoted the role of Ebenezer Green and Charles Murphy in the creation of the first bamboo rods, downgrading the earlier pioneer work of Phillippe. Later articles echoed the Mitchell story, including a piece that was printed in *The New York Times* in 1881. It granted that Phillippe had discovered the utility of split bamboo, but that Green and Murphy had built the first completely bamboo rods after 1860, erroneously crediting Murphy with the creation of the first all-cane trout

FROM THE COLLECTION OF HARRY DARBEE

JOHN KAY   1870   SIX-PIECE ASH AND JACARANDA

J. M. KAUFMANN ROD IN THE COLLECTION OF THE MUSEUM OF AMERICAN FLY FISHING

C. F. MURPHY   1875   FOUR-PIECE CALCUTTA

rod in 1863. Murphy apparently did build his first cane trout rod in that year, although both Samuel and Solon Phillippe preceded him. The following observations were made by Charles Murphy in his letter to James Henshall, and contain some striking facts:

> Mr. Charles Luke, of this city, formerly of Easton, Pennsylvania, used to fish and hunt with Mr. Phillippe, and frequented his workshop, where he saw him use split bamboo for fly rods certainly as far back as 1848.
>
> Luke moved from Easton to Newark in 1850. I am very certain you can give Phillippe credit for the discovery of split bamboo for fly rods without fear of being contradicted. While he was making rods for Andrew Clerk & Company, Mr. Abbey, of that firm, showed Mr. Green and myself a rod made by Mr. Phillippe, the top and second joint made of split bamboo, with the butt joint made from white ash.

Murphy was clearly a major figure in the history of the bamboo fly rod, and there is evidence that he believed the first complete bass, trout, and salmon rods were his. Perhaps Murphy himself was the source of the contention that Phillippe never built rods entirely made of cane, since his letter to Doctor Henshall is careful to mention a butt section of white ash on the first split-bamboo rod he had seen. It is interesting that Murphy places Ebenezer Green with him that day at Andrew Clerk & Company, when they both examined the Phillippe rod.

Thaddeus Norris and Ebenezer Green were both making split-cane rods for their own fishing in 1860, after earlier contact with Phillippe and his work. Charles Murphy started selling split-cane trout rods in considerable numbers in 1863, marketing many of them through Andrew Clerk. Two years later, Murphy made the first bamboo salmon rod, using the four-strip method. This rod was carried to Scotland by Andrew Clerk, where it was quickly admired and copied. Murphy also used four-strip construction for the first cane bass rod in 1865. Until it was dissolved in 1875, Andrew Clerk & Company exported surprising numbers of American six-strip, eight-strip, and twelve-strip rods to the United Kingdom.

Ebenezer Green was a fine cabinetmaker in Newark, and many of his practical skills undoubtedly influenced Murphy in the period just before the Civil War. Green built excellent rods, but largely for himself and his fishing friends, and few apparently survive today.

Charles Murphy is not the most celebrated rodmaker in the evolution of American fly-fishing, since that position clearly belongs to the younger Hiram Leonard, who followed in 1870. Murphy did not build the first trout rods made entirely of split bamboo, since both Samuel Phillippe and his son have that honor. However, the design and casting qualities and calibrations of his rods unquestionably influenced later craftsmen, including the younger Leonard himself. Murphy also was thoroughly versed in the theory and technology of rod construction.

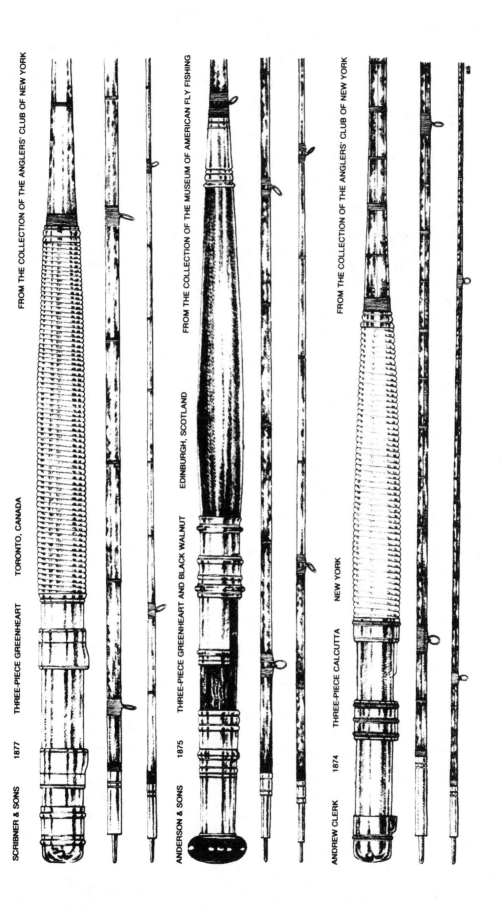

SCRIBNER & SONS   1877   THREE-PIECE GREENHEART   TORONTO, CANADA   FROM THE COLLECTION OF THE ANGLERS' CLUB OF NEW YORK

ANDERSON & SONS   1875   THREE-PIECE GREENHEART AND BLACK WALNUT   EDINBURGH, SCOTLAND   FROM THE COLLECTION OF THE MUSEUM OF AMERICAN FLY FISHING

ANDREW CLERK   1874   THREE-PIECE CALCUTTA   NEW YORK   FROM THE COLLECTION OF THE ANGLERS' CLUB OF NEW YORK

Fred Mather was the distinguished fisherman and pioneer ichthyologist who later imported the brown trout to the United States, and his book *My Angling Friends* describes meeting the talkative Murphy at the Manhattan tackle shop of J. C. Conroy in 1865:

> I listened with wonder to the talk of angles, tapers, gluing, and other details, until I thought that the building up of a split-bamboo rod required more careful attention than the grinding of a lens for a great telescope.

Murphy was posturing and voluble in his encounter with Mather, claiming full credit for the development of the bamboo rod, and adding that he was experimenting with six-strip construction. Genio Scott fished the four-strip Murphy salmon rod with Andrew Clerk in Canada, and praised its casting qualities in *Fishing in American Waters*.

Later in his life, Murphy became increasingly insular and cantankerous, perhaps echoing his combative Irish heritage. It was commonly said that Murphy would rather quarrel than eat, although he was a relatively small man. His sullen moodiness led to increasing claims that he alone had invented split-cane construction, contradicting his earlier letter to Doctor Henshall. His combativeness and ego eventually annoyed Charles Imbrie so completely that their long-standing business relationship was ended. Imbrie believed that Murphy might have been a splendid rodmaker, perhaps the equal of Hiram Leonard, had he exercised more self-discipline—adding in his letter to Henshall that Murphy failed to grow after 1870, in terms of both his craftsmanship and his character.

Murphy failed to compete in the mercantile atmosphere that followed the Civil War, the split-cane production coming from the shops of rodmakers like Orvis, Leonard, and Chubb. Other craftsmen were able to organize and direct the work in their shops, while Murphy trusted only himself, and was still working alone in his home in 1881. Such solitary craftsmen seem romantic now, but Murphy's disposition and pride both cost him a chance at greatness, and his historical position unquestionably suffered from a limited output during the years when his skills should have matured and flowered.

The famous Murphy trout rod from the Kauffmann collection that is displayed at the Museum of American Fly-Fishing shows that Murphy was a superb craftsman. The Kauffmann rod was made about 1867 for Samuel Kauffmann of Washington, and was apparently used primarily at the Oquossoc Club in Maine, which was formed in 1869. Its workmanship equals the best of the early Leonard rods and clearly displays the promise that Charles Imbrie encouraged before he subsequently quarrelled with Murphy at Abbey & Imbrie in New York.

The Kauffmann rod is made in three sections and measures a full twelve feet. Despite its length it surprisingly weighs only seven and a half ounces. The Murphy is a delicate two thirty-seconds of an inch at its tip ring, four thirty-seconds of an inch at the midpoint of the tip joint, and measures a slender six thirty-seconds at its upper ferrule. Unlike the Norris and Phillippe patterns, the Murphy tapers apparently held constant across a ferrule, at least in the Kauffmann rod, indicating that Murphy better understood the dynamics of the casting stress between rod sections than either Norris or Phillippe. The middle joint tapered from six thirty-seconds to ten thirty-seconds at the lower ferrule. The butt section calibrated ten thirty-seconds at the ferrule, tapering to fourteen thirty-seconds approximately four inches above the German-silver grip check, and swelling to twenty-four thirty-seconds at the check itself. Such swelled grips had originated with the Phillippes before 1860, and a swelled bamboo grip checkered like a gunstock had been a striking detail of the Oldenwalder rod. Such swelled grips were quite difficult to make, since each bamboo strip was sharply widened so the handle swelled gracefully over a cedar core. Anyone who has ever worked with split-cane construction respects the high degree of skill needed to finish a swelled grip, instead of the modern method of concealing the butt inside its reel seat and cork. The Murphy rod was distinguished by the elegance and surprisingly modern proportions of its grip design. Its butt cap was gracefully shaped and engraved, measuring about an inch, and showing a brief length of swelled bamboo between its upper edge and the handsome welt of the check that secured the sliding reel band. The reel band itself measured about three-quarters of an inch and was engraved with six ornamental rings. The grip itself was wound with rattan, split and laid with great precision in a shallow spiral, its ends concealed under a pair of half-inch rings.

The Murphy rod made for Kauffmaun is in exquisite condition and could easily be fished today. Its silk windings have grown a little brittle in the past century, and its guides are ring-and-keeper fittings of brass. The German-silver ferrules are probably frail, enclosing their dowelled slides in a tube formed of a rolled and soldered plate of thin alloy. The sections are round, their hexagonal corners planed off until only the delicate glue lines reveal the number of split-cane strips. It is curious that the butt and middle sections are six-strip work, while the delicate tip uses four-strip construction. Murphy probably chose this hybrid design because such tips were much easier to make, but the Oldenwalder Phillippe rod had used six-strip construction throughout its length fifteen years earlier, clearly demonstrating that the controversial Murphy was not the only wellspring of craftsmanship in bamboo. The famous 1873 Leonard, in the Howells collection at San Francisco, also incorporates the more difficult six-strip construction throughout its length.

The Kauffmann rod is a superb example of Murphy's work, and its great value extends beyond its actual worth, since it teaches us much about the history of American fly rods. It closely resembles the vintage Leonards that appeared a decade later, with their grip fittings and rattan handles, their bayonet ferrules, and their bamboo culm cases with caps of elegantly machined brass. The Murphy rod is surprisingly modern, and although Leonard is better known because several of his apprentices later became fine rodmakers in their own right, Murphy unmistakably influenced the future.

No roster of early American rodmakers would be complete without Charles F. Orvis, who founded the present tackle company in 1856. Orvis was born at Manchester in 1831, along the Battenkill in central Vermont. It is a lovely New England village sheltered in a beautiful valley, and fishing between Manchester and Arlington occupied most of his boyhood summers, mixed with woodcock and grouse shooting in the fall. Orvis was a precocious craftsman, tirelessly repairing clocks and toys in his youth, and turning to fly rods and reels in later years. His first rods were made in about 1854, using butts of white ash and upper sections of lancewood, much like the early work of Norris and Phillippe. Orvis enjoyed a superb reputation with his contemporaries, leading James Henshall to comment in his *Book of the Black Bass* that Orvis was among the finest and most honest tacklemakers of his time.

CHARLES F. ORVIS

Orvis was fully aware of the developments in the workshops of Phillippe, Green, Murphy, and Leonard, and his company was producing split-bamboo rods as early as 1874, the same year that Orvis patented the first perforated-spool reel for fly-fishing. Orvis produced sixteen catalogues before 1884, the probable date of the remarkable Orvis publication reproduced in *Great Fishing Catalogs of the Golden Age.* That 1884 catalogue was a Victorian classic, with its embossed and gilded cover secured by a silk binding cord and tassel. It offered fly rods of hornbeam, lancewood, and lancewood with a white-ash butt, as well as hexagonal split-cane designs of the Leonard type. The common grips were wound rattan, walnut with longitudinal flutings, and lightweight sumac that had a florid grain pattern clearly appealing to the Victorian eye. Orvis also offered cork grips on its so-called ladies' rods of lancewood and hexagonal cane, when they were introduced in the United States in 1880. Cork proved popular with fishermen too, and the specie-cork handle was king after only a decade. It still reigns today, although first-quality cork is increasingly difficult to import for rodmaking.

The style of the most expensive Orvis rods was still unmistakably derived from the bamboo prototypes of Murphy and Leonard, with their swelled cane handles wound in rattan, and their German-silver fittings. These premium Orvis rods included a patented internal spring which secured the sliding reel band. The walnut, cork and sumac grips were fitted along the rod shaft itself, an easier task than tapering a swelled handle of split bamboo, and their designs were a prelude to the modern Orvis rods. The 1884 catalogue also includes the Orvis patent reel, with its fully perforated drum, as well as two elegant Vom Hofe reels of the period.

Orvis was building relatively modern fly rods of hexagonal split bamboo in 1900, concentrating on three-piece designs as light as four ounces. The entire Orvis stock now featured cork grips exclusively. There were bargain models selling at less than five dollars, with nickel-plated ferrules and metal reel seats. These rods were still fitted with ring-and-keeper guides, varied between ten and ten and a half feet, and weighed from six and a half to seven and a half ounces. The Orvis five-dollar grade had similar fittings, but offered more delicate tapers. Its rods were nine to ten and a half feet in length, and weighed between five and six and three-quarters ounces. The ten-dollar series ranged from nine to eleven feet, and offered weights from five to seven and one-quarter ounces. The most expensive fly rod offered English snake guides, which first appeared on American rods late in the nineteenth century. Its ferrules, reel bands, grip check, and butt cap were all machined of German silver. It sold for only fifteen dollars, measured eight feet three inches, and weighed only four ounces. Except for its relatively soft action, its length and weight compare favorably with a modern Orvis Battenkill, which sells at twelve times the price. It is interesting to note that the Orvis catalogue found it necessary to comment that a rod weighing only four ounces was not a toy.

The reputation of Orvis bamboo rods was already excellent in 1881, beginning a tradition for quality that endures today. Ned Buntline was famous in the late nineteenth century for popular novels extolling figures like Wyatt Earp and Buffalo Bill Cody on the American frontier. His 1881 article in *Turf, Field and Farm*, a major periodical in those years, described a day along the Beaverkill with his favorite Orvis. Buntline died in 1886, and from his final sickroom he wrote these lines for opening day:

> Tomorrow a hundred rods will bend over bright waters in my happy Catskills, yet I can only stare at my Orvis in the corner, and let its bamboo rest.

Hiram Lewis Leonard is the father of the modern fly rod, both in the remarkable technical knowledge and craftsmanship his work displayed and in the great rodmakers he trained in his shop. Leonard was born in Maine in 1833, on the estuary of the Penobscot at Bangor. His early apprenticeships taught him metalworking and cabinetmaking skills, and Leonard had subsequent training as an engineer.

His rodmaking career started at Bangor in 1871, with his first efforts constructed of white ash and lancewood. Since Leonard loved fishing and made the rod for himself, his career almost remained a hobby but a friend suggested that the rod should be shown to Bradford & Anthony, the famous sporting goods house in Boston. Its partners were so impressed that Bradford & Anthony agreed to market his entire production and encouraged Leonard to experiment with cane. Leonard also built many lancewood rods in these early years, although Bradford & Anthony soon talked him into building rods in four-strip bamboo. The early Leonard in the Howells collection is exquisite proof that Hiram Leonard was building six-strip rods as early as 1873.

The Howells Leonard was built in Bangor in 1873; its fixed-reel band is inscribed from H. L. Leonard to H. H. Howells and the date is unmistakably engraved underneath. It is the oldest known Leonard in any collection, and H. H. Howells was an attorney in Maine when the rod was built. Since it is obviously a presentation rod from its maker, Howells apparently performed the legal services in securing the first ferrule patents for Leonard. Howells went west about 1875, practicing law in Wyoming for many years before finally travelling to San Francisco, where he was ultimately appointed to the bench. Judge Howells was the grandfather of Gary Howells, one of our finest American rodmakers.

The Howells rod itself is remarkable. Its calibrations are surprisingly modern considering its age. It measures ten feet and was made in three sections, weighing approximately nine ounces. The reel seat is cut into the laminated handle and measures two and seven-eighths inches, and the slender grip is nine and seven-eighths inches in length. The shaft itself is only two thirty-seconds of an inch at its tip guide, reaches three thirty-seconds of an inch at the middle of the tip section, and five thirty-seconds at the ferrule. The middle joint is six thirty-seconds at its upper ferrule, eight thirty-seconds at its midpoint, and nine thirty-seconds

HIRAM LEWIS LEONARD

at its lower ferrule. The butt calibrates ten thirty-seconds at the ferrule, twelve thirty-seconds halfway to the handle, and fourteen thirty-seconds at the grip check. The swelled handle tapers from fourteen thirty-seconds of an inch at the check to twenty-eight thirty-seconds of an inch at its thickest point, tapering back to twenty-five thirty-seconds at the fixed band of the reel seat. The handle is only eighteen thirty-seconds of an inch at the butt cap. These calibrations would probably produce a ten-foot rod weighing only four to five ounces, except for the weight of its swelled, laminated grip.

The ferrules were originally the slender dowel-type patented for Leonard two years later. The tubing was rolled and soldered from a thin sheet of German silver and reinforced at the throat with a simple welt. There were two ornamental rings engraved at the base, the ferrules were pinned with brass, and there were still no serrations. Ring-and-keeper guides were used throughout. The reel seat is fitted with a small hole, perhaps to receive a particular reel. Elegantly machined fittings of German silver form the grip check, the fixed-reel band, and the sliding reel-seat ring. The butt cap is also shaped from nickel silver into an elegant ornamental cup, and the fixed bands are so tightly fitted into the handle that a rattan covering seems unlikely. The exquisite laminated handle with its six strips of cane swelling with alternating splines of Port Orford cedar is quite ornamental and unique. This 1873 Leonard in the Howells collection is one of the rare bench marks in our angling history.

Hiram Leonard loved the hunting and fishing in those early years in Maine and was such a skilled angler that he fully understood the dynamics of fly casting. It is obvious that Leonard also possessed the rare ability to communicate his skills and knowledge and love of rodmaking to others. Several young Bangor craftsmen joined his shop crew as apprentices, and a surprising number ultimately became famous rod builders—men like Edward Payne, Fred Divine, Eustis Edwards, Thomas Chubb, Fred Thomas, and the Hawes brothers all made rods in later years.

During their Bangor years, the Leonard staff was a happy family that fished and hunted together across Maine. Hiram Leonard also loved music, and his shop repaired and made musical instruments. The staff had its own musical group and played together often.

It was pretty well known, Arthur Mills explained many years ago, at William Mills & Son in downtown New York, *that you had to play some instrument to work for Leonard.*

Unfortunately, their idyllic life together began to sour. The principal markets for their work lay in New York and Philadelphia, and a business relationship for selling Leonard rods was forged with Thomas Bate Mills of William Mills & Son. Leonard suffered money problems in 1878 and grudgingly surrendered a controlling interest to the Mills family. Thomas Bate Mills moved Leonard south to a new rod plant in Central Valley, fifty-odd miles above Manhattan, in the summer of 1881. Leonard and his staff moved reluctantly, in spite of their new proximity to famous Catskill rivers like the Beaverkill and Willowemoc, and the mood of their workrooms never matched the bucolic years in Maine. However, the Catskill trout ultimately did become the yardstick for Leonard's achievements, and their rivers became the perfect proving grounds for the evolving Leonard rods.

Thomas Chubb decided against the move to southern New York, and chose to establish his own tackle company in Vermont. His boldness paid off, and Chubb had established a thriving plant at Post Mills in 1886. Fred Thomas and Eustis Edwards agreed to leave Bangor. Thomas became the foreman, and soon enticed Edward Payne to join them with his glowing descriptions of the trout streams and bird shooting. Payne soon found himself homesick for Maine and went back, but his wife had been born near Central Valley, and loved its milder winters. Her arguments finally persuaded Payne to rejoin Leonard. But the camaraderie they had found together in Maine was never rekindled, and their growing skills made several members of the Leonard staff restless. Thomas, Edwards, and Payne soon left and formed their own partnership. The following year they sold their budding firm to the United States Net and Twine Company, in concert with several other wealthy backers, and their rodmaking operations were moved to Brooklyn. It seems their new facilities were the property of their backers, and the Wilkinson Company was chosen as the primary sales outlet, but the new ownership had misjudged its new employees. Fred Thomas soon resigned and started making his own rods with his son Leon in Bangor. Eustis Edwards followed Thomas to Maine, and moved later to Connecticut, where he built rods with his sons William and Eugene Edwards.

Edward Payne had finally adjusted to leaving his native Maine for the Hudson Valley, but commuting each day to Brooklyn was the final straw. Payne finally exploded under the abrasive pressures of Brooklyn and bought back his remaining interest in the new rod company. Payne joined the Leonard foreman Frank Oram in a fresh partnership under his own name. The fledgling Payne rod company was located at Highland Mills, a few miles north from Central Valley. His son James and other apprentices joined the Payne operation, and the younger Payne continued in the family business after his father's death. It was James Payne who ultimately became the principal heir of Hiram Leonard, and perhaps the finest rodmaking craftsman who ever split a culm and worked a planing block—although many fine fishermen would argue that perhaps Everett Garrison also deserves that title, without diminishing the exquisite work of Payne and his incredible skills.

Loman and Hiram Hawes were Leonard's nephews, and remained loyal associates until Hiram Leonard died in 1907. Thomas Bate Mills acquired the last outstanding shares of Leonard after its founder's death, and most of the employees skilled enough to make an entire rod themselves soon left. Loman Hawes was the mechanical genius who had conceived the Leonard bevel cutter that still remains one of the finest ever designed, and a partnership with his brother Hiram was soon established. It was a marriage of creativity and skills that held great promise, but Loman Hawes died suddenly, before that promise was tested or fulfilled. Hiram Hawes was a fine tournament caster and craftsman who had married one of Leonard's daughters, and he ultimately produced a number of excellent rods under his family trademark. The most successful years for the Hawes rods probably occurred after the First World War, when Abercrombie & Fitch sold them in good numbers.

Fred Divine was perhaps the only former employee who failed to follow in the Leonard tradition, although he clearly had the skills to equal the work of his colleagues. Divine held a unique patent on a spiral-laminated bamboo rod, which had been granted in 1892, but it never became popular. Such rods were tapered, glued, and pressure-wrapped like conventional cane sections. The freshly wrapped bamboo was then twisted and held in tension until it dried. The result was an extremely stiff rod section of great strength, and many are still fishable today. However, the Divine patent is rather difficult to implement, and many finished sections must be rejected. His only disciple was probably Letcher Lambuth, the famous amateur rodmaker and fishing companion of Roderick Haig-Brown in the Pacific Northwest. Lambuth rods fabricated with the Divine spiral patent are rare, but owners like Steven Raymond are sold on their performance on brawling steelhead rivers from northern California to British Columbia.

Divine had pliable standards of workmanship and design, and his rods varied radically in quality over the years. Divine made large numbers of lancewood and lemonwood rods after his departure from Leonard, using proportions and fittings of surprising elegance. Their workmanship and performance were good. Divine probably knew bamboo was better, but he eagerly supplied what his buyers wanted. His catholic tastes included four-strip and eight-strip cane, although as a former Leonard employee, Divine unquestionably knew six-strip rods were better. He also worked his rods from Calcutta and Tonkin cane with equal relish.

Tonkin cane was first imported through New York in 1895, and few knowledgeable craftsmen used anything else after 1910. Divine made six-strip and eight-strip rods in large numbers for Abercrombie & Fitch in 1911, charging more for the eight-strip rods, and telling his customers that octagonal sections cast better because they were round. His eight-strip rods varied from eight to ten feet, and between four and a half and eight ounces. The six-strip series weighed from a delicate three and a half ounces to eight and one-quarter ounces, and measured between eight and ten and a half feet. The most expensive rods that Divine made for Abercrombie & Fitch weighed three and three-quarters ounces to six and one-quarter ounces, and varied from eight to nine and a half feet. Their cost stemmed from being completely wrapped in white silk from grip check to tip guide. The silk virtually disappeared when the rod was varnished, revealing the nodes and graining in the bamboo, and its varnish-soaked weight was enough to deaden the spirit of the finest cane.

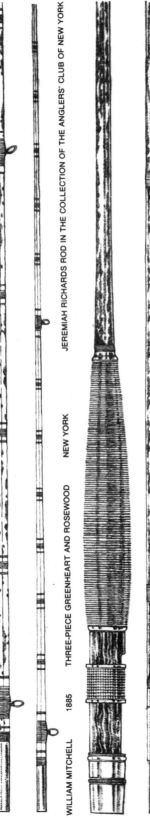

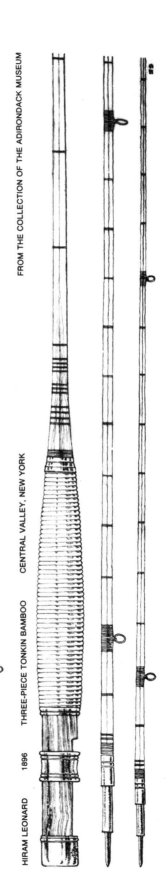

SOLON PHILLIPPE   1881   THREE-PIECE CALCUTTA AND BLACK WALNUT   EASTON, PENNSYLVANIA

JOHN FARQUAR ROD IN THE COLLECTION OF
THE ANGLERS' CLUB OF NEW YORK

WILLIAM MITCHELL   1885   THREE-PIECE GREENHEART AND ROSEWOOD   NEW YORK

JEREMIAH RICHARDS ROD IN THE COLLECTION OF THE ANGLERS' CLUB OF NEW YORK

HIRAM LEONARD   1896   THREE-PIECE TONKIN BAMBOO   CENTRAL VALLEY, NEW YORK

FROM THE COLLECTION OF THE ADIRONDACK MUSEUM

African steel-vine rods appeared shortly before the First World War and were an utter and laughable fraud. Catalogue copy touted African steel vine as the strongest rod material in the world. Steel vine simply did not exist. It was actually Calcutta bamboo formed into a six-strip taper and planed round into its pith core. Theodore Gordon was the first to observe that African steel vine looked like the internal fibers of Calcutta bamboo, but except for Gordon, the steel-vine hoax went undetected for twenty-odd years. It is typical of Divine that he willingly made African steel-vine rods in large numbers after his rod company was absorbed by Horrocks-Ibbotson in New York.

The eighty years between Samuel Phillippe and the accomplishments of Hiram Leonard and his disciples are the Golden Age of American rod building. Leonard died before his company had started working in Tonkin cane, although his younger colleagues and their sons would ultimately build rods of the new Chinese bamboo that easily surpassed the performance of the earlier Leonards.

The vintage years had passed, and their fingerprints are found in the specifications and fittings of the vintage rods. The history of fly-fishing is written in such tackle. The principal clues indicating the age and historical importance of a particular fly rod are found in its tip guide, running guides, ferrules, shaft materials, grip and reel-seat design, and ornamental wrappings. These bench marks identifying both the maker and birth of any rod are only found in the physical character of the rod and its fittings.

Tip guides have varied surprisingly over the years. Several curious designs evolved in the beginning, particularly the Chubb-patent type, which looked a little like a golf tee. Its top was cupped and its sides were perforated to receive the line. The three-ring top was a skeletal version of the same concept. Two German-silver rings were set on edge and flared out like a yoke, receiving a third ring set flat on top. Another version set a ring of agate or agatine on top, seating it in a band of nickel silver. The early Phillippe, Green, Murphy, Leonard, and Chubb rods all used a simple ring guide with its delicate ring set in the plane of the rod and not turned down like a modern tip guide. Later Leonards used a ring of agate soldered at a ninety-degree angle to its tubing. Early Hardy rods used a similar agate guide, but reinforced it with a pair of slender German-silver supports. Other braced types were also common, and have surfaced again in the modern graphite rods. It was Fred Thomas who developed an intriguing tip guide designed to be secured to the cane even when the glue deteriorated. To the regular tubing it added a slender tongue of German silver that lay along the top face of the rod concealed under the usually ornamental silk wraps. Modern rodmakers have almost universally accepted the so-called perfection tops, which consist of a slender tube with a pear-shaped guide bending down to align with the snake guides—limiting their creative energies merely to optional finishes in silver, oxidized silver and black.

The running guides have experienced a similar evolution. Before fly reels were widely used, only a flat-ring top was needed. Early rods largely

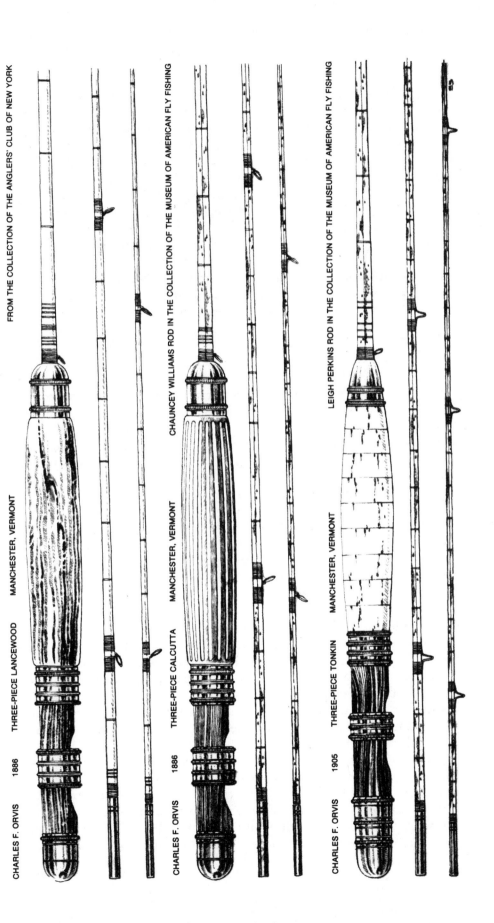

FROM THE COLLECTION OF THE ANGLERS' CLUB OF NEW YORK

CHARLES F. ORVIS   1886   THREE-PIECE LANCEWOOD   MANCHESTER, VERMONT

CHAUNCEY WILLIAMS ROD IN THE COLLECTION OF THE MUSEUM OF AMERICAN FLY FISHING

CHARLES F. ORVIS   1886   THREE-PIECE CALCUTTA   MANCHESTER, VERMONT

LEIGH PERKINS ROD IN THE COLLECTION OF THE MUSEUM OF AMERICAN FLY FISHING

CHARLES F. ORVIS   1905   THREE-PIECE TONKIN   MANCHESTER, VERMONT

employed ring-and-keeper guides of various metals, although they often collapsed and pinched a shooting line, quickly killing the velocity and distance of the cast. Such guides were typical between 1800 and 1900. Tunnel guides soon followed, although their openings were too small for good casting performance. The double twist guide was a curiously intricate ancestor of the English snake guide that first appeared about 1900, and the simpler single-wire snake guides quickly doomed the double twist design. English snake guides are formed with their openings toward the right, while a modern American type opens to the left. Double ring guides achieved a brief popularity between 1890 and 1900. American snake guides were used almost exclusively in this country after 1915, when the First World War interrupted trade in such items—except for the independent Fred Thomas, who stubbornly continued to use the English snakes until he died, perhaps because he knew it would identify his work in the future.

Ferrules are another clue to the origins of an antique rod. Their quality is often indicative of the quality of the rod itself. German silver has been the hallmark of rod quality since the Civil War, although brass and copper alloys sometimes were used earlier. Some modern builders like Paul Young have used first-grade aluminum ferrules in their passion for reducing weight, and western artisans like Lew Stoner, Doug Merrick and Gary Howells prefer duronze alloy. Nickel-plated and lacquered brass clearly indicate poor rod quality or poor judgment on the part of its maker.

Dowel-type ferrules were popular throughout the nineteenth century. Sometimes they were also called spike, bayonet, and dowel-and-pin ferrules. The names came from a tapered pin projecting axially from the end of the male ferrule. Before the Civil War, most of these ferrules were merely straight tubing rolled from a thin sheet of German silver. Their solder lines were clearly visible. No welts or raised shoulders were used. Sometimes delicate rings were engraved to embellish these primitive ferrules, and nothing prevented water from reaching inside the female socket to penetrate and damage the cane. Simple ferrules without dowels were also used on many rods, exposing the bamboo to moisture and fungus both inside the female ferrule and at the bottom of the male. More sophisticated ferrules began to evolve about 1860. The open ends of the female ferrules were reinforced with soldered welts, both strengthening them and improving their appearance. The two-piece male ferrule soon followed; it was shaped from two nickel-silver tubes of different sizes, fixing the smaller inside the larger with solder. The smaller tube was polished to fit inside the female ferrule, while the larger formed a shoulder to control the depth of its penetration.

Hiram Leonard introduced his ferrule patents in 1875, which seated the dowel pin in a waterproof socket. The water stop was conceived to protect the cane. The split-shoulder ferrule was also introduced by Leonard three years later. Its sliced edges were designed to permit the smooth transition of bending stress through the entire rod, eliminating the cutting wear of a rigid ferrule. These concepts were revolutionary in their time, and

Leonard engraved his two patent markings on every female ferrule manufactured between 1878 and 1925.

Many variations soon emerged from other rod shops, as the several Leonard competitors scrambled to work out similar designs. W. H. Reed introduced a ferrule in 1885 which tapered its tubing to a paper-thin edge under its silk wrappings and was swaged or die-formed to create a shouldered ferrule from a single piece of tubing. In 1890, George Varney patented a fully serrated ferrule in which long triangular slots were filed into the thin wall of the ferrule. Fully serrated ferrules are excellent, but demand a lot of handwork and are expensive. Varney was a relatively obscure member of the Leonard team after the move to Central Valley, but his later independent career ultimately led to managing rod production at Montague. Eustis Edwards was awarded his patent for the curiously named Kosmic ferrule in 1890, and it was briefly machined by Edward Payne at the old self-winding-clock factory in Brooklyn. It was used on the Wilkinson Kosmic rods, which were made in limited numbers there after 1895. The Kosmic ferrule abandoned the dowel pins altogether, added an intriguing water stop and gluing joint inside the female ferrule, and flared the edge of the ferrule away from the rod over a tapered collar of celluloid.

British rods are often fitted with the so-called lock-fast ferrules that appeared just after the turn of the century and added a locking hook to the male ferrule designed to engage a raised spiral thread at the mouth of the female ferrule. It still retained a dowel center pin on the male. It was the ancestor of dozens of ingenious screw-thread, latching, and snap-catch ferrules that later flooded the market, particularly in the United Kingdom. Such ferrules were an abomination, unnecessarily heavy, and prone to oxidize and stick after surprisingly little use. The lock-fast type was seated by twisting it into place, placing dangerous twisting forces on the cane and wearing the ferrules spirally. However, it did embrace the watertight cup principle invented by Leonard, and it improved the split corners fitted to the cane. That Hardy feature still dominates modern ferrule work seventy-odd years later.

The stolid British refusal to trust the simple friction ferrule persists even today. It led Halford to design a special trout ferrule for Hardy in 1913 that was a masterpiece of overcomplication. It still retained the dowel pin, adding a split female mouth that was machined inside to close over a raised ring formed on the male ferrule. There was a sliding lock ring outside the female ferrule which was slipped toward the male when the two were seated, tightening the mouth of the female until it engaged the locking ring on the male. It was elaborate, secure, and completely unnecessary in the design of a foolproof ferrule since the modern friction-type was already well known—and being used by Hiram Leonard and most of his skilled protégés in the United States.

The modern ferrules we take for granted evolved quite slowly across the past 150 years, and all fine rods incorporate the waterproof plugs and serrations first introduced by Hiram Leonard. Rodmakers that were technically trained in dynamic stress theory fully understood the advantages of these principles, and European craftsmen made another important contribution to ferrule theory after the First World War. The reverse-stepped ferrule that has no shoulder on its male plug is believed to have developed in Bavaria or Austria, but it has firmly become entrenched in American rod theory as the Swiss-type ferrule. Its design is intended to create a ferrule in which minimal cutting of the bamboo, for both the male and female fittings, is required. The male ferrule is simply a straight German-silver tube with six serrated cuts. It fits into a female socket larger than the male diameter or the bamboo itself, which necks down to a serrated diameter designed to fit the rod. The Swiss-type ferrule is clearly best in terms of a rod's stress performance and life span, but it is clumsy-looking and expensive to make. It failed to achieve popularity for those reasons, but is still·used on the rods built by Walton Powell.

Louis Feierabend is the rodmaker who designed the famous Super Z ferrules, attempting to adapt the principles of the Swiss-type into a fitting that was more conventional in appearance. Feierabend was so successful that a cavalcade of fine rod builders, including the late Paul Young and Everett Garrison, quickly relied on his ferrules. The design was simple. It consisted of a male ferrule with six serrations and no shoulder, either swaged or stepped of separate tubing. The female ferrule was formed of separate German-silver tubes, the larger forming the socket and housing the waterproof plug. The outside tube was gradually tapered until its final edge was thin enough to form a winding stop. The Feierabend ferrule company was finally bought by the larger Garcia Corporation, which soon found its minuscule profits unacceptable and discontinued the production of these remarkable ferrules.

Perhaps the most unusual modern ferrule was developed by William Edwards for his four-strip quadrate rods. Hexagonal rods are virtually round and readily accept a conventional ferrule, but a square section is a problem. Virtually all the power fibers would be lost in turning down a four-strip rod to receive a tubular ferrule, and the transition between its round configuration and the rectangular rod was clumsy at best. Edwards ultimately designed a beautiful ferrule, utterly unique in its appearance, with a square neck receiving the cane and tapering smoothly into its round socket and plug. The water stop was fitted in the round female socket, and a handsome welt reinforced its throat. The quadrate ferrules were slotted at the corners. The male ferrules were embellished with an engraved ring, and both males and females were oxidized German silver. These quadrate ferrules are still being used on the exceptionally handsome four-strip rods made by Samuel Carlson in Connecticut, who now owns the Edwards patents and equipment.

The bamboo work and its coloring are often important clues to the origins of a fine fly rod. The species of cane is critical, since the transition from lath-turned Calcutta to Tonkin bamboo was clear-cut, except for the fraudulent African steel-vine rods. Configuration and node placement are

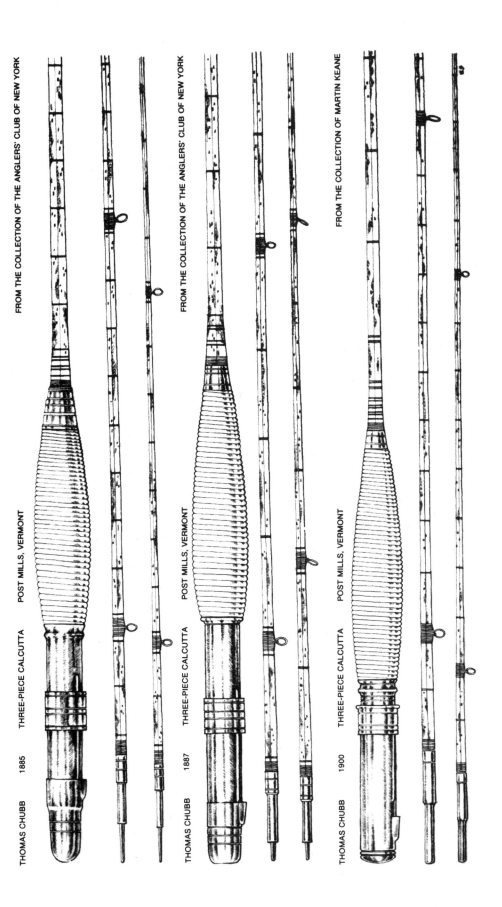

FROM THE COLLECTION OF THE ANGLERS' CLUB OF NEW YORK

THOMAS CHUBB   1885   THREE-PIECE CALCUTTA   POST MILLS, VERMONT

FROM THE COLLECTION OF THE ANGLERS' CLUB OF NEW YORK

THOMAS CHUBB   1887   THREE-PIECE CALCUTTA   POST MILLS, VERMONT

FROM THE COLLECTION OF MARTIN KEANE

THOMAS CHUBB   1900   THREE-PIECE CALCUTTA   POST MILLS, VERMONT

important too. Until the middle of the nineteenth century, rod tapers were more like billiard cues, working straight from tip to handle. Hickory and ash were common in both butts and midsections, with tips of lemonwood and lancewood; greenheart made up entire rods. There were also some bamboo rods of three-strip and four-strip construction, but these were limited to a handful of makers in England and the United States. Such rods were surprisingly clumsy.

After the Civil War, rod shafts became more slender and sophisticated in their tapers. Such sections flexed much farther toward the grip. Complete six-strip rods were produced in the Phillippe shop, particularly by Solon Phillippe, as early as 1857. However, six-strip construction first appeared in the butts and middle sections while the tips were still made of four strips. It was not until almost 1870, that rodmaking skills had evolved that could produce a really delicate six-strip tip. Specimens of these early bamboo rods are rare collectors' items today, particularly the rods of Phillippe, Green, Murphy, and Leonard.

However, these rods were Calcutta cane with their corners rounded off, and the advantages of rods constructed fully of hexagonal sections were not widely understood until 1880. Leonard was the first to discover such concepts, perhaps learning them first from his own six-strip tips, since the classic Howells Leonard has an hexagonal cane tip above its lower joints of rounded bamboo. It was built in 1873. After 1878, when Leonard became convinced that hexagonal sections were better, he built round rods on special order only. Other makers continued to work with hickory, ash, bethabara, greenheart, snakewood, lemonwood, and lancewood and had a stolid following of anglers slow to accept the advantages of split bamboo. Such exotic woods were used until well after the First World War and were found in the catalogues of first-rate tackle firms like Thomas Chubb, Von Lengerke & Detmold, and the celebrated William Mills & Son.

Tonkin cane was first imported in 1895, and was not received with any particular enthusiasm. Fishermen adapt slowly and stubbornly, and insisted on Calcutta bamboo with its darkly mottled sections, instead of Tonkin cane and its pale node patterns. Tonkin cane took about twenty years to displace its rivals, and after the First World War, Calcutta was finally relegated with lemonwood, greenheart and lancewood to the back pages of the catalogues—except for its resurrection in the African steel-vine rods.

Grip proportions and design are certainly the most obvious signature of a particular craftsman. Each rod handle holds myriad clues concerning its origins and the craftsmanship and sense of design possessed by its maker. Before 1850, rods had changed surprisingly little from the weapons described by Berners in her *Treatyse of Fysshynge wyth an Angle*. Such rods measured from ten to twenty feet in length. Tightly grained and elegantly finished, these javelins lacked grips or handles in modern terms. The wood itself was simply tapered into a butt thick enough to serve as a handle. The reel was typically seated in the upper or middle part of the grip—not unlike a two-handled salmon rod—so a fisherman could wield his weapon.

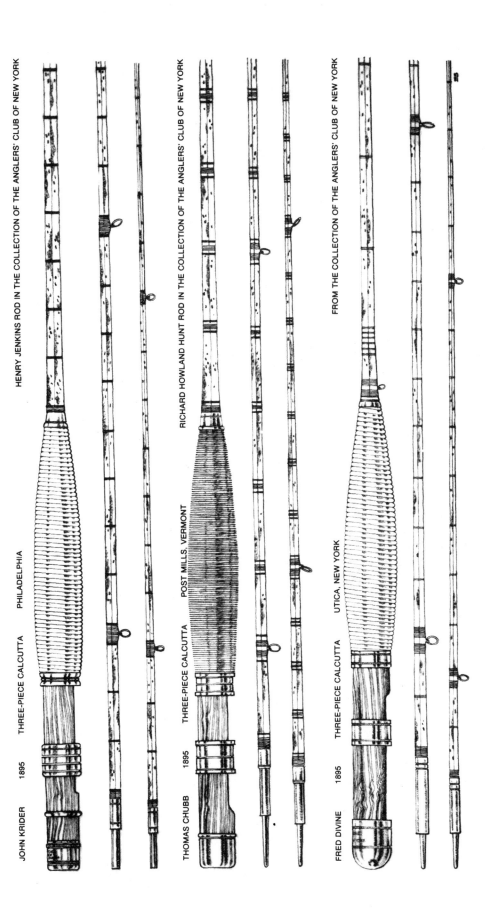

HENRY JENKINS ROD IN THE COLLECTION OF THE ANGLERS' CLUB OF NEW YORK

JOHN KRIDER   1895   THREE-PIECE CALCUTTA   PHILADELPHIA

RICHARD HOWLAND HUNT ROD IN THE COLLECTION OF THE ANGLERS' CLUB OF NEW YORK

THOMAS CHUBB   1895   THREE-PIECE CALCUTTA   POST MILLS, VERMONT

FROM THE COLLECTION OF THE ANGLERS' CLUB OF NEW YORK

FRED DIVINE   1895   THREE-PIECE CALCUTTA   UTICA, NEW YORK

Later rods became slender and more graceful. Although many manufacturers continued to place the reel above the grip as late as 1875, the more creative makers started seating it below the handle like our modern rods. Phillippe, Green, Murphy, and Leonard are all typical of this climate of change. The character of the bigger, traditional rods still echoed in the work of these men, although their grips were smaller and their specifications were designed for one-hand casting. The new grips were sometimes left bare, alternating the split cane with snakewood or cedar or walnut, and sometimes they were wrapped with a spiral of dark celluloid or pale rattan. Other makers soon adopted grips completely covered with tightly wound celluloid or lacquer-finished twine or rattan, and the evolution of the modern grip had started.

Fine craftsmanship and elegant proportions became the watchword of rodmakers. The German-silver grip check appeared after 1860, and some workmen soon discovered that rare grip materials like tiger maple, cherry, fruitwood, butternut, walnut, and Brazilian rosewood greatly enhanced their work. Sterling silver fittings and rich engraving enjoyed a vogue in the Victorian period, and some almost baroque presentation rods were made for royalty and captains of industry and politicians, heavy with expensive brightwork and other embellishments.

The period after 1875 witnessed a cornucopia of changes in grip and reel seat design. Hollow butt sections were devised for storing an extra tip. Cork grips were introduced at Orvis in 1880, and seamless German-silver reel seats appeared about that time. Detachable handles also enjoyed a brief period of popularity. Grips of fluted or checkered wood, celluloid or rattan winding, rubber, and cork veneer were common. Cork rings followed in about 1886, usually cut from sheets less than half an inch thick. Mills patented a locking reel seat that appeared on salmon rods in 1893. Screw-locking reel seats apparently developed on trout rods in England well before the First World War, since there are Hardy DeLuxe rods in this country with serial numbers old enough to place their origins slightly before 1900. Handsome screw-locking seats had evolved for trout rods on both sides of the Atlantic before 1925, with exposed fillers of hard rubber and elegant woods replacing the heavier full metal seats of German silver—except on the work of isolated craftsmen like Cross in the Middle West and Goodwin Granger in Colorado.

Hiram Leonard refined the earlier work of Phillippe, Green, and Murphy into a polished art and contributed pivotal concepts in the design of ferrules and six-strip sections, yet Leonard did not live to witness the fruition of his work in Tonkin cane. Leonard worked largely in Calcutta, which is slender porch-furniture bamboo, incapable of being made into a modern split-cane rod.

Calcutta bamboo is the slender *Dendrocalamus strictus* and is principally found in the rain forests of southern India, as well as other coastal regions in Burma, Thailand, and Malaysia. It grows to surprising heights, as much as thirty to sixty feet in optimal habitat, and its culms can measure two to four inches in diameter. The culms are almost solid, but they lack the strength of the so-called Tonkin canes. Calcutta is no longer used in fly rods, except in a few cheap Asian imports.

Tonkin bamboo is not actually found in the Tonkin Province of North Vietnam, but is cultivated in a surprisingly small area in the Kwangtung and Kwangsi provinces of southern China. Calcutta became available in Europe and the United States much earlier because of the British trade in India, and the Chinese cane later reached the Western world through Macao and Canton. Portuguese influence in Macao is extremely old, and had Portugal played a role in the history of rodmaking, we might have used Tonkin cane earlier than the first British commerce in Calcutta from India. Most Tonkin now reaches Europe and the United States through the British colony at Hong Kong and is known as Tsing Li bamboo there. Its scientific name is *Arundaria amabilis*, and the taxonomist who first classified it was perhaps an angler since its Latin name describes it as the lovely reed, and it is fitting that such a poetic material should find its ultimate purpose in an elegant split-cane rod.

The monsoon winds howl fiercely off the South China seas, driving the storm tides into the coastal lowlands behind Macao, and the yearly rainfall can reach several hundred inches. Fishing mythology holds that the finest bamboo for rodmaking grows on the hilltops, where its culms are wildly bent and tempered by the wind. Whether it is the climate that tests the canebrakes above Canton, or whether the resilient bamboo itself has evolved to test the violent winds and rain, we cannot be certain. Many anglers would prefer the obvious poetry of the latter. Whatever the cause, it is clear that some happy alchemy is wrought in this remote corner of the world. The vigorous shoots of bamboo that grow there, reaching toward the rainswept monsoon skies, have drawn the best from their climate and soil. And the artisans who have lovingly cured and shaped such bamboo into fly rods have learned to draw the best from its qualities.

The peculiar climate and other conditions that apparently limit *Arundaria amabilis* to its tiny corner of the world are not fully understood. The provinces where it thrives are hot and semitropical during most of the year, although the winters are dry and surprisingly cold. Its growers call it tea-stick bamboo. Too much summer heat and humidity are apparently poor for the cultivation of rod-quality cane, and the excessive heat and humidity found in the Tonkin Province of North Vietnam make it unsuitable for the tea-stick species.

The soils of Kwangtung and Kwangsi are varied. The river bottoms are richly fertile, although the foothills are rugged and barren. *Arundaria amabilis* is a plant species that grows best in the uplands, and fertile soils are not critical to its cultivation. Botanists believe that climate and drainage properties are more critical than soil quality. The molecular structure of the cane and the remarkable definition of its tension and compression fibers indicate that the strong prevailing winds of the rainy season do play a role in its rodmaking qualities.

The principal expert in the botany and cultivation of the Tsing Li bamboo was probably Doctor F. A. McClure, who served in the Biology Department of Lingnan University at Canton. It was McClure who worked out the taxonomy of *Arundaria amabilis* and published the definitive technical papers on this species of bamboo. McClure concluded that his new species was perhaps limited in its distribution because it was cultivated largely in its original habitat, and that its growers lacked the technology and resources to search for other equally suited growing regions—let alone the time necessary for experimental plantings.

Such new groves were established in its original range, however, to meet the demand of Western rodmakers. New sites for planting were usually chosen on southern or southeasterly slopes of steep hillsides or mountains, to provide good solar orientation and exposure to the monsoon winds. Southwest sites provided too much sun and less direct exposure to the seasonal storms tracking off the Pacific from the southeast. The jungle and scrub are cleared and burned to prepare a new grove. Clusters of travelling rhizome roots containing one or two upright culms are planted in a geometric grid, six to ten feet on centers. The freshly tilled earth is firmly tamped with the feet. Subsequent growth is monopodial, covering the open spaces with its travelling root systems. Bamboo roots travel just below the surface, parallel with the ground level, and send up new stems at fairly regular intervals. The stems are surprisingly larger than the roots themselves, and they quickly grow straight and uncrowded into the air. The rhizomes spread and sprout fresh shoots aggressively. The new grove expands quickly, bearing larger culms until optimal growth is reached. However, development of a mature grove is relatively slow. Ten years are required to reach the point of first harvest. Such a grove is productive for about fifty years, except when the bamboo is flowering.

Flowering occurs at irregular intervals, unpredictable even to the growers themselves, and during these periods a grove ceases to produce. Folklore once held that a grove lost its commercial value once it had flowered, but Professor McClure proved that a mature stand of cane will recover from flowering and resume production much sooner than a freshly planted grove. However, extensive periods of flowering triggered a great financial loss to the growers.

Freshly planted groves require no irrigation and remarkably little attention between harvests. The stands grow straight and tapering slightly to heights of forty to fifty feet, with maximum diameters of two and one-quarter inches. Most culms reach about half that height. Green culms are often marked to identify them for cutting three to four years later. Bamboo culms grow dense and hard with maturity. Their deep olive color gradually becomes a pale primrose yellow. Harvesting is done all year, although the best growers confine their cutting to autumn. The growth and health following the monsoons is optimal, but such culms must be thoroughly dried. The cane is cut with a heavy sharp-bladed machete that slices the culms with a steeply angled blow at the base.

Harvested culms are tied into bundles of convenient size for transportation by hand to the nearby rivers. Sometimes the bundles are assembled into rafts, although the most knowledgeable growers carry them overland to keep their moisture content low. The bundles are taken to sandbars along the rivers, where they are scoured to remove the fungus and lichens and stains. Some growers scrub the cane in the shallows, while others use only dry sand to keep the culms dry. Fresh bundles are assembled after scouring into equal numbers, loosely bound around the middle, and spread in an hourglass-shaped fan to dry and bleach. The bundles are placed under shelter at night and in rainy weather. Such first curing takes about a week in good weather, after which the cane is ready to start its journey.

The bundles are carefully sized and cut to lengths specified by the export agents in Canton and Hong Kong. These bundles are shipped by sampan down the Bambus and Sui Kong rivers to Fatshan. The culms are heat treated and straightened over earthen fire pots in the warehouses of the exporters. The Chinese workmen sort the culms into bales, wrapping each bale in tea mats for shipment down the Pearl River in junks to Canton and Macao. Ultimately these bundles reach exporters in Hong Kong, where they are sold to importers in Europe and the United States. Before the Second World War, when bamboo-rod production was at its zenith, more than $1,000,000 in tea-stick cane was exported annually for split-cane work. Consular records indicate that in 1937 almost $700,000 worth of *Arundaria amabilis* was exported to the United States alone.

It is probable that vintage bamboo rods had adventures long before they reached the shops of their makers in Europe and the United States or throbbed in response to a cartwheeling rainbow. The sampans and junks that carried the bundled culms to Canton were often stopped by river pirates demanding tribute, and similar extortion was frequent in the coastal seas between Canton and Hong Kong.

The Sino-Japanese War found both Canton and Fatshan under Japanese occupation in 1940. Japanese control of the Pearl River estuary was so complete in the autumn of 1938 and their gunboats patrolled so mercilessly that no cane reached Hong Kong for months. However, the enterprising Chinese soon found overland routes, wrapped the cane in smaller bundles, and transported them on the backs of coolies to several remote inlets along the coast between Canton and Hong Kong. Sampans transported the bamboo from those secret beaches to junks offshore, which carried it through the Japanese blockade. It was tortuously slow and expensive. It was hazardous too, since Chinese hill bandits demanded tribute and there were frequent patrols of Japanese soldiers. History tells us that more than one caravan was ambushed by the Japanese, and many of the coolies were killed. The flow of bamboo to Europe and the United States had dwindled to less than half of the normal trade by 1940, and with the Japanese attack on Pearl Harbor the following year, the cane trade virtually ended altogether.

Some bamboo trade resumed with the Japanese surrender in 1945, but the war in China had so disrupted the cultivation of rod-quality cane that shipments were unpredictable. Much of the cane imported in those years was virtually useless, although a trickle of first-rate bamboo continued to arrive in Europe and the United States through the Panama Canal. This rebirth of the cane market was brief, at least for American importers and tacklemakers. The wartime truce between Chiang Kai-shek and the powerful forces of Mao Tse-tung dissolved into open warfare in 1946, and China was wracked by civil war until 1949, when the defeated Chiang Kai-shek was driven into exile. The United States proclaimed an embargo against the government of Mao Tse-tung, ending all American trade with mainland China.

Practically all of the tea-stick cane imported into the United States after 1895 was handled by the late Charles Demarest, who began his career in the bamboo trade as a clerk with the D. A. Shaw & Company. Demarest subsequently acquired that firm and played a major role in the rise of Tonkin cane in American rod manufacturing. Harold Demarest served for many years in his father's business and was in Hong Kong early in 1950, when he acquired the last shipment of *Arundaria amabilis* that legally entered the United States.

It was just a matter of luck, Demarest later described his good fortune. *I happened on a bamboo shipment in a Hong Kong godown in April, and it was our last shipment out of China.*

The United Kingdom had recognized Mao Tse-tung earlier in 1950, and the American embargo was imposed in December, so limited amounts of bamboo continued to arrive via England. It was second-rate cane, however, because British rodmakers like Hardy and Millward and Sharpe understandably kept the best culms for themselves. Fortunately, there were large supplies of aging Tonkin on hand in many shops, and major tackle manufacturers often bought supplemental cane from smaller rod builders. Some stocks of bamboo were lost when large companies abandoned cane for fiberglass, and priceless inventories of aged Tonkin were tragically destroyed. Because of its embargo of Chinese goods, no first-quality culms of bamboo entered the United States until Leigh Perkins of the Charles Orvis Company succeeded in receiving a waiver on tea-stick bamboo—demonstrating with the technical assistance of David Ledlie, a knowledgeable biology professor at Middlebury College, that Orvis could not function without Chinese cane.

However, the bamboo shipments that have arrived thus far are erratic in quality, and it is apparent that skilled cultivation and preparation of the tea-stick bamboo has been a casualty of the traumatic events in recent Chinese history. Hopefully, the Chinese growers will recultivate the horticultural and handling skills their countrymen possessed before the Second World War.

Much experimenting with cultivation of *Arundaria amabilis* in the United States has been done, starting in about 1933 with the successful shipment of living shoots and rhizomes. Propagation was disappointingly

FRED DIVINE 1900 THREE-PIECE CALCUTTA UTICA, NEW YORK

JOSEPH JEFFERSON ROD IN THE COLLECTION OF THE MUSEUM OF AMERICAN FLY FISHING

J. B. CROOK 1890 THREE-PIECE CALCUTTA NEW YORK

FROM THE COLLECTION OF THE ANGLERS' CLUB OF NEW YORK

B. F. NICHOLS 1890 THREE-PIECE CALCUTTA BOSTON

WINSLOW HOMER ROD IN THE COLLECTION OF THE MUSEUM OF AMERICAN FLY FISHING

slow, and groves being cultivated by the Department of Agriculture flowered only a half-dozen years after planting. The second planting in Louisiana did not flower, but bamboo of first-rate quality in commercial quantities was not obtained. These experiments in the American cultivation of tea-stick bamboo lost their impetus when fiberglass replaced cane in volume rod production, but our increasing interest in bamboo might reawaken the interest once shown in growing rod-quality Tsing Li in our southern states. Prices continue to rise sharply, the quality of Chinese cane remains unpredictable, and more bamboo rods are being made and sold each year.

The yardsticks of quality for raw Tsing Li are that the culms are ripe and yellow. Their graining and shafts must be relatively straight and should rend cleanly in linear splits and checks. The cane must be clean and free of worms or decay. The culms should average six feet in length and exceed one and one-quarter inches in diameter. The manufacturers must hold sufficient stocks of cane to insure that they are working with seasoned culms averaging three to five years in age. The finest culms are hard and resilient, relatively uniform in size, and densely grained. Good bamboo tends to split straight down the length of the culm. Seasoned culms are a perfect straw color, free of stains and bad water marks. The enamel and its underlying power fibers are hard and abrasion resistant, and a fine stick will ring with a clear bell-like tone when struck.

Skilled rodmakers have an eye for a fine culm of tea-stick cane. Such judgment is perhaps their finest skill since even the best bamboo varies widely in quality. Each stick is carefully examined for irregularities in graining, dents, scratches, mold, dry rot, insect damage, sand cuts, and variations in wall thickness and density. There is also a sixth sense.

You can tell a good culm by its heft, Wes Jordan of Orvis explains, holding a length of tea stick reverently. *It has a certain feel and strength you can unmistakably sense with your fingers.*

Fully half the culms in a bundle of fifty are rejected in their first shoring at the factory, and others are rejected later, when cutting and milling reveal other imperfections. The best culm has a hard enamel underneath its waxiness. The density of these longitudinal fibers gradually decreases toward the inner wall of the culm, although the inner fibers are pithy and less resilient. The nodes of the cane, which are the leaf rings of the living plant, occur at regular intervals along its length. These nodes form weak points in the culm, once they are worked flat and their inner bulkheads are removed. These nodes give the exterior of the raw culm the characteristic jointed look of bamboo, like the fishing poles on the sunfish ponds of our youth.

It's painstaking work, the late Jim Payne gestured toward his stock of aging bamboo. *It takes a hundred and forty-five separate operations and two months from the raw cane to a finished fly rod.*

These basic operations of rod building are common to virtually each of the makers, although each also has personal variations on these basic

WILKINSON KOSMIC   1891   THREE-PIECE CALCUTTA   BROOKLYN, NEW YORK

FROM THE COLLECTION OF LEN CODELLA

WILKINSON KOSMIC   1895   THREE-PIECE TONKIN   BROOKLYN, NEW YORK

FROM THE COLLECTION OF MARTIN KEANE

UNITED STATES NET & TWINE KOSMIC   1900   THREE-PIECE TONKIN   BROOKLYN, NEW YORK

FROM THE COLLECTION OF THE MUSEUM OF AMERICAN FLY FISHING

themes. Choice culms are chosen for seasoning, and are split along one wall full length. The prepared culms are cured under precisely controlled temperature and humidity. Several famous makers age their cane as much as twenty years, and some allow the cane to season another full year after it is split into rough splines.

Once his seasoning period is complete, the rodmaker culls through his stocks for culms of the proper wall thickness for the size rod being made. Straight culms with widely spaced nodes, free of blemishes and water stains and checks, are selected for splitting. The strips or splines are split longitudinally from the culms with a knife or cane wedge in the best shops, and sawn into rough cuts in factory operations. Either method is workable, although a serious connoisseur of bamboo work will argue that hand-splitting will work along the natural grain of the culm, while a machine-cut is likely to cut across the grain at a shallow angle in a slightly twisted culm. Good bamboo will invariably split straight along its grain.

Skilled hands and eyes play a primary role in inspecting each roughly split strip of cane. The splines are closely examined for irregular graining and serious flaws. Each is carefully flexed to observe its resilience and rate of recovery from stress. Sluggish or soft strips are discarded, along with any spline that fails to bend in a constant curve.

The select strips are finally filed carefully to remove the nodes without damaging the adjacent power fibers. The inner nodal walls are removed with a gouge. The edges are planed smooth, and preliminary cuts are made to remove the excess pith before final cutting of the tapers. Some rough splines display slight twists and warping at this stage of work. These strips are perfectly workable, and are delicately heated and straightened while still warm. Final planing and bevelling follows when they have cooled.

Heat tempering can occur at various stages of work. Orvis tempers its cane in the raw culms once they are properly seasoned in controlled storage. Its rich brown color comes from this delicate heat tempering. Craftsmen like the late Lew Stoner and Everett Garrison temper their cane much less, Gary Howells oven tempers his cane slightly more, and the late Paul Young actually flame-tempered his culms in a ring-shaped gas jet. Pezon & Michel use a sensitive electric kiln of French design. Other makers oven temper the rough-cut splines before the final tapers are made.

Some heat tempering is absolutely necessary, but it must be carefully executed. Too much heat and the cane is literally robbed of its moisture and strength, and excessive tempering can make a rod short-lived and brittle. Controlled application of heat increases bamboo strength and stiffness. Moisture content is reduced and the tendency to set is reduced. The cane fibers are partially sealed against the later penetration of moisture by polymerization of their natural resins. The precise formulas for heat tempering are often closely guarded secrets.

Hand tapering is usually accomplished by placing the rough splines in a steel or hardwood planing form. Sharp planes are used to shape them into triangular strips. The grooves in the planing forms are tapered along their length, deep enough to accommodate the butt tapers of the largest salt-water calibrations, and delicate enough at their shallow ends to shape the minuscule strips that make up into tip sections of three sixty-fourths and four sixty-fourths of an inch. The planing is done on the two pith faces of the splines. Each pass of the plane cuts away the coarse, relatively weak inner fibers of the cane. The dense exterior fibers are carefully preserved, and the rough strips are staggered to mismatch the nodes before final bevelling. Some makers offset their splines to place the brittle nodes in alternating faces of the finished cane, since aligning nodes in adjacent faces results in a fatally weak spot in the rod. Other makers spiral their nodal patterns before final tapering in their planing forms, and Everett Garrison is perhaps the last craftsman to rely entirely on handwork.

It's both difficult and simple, Garrison smiles faintly and his eyes twinkle with years of knowledge. *You work the rod into the planing grooves at the right design tapers and keep planing until the blade fails to touch the bamboo.*

Other rodmakers use machines to cut their tapers. Milling is usually accomplished in two operations. The first machine cuts an approximate taper and strips off the excess pith fiber. The finish milling machine usually employs a cutting wheel formed with a series of precise cutting teeth. Some machines place the tungsten carbide cutter vertically above the spline being tapered, while the Orvis cutter passes each strip horizontally past its cutting head. Extremely fine tolerances are possible with such milling machines, although the cutting heads are quite costly and difficult to sharpen. Cheap cane rods were often made with cutting heads designed to mill each strip at an angle of slightly more than sixty-one degrees. Poor workmanship and ill-fitting tolerances could easily be concealed in the exaggerated glue joints between such strips, while the glue faces of splines cut to exactly sixty degrees must fit with remarkable precision. No reputable manufacturer uses exaggerated glue joints today.

It was Loman Hawes who designed and built the famous milling machine still used at Leonard. It survived the disastrous fire that almost ended the company after a century of production, and is still mounted on its fluted cast-iron bases. Instead of placing a rough spline on its back and milling its pithy fibers into an equilateral triangle, thereby processing it through a single cutting head, the Hawes milling machine places the rough strip with its power fibers up. Two interlocking cutters then form the finished spline, shaping the cane with its pithy apex down. William Edwards designed and built his milling machine on similar principles, although the exact specifications of such machinery are usually trade secrets, and the finish milling rooms are often forbidden territory.

Please, an embarrassed Arthur Mills often stopped casual visitors to the Leonard shop, *we don't permit anyone to see our Leonard milling machines—we're awfully sorry, but it's been off limits for seventy-five years!*

Other methods of tapering are also used. The Randle bevelling system used adjustable, interlocking boards of hard mahogany on a base of seasoned long-leaf yellow pine. Four-sided measuring blocks were common thirty years ago, with different increment of a design taper cut into each face. The Moss forming block also enjoyed a brief vogue after the Second World War. It was a triangular block slightly longer than each section, with its apex slightly fluted to receive a rough-cut spline of bamboo with its power fibers down. The enamel surface is glued to the forming block, its tapers are carefully shaped to match the bevelled surfaces of the Moss template, the temporary glue joint is worked free, and the strip is ready. Adjustable steel planing blocks are very expensive to make, and few machinists have the necessary skills. Track-type planing blocks are designed to control the shaping strokes with precision.

Whatever the method used in tapering a spline, it must frequently be checked closely with a micrometer to insure that each strip has the same taper. The tungsten carbide cutting heads or planing blades must constantly be sharpened, since fine bamboo quickly dulls even the finest steels. Precision of the highest order is needed, particularly to avoid pocking or shearing the glue faces. Cautious grinding removes any rough corners, and at their final assembly and gluing, these strips will calibrate within an incredible .001 inch. The differences in workmanship between a fine split-cane rod and its cheaper competitors are minuscule, but are absolutely critical to its performance.

Once careful checking of the splines with a micrometer has established that they meet the .001 tolerances demanded by a fine rod, they are glued together and tightly wrapped. The early adhesives used were hot fish or animal glues, particularly the fine glue made from the air bladders of the Caspian sturgeon. However, such hot glues are greatly affected by weather changes, and rods assembled in rainy weather are softer than rods made up with hot glues during dry weather. Hot adhesives keep for long periods in a glue tank and are heated when a rod is ready for gluing. The finished splines are assembled and taped lightly at the heavy end. The assembled splines are dipped in the glue tank, the surplus glue is quickly wiped off, and the stick is slowly run through a pressure-wrapping machine.

The basic process is similar with most contemporary rods, except for their use of modern adhesives. Fish and animal glues remain water soluble after they have set, and without their protective varnish, rods assembled with the hot glues could come apart in rainy weather. Synthetic adhesives have solved that problem although they are considerably more difficult to use. Their fully cured strength is incredible. The glue faces in a modern rod are much stronger than in the rod itself. Synthetics are also costly and each batch must be mixed immediately before gluing. The rod splines are assembled with tapes, the tapes are slit through one corner, and the splines are laid flat still adhering to the tapes. The synthetic resins must then be brushed on the strips by hand. Orvis, Young, Sharpe's, and many other firms are using Bakelite resins to glue their rods, while Everett Garrison and the late Pinky Gillum preferred compounds. Most reputable builders are using synthetic adhesives now.

Pressure wrapping is a standard procedure in all split-cane rod shops, although pressure-wrapping equipment varies widely from builder to builder. Small bench wrappers are still used by several rodmakers. Cotton cord is used since the stronger linen and nylon can fray and break under pressure, or actually mar the cane at its corners. The bench wrapper lays uniform windings from end to end, always working from the larger calibrations to the smaller. Working both clockwise and counterclockwise, the finish wrappings are a spiral cross wind. The larger firms use heavy pressure wrapping benches in assembling and gluing their rods, and the late Paul Young built his wrapper with the components of a war surplus B-29 bomb hoist. Some variations in the angle of wrapping, the tensile forces applied, and the uniformity of pressure occur from shop to shop, but the basic principles are always the same.

Freshly wrapped sections sometimes are warped or display a slight twist. Such deformation is not unusual. There are several ways of correcting these problems before the glues have set. Middle and butt sections are often struck gently across a flat workbench to realign the strips inside the pressure windings. Minor twists or warps can often be hand-straightened by simply bending the section carefully. Such corrections must be made in the first five minutes after wrapping, before the adhesives can start curing. Some of the modern adhesives set so quickly that corrections are impossible once the splines are wrapped. Some makers hang weights from their suspended sections, insuring that these postwrapping corrections remain in the stick.

The pressure wrappings are not removed from a stick for about a week, and after they are stripped the section is stored in a dry temperature-controlled room for three to six months. Such final curing allows the stresses in the fibers to equalize, and the moisture of the glue is finally dried out. The excess moisture both softens the action of a finished rod and slightly expands its calibrations, making a permanent ferrule fit difficult. Final straightening of a bamboo section can be accomplished by hand over a small steam jet or bunsen burner after the pressure wraps are stripped, and careful application of heat can also straighten a finished rod.

Once a wrapped section is stripped of its windings, it must be carefully scraped by hand to remove the excess glue. Cheap rods were often cleaned with power equipment, both to remove the glue and to sand off the bamboo enamel layers. These enamel layers contribute nothing to the performance or appearance of the finished rod. However, the use of power tools always risks damaging the thin layer of power fibers lying just under the enamel, seriously injuring the bamboo itself. The glues and enamels are always scraped, filed, and carefully hand-sanded from a fine rod section to protect its power cells. The section is finally polished with the finest steel wool, and a first-rate piece of cane will have no glue lines visible along the entire length of the rod—except in rods using the dark synthetic glues.

The cleaned sections are checked with a micrometer to verify their calibrations and straightened again with heat. Orvis, Phillipson, and Sharpe's immerse their finished sections in pressure-impregnation tanks at this point in their manufacture, sealing the cellular structure of the cane with Bakelite resin. Impregnation takes about a week. It makes the rod so impervious to heat, moisture and fungus that no varnish is needed to protect it once the rod is finished.

Impregnation will stand most anything, Wes Jordan insists with obvious pride in his Orvis rods. *It will stand up to ice, boiling water, rain, sun, blizzards, bug dope—even a spilled nine-to-one martini!* Such rods are not ultimately varnished, but are simply buffed to a deep polish, since the Bakelite finish lies in the cells of the cane itself.

Other builders subject their finished rod sticks to another drying cycle of several months, although some shorten this final curing with thermostatically controlled ovens. Properly seasoned cane will shrink much less than .001 inch in this final drying period. Most rodmakers stockpile their most popular rods in the form of glued and fully seasoned sticks, selecting them from the curing racks as needed for assembly.

Seating the ferrules comes next. The cane is checked to insure that no bamboo enamel remains, and the section is measured to verify its length. Since the female ferrule is hollow, its socket length must be calculated into the finished length of each piece. Final cutting of sticks to length should always occur at their butt calibrations. Fitting the ferrule to the bamboo properly is a difficult operation, as anyone attempting to fit a ferrule himself soon discovers.

Female ferrules are mounted simply by shaping a distance along the rod shaft equal to the depth of the tubing to the water plug inside the throat. Many craftsmen employ a small metal lathe, using its hole gauge and tool-post fitting and carriage, turning the ferrule seat to a diameter .002 above the ferrule itself, and feathering the corners of the cane in transition between the ferrule and its five- or six-strip section. Four-strip ferrules of the Edwards type require almost no feathering. Male ferrules of the Swiss-type or Feierabend design lack the internal stepped shoulders typical of other quality ferrules and are seated just like a female type.

Stepped male ferrules require an additional cutting operation. Using a medium-fine metal file, the cane is shaped in a lathe to fit the ferrule tubing below the step. The fit should be precise and tight prior to final gluing and seating on the finished sections.

Modern rodmakers are using synthetic ferrule cements like Pliobond and Silhower, which remain slightly elastic after setting and flex in harmony with the rod. Some maintain that their ferrules are heated and driven home with a dry fit so precise that no cement is required. Others still use the stick-type cement that was common in my boyhood years, melting it with a controlled flame and coating the cane quickly to seat the ferrule before the adhesive cools. The synthetic cements take from two to four weeks to dry.

Several methods for seating ferrules are used. Some builders simply start the ferrule over its carefully worked seat and press it home firmly against a workbench. Ferrule-driving plugs are also common. Properly

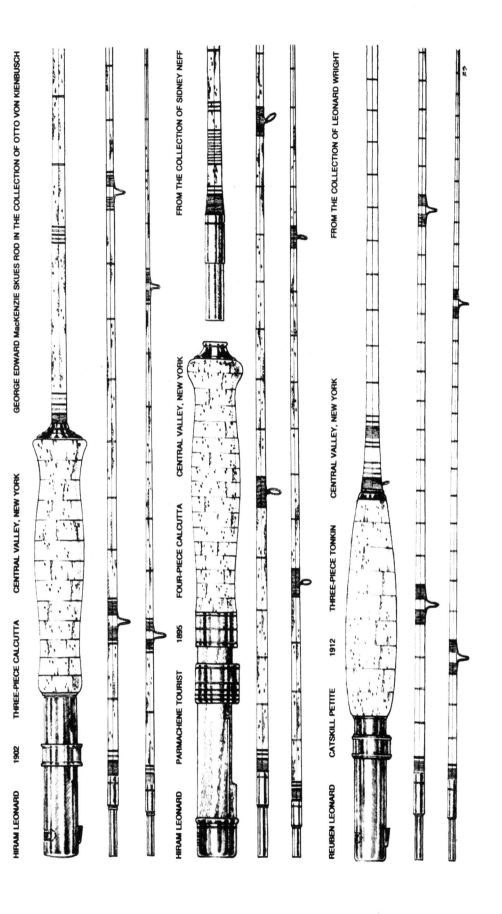

HIRAM LEONARD   1902   THREE-PIECE CALCUTTA   CENTRAL VALLEY, NEW YORK   GEORGE EDWARD MacKENZIE SKUES ROD IN THE COLLECTION OF OTTO VON KIENBUSCH

HIRAM LEONARD   PARMACHENE TOURIST   1895   FOUR-PIECE CALCUTTA   CENTRAL VALLEY, NEW YORK   FROM THE COLLECTION OF SIDNEY NEFF

REUBEN LEONARD   CATSKILL PETITE   1912   THREE-PIECE TONKIN   CENTRAL VALLEY, NEW YORK   FROM THE COLLECTION OF LEONARD WRIGHT

machined driving plugs fit inside a female ferrule and enclose a male fitting, supporting and protecting the fitting as it is driven home. Separate driving plugs are required for each diameter ferrule. The ferrule is started by hand, then fitted with a driving plug that matches its size, and the plug is tapped home with a soft mallet. Most large firms use driving plugs in concert with a small metalworking lathe that starts the ferrule and fits it with a driving plug. The ferrule is seated with a hardwood block placed between its plug and the lathe. It is forced home by turning the tailstock.

The cork grip follows the ferrules. Some makers prefabricate their handles by gluing the rings with a tension bolt and end washers. The best rodmakers make their grips by seating only a single ring of specie cork at a time. Each ring is tightly set in glue against the last. Many factory rod grips were often shaped with a grinding wheel designed to produce the desired shape. Twenty-four hours are needed for the glue to dry. Prefabricated handles are forced over the ferrule end of the butt section, and the cane is coated with glue at its final grip position. The grip is then pressed steadily and firmly into place, using a template block to reserve enough space for the reel seat filler. Grips assembled and glued on the rod shaft are usually shaped with a file and sandpaper on a small metal lathe, using fine garnet paper to finish the cork by hand.

There are many grip configurations, and most originated with famous anglers and rodmakers. The classic full Wells style is named for Henry Wells, the nineteenth-century author of *Fly Rods and Fly Tackle*. It has been used by many craftsmen over the years, and variations on the standard Wells are found on Winston, Powell, Young, Uslan, Montague, Phillipson, and some rods built in the shops of makers like Hardy, Sharpe's, and Howells. Half-Wells grips are found on many rods built by Hardy, Sharpe's, Young, Montague, Dickerson, Heddon, South Bend, and several others. Reverse Wells are popular with makers who like to conceal their hooded caps in the cork itself. These grip designs are found on the rods built by Edwards, Carlson, Thomas, Heddon, Payne, Montague, Granger, Gillum, Leonard, Hardy, and Howells.

The classic cigar-type handle is attributed to Samuel Phillippe, although the historical ties are tenuous at best. Modern craftsmen sometimes using the Phillippe cigar grip or minor modifications clearly based on its original design are Leonard, Payne, Hardy, Sharpe's, Divine, Edwards, Uslan, Orvis, Dunton, Jenkins, Cross, Jordan, Thomas, Montague, Heddon, Young, and Thomas & Thomas.

Hardy is probably responsible for both the classic Hardy fishtail grip, which combines a reverse Wells silhouette at the reel seat and tapers to a slender taper at the grip check. It was found on a galaxy of Hardy rods like the Houghton, Halford, Tournament, Perfection, Pope, Viscount Grey, J. J. Hardy, L. R. Hardy, Crown Houghton, and the classic Fairy model—the favorite rod used by Ernest Hemingway, on rivers from Silver Creek in Idaho to the Black Forest in southern Germany.

Some historians also credit Hardy with the slender reverse cigar grips that appeared after the First World War, particularly on models like the

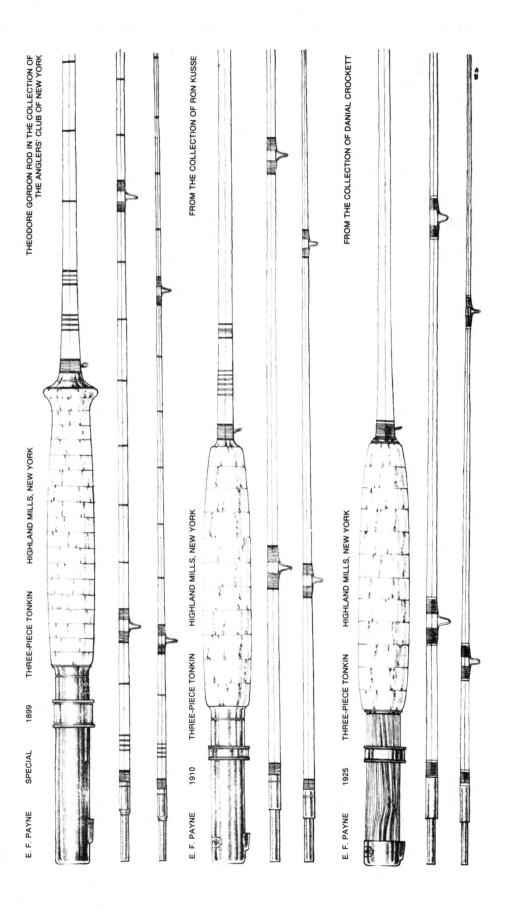

THEODORE GORDON ROD IN THE COLLECTION OF
THE ANGLERS' CLUB OF NEW YORK

FROM THE COLLECTION OF RON KUSSE

FROM THE COLLECTION OF DANIAL CROCKETT

E. F. PAYNE   SPECIAL   1899   THREE-PIECE TONKIN   HIGHLAND MILLS, NEW YORK

E. F. PAYNE   1910   THREE-PIECE TONKIN   HIGHLAND MILLS, NEW YORK

E. F. PAYNE   1925   THREE-PIECE TONKIN   HIGHLAND MILLS, NEW YORK

Casting Club de France, Mainwaring Sussex, Fairchild, Marvel, and the contemporary Palakona line. These grips are still found on the modern Hardy Lightweights, and are also found on rods like the Orvis Flea or the Thomas & Thomas Paradigm and Individualist.

Other variations of these designs are found on the rods of other great craftsmen. Charles Ritz prefers a simplified Phillippe taper grip which increases in diameter from the reel seat to the grip check. Such handles provide a working taper for the thumb and hand to generate the high-speed, high-line stroke in the Ritz style of casting. Everett Garrison has evolved from his original cigar grips to a similar increasing grip taper, although its diameter increases only one thirty-second of an inch in its full length. Halstead and Summers rods use a slender grip similar to the Garrison design. Hiram Hawes was a tournament caster and developed a strangely tapering grip with a swelled thumb stop as a fulcrum for his powerful casting style.

It was the late Paul Young who first developed a specially shaped thumb depression in his grips. The idea was later adapted by Wes Jordan in the postwar rods developed for South Bend and is still found on his special series of autographed rods for Orvis. Young continually experimented with variations in grip design, from his graceful Perfectionist and half-Wells designs to the flat bull-nose grips often found on his Parabolic 15 and Parabolic 17 tapers. Paul Young clearly favored utility over esthetics, although most rodmakers lean toward traditionally slender elegance in their rod-grip design.

Reel seats precede cork grips on many rods, depending on their size and design. Trout rods are generally fitted with reel seats measuring three-quarters and five-eighths of an inch, although some midge rods can be smaller, with their cork fillers and delicate aluminum reel bands. Solid metal reel seats are usually fitted with a wood core; birch, sumac, cedar, and basswood are commonly used. The filler plug is seated first, its cement allowed to dry thoroughly, and the reel seat barrel follows. Some tubular reel seats were fixed and pinned with German-silver wire. Fine rodmakers like Goodwin Granger, Hiram Leonard, Wes Jordan, Heddon, and Cross all used solid metal reel seats, although such full-metal seats are seldom used today.

Skeletal screw-locking seats with functional specie-cork fillers are common, along with ornamental fillers of various hardwoods like butternut and American walnut. Other exotic woods are often used: fine burled walnut and Macassar ebony are found on the exquisite Heddon rods, rosewood fillers are used on some of the finest Wes Jordan rods made at Orvis, and the talented Gary Howells likes zebrawood for his exquisite, darkly grained reel seats. Some reel seats require fixing the hooded butt cap with a pin or screw set into the cane on its longitudinal axis, and the rodmakers sometimes reinforce the butt of the section with a small collar of thin aluminum tubing. The skillful young rod builders at Thomas &

Thomas are making unusually functional reel seats which cut away the barrel of a locking seat until only the threads remain, and the threaded sleeve is morticed into the walnut seats. The skeletal sliding-ring seats built at Thomas & Thomas do not use a butt plate to protect the flared seat, preferring the look of the cane itself exposed inside the cork.

Richard Held is a private rodmaker who mortices cork into the hardwood of his sliding-band seats, using its resilience to hold the reel tightly in place, in a uniquely handsome design. For twenty years I have been experimenting with a reversed sliding-ring seat which conceals a hooded cap inside the cork handle, and uses a single ring that is tightened from below. It is a system that is unusually secure, since the weight of the reel is self-tightening. My own rods include a fine Leonard ACM 38 and an exquisite seven-and-a-half-foot Young Princess that are fitted with my skeletal grips, and Robert Summers is building excellent bamboo rods with a similar handle design on both his cork and hardwood seats.

Several makers finish the entire rod with a thin first coat of tung-oil varnish, polyurethane, or tung oil itself at this final stage of assembly, achieving a remarkably smooth finish base before the guides are seated and wrapped. Others buff their impregnated sections before winding.

The grip check is slipped down the butt section of the rod and seated against the cork handle. Neither the reel seat nor the guides can be aligned and placed until the stiffest bending profile of the rod has been tested. Some makers check the stiffness of each section on a deflection board, while others use less sophisticated methods. It is possible to hold a rod section at a forty-five-degree angle with its butt on a table and its upper end in the left hand. The section is then rolled with the right hand, making it possible to feel the stiffest bending face. The reel seat and guides are aligned opposite that stiffest side in a fly rod, so the strongest bending fibers are subjected to maximum stress during the pickup and the forward casting stroke. These fibers in the top face of the rod are placed in tension during the high-lift stroke and are radically compressed in delivering a cast.

Guides are made from several materials, and a number of designs have evolved since the ring-and-keeper fittings of the nineteenth century. Tungsten, monel, stainless steel, chrome-plated beryllium copper, and chromium-plated brass have all been used. Tungsten and chromium-plated tungsten are probably best, since they are remarkably hard and resist line wear. English snake guides, which are formed in a configuration opposite to that of American guides, and the side-supported ring guides are all popular. Side-supported guides are most commonly found on rods intended for big-water and long casts. Butt guides are usually metal ring-mounted guides of stainless steel, carboloy, chrome-plated beryllium copper, and tungsten. Such guides are common on virtually all fly rods, although the late R. W. Crompton used an ordinary snake guide in place of a heavier stripping guide. Older rods often used butt guides lined with agate or agatine, and some of the new English and Scottish rods are using synthetics like aqualite and sintox. The new carbon graphite rods are using butt- and tip-guide rings lined with a black aerospace ceramic originally developed for missile nose cones and rocket nozzles.

Tip guides of the American type with a simple pear-shaped configuration are probably best. The finest are made from tungsten, chromium, or stainless steel. Tip guides should be large enough to permit the leader knot to enter the guides readily when a fish is worked close. All of the guides should be large enough to facilitate long casts, and the butt guide should not be too close to the grip. It should be easily reached with the left hand, yet far enough up the butt section to take the exaggerated line shoot of the left-hand haul. Many butt guides are too close to the grip. The feet of the guides are usually filed or ground down to a razor-fine edge, making the silk wrappings absolutely smooth when they are wound. Most rodmakers include a fly-keeper ring or guide or bent wire loop in the windings at the grip check.

Several methods of placing guides are used. R. W. Crompton liked the same number of guides as there were feet in the rod so that nine guides were required for a three-piece rod of nine feet. However, Crompton spaced his guides with one important difference. The butt guide on the butt joint was completely omitted. Four guides were used on the middle section, and five were placed on the tip. The American standard technique uses a stripping guide on the butt section, five snake guides on the middle section, and five on the tip. Using one more snake guide than the rod length is a fine rule of thumb. Samuel Phillippe developed a method used by many American manufacturers. One stripping guide was placed on the butt, four were placed on the middle joint, and five guides were seated on the tip. Many European makers use guide spacings identical to the Phillippe method, although some British and Scottish manufacturers use only three guides on the middle joint and four on the tip. Seven or eight guides are clearly too few on a nine-foot rod. Such rods should be fitted with a nine thirty-seconds of an inch stripping guide, number two snake guides on the middle section, and number one guides on the tip. Snake guides smaller than size 2/0 should not be used, and stripping guides under five thirty-seconds of an inch do not shoot a cast readily.

Guides are wound by hand on the best-quality rods. The guide is placed in its proper position and temporarily held with masking tape. The winding silk is started about one-sixteenth of an inch in front of the first foot of the guide. The thread is wound over itself. The silk is wound carefully up the sloping foot of the guide, each winding being laid tightly against the last, until the wrapping lies about one thirty-second of an inch past the shoe. Then a loop of winding thread is wound under the last few turns, the free end of the silk is threaded into the loop, and the loop is used to pull the thread back under itself. The remaining silk is trimmed carefully with a razor blade. The tape is stripped from the other foot, and it is secured with winding silk. Rodmakers like Winston and Howells double-wrap their guides, working back along the wire toward the feet. The ferrule serrations or splits are firmly wound too, with small ornamental wraps at the tip guide and above the grip check. In the days when fish and animal glues were common, regularly spaced wrappings of silk were necessary to hold the bamboo splines together. The only relatively modern rodmaker who used intermediate wraps was Edwin Powell, and his wraps were actually needed to reinforce his patented method of hollow construction. Rod windings vary widely from maker to maker, from the simplicity of Garrison transparent wrappings at the guides to the intricate silk embellishments on the butt sections of Thomas and Edwards.

The windings are set with a color preservative in most shops, and then coated with tung varnish, epoxy, or polyurethane. Once the guides are dried, it is time for the final finish of tung oil, polyurethane, epoxy, or rod varnish. Four hand-rubbed coats of hot varnish are still perhaps the finest protective finish, although a modern dipped finish is better looking. Everett Garrison finishes his rods in an ingenious tubular dipping tank about two inches in diameter, and a timing mechanism designed to remove a rod section slowly—its rate of withdrawal synchronized with the drying rate of the finish, producing a gleaming surface as perfect as a mirror.

Hand-applied coats of varnish are usually rubbed with lava stone and felt, making them smooth and hard. The final coat is left bright by some makers, who like its brilliant glitter, and rubbed to a dull matte finish by others. Ten days to two weeks are required for a fine tung-oil varnish to dry completely, particularly before rubbing down between coats. Once the final coat is dry, the rod is ready for fishing in all types of weather, and its beauty is remarkably enhanced, particularly in the work of builders like Payne and Carlson and Howells, who are famous for the quality of their finishes.

The late Lew Stoner believed that varnishing was far more important than many anglers believe. Stoner argued that too much varnish can deaden a rod and increase its tendency to set, and that too little varnish can leave the cane without adequate protection from mildew and rot.

Found out the hard way years ago, Stoner always explained. *Unless the finish is as elastic and hard as the cane itself, it soft-sleeves the rod and deadens its action—it gets bent and stays bent beyond the power of the cane to force it back into shape after a hard day of fishing.*

The basic operations are similar with all rodmakers, but in matters of casting action and the structure of the rod, there is considerable difference in rod theory and construction. Some builders prefer a fast, crisp action in their rods, others like the traditional delicate tip and stiff butt tapers, and still others lean toward a compound taper that flexes more in the butt than in the upper calibrations. Modern rods are still built in four-strip and five-strip sections, although most are still the common six-strip construction, and each of these types displays its own distinctive character under casting stress. Preferences in rod action are highly personal. Some fishermen prefer an extremely fast action, like many of the rods built by Pinky Gillum and Lyle Dickerson. Others like a slower rod, the exquisite compound tapers found in the work of men like Garrison and Young.

It's a question of personality, insists Art Neumann of the Wanigas Rod

Company. *The ulcer type is a driver, and needs a fast rod to keep up with his choppy casting strokes—the more relaxed fisherman is the one who likes the Parabolics, and their deliberate casting rhythms.*

Minor variations in rod tapers result in these major differences in casting performance. Each of the manufacturers tapers its rods to carefully engineered calibrations that vary surprisingly from maker to maker. Such tapers are a highly competitive aspect of the rod-building business, and some manufacturers are endlessly experimenting with new theories and rod actions. Many craftsmen will make special tapers to suit a knowledgeable fisherman's specifications, providing he is willing to pay the price.

It is surprising how few anglers realize that rod tapers are milled at extremely fine tolerances, and that differences of only .005 inch can make the difference between a fast and slow butt action. Differences of less than .002 can make a radical change in the casting and hooking delicacy of a tip section. Two rods of identical calibrations from the workbench of a single craftsman can also vary radically. Bamboo is a variable wood, quite heterogeneous in its molecular structure and varying widely in its wall thickness from culm to culm. Heat treatment of the cane can also produce variables in its casting performance. It is this combination of variables that can make a rod great—its sweetness a poetry impossible to describe—or merely another fine casting tool. There are two excellent Young Parabolic 15s in my collection that demonstrate this fact perfectly. One is a surprisingly fast Parabolic action, while the same compound taper in the other produces a slow casting rhythm that works well into the butt. Such subtle differences are impossible to predict—just as the tonality in a particularly fine Stradivarius never quite duplicates the richness or brilliance found in another made by the same master.

There are also surprising variations in rod behavior between four-strip, five-strip and six-strip rods of identical weight. Both cross section and taper profile are factors in rod performance. The quality of its cane will determine how a rod might perform, but it is taper and construction that largely determine the character of that performance. Fly rods are forced to bend in almost every plane while casting, since few anglers cast without bad habits and torque, so any rod must perform both across its flats and its corners. Many anglers believe their cane rods will not bend in the diagonal planes of their corners. Early rod builders thought so too, and rounded their bamboo rods to eliminate the corners. It took many years before they discovered that turning their rods down ruined the power fibers of their cane. Four-strip rods were easily milled, and involved much less work than six-strip, eight-strip, ten-strip, or twelve-strip sections. Six-strip rods soon eliminated the more complicated designs, and their casting strokes were less demanding than four-strip tapers. Three-strip rods were tried and abandoned before 1850, but the five-strip theory did not evolve until the late R. W. Crompton proposed its superiority forty-odd years ago.

Crompton planed his first five-strip rod in a specially made tapering block that required two grooves for each section, milling the splines at

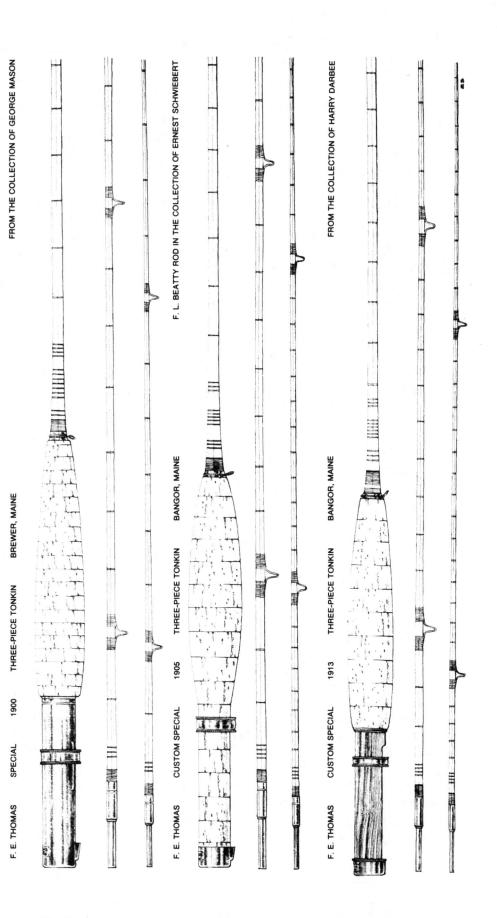

F. E. THOMAS   SPECIAL   1900   THREE-PIECE TONKIN   BREWER, MAINE

FROM THE COLLECTION OF GEORGE MASON

F. E. THOMAS   CUSTOM SPECIAL   1905   THREE-PIECE TONKIN   BANGOR, MAINE

F. L. BEATTY ROD IN THE COLLECTION OF ERNEST SCHWIEBERT

F. E. THOMAS   CUSTOM SPECIAL   1913   THREE-PIECE TONKIN   BANGOR, MAINE

FROM THE COLLECTION OF HARRY DARBEE

precisely fifty-four degrees. Each spline is an isosceles triangle in cross section, measuring fifty-four degrees at its outer corners and seventy-two degrees at its apex inside the rod. A five-strip section has a corner opposite its bending plane, stiffening and reinforcing its character. Such rods are much stiffer than four- or six-strip rods of equal weight and similar tapers. However, five-strip rods often respond with considerable eccentricity under casting loads, and sometimes fracture in the hands of anglers with erratic casting habits. The bending behavior of these five-strip rods is difficult for an average fisherman, and they have never achieved wide popularity. Nathaniel Uslan, who once worked in the Payne shop, is the best-known disciple of R. W. Crompton and his five-strip tapers—although the late Frank Wire on the Pacific Coast was also an advocate of the Crompton five-strip theory.

Four-strip rods are also demanding in their casting behavior, and never achieved much popularity, although they require much less work than either five- or six-strip tapers. The principal arguments for four-strip fabrication lie in easier construction, the fact that it has more power fibers per diameter than the other cross sections, and that its power fibers are concentrated slightly farther from the neutral bending plane of the rod. However, a four-strip taper is slightly heavier per diameter than a similar five- or six-strip taper, and the extra power fibers are often fully occupied in compensating for the additional weight. The principal advocate of four-strip design was the late William Edwards—although his father Eustis Edwards and his brother Gene Edwards were both six-strip partisans—and his famous Edwards Quadrate rods are beautiful. Samuel Carlson is presently building equally fine four-strip rods in his Connecticut shop, using the superb Edwards tapers.

Six-strip rods are more difficult to make, having twelve gluing faces that must be precisely milled, instead of the ten faces in a five-strip taper and only eight in a four-strip design. However, their bending character makes them easier to cast in the hands of an average fisherman, and they dominate modern rod building. Six-strip rods are more nearly round, and flex almost as readily across the corners as the bending planes. The flexing stresses are also more uniformly distributed in a six-strip rod, and the principal manufacturers in both Europe and the United States all use six-strip construction.

However, the arguments between the adherents of four-strip, five-strip, and six-strip construction still continue. Their prelude came in the first exchanges between R. W. Crompton and authors on split-cane construction like Perry Frazer and George Parker Holden. Crompton argued that his five-strip method was theoretically superior, although it took him almost fifty years to work out practical tapers. His theories held that there was no continuous glue line across the median bending plane as there was in a six-strip rod. There was approximately fifteen percent less glue, and the extra glue in rods built with six to twelve strips was a liability contributing nothing to their action. A. J. McClane added his experience to the

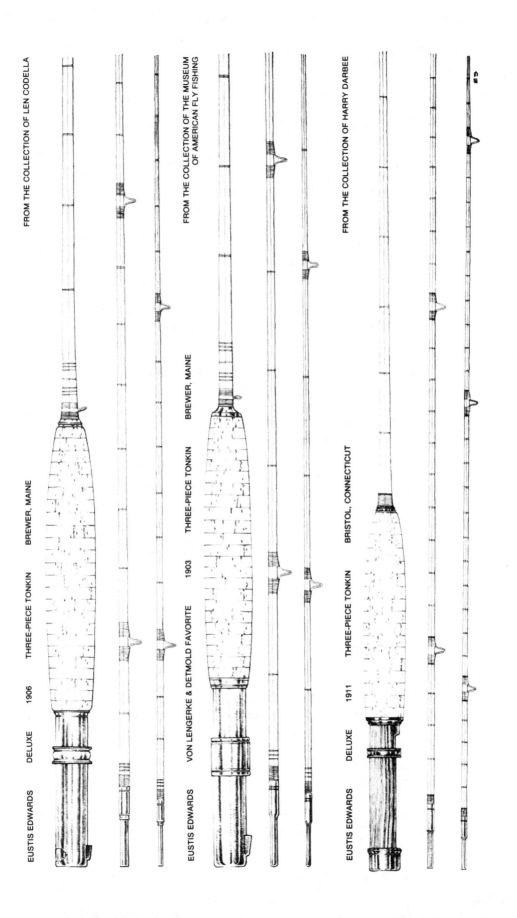

FROM THE COLLECTION OF LEN CODELLA

EUSTIS EDWARDS   DELUXE   1906   THREE-PIECE TONKIN   BREWER, MAINE

FROM THE COLLECTION OF THE MUSEUM
OF AMERICAN FLY FISHING

EUSTIS EDWARDS   VON LENGERKE & DETMOLD FAVORITE   1903   THREE-PIECE TONKIN   BREWER, MAINE

FROM THE COLLECTION OF HARRY DARBEE

EUSTIS EDWARDS   DELUXE   1911   THREE-PIECE TONKIN   BRISTOL, CONNECTICUT

controversy in *The Practical Fly Fisherman*, and his observations are interesting:

> The corners in a five-strip rod act as backbones extending the length of the rod, but in four- and six-strip rods they are in the same plane, directly opposite each other. Since there are three pairs of flats, it follows that the action, or bending, will occur in one or more of these planes.
>
> In theory, if the fisherman forces a corner to take some of the load, it simply shrugs the load over to one of the adjacent flat sides, with the result that the cast doesn't go exactly where he directs it. This is an inherent characteristic of all rods having an even number of sides according to the pentagonal theorists.
>
> A five-strip rod doesn't respond in such a manner. In this case each weak flat has a reinforcing backbone on the opposite side. Naturally, the strengthening is greatest right at the five corners. At points slightly to one side or the other of these corners the effect diminishes slightly, only to increase again to full value as the center of the bordering flat side (remember that there is a corner opposite this flat) is reached. A four-sided rod prefers to bend up-and-down and sideways. To use shooter's parlance, it wants to swing directly from twelve to six o'clock or from three to nine, but it resists bending slightly more in any other combination of bending stress.
>
> By the same reasoning a rod of six-strip construction will flex evenly from twelve to six, from two to eight, and from four to ten. It is reluctant to bend in any other direction. The five-strip rod is no exception to this tendency to bend in any other direction.
>
> But where are these paths and how many of them are there? According to Nat Uslan they're not at the corners because these regions are strongest; nor are they at the flats because, as pointed out before, there is always a corner opposite a flat. Since there are ten such combinations of corners and flats, we can assume that a five-strip rod doesn't care which way you shoot your cast.

Stream experience with all three types of rod cross sections tends to verify some of these theoretical arguments and to discount others unmistakably. Four-strip rods are poetry in motion, sweet and smooth in their casting planes, but any deviation from those planes and the poetry is broken. The rod reacts almost roughly, forcing the casting loads back toward the bending faces, and it is unforgiving in the hands of a careless fisherman. Five-strip rods are undeniably stiff for their weight, since they increase the moment of inertia in cross sections of equal area. The moment of inertia in a circle is a function of its diameter to the fourth power. The circular perimeter in a five-strip rod is slightly larger than the circumference of a six-strip cross section having an equal area, which means that if its diameter is only one-tenth larger, its moment of inertia and stiffness are increased almost fifty percent. These mathematical relationships are expressed in the following equations for the three types of construction:

$$D_1^4 = 1.0 \times 1.0 \times 1.0 \times 1.0 = 1.0 \text{ (six-strip)}$$

$$D_2^4 = 1.1 \times 1.1 \times 1.1 \times 1.1 = 1.46 \text{ (five-strip)}$$

$$D_3^4 = 1.12 \times 1.12 \times 1.12 \times 1.12 = 1.57 \text{ (four-strip)}$$

The moment of inertia and theoretical stiffness of the three cross sections seem to point toward optimal stiffness in the four-strip sections, although the placement of the glue lines, the relativity of corners and flats, and the heterogeneity of bamboo are equally critical in rod action. Actual rod behavior under casting loads involves other factors too. The alignment of the reel seat and the guides stresses a rod with eccentric loads in a clearly preferred bending plane. The guides themselves displace a rod's center of gravity from its longitudinal axis and affect bending dynamics.

Stiffness and performance under stress are not just functions of moment of inertia, since the modulus of elasticity implicit in a rod's material is equally important. Its dynamics are not like those of a spring or cantilever beam, as early mathematical analysis usually sought to prove.

Rods stress according to wave linear equations, Everett Garrison explains, *like the progressive uncoiling of a bullwhip.*

The loads of casting are complex. When the line is being picked up off the water, the primary forces are its hydraulic friction, line weight and atmospheric drag, air resistance against the rod, and the casting energy imparted by the caster. Line weight and its mixture of hydraulic and atmospheric drag are distributed through the guides to the rod in a series of concentrated loads. Secondary forces are the impact load of the pickup haul on the stripping guide, the inertial forces of rod and reel weight, and the choppy torque that comes from poor casting habits.

The loads of the forward stroke are slightly different. Line weight remains the same, but line drag is entirely atmospheric unless a careless backcast hits the water. Rod inertia and atmospheric drag on its length remain the same, unless the variables of wind direction and velocity intrude. The combined line forces are more uniformly distributed along the rod, since during the forward cast, the line rides back against the cane itself. The impact load of a strong left-hand haul begins parallel to the rod, but quickly exerts force vectors on the butt guide as the stroke starts forward. The inertial forces of the reel remain the same, except that they may take the form of counterclockwise torque on the forward cast. Many skilled distance casters allow the reel to ride out sideways during the backcast, while the line is extending, and its twisting loads are clockwise. Poor casting habits can also exert a minor counterclockwise load on the butt section. Arm force is usually equally distributed on both the backcast and the forward stroke, although the final left-hand haul in the forward cast exerts an accelerating impact load on the rod and its butt guide.

The arm stroke is not a constantly accelerating load either. The pickup starts gently to break the hydraulic friction of the surface film and finishes with a sharply accelerating stroke once the line is skimming lightly across the surface. The forward cast accelerates powerfully and ends with a sharp wrist snap in the follow-through. The cumulative force in both strokes is roughly equal, although that force is not delivered in the same way.

Many anglers may find such stress analysis disturbing and dislike any attempt to explain the poetry of a fly rod with mathematical equations. The pleasure transmitted through a fine rod to our senses defies mathematical explanations, but many rodmakers do argue about their work in scientific terms. Our brief discussion will at least make the reader aware of their conflicting theories and the performance variables of their rods. However, didactic sermons about moment of inertia, bamboo and its modulus of elasticity, and the number of strips in a rod are infinitely less important than its taper; and rod tapers are seldom openly discussed. There are surprising differences in rod calibrations and tapers from one manufacturer to another—ranging from the soft actions found in the classical Leonards to the extremely stiff tapers typical of Lyle Dickerson or the exaggerated tip actions built by Sewell Dunton.

Several engineers have worked out methods of comparing rod actions in past years. Systems of measuring the vibrations of a rod have not proven significant since they often fail to describe the variables in radically different tapers. Perhaps the best known of these systems was the Montague Free Deflection Method, which sought to evaluate rods in terms of their oscillations per minute. The tensile stress a rod exerts against a scale is meaningless in terms of casting qualities, although it was widely used for many years. The British system, which loaded a rod in deflection until fracture occurred, was also quite meaningless in evaluating its fishing qualities. The Crompton Deflection Board was perhaps the best method used in judging the character of fly rods. It placed a test rod on a graphic grid, fixing its grip and reel seat on the base line and attaching a four-ounce weight to its tip. The curvature of the various rods could then be photographed or plotted for ready comparison, and their stiffness profile was clearly pinpointed.

In recent years, Don Phillips has developed another method of comparing fly rods. The Phillips Stiffness Profile is clearly the most knowledgeable and scientific approach to the comparison of rod behavior under stress. Few of our past rod builders were technically trained in the modern sense of understanding stress analysis, and since the essential mathematics governing a fly rod in casting lie in both aerodynamics and static structures, it should not be surprising that an aerospace engineer like Don Phillips has married these disciplines in analyzing rods. Most of our famous rodmakers, including formally trained engineers like Hiram Leonard, were incapable of real stress analysis. Their finest tapers were largely empirical designs, painstakingly evolved over the years by trial and error. Even famous Payne tapers like the eight-and-a-half-foot dry-fly rod that virtually became the company's trademark were largely accidental.

ALBERT EVERETT HENDRICKSON

Jim Payne was forever building salmon rods for Albert Everett Hendrickson, the man for whom the Hendrickson fly patterns are named, and once built forty-eight ten-foot tapers before Hendrickson was satisfied. Hendrickson also had a twelve-foot salmon rod that Roy Steenrod, who developed the Hendricksons, and Jim Payne were trying out at Four Maples on the Esopus. When they had finished, and Steenrod was taking it apart, he happened to flex the tip and middle section in a casting stroke.

That's it, Jim! he exclaimed to Payne. *You add a handle to that and you've got the perfect dry-fly taper!*

The tapers of other famous rods were often accidents too. The superb Ritz design called the Fario Club evolved from a traumatic encounter with a bicycle. Charles Ritz was planning a trip to the Lech in Bavaria and had sent a favorite rod to the shop of Pezon & Michel for some minor repairs. It was a conventional nine-foot rod, fairly stiff in the butt tapers at the grip and too soft in its tip calibrations. It was also a travel rod, built with a detachable grip that received a male ferrule fitted to the bottom of its butt section. There was no extra tip and the rod was protected with only a simple poplin rod sack. When it was ready, Pezon & Michel sent it over to the Hotel Ritz with a messenger on a bicycle.

It was a mistake. During the trip from the shop to the Place Vendôme, the messenger boy allowed the cloth rod sack to catch in the spokes of his bicycle. Its front wheel was damaged, and the boy hurt his elbow and knee in the resulting tumble.

But the rascal said nothing about catching the rod in the spokes, Ritz laughs today. *He simply delivered the cloth sack to the hotel concierge, and left the Place Vendôme as quickly as possible!*

Ritz failed to examine the rod and simply packed it in his little Lancia when he left for Germany. When his party arrived on the Lech, Ritz was dismayed to find that both the tip section and butt joint of his rod were completely sheared off. The tip had lost about three inches at its top guide and another three inches were gone at the butt ferrule just above the grip.

It was a disaster! Ritz shrugs eloquently.

Ritz had no extra rod along, and no one else had thought to bring a spare. There was no alternative to making temporary repairs on the damaged rod, and Ritz quickly stripped off a snake guide and fitted the tip top in its place. The ferrule was heated and removed from the broken butt section, and refitted on the remaining cane. The resurrected rod measured about eight and a half feet, and Ritz half-heartedly walked down to the Lech to test it. Ritz is one of the finest casting stylists who ever lived, and the rod behaved strangely after its surgery in the field, but he soon adjusted to its unusual rhythms. Its stroke was slow and exotic, with most of the bending in its butt section, and the tip a little stiff and top heavy.

Fantastic! Ritz explains excitedly.

The modified rod could carry a remarkable line load in its false casting and lift a surprising length from the water. It did both of these things better than before. Its timing was exotic and slow, but the reduction of tip flexing made the butt function in bending and the tip perform like a lever. The upper two-thirds of the rod delivered full casting power to the line at the point of release with almost no oscillation or follow-through.

The rod was a revelation then, Ritz continues. *It would deliver an absolutely straight line at eighty feet!*

It was a happy accident, and although its action was a little clumsy and difficult to master in its timing, the half-crippled Pezon & Michel was one ancestor of the modern semiparabolic tapers found in the work of master craftsmen like Everett Garrison, Lew Stoner, Jim Payne, Paul Young, Edwin Powell, Doug Merrick, and Gary Howells.

Don Phillips has been working out a more disciplined approach to the design and analysis of rod tapers. His stiffness profile is a static method of analysis which merely treats a rod like a deflecting cantilever beam. Although such analogies are too simple, since they exclude the radical dynamics of casting, they do offer some preliminary bench marks for evaluating and comparing rods. Phillips even grants some credibility to a rudimentary deflection board analysis, although he has a number of reservations about its usefulness. Perhaps the most obvious flaw in deflection analysis is the fact that a rod has a constantly varying cross section throughout its length. The grip and lower butt section are not fixed during a casting stroke, like the rod butt is fixed on a deflection board, but are constantly moving and subject to wrist torque. The inertial forces imposed by the weight of the rod itself vary along its entire length, and local variables in acceleration also occur.

Atmospheric drag varies with rod diameter, and wind direction can produce intriguing variables in the atmospheric loads imposed on a rod. Lateral winds can cause eccentric loads and compensating torque well into the delicate calibrations of a rod, and buffetting and gusts in variable winds are another complexity affecting the stress analysis of actual casting performance. The static load of a lead weight in simple deflection analysis is not a viable simulation of the accelerating dynamics and momentary impact loads of either line work or a hooked and fighting fish. These loads are also erratic, being transmitted back into the rod through its guides. The direction of these loads is dependent on the constantly changing position of each guide, and the angles of the line entering and leaving it. Phillips also argues that the relatively minor deflection caused by a four-ounce weight on the tip is a faint echo of the radical deflections that occur in long-range casting or playing a strong fish.

There are two basic equations in analyzing such static deflection, and both are derived from common structural design. The first defines total tip deflection, and is expressed in the following terms:

$$\text{Deflection in inches} = \frac{0.25 \text{ pounds} \times \text{rod length in inches}^3}{3 \times \text{modulus of elasticity} \times \text{moment of inertia}}$$

The modulus of elasticity is expressed in pounds per square inch, while the moment of inertia for a given cross section is defined in inches to the fourth power. Moment of inertia is critical to all structural analysis and is often derived as follows:

$$\text{Moment of inertia} = \frac{3.1416 \times \text{rod diameter in inches}^4}{64}$$

Don Phillips is quick to point out that these classical equations of stress analysis are useful in describing fly-rod behavior only when the deflection is minor. Their relationships apply to a cantilever with a load concentrated ninety degrees to its axis. It is obvious that in exaggerated deflection, when the tip bends down to align with the direction of the load, it is entirely subjected to tensile loads rather than the mixture of tension and compression found in less radical bending behavior. Since a four-ounce weight will easily cause exaggerated deflection in most light rods, Phillips pinpoints this as the principal limitation of using a deflection board in analyzing rod actions. However, modulus of elasticity and moment of inertia are the only forces affecting a rod's deflection and resistance to deformation.

Other factors are external, Phillips insists, *and lie outside the parameters of static deflection analysis.*

Phillips believes that a well-designed rod taper behaves in a series of wave-linear deflections, permitting its tip to oscillate back and forth in a crisply defined path. When the casting rhythms are broken and that path is not relatively straight, wavy loops will form in the line that kill both accuracy and distance. High concentrations of bending stress can occur in distance casting, with the bending moment in rod deformation as follows:

$$\text{Bending moment in inch/pounds} = \frac{\text{Stiffness factor in pounds/inch}^2}{\text{Radius of curvature in inches}}$$

The stiffness factor is a constant in this equation, and the maximum stresses occur in the tensile forces along the outside curvature of the power fibers, and in the compressive forces concentrated in the inside curvature of the rod. Standard stress analysis tells us that these stresses occur at the extremities of the cane, while the bending stresses along its axis remain neutral. Years ago I had an engineering professor who described such bending phenomena with his hand extended palm down, with his fingers together and straight. Bending his fingers up, he demonstrated the tensile stresses in a deflecting beam with the tightly stretched skin across his palm and compressive stresses with the wrinkled skin that formed across the back of his hand. Bending his fingers down wrinkled the skin in his palm and tightened the skin across the tendons in his hand, and I never forgot that simple lesson in the dynamics of bending stresses. Maximum tension and compression in bending is determined with this equation:

$$\text{Bending stress in pounds/inch}^2 = \frac{\text{Bending moment} \times \text{radius of rod}}{\text{Moment of inertia}}$$

Don Phillips argues that these mathematical expressions of bending moment and bending stress can be combined in a new equation that better defines the maximum stress at the maximum distance from the neutral axis of the rod. His new equation shows that in any radius of rod curvature, stress can be reduced by using materials with a lower modulus of elasticity or designing rods of smaller diameter. Phillips' equation is as follows:

$$\text{Bending stress in pounds/inch}^2 = \frac{\text{Modulus of elasticity} \times \text{radius of rod}}{\text{Radius of curvature}}$$

Radius and modulus of elasticity have obvious limits in split-cane construction, but engineers like Don Phillips are working beyond bamboo and fiberglass to exotic materials like carbon graphite, boron, PRD-49, and various hybrid structures using these synthetic fibers with glass.

Phillips is correct in insisting that both stress and stiffness must be considered in terms of simultaneous interaction, and an integral part of the design process. Stress should be permitted to reach relatively high levels, as long as the material has a sufficient safety factor between maximum stress and its fracture point. Phillips points out that the maximum rod curvature in fiberglass is much greater than the allowable curvature in bamboo, a material with a much higher modulus of elasticity. The fracture behavior of cane suggests that future synthetic rod materials demand close attention to these relationships between maximum bending stresses and their structural limits, since they have a modulus of elasticity that lies well beyond the finest Chinese bamboo.

Phillips' theories clearly recognize the complex relationships involved in casting stresses, and that a rod is not subject to static loads but performs in a series of dynamic wave-linear vibrations. The tensile stresses affecting the tip during the pickup, false casting, and the forward casting stroke are filled with variables that virtually define numerical analysis. Cyclical variations occur throughout these casting oscillations as the line loops accelerate and form and extend in both directions. Phillips has evolved this equation to describe for the frequency of these oscillations:

$$\text{Casting frequency } F_n = \frac{1}{2\pi} \sqrt{\frac{3EIg}{PL^3}}$$

Don Phillips defines EI as the stiffness factor in pounds per square inch, and multiplies it with a constant gravitational factor of 386 inches per second squared. The value of π is 3.1416, and the combination of 0.25 pounds P multiplied by the rod length in inches to the third power has its origins in our first equation for tip deflection.

The Phillips frequency equation establishes the oscillatory behavior of any rod in cycles per second, and is a workable simulation of its character, provided the distributed loads are negligible and dampening action is not a major factor. However, it should be understood that the Phillips concept of natural frequency is limited to a rod's recovery from bending stresses, consciously excluding its inertial factors and atmospheric loads. It can be argued that rod stiffness and length, as well as the distribution of that stiffness through taper calibrations, are the basic factors in fly-rod design. The other primary factors are external forces imposed on the rod by the dynamics of the working line, the atmosphere and hydraulic friction, and casting skills.

However, these external forces cannot be ignored. Fly casting involves muscular energy that either accelerates or decelerates the rod in its normal casting cycles. Its velocity varies constantly throughout its length. The basic laws of Newtonian physics state that an accelerating force in one direction always occurs in concert with an equal inertial force in the opposite direction. During the early moments of a forward casting stroke, the rod accelerates at increasing speeds toward the tip because of its proportionately increasing moment-arm distances above the grip. Rod length and simple rotation are the forces involved. Comparable inertial forces occur at each point along a rod taper, matching each increasing vector of acceleration. Phillips uses a surprisingly simple equation to describe the total force concentrated at such points along the rod in question. It divides the weight of the rod segment, multiplied with its acceleration in inches per square second, by the gravitational constant of 386 inches per square second. The equation is as follows:

$$\text{Total force in pounds} = \frac{\text{Weight in pounds} \times \text{acceleration}}{\text{Gravitational constant}}$$

It is important to understand that inertial forces occur only when the rod is accelerating or decelerating, and its composite velocities are changing. No inertial loads are generated by a rod oscillating at a constant rate of speed. Weight and diameter are therefore the factors that affect bending performance through inertial loads, while acceleration depends directly on the angler.

Atmospheric drag imposed by air density, wind velocity and direction, and the hydraulic drag that occurs when the line is lifted from the water are other external forces with a primary influence on casting performance. These factors of drag are exerted on the line and transmitted to the rod, as well as exerted directly in terms of atmospheric resistance on the rod itself. Aircraft designers and naval architects are perhaps best acquainted with

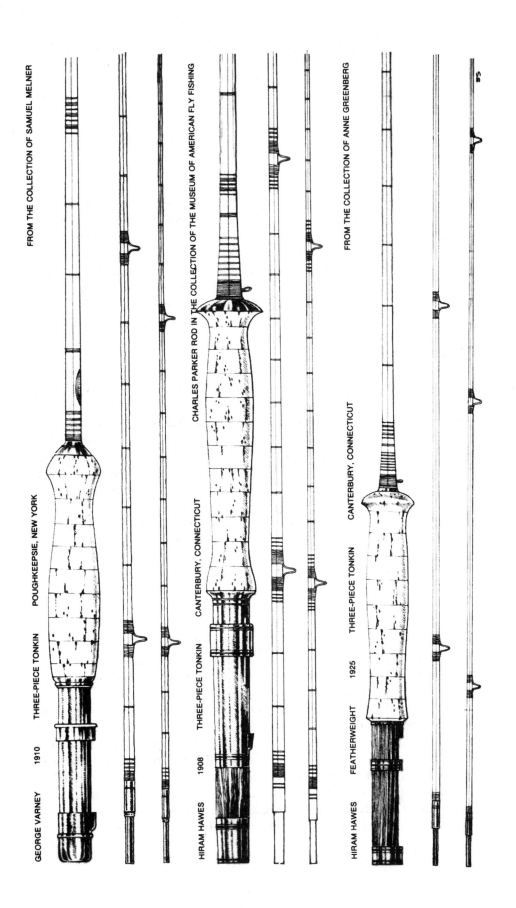

FROM THE COLLECTION OF SAMUEL MELNER

GEORGE VARNEY   1910   THREE-PIECE TONKIN   POUGHKEEPSIE, NEW YORK

CHARLES PARKER ROD IN THE COLLECTION OF THE MUSEUM OF AMERICAN FLY FISHING

HIRAM HAWES   1908   THREE-PIECE TONKIN   CANTERBURY, CONNECTICUT

FROM THE COLLECTION OF ANNE GREENBERG

HIRAM HAWES   FEATHERWEIGHT   1925   THREE-PIECE TONKIN   CANTERBURY, CONNECTICUT

such drag analysis, and their accepted formula for computing drag is the following:

$$\text{Drag in pounds} = C_d V^2 L_d \frac{W}{2g}$$

This equation predicts drag forces in terms of an empirically determined coefficient of drag, the velocity of the rod itself in feet per second, the diameter and length of the rod, and a factor consisting of atmospheric or hydraulic density in pounds per cubic foot divided by the gravitational constant times two. Effective rod length is less than the full length of the rod at rest, and is measured between the hand and tip when it is subjected to bending stresses. Since velocity is not equal at any two points along a rod in flexure, drag is also distributed unevenly along its length. Unlike inertial forces, which both resist acceleration in a rod at rest and multiply once the casting stroke is fully started, drag always acts in direct opposition to rod casting-stroke velocity.

Because of its negative influences on rod dynamics, drag is still fighting the casting stroke near the completion of its forward extension, while its inertial forces have joined in its velocity. Phillips is quick to call our attention to an intriguing facet of drag and its effect on casting. The drag equation makes it clear that atmospheric drag is directly proportional to the square of the rod's casting velocity. Practically speaking, atmospheric drag is radically multiplied when a skilled caster really powers his stroke. It means that mere casting strength has an unmistakable point of marginal return, and that manipulating line speed with a delicately timed double haul is more important in distance work than muscle. The factors of drag imposed on a rod are clearly related to its diameter and length—and the velocity of its working rhythms is a function of the fly caster.

Although each of these equations describes an important facet of rod performance, Don Phillips agrees that understanding them is not critical to your fishing skills. Stress analysis and casting dynamics are really the territory of skilled engineers. However, Phillips is correct in his contention that the length of a rod, its stiffness profile, the factors of diameter and weight implicit in its tapers, its capacity for deflection without fracture, and its inherent recovery from stress are the principal components of fly-rod behavior while casting.

Rod length affects casting performance in several ways. Longer rods keep the line higher above the water, free of the atmospheric turbulence there, although their diameter and length make them subject to greater drag. Their frequency of oscillation is slower. Short rods are fast because of their higher frequency, less atmospheric resistance, and less deflection. The optimum profile of stiffness is more elusive. Most anglers agree that a limp taper without backbone is just as abominable as a rod that is too stiff.

But there are a multitude of stiffness profiles in between, Don Phillips observes,

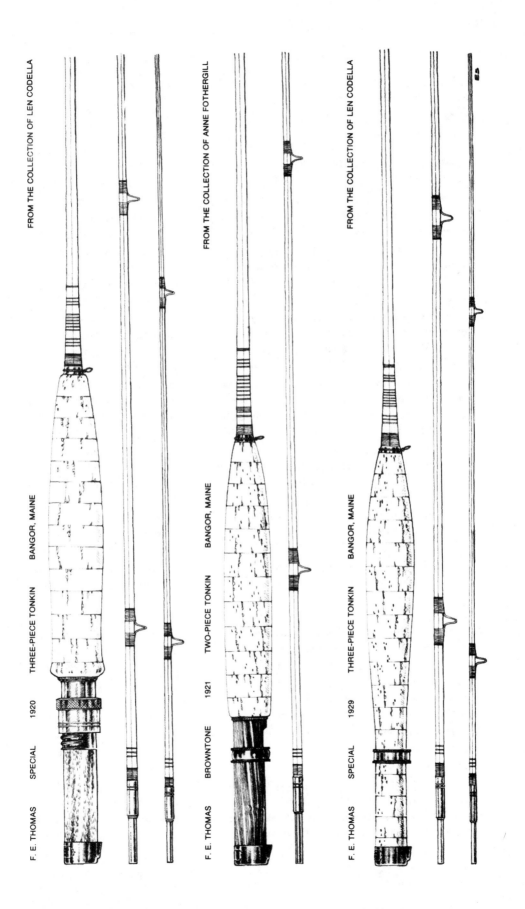

FROM THE COLLECTION OF LEN CODELLA

F. E. THOMAS   SPECIAL   1920   THREE-PIECE TONKIN   BANGOR, MAINE

FROM THE COLLECTION OF ANNE FOTHERGILL

F. E. THOMAS   BROWNTONE   1921   TWO-PIECE TONKIN   BANGOR, MAINE

FROM THE COLLECTION OF LEN CODELLA

F. E. THOMAS   SPECIAL   1929   THREE-PIECE TONKIN   BANGOR, MAINE

and they all have their fans—the principal variables in such choices are the character of the water being fished, the shyness and selectivity of the fish, and the personality and character of the fisherman himself—expressed in his casting style.

Stiffness is a result of two independent variables, as we have discussed earlier: the modulus of elasticity implicit in a material and the moment of inertia of its cross section. The modulus of elasticity in bamboo varies with the density of its power fibers and wall thickness, and the moment of inertia varies in four-strip, five-strip, and six-strip rods of equal weight. More dramatic variables occur in synthetic materials like carbon graphite, boron, fiberglass, and PRD-49. It is possible to obtain similar stiffness profiles using a high modulus fiber like boron in a small-diameter section or with a low modulus material like fiberglass in a much larger diameter.

The distribution of rod weight involves the volume and density of its material, and in the calibrations of its tapers. The physical volume of any rod varies with its tapers and the geometry of its structure. Rod density obviously varies with the quality of its bamboo and with the density of the several synthetic fibers. Both volume and density play a role in moment of inertia, and therefore in the relative stiffness of any rod. The laws of physics demonstrate that any increase in rod weight, particularly in the middle and tip calibrations, will slow its casting rhythms because of increased inertial loads. Parabolic tapers and the hollow-cane construction used by California rod builders like Stoner, Powell, Merrick, and Howells are typical examples of such stress behavior.

Moment of inertia is also closely related to the variables of rod diameter, both in the number of strips and their geometry and in the particular design tapers involved. Atmospheric drag is also directly proportional to the size and distribution of rod diameter. Both Don Phillips and the late Peter Schwab, who was one of the finest steelhead fishermen and distance casters on the Pacific Coast, agreed that atmospheric drag is the primary factor affecting the power stroke in distance casting. Schwab played a major role in the evolution of both the weight-forward line and the early Stoner patents for the fluted hollow construction.

Wind resistance and drag are almost the whole thing in casting, Schwab always argued persistently, *and they are murder on achieving high tip speed—that's why the same casting stroke will sometimes get more distance with a lighter rod!*

Deflection is actually a series of overlapping stress curvatures, and optimal flexure in any rod is achieved through cane tapers that resolve the problems of equilibrium between its diameter, its varied modulus of elasticity, and the bending capacity of its shaft material in pounds per square inch. Maximum rod deflection without fracture is also closely related to its stiffness profile and the relationships between its diameters and its distribution of stress.

Dampening is also an important factor in any structure designed to vibrate with a regular frequency. It is the tendency of any material to recover from oscillatory stresses, as its molecular structure and flexural properties tend to inhibit and control vibration. The rate of recovery from stress through dampening is important in fly rods, because a taper that continues to vibrate after a cast has been delivered is trouble. Its oscillations transmit waves into the line that kill velocity, and the slap of the line inside the guides and against the rod also affect the shoot.

Several factors affect dampening action in rods during the dynamics of casting. Atmospheric drag on tip speed is primary. Some casting forces are absorbed in the physiology of the caster himself, as well as the handle, reel seat, and inertial counterweight of the reel. Some dampening occurs in the glue joints of the cane, which is one of the reasons why eight- to twelve-strip rods were finally abandoned. Normal line friction in the guides also dampens rod vibrations. There is also considerable dampening through cellular friction implicit in bamboo itself, including the molecular behavior called hysteresis. Some dampening also occurs in the friction surfaces of the male and female ferrules. Don Phillips has performed a number of experiments in rod dampening which indicate that internal dampening forces are relatively minor, compared with the external stresses.

Phillips summarizes his work with the observation that length, stiffness, weight, diameter, and bending properties are the five basic parameters of fly-rod action. Stiffness is largely a function of moment of inertia and the modulus of elasticity implicit in a rod material. Weight is defined in terms of density and volume. Bending properties are derived from diameter, the modulus of elasticity, and the maximum acceptable stress of the material in question. It is interesting to observe that rod length, moment of inertia, volume of structure, diameter and calibrations are variables of design and fabrication, while the modulus of elasticity, strength and density of a rod's structure are properties implicit in the material itself.

Focusing on these properties of density, strength, and elasticity, Don Phillips has worked out a simple system for measuring stiffness profile in fly-rod design. Theoretical analysis is clearly beyond most fishermen, particularly considering the variable properties in any two culms of bamboo. It is much easier to calibrate a rod's stiffness profile directly, using a series of rudimentary deflection tests made at regular intervals along its length. The rod is firmly clamped on a test frame, and the test gauge is secured at the first calibration point. The test weight is suspended from each testing point, and deflection is measured on the gauge. Average stiffness between the bench clamp and the test point can be calculated with this formula for stiffness:

$$\text{Rod stiffness} = \frac{\text{Test weight} \times \text{section length}^3}{3 \times \text{observed deflection}}$$

The equation is derived from the classic structural equation describing static deflection in a fixed-end cantilever with a concentrated load. The deflection tests are then repeated at twelve-inch intervals along the full length of the rod, and the average stiffness of each foot-long section is plotted in units of pound-inches squared on a logarithmic scale so the stiffness behavior of any rod is graphically delineated. The stiffness profiles of several rods can be plotted on the same graph, making comparisons remarkably easy.

Many craftsmen have explored a remarkable number of ways to multiply the stiffness profile of their rods beyond their usual casting properties. Double-built and triple-built sections were tried to create a rod composed entirely of bamboo power fibers, completely eliminating the pithy layers, and increasing both density and strength. Cross is best known for his double-built rods, which planed away the pith of two splines, glued them together with their power fibers toward the outside, and milled the resulting laminated strip into a final taper. Eugene Edwards patented another method of double-built construction in 1885. It laminated two splines back to back, concentrating the dense power fibers at the surface and the core. It did not prove popular with either anglers or rodmakers. Fred Divine patented his spiral construction in 1892, and although it unmistakably stiffened a rod by concentrating more power fibers in a slightly reduced length, it involved too much extra work. British manufacturers experimented extensively with wrapping or centering rods with steel. Their wrapped designs included both cross-wrapping and rods covered with a continuous spiral, like the bamboo and lancewood rods completely wrapped in varnished silk. Foster rods were perhaps the best known of the steel-ribbed types, and although the Foster patent clearly improved the loading capacity of a rod, breaking strength has little relationship to casting performance. Hardy was briefly fascinated with steel-core construction, and milled the bamboo strips to house a steel center; but even though such sections were quite strong, the added weight also greatly multiplied their inertial forces and deadened their actions.

Two other surprising innovations were introduced in 1933, and both were based on the same principles. Making a tubular split-cane rod could theoretically eliminate the pithy fibers and their unnecessary weight, retain all of the power fibers in the outer surfaces, and increase the effective moment of inertia by permitting larger rod diameter at the same weight. Various methods of hollow construction were tried, but planing away the core layers of pithy fibers also reduced the effective gluing surfaces between the bamboo splines, and such rods were fragile.

It was the incomparable Lew Stoner who first solved the problem successfully, with the patent he developed for his superb Winston rod. Stoner developed a technique which milled a small U-shaped groove from the apex of each spline removing considerable pith and reducing weight while leaving relatively large glue faces between adjacent strips. These fluted hollow-built rods were an immense success, setting a new distance record of 147 feet in the hands of Marvin Hedge in 1934. Two years later, G. L. McLeod extended that record two feet, and Dick Miller used his Winston to reach an amazing 183 feet during tournament competition in 1938. Winston rods and their fluted construction have dominated tournament casting ever since their baptism in competition at Saint Louis forty years ago, particularly in the skilled hands of men like Steven Rajeff, Myron Gregory, and the late Jon Tarentino of San Francisco.

Edwin Powell instantly recognized the unique potential of the Stoner patents, and patented his own method of building a semihollow bamboo rod later that same year. The Powell system did not attempt a continuously hollow core, but cut away the pith in a series of semicircular arcs. Between these semicircular cuts, the splines remained intact. The rods were relatively fragile, and their hollow sections were always reinforced with wrappings of silk, but a fine Powell rod is an exquisite fishing tool.

These hollow-built rods were a revelation, explains Doug Merrick of Winston, *in both distance and accuracy competition.*

Edward Hewitt played a major role in the evolution of American rods after 1900, often working closely with Hiram and Reuben Leonard. Early fast-action tapers for dry-fly work were the legacy of writers like Halford and Marston, and in the beginning Hewitt unquestioningly echoed their opinions on rod action. His legacy is still found in the fast action rods of craftsmen like Dunton, Dickerson, and Gillum.

Hewitt advocated the rapier flick-flick rhythms of a steep-taper design for false casting the moisture from a dry fly, although he apparently abandoned his fast-action theories in the last years of his life. The old master had reached his eighties when *A Trout and Salmon Fisherman for Seventy-five Years* was published in 1948, and it tells us that he no longer preferred the stiff butt tapers and soft tip actions he recommended half a century earlier.

Hewitt and many other experts of his generation preferred three-piece rods because the shorter sections were more easily transported, although most knowledgeable casters agreed that the single ferrule in a two-piece design weighed less and placed only one dead point in the flow of its bending action. Hewitt argued that a single ferrule at the midpoint also occurred at a critical nodal point in its flexing under stress. Since his books have become less influential in the years past midcentury, modern rodmakers and fishermen have turned increasingly to two-piece construction. The trend represents both a desire to reduce weight and a search for optimal power flow.

Most fishermen believe that two-piece designs are superior. It is certainly true that a single ferrule reduces the weight of a delicate rod, and it means slightly more power in ratio to that weight. Such concepts are clearly more significant in rods under eight feet, and for most rods they are more theoretical than practical considerations. Contemporary rodmakers are almost universally committed to two-piece rods under nine feet, except perhaps for the young tradition-conscious artisans working at Leonard. However, the practical superiority of two-piece rods over the older three-piece designs is probably more critical in the minds of modern anglers than it is demonstrable in actual fly-rod dynamics or performance.

Hewitt and George La Branche pioneered a number of modern concepts in rod fitting too. Their sense of craftsmanship and elegance is obvious in the beautifully-machined reel fittings on the rods built by Reuben Leonard and Edward Payne in later years. Larger snake guides with a much closer spacing were another Hewitt suggestion, along with an oversized stripping guide, placed well out from the grip to facilitate shooting the line. Such placement of the butt guide also helps with the line work in the double-haul. Closely spaced guides distribute both casting and fish-playing stress more evenly along a delicate rod. Their spacing must achieve an equilibrium between the effects of cumulative guide friction on a cast and its line slap against the rod.

Early in this chapter, the influence of Hiram Leonard on American rodmaking was discussed at length, tracing the subsequent careers of his early Bangor disciples. Most of those early apprentices left the Leonard shop before 1900, except for the Hawes brothers, who were related to Leonard and remained until his death in 1907. However, the loss of exceptional craftsmen like Fred Thomas, Eustis Edwards, and Edward Payne did not end the production of fine rods at Leonard. Reuben Leonard ably continued his father's tradition of excellence after 1907. His principal assistant in the period just before the First World War was George Reynolds, and when Reuben Leonard finally died, Reynolds took the helm. His son Harold Reynolds ultimately followed in his footsteps at the Leonard shop in Central Valley, producing superb rods from before the Second World War until his retirement in 1965. Reynolds himself retired after a disastrous fire swept the Leonard plant, and it seemed the Bangor tradition had died. Arthur Mills greeted me in the store his family had operated since 1826, and his eyes glistened with tears.

It's terrible! Mills shook his head sadly. *The factory at Central Valley burned down last week—the Hawes milling machine was almost destroyed too, and Leonard may be finished completely!*

His predictions were happily premature, for knowledge and craftsmanship had always been passed on in the Leonard shop like the secrets of a medieval guild, and another generation of artisans was waiting in the wings. Hap Mills had cast his lot with rodmaking in 1957, choosing the Leonard shop instead of the family store, the famous William Mills & Son in lower Manhattan. Mills was determined that Leonard should not die after a century of rodmaking, and soon embarked on a process of resurrection. The Leonard shop was rebuilt, including the vintage bevel originally designed by Loman Hawes, and Tom Bailey was persuaded to return to making his elegant German-silver fittings. Mills was soon joined by Ted Simroe, a former professor of literature at West Point, and a superb bamboo craftsman in his own right. Several other fine young craftsmen have joined them, new bevels and other equipment have been added, and Mills and Simroe are plunging into the reams of back orders that have always plagued Leonard—building exquisite fly rods in the tradition that started in a little workshop at Bangor more than a century ago.

Hiram Leonard had already established the basic character of the modern Leonard rod by 1894. The William Mills & Son catalogue issued in

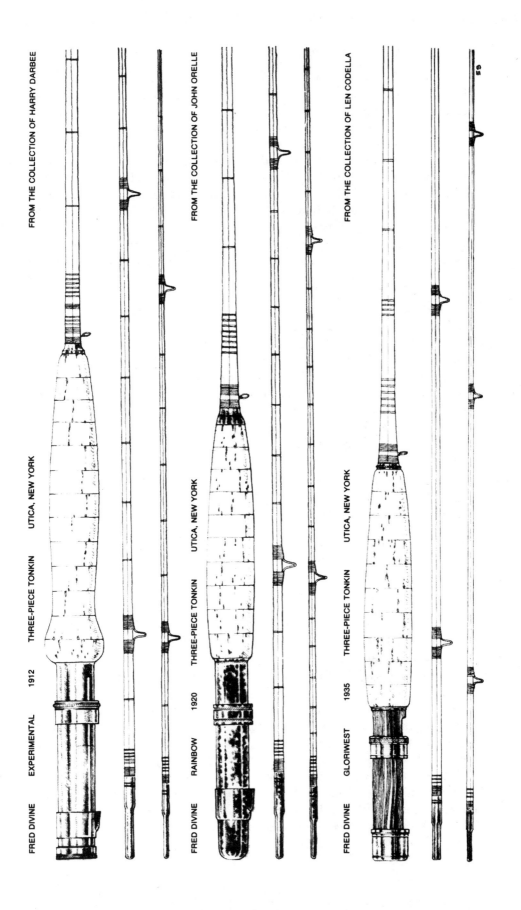

FROM THE COLLECTION OF HARRY DARBEE

FRED DIVINE   EXPERIMENTAL   1912   THREE-PIECE TONKIN   UTICA, NEW YORK

FROM THE COLLECTION OF JOHN ORELLE

FRED DIVINE   RAINBOW   1920   THREE-PIECE TONKIN   UTICA, NEW YORK

FROM THE COLLECTION OF LEN CODELLA

FRED DIVINE   GLORIWEST   1935   THREE-PIECE TONKIN   UTICA, NEW YORK

59

that year included skeletal reel seats with hardwood fillers, butt caps, and sliding bands. There were luggage rods made with full Wells-type detachable handles, trout rods with slender cigar grips and reel seats of German-silver tubing, and the Catskill Fairy had already made its debut in a three-piece design weighing only two ounces.

It was under Reuben Leonard that the modern cigar grip typical of the modern Leonards first appeared, with full metal reel seats of German silver, sliding bands, and a reel hood soldered to its barrel. These rods were embellished with intermediate wraps and intricate silk windings above the grip check. Like the earlier Leonards, they were provided with tip cases of Calcutta with machined butt fittings and screw caps of brass. Most rods of this period were three-piece designs, ranging from eight to nine and a half feet, although I recently examined a beautiful, two-ounce Catskill Fairy of seven and a half feet that was built in 1914. Except for its intricate silk windings and heavier reel-seat fittings with their richly ornamental machining, the rod looks surprisingly like a modern Leonard.

The Leonard tournament rods built in this same period featured slightly longer cigar grips and full metal reel seats with soldered caps and sliding bands. The examples I have seen were usually nine feet and weighed between five and one-quarter and six ounces, although I recently examined a special tournament Leonard of nine and a half feet that weighed six ounces. These special tournament rods introduced the bright scarlet silk and black trim found on the contemporary Leonards, although their intermediate wraps reveal their true vintage.

The classic screw-locking seat found on the modern Leonards apparently evolved after Reuben Leonard died, and its design is attributed to George Reynolds. It has embellished a generation of rods like the three-piece 50DF, which weighed four ounces and measured eight feet, or the famous Hunt pattern that was also an eight-footer. It had a slightly faster action at four and five-eighths ounces, and had oxidized ferrules and reel fittings. It was designed by the late Richard Hunt, author of the classic *Salmon in Low Water* and a familiar figure on the Brodheads before the Second World War. The Hewitt pattern built by Leonard was also an eight-footer, with a cane taper that weighed four and a half ounces. Hewitt originally liked rods with fairly stiff butts and fast tips when he first made the transition to dry-fly fishing, which his book *A Trout and Salmon Fisherman for Seventy-Five Years* tells us also took place on the Brodheads. His Hewitt-pattern rods flex most in the butt and the lower third of the middle section, with fairly level tapers halfway through the tip. Such calibrations make the middle and tip less flexible and a little tip-heavy in feeling, adding a steep taper to a relatively delicate hooking tip that permitted Hewitt to use his patented nitrate-stained tippets of 5X gut.

Before the Leonard fire in 1964, both the Hewitt- and Hunt-pattern rods were still made, and the Leonard 50DF was unquestionably the most popular model in the entire line. Some of the 50DF rods made after the Second World War were fitted with graceful reverse cigar grips that

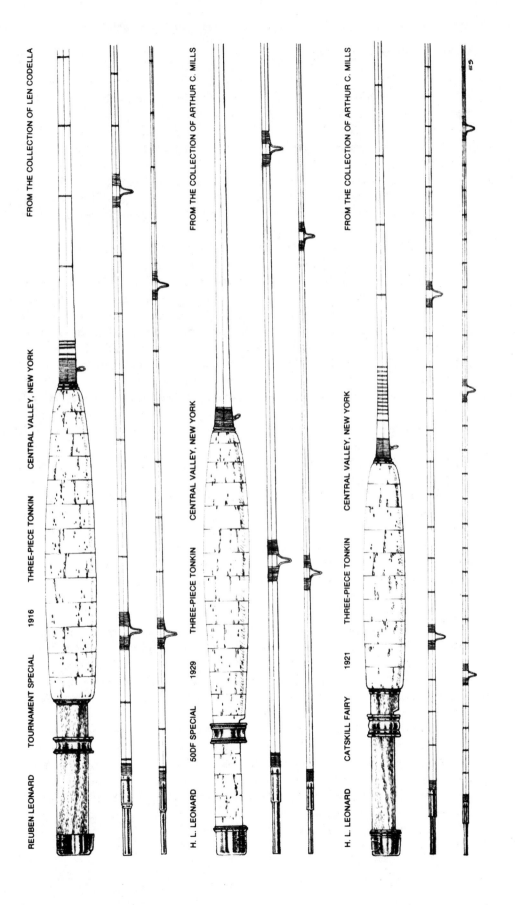

REUBEN LEONARD   TOURNAMENT SPECIAL   1916   THREE-PIECE TONKIN   CENTRAL VALLEY, NEW YORK   FROM THE COLLECTION OF LEN CODELLA

H. L. LEONARD   50DF SPECIAL   1929   THREE-PIECE TONKIN   CENTRAL VALLEY, NEW YORK   FROM THE COLLECTION OF ARTHUR C. MILLS

H. L. LEONARD   CATSKILL FAIRY   1921   THREE-PIECE TONKIN   CENTRAL VALLEY, NEW YORK   FROM THE COLLECTION OF ARTHUR C. MILLS

tapered directly to the hooded butt cap, with a sliding ring on the continuous cork handle. It was the favorite dry-fly rod of Arthur Mills after its introduction in 1915, although two-piece rods of lighter construction were gradually becoming popular at midcentury, and Leonard Catskill models like the elegant ACM 38 dominated sales by the time the original Leonard shop perished in the fire. Arthur Mills was responsible for the ACM 38, just as his father Thomas Bate Mills had suggested that Hiram Leonard should design the original Catskill Fairy in 1890. The Leonard ACM 38 was a seven-footer weighing two and one-quarter ounces, and was the jewel in a series of fine two-piece designs.

The Baby Catskill line ranged from the 37L at six feet and a single ounce to the 38H, which measured seven feet and weighed two and three-quarters ounces. It also included the Arthur Mills ACM 37, which took a three-weight line and weighed one and a half ounces. These rods were usually fitted with the standard cigar grip and skeletal butternut reel seat, although after 1960, many were made with the reversed cigar handles shaped entirely of cork and fitted with extralight reel bands. Recently I fished an exquisite 38L of this type which weighed only one and three-quarters ounces. It took a three-weight silk and had oxidized fittings. One of my favorite rods is an experimental version of the lovely ACM 38, measuring seven feet and weighing only two and one-quarter ounces. It has calibrations one ferrule size larger than comparable Catskill Fairy tapers, but eliminates the swelled butt and holds a surprisingly flat taper into the grip. The tip guide is a delicate four sixty-fourths of an inch and takes a DT4F—it was originally intended to fish terrestrials on cobweb-fine tippets of .003 and .004, and it has performed that function perfectly on many streams.

Before the fire, Leonard also made a series of three-piece rods with a delicate three-piece action suited to traditional wet-fly work. These designs ranged from the 35 model at seven feet and two and three-quarters ounces to the Leonard 46, which weighed five and a half ounces and reached a full nine and a half feet. The Leonard 36 was a seven-and-a-half-footer that weighed three and one-eighth ounces, and the 40 design was a fine eight-foot rod at only three and a half ounces. Both were extremely popular rods in their day, although modern fishermen now find them a little too soft. Yet these rods had some important partisans in the past half century.

It's hard to believe, Arthur Mills once told me with a note of quiet pride, *but George La Branche once had forty Leonards in the shop for refitting and refinishing at the same time!*

Leonard was also making two-piece rods larger than the Catskill series after midcentury. These rods were available in eight sizes, from the 65 model at seven and a half feet and three and a half ounces to the powerful Leonard 67H at six ounces and nine feet. These rods were usually fitted with the standard screw-locking seat, and they are superb fishing tools. Charles De Feo always liked the Leonard 51W rods, which weighed only six ounces at a full nine and a half feet, even with the oversized grips originally found on the special tournament rods built before the First World War. But the apogee of the Leonard tradition was perhaps found in the one-piece bamboo rods they built over the years. Other builders have made six-foot rods without ferrules, but not like the Leonards, weighing less than an ounce—let alone one-piece rods of seven, eight, and eight and a half feet.

It's unthinkable that we once had culms long enough to make rods like that, Hap Mills shakes his head unhappily, *and we lost most of them in the fire.*

Since the fire and the subsequent resurrection, Leonard has completely revised many of its rod designs and tapers, although attention to quality and craftsmanship remain unchanged. Four groups of fly rods are included. The Letort series is named for Letort Spring Run in Pennsylvania, the temple of light-tackle fishing, while the Ausable series is named for that famous Adirondack stream. Heavier trout rods ideally suited to big water are found in the Miramichi tapers, and the Leonard Duracane series is intended to provide a full range of weights and tapers with first-quality Leonard fittings at a moderate price.

The ancestry of the Letort series is unmistakable. Their grips and butternut reel seats have obvious roots in the rods that Reuben Leonard started building before the First World War. The butt caps and sliding bands are a little simpler in their machining, but the grip checks are virtually unchanged. The silk wrappings are rich scarlet tipped with black. The Letort rods are all two-piece designs. The remarkable Letort 36L is six feet long and weighs only one ounce, taking a level L2F line. The 40L taper is the heaviest at eight feet and three and three-quarters ounces, taking a four-weight line perfectly. Two years ago, Leonard built a special three-piece rod of eight feet that weighed three and three-quarters ounces and was designed to fish a four-weight line because of its delicate tip calibrations. It lies between the delicacy of the eight-foot 40L in the Letort series and the 50 series rods designed for six-weight lines.

The first time I saw the rod it was merely culms of dense-walled Tonkin bamboo, and on my second trip to the Leonard shop it had become four split-cane sections newly mounted with ferrules and tip guides. Hap Mills and Ted Simroe fitted it together, and Tom Bailey came over from his lathe where a delicate German-silver ferrule was being finished. Simroe happily waggled the unfinished sticks and handed it to me.

It's really sweet, Simroe grinned. *It's so lovely I wish I could own it myself.* Hap Mills nodded in agreement.

It's beautiful, I sighed happily.

It was ultimately finished with a butternut reel seat and a silver butt cap and sliding ring. Although it was a new Leonard, its guides and ferrules and keeper were wound in traditional lime green silk with yellow trim. Its action was poetic, fishing perfectly in close and handling distances of eighty to ninety feet with ease; and its baptism came on a late summer evening near Sun Valley in Idaho.

André Puyans and David Inks had taken me to try the difficult rainbows of Silver Creek, and I had planned to use a smaller rod designed for fishing a 6X tippet, because there was no wind and the current was mirror-smooth.

You going to try the new Leonard? Puyans asked.

Why not? I laughed.

Since the big rainbows were selective and shy, it seemed like too much rod—until I tried it. We had to fish .005 tippets and some of the fish were lying sixty to eighty feet away. There were also tall reeds along one reach of water, and I found its full eight feet valuable in keeping the backcasts high. The trout were porpoising steadily to a parade of tiny *Callibaetis* flies, and we took fish after fish that evening. The special 50L performed perfectly, taking a fine three-pound rainbow sixty feet out on a size 20 nymph imitation. There was a smaller fish that broke off when it took as I started to lift for another cast, but otherwise it fished the fine nylon tippet without problems.

The Ausable series is also typical of fine Leonard rods since the First World War. The sizes under seven feet are normally fitted with skeletal sliding-band seats, while the models between seven and a half and nine feet are made with Leonard screw-locking hardware. It is possible to have the seven-and-a-half- and eight-foot rods made with skeletal seats on special order, although the Leonard craftsmen believe the larger reels balancing their eight-and-a-half- and nine-foot tapers require the security of a locking seat.

Two-piece rods in the Ausable series range from the Leonard 36 model at six feet and less than two ounces, to the Ausable 41H weighing five and a quarter ounces and measuring eight and a half feet. The six-footer takes a DT3F and the eight-and-a-half-foot taper takes an eight-weight line. There are two models for different line weights in each length, offering a total of twelve rod choices in the two-piece Ausable weights. Seven other three-piece rods complete the Ausable series. The 48H model is a seven-foot taper taking a four-weight line and weighing three and one-quarter ounces, and is the smallest three-piece rod in the present Leonard weight line. The larger seven-and-a-half- and eight-foot designs take five- and six-weight lines. There are also three rods taking seven- to nine-weight forward tapers perfectly, the largest a nine-foot rod weighing five and seven-eighths ounces. My favorite rods in the Ausable series are probably the model 39, which is a seven-and-a-half-footer for a five-weight line, and the 40 and 50 designs, which are eight-foot rods for six-weight tapers in both two- and three-piece constructions. These are extremely versatile rods for all-around trout fishing.

The Miramichi series was developed by Ted Simroe. Although it is intended for salmon fishing, its rods are superbly adapted to big western rivers like the Snake and Yellowstone and Big Hole. Simroe designed the reversed half-Wells grips and reel-seat hardware, adding a two-inch fixed-cork extension. The eight-foot rod for a weight-forward seven weighs four and three-quarters ounces, and the eight-and-a-half-foot 61 model weighs five and a half ounces with a taper intended for eight-weight lines. Both the Miramichi 60 and 61 are two-piece rods. The 71 model is a three-piece design of eight and a half feet, weighing five and five-eighths ounces and taking a weight-forward eight. These are excellent big-water outfits.

The Duracane series of rods represents a departure for Leonard, since they replace the moderately priced Mills rods once sold through William Mills & Sons with a line of fine impregnated fly rods. These Duracanes are heat-treated bamboo with a rich brown tone produced for Leonard in Europe, fitted with the excellent screw-locking hardware typical of the more expensive Leonards, and finished with emerald silk windings. The lightest rod in the Duracane group is the seven-foot 700 model, which weighs two and seven-eighths ounces and takes a four-weight line. The seven-and-a-half-foot rod for a four-weight and the eight-foot model designed for five-weight are both particularly fine rods. The eight-foot Duracane 800 at four and one-eighth ounces takes an eight-weight taper and is an excellent all-around rod. There are also Duracane models comparable to the more expensive Miramichi rods, with their reverse screw-lock seats and extension butts, taking seven- to nine-weight forward tapers.

Appalachian pack rods are available in the Duracane grade, made in four pieces for easy backpacking and with full-cork reel seats and grips of the reverse cigar style. The Appalachian 700P is a seven-footer for a four-weight line, and the 800P is a versatile eight-foot rod that takes a six-weight taper. Like the other Duracane rods, the Appalachian trail rods are normally furnished with a single tip.

The Leonard tradition reaches both sides of the Atlantic, since the famous Skues used them extensively during most of his fishing career. Skues acquired his first Leonard through an American friend Walter Durfee Coggeshall in 1903. It was a ten-footer weighing six ounces, and it whetted his appetite for a smaller version.

Edward Hewitt and young Edward Bate Mills journeyed to the Crystal Palace at London in 1904, participating in the international casting tournament. Hewitt demonstrated a classic nine-foot Leonard weighing five and a half ounces to Skues during the tournament. Mills was part of William Mills & Sons, the principal agents for the Leonard rods, and showed Skues his catalogues. The following winter Skues completed a particularly successful case for his clients, and in gratitude for his legal expertise, Skues was offered the finest rod that British sterling could purchase. His clients and fishing colleagues were shocked when Skues immediately chose a fine nine-foot Leonard.

Skues observed that his new Leonard possessed a smooth, fluid action that was a marked contrast to the relatively stiff dry-fly tapers made fashionable by men like Halford and Marryat. Such rods were conceived to switch-cast the moisture from a floating fly before it is cast again. Skues observed that Hardy rods like the Halford and Houghton Club and Marston patterns seemed like weaver's beams once he had fished his first nine-foot Leonard. Its smooth rhythms permitted him to false cast without drying his delicate nymphs. Skues tells us in his book *Nymph Fishing for Chalk*

Stream Trout that its poetry and precise character were a major factor in the Itchen experiments that originated nymph fishing, and the old master fished his Leonard happily for half a century.

It caused a lot of talk, Dermot Wilson explained at his fishing hut on the Itchen, where Skues once walked the banks, *but Skues was convinced that Leonard made the best rods.*

Must have made your rodmakers unhappy, I said.

It did! he agreed. *It did!*

This past spring I have been fishing with Dermot Wilson on both the Itchen and its sister Hampshire river, the legendary Test at Stockbridge. When the young artisans at Leonard heard that I would be fishing the Itchen at Abbots Worthy, where Skues himself had often fished his nymphs, they insisted that we collaborate on a modern version of Skues' favorite Leonard rods.

What should it do? they asked.

Well, I began thoughtfully, *the fish are shy enough to make a 6X or 7X tippet necessary and the hatches are tiny.*

How tiny is tiny? Hap Mills interjected.

Twenty or twenty-two, I said, *because the fish will be on the little Iron Blues and Pale Waterys and Olives–and the rod has to be long enough to keep the backcast out of the bankgrass and weeds.*

And how long do you cast? Simroe asked.

Twenty to thirty feet on most beats, I replied, *but at Testcombe House on the Chilbolton beats, there's a reach of water where the big fish dimple steadily at least eighty to ninety feet away–lying right against the reeds.*

It's a tough prescription, Simroe sighed.

Their solution is a unique fly rod, even considering the rod quality that distinguishes the Leonard shop. The rod is a full eight-and-a-half-footer, long enough to hold a backcast above the fences and bullock herds and weeds that plague the backcasts of the chalkstream angler. Its tapers are slender enough, particularly at the delicate four sixty-fourths tip, to fish leaders testing under a pound. Yet it also has the power to punch out ninety-foot casts with accuracy and hook a good fish on 7X nylon without breaking off. It is finished with the Reynolds screw-locking seat and butternut filler traditional at Leonard for more than fifty years.

I know it's light enough for a four-weight, Simroe argues, *but an eight-and-a-half-foot Leonard looks better with a locking seat.*

Three weeks later, where the manicured lawns sweep down to the Chilbolton water from the richly timbered Elizabethan gables of the Testcombe, the rod had its baptism on the storied Test. Its trout were working steadily against the reeds, sipping nymphs in the smooth pondlike currents. Several times that day, casts were necessary that left the backing knot hanging just below the butt guide or left just a few turns of line on the reel. Many fish refused my tiny nymphs until I added a 7X tippet, yet the rod did not break off a beautiful three-pound brown that took more than eighty feet out. The Itchen fish at Chilland and Abbots Worthy are smaller,

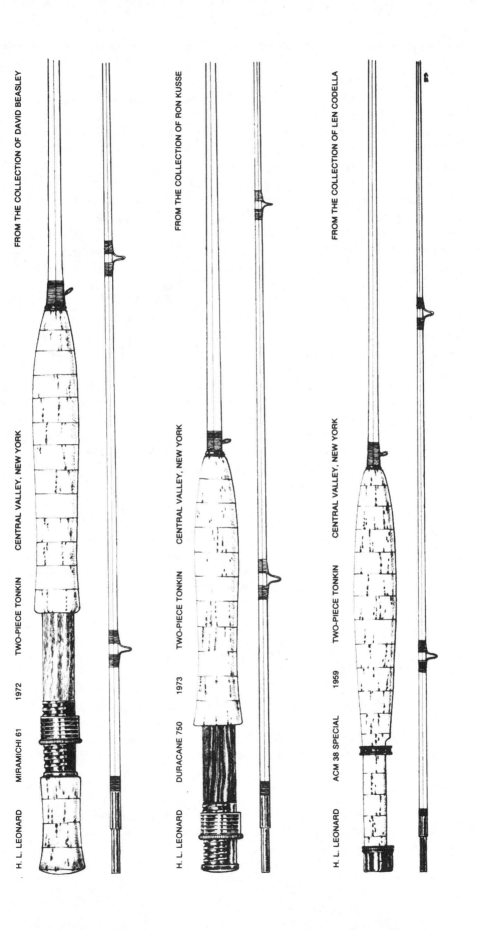

FROM THE COLLECTION OF DAVID BEASLEY

FROM THE COLLECTION OF RON KUSSE

FROM THE COLLECTION OF LEN CODELLA

H. L. LEONARD   MIRAMICHI 61   1972   TWO-PIECE TONKIN   CENTRAL VALLEY, NEW YORK

H. L. LEONARD   DURACANE 750   1973   TWO-PIECE TONKIN   CENTRAL VALLEY, NEW YORK

H. L. LEONARD   ACM 38 SPECIAL   1959   TWO-PIECE TONKIN   CENTRAL VALLEY, NEW YORK

since there is no supplemental stocking on that mileage, but I took several sixteen-inch fish on both beats, fishing at similar ranges with light tippets. The delicacy and distance were an unusual mixture of qualities, but the special Leonard admirably followed in the footsteps of the rods that Skues first used on the Itchen.

It's a remarkable rod, Dermot Wilson agreed. *It's delicacy and length are ideally suited to our chalkstreams—maybe Leonard should think about making more of them for your spring creeks, but trade on tradition and name it after Skues.*

Charles F. Orvis started his rodmaking company much earlier than Hiram Leonard, having founded Orvis more than twenty years before. The workshop where he produced the first Orvis rods is still standing in Manchester, less than a half mile from the Vermont headwaters of the Battenkill. However, Orvis had declined over the years until it was rescued from oblivion under the ownership of E. C. Corkran just before the Second World War, and it is the peripatetic Leigh Perkins who has pumped new life into Orvis in recent years—since the demise of William Mills & Sons, which had flourished in New York since 1822, Orvis has rapidly become the finest fishing tackle house in the United States.

Their early reputation was based as much on the quality of their flies as well as their first lancewood and lemonwood rods. The Orvis flies were the work of Mary Orvis Marbury, who had first learned the secrets of fly dressing at the insistence of her father. It must be remembered that skilled fly making was an occult art as late as the First World War—and how closely tiers like Theodore Gordon shielded their secrets.

When Mary Orvis Marbury learned to dress fiies, it had all the trappings of a medieval guild. But she obviously had great talent, and Orvis flies were soon competing with the imported patterns sold at William Mills & Sons. Marbury published her encyclopedic *Favorite Flies and Their Histories* in 1892. Its exquisite lithography was a revelation, and its plates are still the classic reference for the garish flies fashionable on American rivers after the Civil War. Before her influence most American tackle dealers gave their patterns numbers rather than names, like the Mills No. 1, famous among the brook-trout fishermen on the Nissequogue at the Wyandanche Club. Orvis insisted on making standard patterns and giving them names rather than numbers, and we owe that institution to Mary Orvis Marbury.

The familiar Royal Coachman was one of those patterns, and it is perhaps the best known of the American flies. It was first dressed in 1878 in the New York shop of John Haily, who tied trout flies to order, and was the first American supplier of fly-tying materials. It was John Haily who journeyed to Vermont to teach Mary Orvis Marbury the secrets of his profession. Fred Mather received the following information from her father in a letter written in 1885:

> I had for many years made fishing rods and reels, and in filling orders for the same, had frequent requests for other tackle to be sent in the same package.

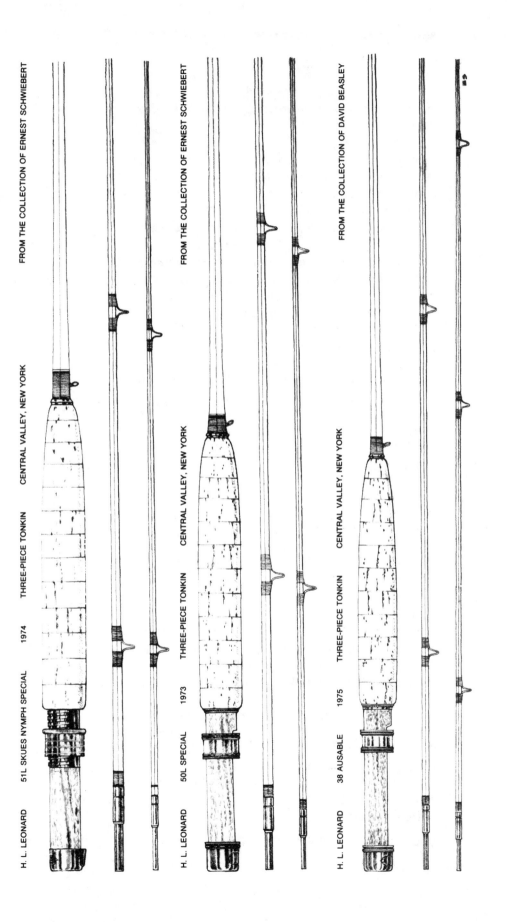

H. L. LEONARD   51L SKUES NYMPH SPECIAL   1974   THREE-PIECE TONKIN   CENTRAL VALLEY, NEW YORK   FROM THE COLLECTION OF ERNEST SCHWIEBERT

H. L. LEONARD   50L SPECIAL   1973   THREE-PIECE TONKIN   CENTRAL VALLEY, NEW YORK   FROM THE COLLECTION OF ERNEST SCHWIEBERT

H. L. LEONARD   38 AUSABLE   1975   THREE-PIECE TONKIN   CENTRAL VALLEY, NEW YORK   FROM THE COLLECTION OF DAVID BEASLEY

I then ordered, to supply these demands, small quantities of flies from dealers—first ordering a complete line of samples with the names attached.

These I received, but soon found it utterly impossible to duplicate my orders. I was continually disappointed by the substituting of other flies or sizes than the ones I had ordered, and in turn, I was forced to disappoint and apologize to my customers. I then thought that if there was any way out of this dilemma, caused by a confusion in names and a carelessness in copying exactly the pattern fly, I should seek it out.

In time, one of my family viewed with favor the idea of learning to tie flies. To this end, I employed one of the best fly tiers in the city to come to my house and stay until he had imparted his knowledge and skill, and when I felt that we were competent I advertised to fill orders exactly in accordance with a customer's wishes.

The Royal Coachman was first offered to purchasers by me. It did not, however, originate with me. The fly tier I mentioned long ago sent me a sample of the same, saying, "I have just been tying some flies to order for a gentleman. He says he likes the Coachman better than any other fly, but finds it very frail, and wants me to tie some with red silk in the middle, to make them stronger, and he also wants a little sprig of wood duck for a jib. I send you a fly to see, and I think it quite handsome."

The fly enclosed had a white wing, brown hackle, peacock body, bound in the center with red silk, and a tail of woodduck feather with the black and white bars.

One evening a number of us were gathered around a table looking at flies. My family, Mr. Horace Dunn of San Francisco, and Mr. L. C. Orvis of Hartford, were present discussing the propriety of every fly having a name, numbers giving them little or no individuality. I said, "But what is one to do? I do not propose to name flies. We have too many names already."

"Why not," said they, "if you make a new combination name it, else it will never become popular. No one can remember to distinguish flies by numbers. They get confused, but a name fixes a fly in your mind."

"Well," I answered, "that may be true. But look, here is this fly: it is similar to the Coachman, but it is not a Coachman. There is but one Coachman: that is the fly we all know, with a white wing, peacock body and brown hackle."

"I will tell you," exclaimed Mr. L. C. Orvis, "that is an extra-fine Coachman; all that scarlet makes it quite magnificent, indeed—call it—call it the Royal Coachman!"

It is obvious that the Orvis tradition is old and rich, although the modern Orvis rod bears little resemblance to its ancestors in the 1894 catalog. D. C. Corkran was a wealthy Philadelphian whose family had long occupied a summer home at Manchester, and after Corkran acquired Orvis in 1938, he persuaded Wesley Jordan to join him as his master rodmaker in the little shop on Union Street.

For thirty-five years, Orvis bamboo work has been synonymous with Wes Jordan, despite the fact that the company has produced as many as 15,000 rods a year. Jordan was born in 1894, and briefly served in the Royal Flying Corps late in the First World War, training at Hendon in the summer of 1918. Shortly after his discharge from the British Army, Jordan met an American rodmaker named William Forsythe, who introduced him to the mysteries of split bamboo. Jordan had found his metier, and he joined the Cross Rod Company late in 1919, having found his life's work except for a brief period just before the Second World War when he worked with automobiles.

His skills quickly blossomed working with Cross, building famous double-built designs like the Cross Tournament and the delicate seven-foot Sylph. Jordan forged a considerable reputation during his years with Cross, and when Cross died and his company was absorbed by South Bend in northern Indiana, Jordan went along to supervise the bamboo work. The fortunes of the tackle industry slipped badly during the Depression years, and Jordan was working with an automobile agency when Corkran rescued him to supervise rod building at Orvis in 1940.

Wes Jordan has been there ever since, inspecting every rod to come from the two-story clapboard workshop in Manchester. Rods that he built during his early years with Cross show strong influences of the Cross rods in action and reel fittings, but the grips are unmistakably the ancestors of his modern work at Orvis. Corkran introduced the pioneering techniques of impregnating the finished sections of split bamboo, eventually obtaining a patent on the process. It was Jordan who designed the screw-locking reel seat that has distinguished the Orvis rods since 1941 and added the exquisite reel-seat fillers of rich American walnut. His Orvis reel seats were originally designed with a single locking sleeve, like the Leonard and Payne type, but the present Orvis assembly no longer has a hooded butt cap made of a single piece—and the locking sleeve consists of two parts, which are less likely to oxidize and freeze tight on the threads.

The Battenkill series of rods has been justifiably famous since the Second World War and were once made in a large number of lengths, weights, and tapers. However, in recent years Orvis has limited its Battenkills to rods designed for six- to nine-weight lines. The more delicate end of the spectrum has been confined to a fresh palette of highly specialized actions and tapers. The modern Battenkills start with a crisp six-and-a-half-footer for a six-weight line that weighs only two and seven-eighths ounces. The heaviest stick in the series is an eight-and-a-half-foot, five-and-one-eighth-ounce rod designed for a nine-weight forward taper. Most of these rods have a fairly fast action, particularly suited to the fisherman who casts restlessly and likes to cover a lot of water. However, my own preference lies with the slower tapers that flex down into the butt, like the seven-and-a-half-foot, three-and-seven-eighths-ounce Battenkill, which many fishermen call the best overall trout model in the Orvis line. Some western anglers who fish slightly larger streams find the eight-foot, four-and-three-eighths-ounce Battenkill a better all-around rod for their purposes, and both have a smooth medium action.

My favorite Battenkills are slower still. The eight-foot version at four and one-eighth ounces is a fine rod for a six-weight line, and I fish it close with 6X tippets and double tapers, but it seems equally happy fishing the full length of a weight-forward line with a small streamer. It even took a number of salmon on the Nordurá and Grimsá in Iceland, including a fish of twenty-three pounds, and I fish it there often. The late Joseph Brooks liked the eight-and-a-half-foot Battenkill that weighs four and three-quarters ounces and takes a WF8S line perfectly, and he fished it from the Big Hole in Montana to the Boca Chimehuin in Patagonia. It is a rod I have also fished—its slow action working in lazy casting rhythms—from New Zealand to the Labrador.

Orvis still makes three Battenkill rods in three-piece construction for travel convenience. These designs include a seven-and-a-half-foot, four-and-one-quarter-ounce model for a seven-weight line, a popular eight-footer for the same line that weighs four and a half ounces, and a superb eight-and-a-half-foot rod weighing four and five-eighths ounces that is also milled to fish a WF7S or WF7F taper. The extra ferrule in these rods makes them slightly heavier than comparable two-piece designs, but the differences in action are virtually indistinguishable.

Orvis also makes a number of special rods in the Battenkill grade, and several of them fish beautifully under rather difficult conditions. The first of these rods is the Orvis Midge, measuring seven and a half feet and taking a five-weight line at only three and five-eighths ounces. It was designed in response to the difficult fishing on our eastern streams in low water, like the headwaters of the Battenkill in August, and it has become one of the most popular rods in the entire Orvis line. Its smooth semiparabolic action makes it a favorite with skilled anglers on our eastern spring creeks, although many experts who fish often with tippets of .003 and .004 nylon wish that Orvis would make its Midge with a more delicate tip.

The Orvis Flea soon followed the Midge pattern. It fishes with a four-weight line, and is a sensitive little six-and-a-half-foot rod of only two ounces. Its tip calibrations are also a bit too heavy for working 7X and 8X leaders, although its slow action makes 7X tippets possible in skilled hands. However, it is a rod I like in hot weather on small streams, particularly in brushy water where its six-and-a-half-foot length is perfect.

The Orvis Nymph is intended for fishing tiny nymphs and pupal imitations in the surface film, with an emphasis on delicacy instead of distance. It is an extremely slow eight-foot rod weighing three and three-quarters ounces and designed for a four-weight line. Unlike the four-ounce Battenkill at eight feet, it will fish nymphal and pupal patterns on .003 and .004 nylon points. Such refinements can be important for trout that are gorging on minute *Tricorythodes* nymphs on the Battenkill just after daylight or dimpling to the millions of midge pupae in the surface film of a western spring creek. Its tapers are clearly unsuited for windy days, and they lack the muscle to fish a sinking line with real control, but it is capable of exquisite work on smutting fish. It is best with a DT4F, and some anglers even fish it with a DT3F line. Nymphing with tiny imitations is its forte, and anglers having chalkstream conditions on their home waters should consider its unique properties: the eight-foot length permits ready manipulation of a nymph in quiet currents, while the four-weight lines drop softly enough for the most selective trout.

Leigh Perkins designed the Limestone Special after exposure to the difficult fishing on the Maigue near Limerick, which rises in the limestone hills above Killarney. His impressions were later confirmed on chalkstreams like the Itchen and the Test in England. These are smooth-flowing rivers that demand a subtle presentation with four- or five-weight tapers, and a six-weight has the guide angle of a stone when it comes to wild brown trout on the Itchen in bright weather. These rivers also mean relatively long casts, so the ideal rod must have some muscle too, and length is valuable for keeping the backcast out of the foliage.

It's not just for chalkstreams, Perkins explains enthusiastically about his Limestone Special. *We've got a lot of water like the Irish and English fishing, streams like the Pennsylvania limestoners and western spring creeks from California to Montana—and particularly the Henry's Fork of the Snake!*

The Limestone Special is eight and a half feet and weighs four and a half ounces, taking a six-weight long belly to fish delicately as well as long. Its backcast is crisp and high, and it will handle distance work with ease. Its character is smooth and slow, flexing progressively into the grip, and its length and delicacy are ideally suited to fishing the nymph.

We're pleased with the Limestone Special, Leigh Perkins adds, *and we're proud to have it featured in the Nether Wallop shop of Dermot Wilson—he's probably the best of the chalkstream fishermen, and lives in the middle of the chalkstream country only an hour below London.*

Like getting a good Broadway review, I laughed.

Exactly, he said.

The most delicate rod in the Orvis collection is another new design called the Orvis Seven-Three, its name coming from its specifications for a three-weight line and seven-foot length. Its tip calibrations take a four sixty-fourths tip top, much smaller than any other Orvis taper, and it is the only rod in the entire line that will fish .003 and .004 with security. It has been available only three seasons, but true fine-tippet addicts have already hailed the Seven-Three and its performance on difficult fish. The rod is balanced perfectly with a DT3F, and it weighs only two and one-quarter ounces. It has served me well on rivers where long casts were not needed, but 8X tippets were a regular prescription on smutting fish in ankle-deep flats. Its relatively short length is also valuable in tree-sheltered water like the Little Manistee and Little South Pere Marquette in Michigan, or eastern rivers like the Brodheads and Bushkill.

Orvis also makes a line of moderately priced split-cane rods made with impregnated bamboo. The sole difference between the Battenkill and Madison grades is esthetic, with subtle variations in graining or color of bamboo, since any structural seconds are destroyed. The Madison rods are sold with a single tip, although extra tips are available. The same first-quality fittings and walnut fillers are used in both the Battenkill and the Madison, and watermarked cane is often the only reason these rods have been finished in the Madison grade.

Three of the special Orvis tapers—the Flea, the Midge, and the delicate little Seven-Three—are also available in the less expensive grade. Two seven-and-a-half-foot rods for six-weight lines are also included, along with the fine eight-foot taper for a six-weight. The eight-and-a-half-foot Limestone Special taper is also furnished in the Madison price range, as well as the Brooks eight-and-a-half-footer taking an eight-weight line at four and three-quarter ounces. The eight-and-a-half-footer for nine-weight lines is also made in the Madison line.

It is probably fitting that the most expensive rods in the Orvis stable are named for Wes Jordan, the master craftsman who breathed new life into Orvis on the eve of the Second World War. Jordan liked his own rods with a bit more tip-muscle than most and a smoothly powerful action. His tapers are clearly in the American tradition, with oxidized German-silver ferrules and special jewel-finished reel fittings of fine aluminum alloy. The name of the owner is engraved in the butt cap. The cork grip is fitted with a thumb seat, a touch first introduced by the late Paul Young and placed into volume production by Jordan before he left South Bend. However, some Wes Jordan rods are also fitted with a depression shape for the heel of the palm, a feature original with Jordan. Some anglers dislike both designs, since casting fatigue can be partially relieved by changing the placement of the casting hand, and such a shift is impossible with a fully sculptured grip. The Wes Jordan rods are protected by an elegant saddle-leather case, with an aluminum tube lining the inside, plus a buckle top and carrying strap. Perhaps the most elegant touch found in the Wes Jordan lies in the hardwood reel-seat fillers that use exotic materials like rosewood, Circassian walnut, and darkly grained Macassar ebony.

The Wes Jordan series includes a seven-and-a-half-foot rod that takes a six-weight line and weighs three and seven-eighths ounces, and an eight-and-a-half-footer weighing five and one-eighth ounces for a nine-weight. The eight-foot rod has long been the most popular in the three-taper series, patterned after the original fly rod that Jordan designed for himself many years ago. It weighs four and three-eighths ounces and takes an eight-weight line, and its partisans argue that it is the most versatile fly rod ever built.

Orvis is perhaps the only rodmaker making split-cane rods in numbers

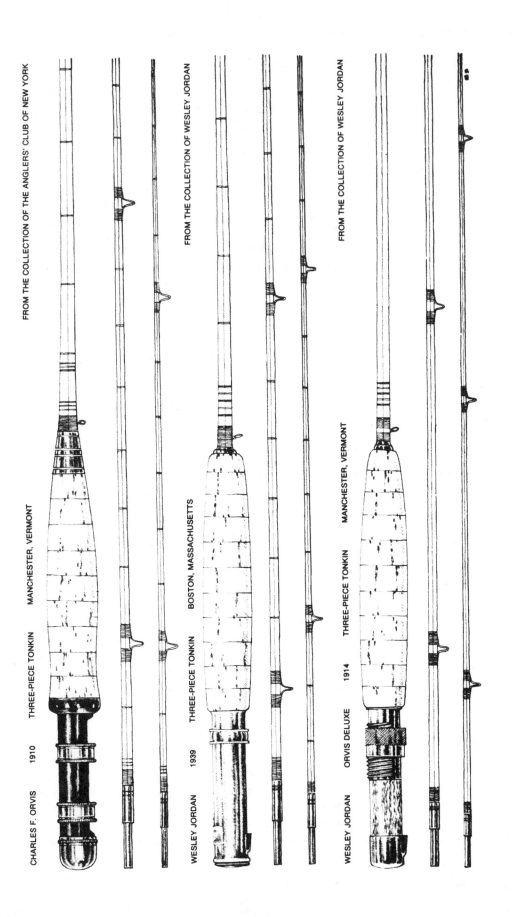

FROM THE COLLECTION OF THE ANGLERS' CLUB OF NEW YORK

FROM THE COLLECTION OF WESLEY JORDAN

FROM THE COLLECTION OF WESLEY JORDAN

CHARLES F. ORVIS   1910   THREE-PIECE TONKIN   MANCHESTER, VERMONT

WESLEY JORDAN   1939   THREE-PIECE TONKIN   BOSTON, MASSACHUSETTS

WESLEY JORDAN   ORVIS DELUXE   1914   THREE-PIECE TONKIN   MANCHESTER, VERMONT

that approach the demand, and much of its production capability comes from the transfusions of fresh energy, ideas, and new equipment provided by the indefatigable Leigh Perkins. His experience at the helm of Orvis clearly belies the pessimism fashionable among many fishermen, particularly about the death of craftsmanship. Perkins writes with eloquence on this argument:

> There are still young men in this day, as in any day, who take a deep abiding pride in fine workmanship. In fact, today, when mass production threatens to make pushbutton automatons out of workers, the best men often gravitate to those relatively few jobs where individual skills and a sense of pride and responsibility are still important.

Earlier in this chapter, we recounted the historic breakup that occurred between Hiram Leonard and his original circle of disciples and apprentices. Many of these men have historic roles in American fly-fishing and became half-legendary craftsmen in their own right. Eustis Edwards, Edward Payne, and the brothers Loman and Hiram Hawes were all superb rodmakers, and Fred Thomas was unquestionably one of the best who ever split a culm.

Fred Thomas returned to Bangor and started making rods under his own name, first in partnership with Edwards, and then with his son Leon helping prepare the sticks for bevelling. Although his Maine customers were often heavy-handed, and fished huge streamers on leaders that could hand-line a six-pound squaretail, Thomas also built a lot of poetic rods that a blank check could not buy from their present owners.

His rods were made in two colors of bamboo, using both the flawless straw-colored cane typical of his earlier experience with Leonard and brown-tone rods the rich color of chocolate. The pale bamboo sticks were fitted with matching reel-seat fillers of butternut, while the darker rods used select black walnut. Most Thomas rods fitted with screw-locking seats used a grip that echoed the Leonard tournament style, although some flared at the reel-seat into a distinctive Thomas fishtail handle. Thomas also made some grips and reel seats entirely of cork, their style offering homage to the Leonard grips that characterized many of the early 50DF designs. Thomas butt caps, which were more delicate than the Leonard type, used bright aluminum on the pale-cane rods and oxidized finishes on the browntones. Thomas used a Leonard-type grip check on his designs, but the grip check at the silk windings was uniquely his. It was more generously proportioned than the comparable Leonard grip check, and its engraved welt included the keeper ring. The silk windings also distinctively bore the Thomas fingerprint. The larger functional wraps that were brown with olive silk trim were typical of his work. Above the grip, Thomas devised an intricate signature of delicate brown windings, grouping the wraps in a series of three, seven, and three, and finishing with a wider ornamental wrap of brown silk. The ferrule wraps were brown tipped with olive, and there were

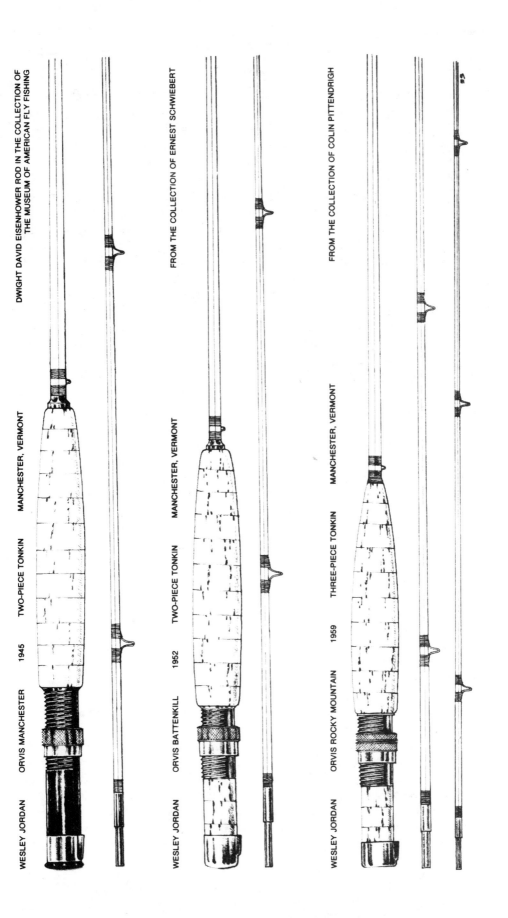

WESLEY JORDAN   ORVIS MANCHESTER   1945   TWO-PIECE TONKIN   MANCHESTER, VERMONT   DWIGHT DAVID EISENHOWER ROD IN THE COLLECTION OF
THE MUSEUM OF AMERICAN FLY FISHING

WESLEY JORDAN   ORVIS BATTENKILL   1952   TWO-PIECE TONKIN   MANCHESTER, VERMONT   FROM THE COLLECTION OF ERNEST SCHWIEBERT

WESLEY JORDAN   ORVIS ROCKY MOUNTAIN   1959   THREE-PIECE TONKIN   MANCHESTER, VERMONT   FROM THE COLLECTION OF COLIN PITTENDRIGH

three fine ornamental windings too, spaced apart from the functional silk. Similar wrappings were used at the top guide, which had a unique little German-silver tongue under the silk. The early Thomas rods used agate tip and stripping guides, while his later products used a bronzed tungsten. Many of the first Thomas designs used a full metal seat, like the early Leonards and Montague rods, but his later work was dominated by skeletal locking and sliding-band designs. The Thomas rods were all supplied with an aluminum case, fitted with brass end caps and screw-locking tops like the cases still used at Leonard. However, Thomas also knurled his caps handsomely. The early reel-seat locks were cut with ornamental rings, while later rods built by Leon Thomas had locking rings that were plain except for the knurling. The Thomas ferrules had a handsome machined welt, and used a split ferrule typical of the Leonard patent issued in 1878. Although Thomas built rods that fully equalled the work of both Hiram and Reuben Leonard, his personal tapers still carried the unmistakable marks of his apprenticeship in Bangor, including the swelled-butt tapers above their cork handles.

The oldest Thomas that I have seen already used the English reverse-loop snake guides that marked his rods until the threshold of the Second World War. It had a full metal seat and was a three-piece eight-and-a-half-footer weighing five and one-quarter ounces, with the relatively strong semiparabolic action typical of Thomas' rod tapers. Similar eight-and-a-half-footers with locking reel seats and butternut fillers weighed about four and three-quarters ounces and are widely coveted among collectors today. Perhaps my favorite Thomas was an eight-foot, three-piece taper of only four and one-eighth ounces, with a skeletal cork reel seat and handle. It was an exquisite piece of split-cane artistry, but it would be difficult to choose between its character and a superb little Thomas browntone of seven feet that I once saw—it was a two-piece rod of only two and a half ounces and a surprising poetry.

Fred Thomas and his son Leon built rods under the Thomas mark for more than forty years, but after the elder Thomas died, the company foundered and passed into receivership. Its cane and cutting blocks and design tapers were subsequently divided between Walter Carpenter, who presently works in the Leonard shop, and Samuel Carlson—who also acquired the equipment of William Edwards, including the specifications and tools for his unique four-strip rods.

Eustis Edwards also made fine fly rods under his own name for a number of years, but it was his sons, William and Eugene, who fully flowered as rodmakers. Eustis Edwards was a cane workman of great skill, and performed the bamboo functions in his brief partnership with Fred Thomas and Edward Payne. Thomas had been the Leonard foreman, while Payne began as a ferrule maker and machinist. The early Edwards rods bear a strong family resemblance to the work of his colleague, the better-known Edward Payne, and the later rods designed and built by his son Eugene Edwards.

The first Eustis Edwards rods were relatively large three-piece tapers in six-strip construction, and I have seen several of nine feet weighing six to six and a half ounces. Edwards was actually more interested in photography than rodmaking, and he often made volume lots of bamboo rods for large companies or sporting goods stores, hoping to start another photographic studio. Such rods were often made for stores like Abbey & Imbrie, Abercrombie & Fitch, and Von Lengerke & Detmold. However, later in his career Edwards built some superbly modern fly rods that had considerable influence. Sparse Grey Hackle tells us in his *Great Fishing Tackle Catalogs of the Golden Age* that Edwards made a run of seven-and-a-half-foot trout rods for the Winchester Repeating Arms Company that were so exceptional that they created a sensation on the Catskill rivers—and the popularity of the seven-and-a-half-foot rod on American rivers has been largely attributed to Eustis Edwards.

His Edwards Special rods were dark, richly colored bamboo with purple wraps tipped in yellow, and most had a poetic medium action that worked down into the grip. Both screw-locking and skeletal seats were common on his later work, and the early rods used full-metal seats. The largest of these early designs was a ten-footer weighing seven and three-quarters ounces, and taking a full ten-weight line. There were also nine-and-a-half-foot tapers weighing five and three-quarters ounces and a particularly delicate eight-and-a-half-foot taper weighing four ounces and taking a DT6F. The collector Martin Keane owns an exceptional Edwards Special built about 1925, that measures eight feet and weighs a mere three and one-eighth ounces. It is a full ounce under a comparable Orvis Battenkill and takes a delicate four-weight floating line.

Its personality is a little exotic and slow, Keane waxes poetic about his Edwards. *But it's my pride and joy!*

It was William Edwards who broke the mold and boldly developed a unique line of four-strip rods. His unusual ferrules and grip checks and reel-seat fittings were singularly his trademark, and his actions were superb. There were a surprising number of these four-strip tapers. Like his father, William Edwards made a lot of fly rods between eight and nine and a half feet with surprisingly delicate tip calibrations. These rods encompassed a wide spectrum of actions, at least in terms of their relative delicacy.

One of the finest eight-foot rods I have ever fished was an Edwards of two-piece construction that weighed only three and one-eighth ounces and took a four-weight silk line perfectly. Edwards also made a three-piece rod of eight and a half feet and four and one-eighth ounces that required a five-weight. His nine- and nine-and-a-half-foot designs in three-piece construction, weighing five and one-quarter and five and three-quarters ounces, are also remarkably smooth rods for seven-weight lines. William Edwards also made a relatively powerful nine-and-a-half-foot three-piece rod, weighing a full seven ounces with the power to punch out a nine-weight forward taper. The late Leroy Whitney had a fine seven-and-a-half-foot Edwards Quadrate that weighed only three ounces and balanced a four-weight Kingfisher silk—one of the finest semiparabolic tapers I have ever been privileged to cast.

It is perhaps in these delicate quadrate tapers that William Edwards most excelled. His seven-foot rod weighing two and five-eighths ounces was a fine action for the four-weight line, and the six-and-a-half-foot Quadrate weighing two and one-eighth ounces was calibrated to handle a three-weight. The most delicate Quadrate was the little six-foot Model 40 that weighed only one and three-quarter ounces and took a DT3F silk. Its ability to handle .003 and .004 nylon make it one of the first true Midge-type rods—and the ability to work with leaders under 6X is the only real measure of such tapers, in spite of the popular definition which includes anything under two ounces.

History often takes curious pathways, surprising knowledgeable observers with its unpredictable patterns of evolution. Since Edward Payne was only the ferrule machinist in the original Leonard shop at Bangor, it is remarkable that it was his E. F. Payne Rod Company that ultimately equalled the bamboo work of his master, and there are vocal Payne disciples who believe that Payne rods became the ultimate in the rod builder's art.

Edward Payne joined forces with Frank Oram, who was a Leonard foreman, after his brief association with the United States Net and Twine Company in Brooklyn. Their new Payne company was started at Highland Mills, a few miles up the highway from Leonard. Their early work was fine enough that a sample Payne won the gold medal at the 1893 World Columbian Exposition in Chicago.

The rods designed and built by Edward Payne at the turn of the century were little different from the rods his company was making fifty years later. Some of the reel fittings were a little more ornate, and the proportions of his early cork grips were less slender and graceful, but there was surprisingly little change in the appearance of the Payne rod in the eighty-year life of the company. When Edward Payne died after the First World War, his interest in the company passed to his son, James Payne, who had worked in the shop since boyhood. The younger Payne had been involved in rodmaking since early childhood, since his father had sternly disciplined his son with an unfinished buff section of split bamboo. The Oram half interest passed to his wife, who had wrapped and finished the Payne rods from the beginning. Except for the Second World War, when James Payne worked for Curtiss-Wright Aircraft, his life was completely consumed with building rods. The design and workmanship of these rods were so remarkable that they command huge prices on the secondhand lists. When James Payne died in 1970, there was a run on the remaining inventory of Payne rods at Abercrombie & Fitch that drove their prices to six times the price of a Payne in 1929, and that had been less than the price of a moderately expensive fiberglass fly rod today.

The early rods built by Edward Payne featured reel seats of solid German silver with a soldered hood and sliding band, although many skeletal seats on black walnut or butternut were assembled before his death. The elder Payne featured both straw-colored cane and brown-finished bamboo. His stripping guides and tip tops were agate, and the balance were bronzed-steel snake guides. The choice of models was limited. The lightest Payne was an eight-footer of three-piece construction that weighed three and one-quarter ounces and took a four-weight line. There was a second

JAMES PAYNE

eight-foot taper of three and three-quarters ounces for five-weight silk and a relatively light eight-and-a-half-footer for a six-weight that weighed four and one-quarter ounces.

There were also several larger tapers. The nine-foot rod weighing only four and one-quarter ounces took a DT6F silk, and a second nine-foot model weighing four and three-quarters ounces was only slightly heavier. There were nine-and-a-half-foot rods weighing five and one-quarter and five and three-quarters ounces, plus a ten-foot model that took a nine-weight line and totaled only six and a half ounces. These rods were the Payne line, and smaller rods did not appear until the Great Depression.

James Payne finally dropped the rods of natural bamboo in favor of the dark finishes that ultimately became his hallmark. The fittings were the same, featuring reel seats of both German silver and oxidized skeletal seats with black walnut fillers. The butternut seats were dropped with the straw-colored cane. The younger Payne also added smaller rods.

The three-piece Paynes then included two seven-foot rods weighing two and seven-eighths ounces and three and one-eighth ounces, and a pair of seven-and-a-half-foot tapers of three and three and one-quarter ounces. The ten-footer had disappeared, but six two-piece rods had replaced them. There was a six-foot wand of only one and a half ounces, and a seven-foot model of two and one-quarter ounces. The seven-and-a-half-foot Payne weighed two and five-eighths ounces, while the eight-footer was three and seven-eighths ounces. The new eight-and-a-half-foot Payne was four and one-quarter ounces, while the nine-foot design went five and one-quarter ounces. The famous screw-locking seat had not yet appeared, even on the Payne salmon rods.

It was the famous little green catalogue that appeared just before the Second World War that introduced both the Payne screw-locking reel seat and a parabolic taper. These changes reflect the influence of famous anglers like George La Branche, Edward Ringwood Hewitt, and John Alden Knight. Payne had stopped building three-piece rods under seven and a half feet, but there were often fifteen rods between seven and a half and nine and a half feet, including five nine-foot models. The two-piece line had expanded. The six-foot taper now weighed one and five-eighths ounces, and the seven-foot design weighed two and three-quarters ounces. The seven-and-a-half-foot Payne weighed three ounces, with a three-and-a-quarter-ounce model available in the same length. Three eight-foot rods dominated the two-piece line, ranging from three and a half to four and one-eighth ounces. The nine-footer went five and a half ounces, and the famous eight-and-a-half-foot Payne that originally evolved from the Hendrickson salmon experiments weighed four and five-eighths ounces.

The Payne parabolics had also appeared. These radical tapers had been developed empirically by Charles Ritz in Europe, and it was John Alden Knight who worked with James Payne to produce American versions. The Payne two-piece parabolics were mounted with full cork reel seats to reduce weight and eliminate inertial damping of an action that flexed right into the handle. The specifications of these new tapers were a little strange. The smallest measured an inch over seven feet and weighed two and seven-eighths ounces, while the seven-and-a-half-footer weighed three and three-eighths ounces. There were two rods of seven feet nine inches that weighed three and three-quarters and four and one-eighth ounces. It was John Alden Knight himself who contributed these paragraphs to a later, more elaborate Payne catalogue:

> When Charles Ritz came to this country in 1936, we compared notes and rods. Then we went to the E. F. Payne Rod Company plant at Highland Mills, and had a talk with Jim Payne. He set up the first American rod in the true parabolic action. This rod, like Ritz's rods, demanded perfect timing but it was a surprising tool for angling. Soon, however, Mr. Payne modified the original patterns and produced a rod more acceptable for general use, and for which, I understand, there is an ever-increasing demand.
>
> Parabolic action means literally this: the working portion of the rod is the lower one-third, next to the grip. The middle one-third acts as a lever, to deliver the power created by the lower rod, while the top one-third imparts the power to the line. The upper third and lower third do most of the bending during the cast. The middle third of the rod bends very little, since it functions as a lever.
>
> True parabolic action is not satisfactory for the average angler. It demands too much in the way of timing and is not a pleasant rod to use. The parabolic rods that are being turned out today are, in effect, semiparabolic in that they are not top-heavy, and permit a certain laxity in timing. They are delightful rods to use in that they handle both short and long casts equally well, in addition to having a high ratio of power to weight.

A. E. Hendrickson was the principal benefactor of the Payne company during the Depression years, although his support was usually concealed in his role as Payne's best customer. Hendrickson was also an occasional financial life preserver, and actually owned four percent of the stock in the company. It was one of his special salmon tapers that led to the eight-and-a-half-foot trout rod—the rod that became the Payne trademark when Roy Steenrod tried casting with its middle and tip section.

Hendrickson also had a role in the ten-foot salmon rod designed for casting single-handed with dry flies. It also became a Payne trademark, and it too was an accident. Hendrickson had commissioned the rod for fishing tarpon at the Gatun Locks in the Panama Canal, but it proved immensely popular for light-tackle salmon work. After Hendrickson died, his small holdings of stock in the E. F. Payne Company were sold to Abercrombie & Fitch. Its management always hoped that holding Payne stock might get them the exclusive selling rights for the Payne rods, but James Payne had always refused. Some years after the Second World War, the Abercrombie

& Fitch holding was acquired by a wealthy manufacturer who subsequently bought the Oram half interest, giving him fifty-two percent of the stock. His dream was to control the production of the best fly rods, reels, and shotguns in the world, but James Payne stubbornly refused to sell—knowing that fifty-two percent of the stock meant nothing when the primary assets of the company were his knowledge and the finest hands that ever held a plane.

His intransigence defeated the dream, although later he sold his remaining stock to the late W. L. Collins, himself a superb fisherman and judge of rods. Collins established a new company with James Payne as its president and himself as vice-president and treasurer, but both Payne and Collins died before they could realize their dream of making the Payne rods a top-quality line with a wide national distribution. James Payne died in the late spring of 1970, having maintained and surpassed the austere standards of his father, himself a craftsman so fine that the legendary Theodore Gordon once bartered thirty-nine dozen of his dry flies to acquire one of the early Payne rods.

Sparse Grey Hackle provides a fitting epitaph for both Paynes in his commentary for *Great Fishing Tackle Catalogs of the Golden Age*, with these observations on their work:

> All the old Leonard workmen who set up their own shops were notable for their rigid adherence to the highest standards of workmanship in spite of small incomes and, often, outright poverty. But I think Jim surpassed them all in his fanatical adherence to his own incredibly high standards of craftsmanship, and his rigid determination to uphold the status of the Payne name as a tribute to his father. Jim was a king of craftsmen, a true friend, and a real gentleman.

The final Payne catalogue is a collector's item, particularly noteworthy if it contains Payne's autograph. It is bound with an uncut rag-paper cover with an exquisite bookplate engraving that adapts a scene from the famous Currier & Ives print of brook-trout fishing in America. It includes brief pieces by such notables as Edward Ringwood Hewitt, George La Branche, Mead Schaeffer, Frederick Barbour, Charles Phair, and Otto von Kienbusch. Their collection of essays alone makes the catalogue a priceless fragment of angling memorabilia.

Its fly-rod lists are the high-water mark in the evolution of the Payne rods, offering a choice of four reel-seat designs. The full-locking hardware added only a half ounce to the listed weight, in spite of its heavy jewel-finished alloys. Both the conventional seat with a hooded butt cap and ornamental end piece and the reverse-locking system with the hooded cap concealed in the grip were still available. The full metal seats of German silver had been dropped, keeping only the skeletal butt cap and band fittings with a select black walnut or cork filler. The three-piece Paynes listed in that final catalogue were the following models:

197	7½ feet	Dry-Fly	3½ to 3⅝ ounces
198	7½ feet	Fast Dry-Fly	3¾ to 3⅞ ounces
200	8 feet	Light Dry-Fly	3⅝ to 3¾ ounces
201	8 feet	Dry-Fly	3⅞ to 4 ounces
202	8 feet	Fast Dry-Fly	4⅛ to 4¼ ounces
204	8½ feet	Light Dry-Fly	4⅛ to 4¼ ounces
205	8½ feet	Medium or Fast	4½ to 4⅝ ounces
206	8½ feet	Medium or Fast	5 to 5¼ ounces
207	9 feet	Slow	4¾ to 4⅞ ounces
208	9 feet	Light Dry-Fly	4¾ to 5 ounces
209	9 feet	Dry-Fly	5¼ to 5¾ ounces
210	9 feet	Medium or Fast	5½ to 5⅝ ounces
212	9½ feet	Medium	5⅝ to 5¾ ounces
214	9½ feet	Fast	6 to 6⅛ ounces

The two-piece list included a six-and-a-half-footer that was missing from the earlier Payne catalogues. These rods are particularly prized among fishermen, and they include the incomparable tapers between six and seven and a half feet not found in the three-piece series:

95	6 feet	Dry-Fly	1⅝ to 1⅞ ounces
96	6½ feet	Dry-Fly	2¼ to 2⅜ ounces
97	7 feet	Dry-Fly	2⅝ to 2¾ ounces
98	7 feet	Fast Dry-Fly	2⅞ to 3 ounces
100	7½ feet	Dry-Fly	3¼ to 3⅜ ounces
101	7½ feet	Fast Dry-Fly	3½ to 3¾ ounces
102	8 feet	Light Dry-Fly	3⅝ to 3⅞ ounces
103	8 feet	Fast Dry-Fly	4 to 4⅛ ounces
104	8½ feet	Light Dry-Fly	4⅛ to 4⅜ ounces
105	8½ feet	Slow	4⅝ to 4¾ ounces
106	8½ feet	Medium or Fast Dry-Fly	4⅝ to 4¾ ounces
108	9 feet	Light Dry-Fly	5 to 5¼ ounces
110	9 feet	Dry-Fly	5⅜ to 5½ ounces

The Parabolics had been reduced to only two models, perhaps in response to the growing fashion of the little rod, although it is in the lengths beyond seven and a half feet that such tapers really excel. These rods had skeletal seats with cork fillers. The seven-foot one-inch model weighed two and seven-eighths ounces, and the seven-foot nine-inch taper weighed three and three-quarters ounces. These rods are similar to the Super Parabolic-PPP tapers that Charles Ritz calls the Featherlight and Colorado, manufactured in France by the firm of Pezon & Michel.

When James Payne left his shop for the last time in the winter of 1969, his customers and disciples were fearful, since Payne was not a man who would quit rodmaking easily. *I'm tired and I don't feel right,* he told Tom Bailey. *Don't really know when I'll be back.*

His company had been acquired by Gladding, primarily to assemble an expensive grade of fiberglass rods using the Payne name and hardware. Payne said little about those rods, although his silence itself was eloquent. Payne hated glass and its contribution to the death of craftsmanship, and it was almost funny to watch him flex one with a silent headshake and grimace that eloquently betrayed his opinion. But like everything else he touched, the glass blanks he fitted with Payne hardware were the finest fiberglass he could find.

There are countless anecdotes about Payne, each recounting his stubborn honesty and integrity or his restless odysscy in search of ultimate perfection. W. L. Collins liked to tell the story about how difficult it became to meet Payne's exacting specifications for German silver after the Second World War.

Big nickel suppliers don't exactly declare a dividend over the size of a rodmaker's order, Collins explained, *and we searched until we found a nickel company with a president who fished–when his rods were held up in delivery we got action!*

Payne himself admitted his fussiness about craftsmanship and detailing, and his solution for finishing the bamboo nodes is typical. The nodes are often marred with minuscule pits and checks that cannot be worked smooth without weakening the section, and they also mar the final varnish work. Payne finishes are legendary for their perfection, and part of their secret lies in his node work.

Getting them down flush with the rest of the stick can make a weak point in the rod when you use a file or sanding block, Payne revealed in his shop a few months before his death. *We worked out a heat-pressure technique that presses the nodes into the rod, and we don't have to risk cutting into the power fibers.*

When Payne finally died, Gladding permitted his apprentice David Decker to continue making rods under the Payne trademark, along with the fittings maker Tom Bailey, who had worked with both Payne and Leonard over the years. Their work used the same cane, milling machines and other equipment, ferrules, reel fittings, and proprietary techniques worked out by the Paynes over the years. Operations are still based in the original shop at Highland Mills. Briefly, the rods were produced under the Decker name, but the fledgling company soon wisely returned to calling itself the E. F. Payne Rod Company. David Decker is an exceptionally talented young craftsman, but it is difficult to honor a legend.

Payne was a tough act to follow, Decker admits grudgingly.

During those gilded years of American rodmaking, several large tackle manufacturers also produced rods of split-bamboo construction, and their premier grades sometimes approached the work of the fine custom builders. Montague was perhaps the first company to trigger this competition in the factory production of cane rods, and other fine equipment was made by Heddon and South Bend.

It is interesting that even this activity often stemmed from the Leonard tradition. George Varney was its primary catalyst at Montague and had served his apprenticeship at Central Valley while Hiram Leonard was still

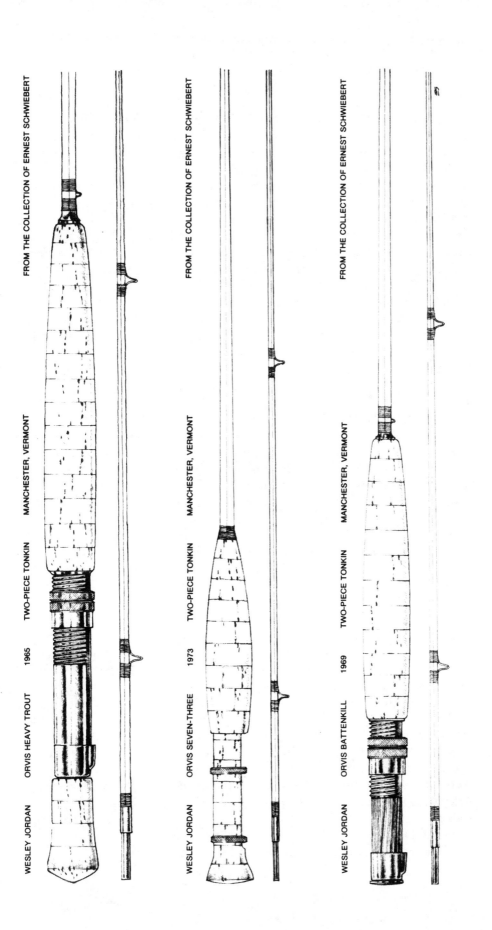

WESLEY JORDAN   ORVIS HEAVY TROUT   1965   TWO-PIECE TONKIN   MANCHESTER, VERMONT   FROM THE COLLECTION OF ERNEST SCHWIEBERT

WESLEY JORDAN   ORVIS SEVEN-THREE   1973   TWO-PIECE TONKIN   MANCHESTER, VERMONT   FROM THE COLLECTION OF ERNEST SCHWIEBERT

WESLEY JORDAN   ORVIS BATTENKILL   1969   TWO-PIECE TONKIN   MANCHESTER, VERMONT   FROM THE COLLECTION OF ERNEST SCHWIEBERT

alive. Montague made a lot of contract rods for major mail-order houses, but its own top-grade Varney rods were special. The oldest I have seen was a nine-foot three-piece rod weighing about six ounces. It featured a full nickel-silver seat with a hooded cap and sliding band as long as the grip itself, which was an exaggerated half-Wells design. Montague rods rivalled the work of Divine for their intricate, polychromatic windings above the grip, and the Varney rods also displayed intermediate wraps, with ornamental silk windings in the middle of the butt section. Later Montague rods included the Redwing, which had a simple Payne-style grip and full metal seat of German silver. The nine-foot Redwing was a three-piece rod weighing five and three-quarters ounces. Its swelled-butt tapers also echo Varney's work with Leonard, and it is typical of cane rods produced before the First World War. Redwing models were also produced which had full locking seats of German silver, combined with garish brass threads and lock-nuts. These were three-piece rods made in eight-and-a-half- and nine-foot lengths. Perhaps the best Montague rods that I have seen are the Fishkill series made just before the Second World War under the direction of Sewell Dunton. These rods had a half-Wells grip with a black locking seat and walnut filler, and were a prelude to the rods that Dunton made in western Massachusetts after he left Montague.

Sewell Dunton produced a series of moderately priced rods in western Massachusetts, both under his own premium trademark and as the Zwirz Favorite that Robert Zwirz sold through his tackle shop in midtown New York. The Dunton tapers were rather fast, featuring a stiff butt and soft tip-action performance. Although the fittings often varied in quality and several grip and reel-seat designs are common, Dunton rods display a number of basic features. The ferrules were drawn instead of machined, and like the reel fittings, they were anodized black. Most grips were a relatively fat Payne-type cigar design. The larger rods, between eight and a half and nine and a half feet, often had full-metal seats anodized black, while the seven and a half to eight and a half foot rods also had skeletal locking hardware with cork or walnut fillers. Dunton used skeletal seats consisting of a hooded butt cap and ring over both walnut and cork on his smaller rods. Black tungsten guides were used, and the silk wrappings were tastefully simple, with a dark brown intended to match the cane and black ornamental tips.

Dunton has since retired and sold his Greenfield shop to the young craftsmen who founded Thomas & Thomas. The company has no relationship to old Fred Thomas and his son Leon, but derives its name from its owners, Thomas Dorsey and Thomas Maxwell. Both are relatively young men who learned rodmaking in boyhood from the grandfather of Thomas Maxwell, and both continued making rods into their college years. They were teaching philosophy at the University of Maryland and building rods as a part-time profession until 1973, when they decided to abandon lecturing for craftsmanship and bought out Dunton.

Thomas & Thomas have now moved their operation from Mary-

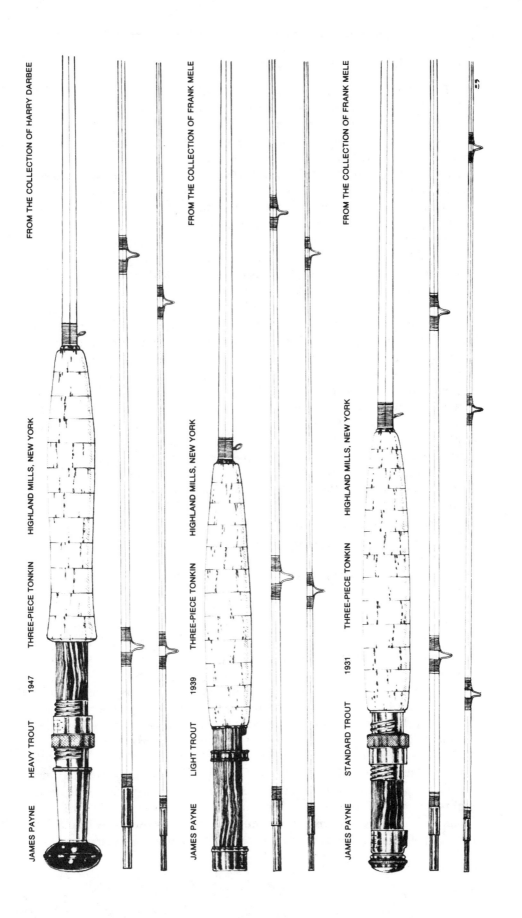

JAMES PAYNE   HEAVY TROUT   1947   THREE-PIECE TONKIN   HIGHLAND MILLS, NEW YORK   FROM THE COLLECTION OF HARRY DARBEE

JAMES PAYNE   LIGHT TROUT   1939   THREE-PIECE TONKIN   HIGHLAND MILLS, NEW YORK   FROM THE COLLECTION OF FRANK MELE

JAMES PAYNE   STANDARD TROUT   1931   THREE-PIECE TONKIN   HIGHLAND MILLS, NEW YORK   FROM THE COLLECTION OF FRANK MELE

land to Dunton's old Greenfield plant and are building rods full time.

We're so awash in back orders, Dorsey explained this past spring, *that we're not really sure what full time means any more!*

Both men are dedicated artisans, determined to pursue their craft with militant fervor, and believe they have been fated to preserve the split-cane tradition. Some of that fanaticism has already been implanted in a growing circle of customers. Armed with the equipment acquired from Sewell Dunton, who still wanders into the shop from time to time, and one of the largest supplies of aged culms in the United States, the future of their fledgling partnership looks bright.

Originally, the Thomas & Thomas rods were impregnated with a polymer resin in a light brown finish, but varnished rods in the natural color bamboo are also available in each model today. The ferrules are handcrafted of nickel silver in a shouldered, hand-lapped design. The reel fittings are machined from first-quality aluminum with a gleaming jewel finish, and full-locking and skeletal seats are available. Oxidized ferrules and reel seats are also furnished. Chromed stainless snake guides and tip tops are used, with carboloy stripping guides. Morticed walnut fillers are supplied with both locking and skeletal seats, along with paired rings on either walnut or cork. The fully skeletal grip of aluminum rings is finished with a butt of delicately sculptured cork. It is typical of their work that the butt of the cane is not covered with a plate in these rods, but is sanded smooth and left exposed in a candid piece of functional design.

Thomas & Thomas have worked in a wide range of grip styles, since they are willing to produce virtually any shape to order, but a number of grips seem to echo the design sense of the makers. Both reverse and standard cigar grips are common in the work of Thomas & Thomas, along with cigar designs having exaggeratedly pointed front tapers ideally suited to the index-finger casting grip.

Thomas & Thomas are building their rods in three price ranges, with the Caenis and Paradigm series the most expensive. The Individualist grade is divided into three groups called the Midge series, the Hendrickson series, and the Montana series. The Thomas & Thomas Classic rods are the least expensive, and include the Gnat series, the Classic Paralights, the Limestoners, the Cahill models, and the Coachman series. These rods are designed to fulfill a remarkable range of fishing problems.

The Caenis series is a unique line of delicate rods designed for fishing terrestrial and minute mayflies on our eastern limestone streams, western spring creeks, and on any river under the fine-tippet conditions of late summer. Caenis tapers for two-weight lines include three models between six and seven feet, weighing from one ounce to one and seven-eighths ounces. There are five rods in the Caenis series for three-weight lines, ranging from the six-footer at one and a half ounces to a surprising eight-foot rod weighing only three and one-quarter ounces. According to Thomas & Thomas, the new Paradigm series is a response to my discussions of parabolic tapers and their particular capabilities with nymphs and delicate tippets. The action is slow and truly parabolic, with the ability to handle a surprisingly long line once its timing is mastered. Paradigm rods are made in lengths between seven and eight feet to provide enough rod to manipulate fly swing in fishing a nymph. There are two designs for four-weight lines, a seven-footer of two and three-eighths ounces and a seven-and-a-half-footer weighing three and one-quarter ounces. Two rods are built for five-weights, one seven-and-a-half-foot taper at three and five-eighths ounces and an eight-foot design at three and three-quarters ounces. The eight-foot Paradigm for a six-weight line weighs only four ounces, and is a superb all-around rod capable of fishing a 6X tippet and punching out a weighted nymph with authority. These Paradigm compound tapers are exquisitely conceived and constructed, and a welcome addition to our sport.

The Individualist Midge series was part of the original Thomas & Thomas line. It is characterized by its extremely fine tip calibrations in each of its several tapers. There are four designs taking four-weight lines. The lightest is six and a half feet long and weighs three and a half ounces. Two of the Midge series are balanced with five-weight tapers, the seven-and-a-half-footer weighing three and one-quarter ounces and the eight-footer weighing three and three-quarters ounces.

The Thomas & Thomas Hendrickson series is designed to serve a versatile spectrum of needs, using three- to six-weight lines. There is a seven-foot Hendrickson at two and one-quarter ounces for DT3F. The three designs for four-weight lines include a six-foot rod at one and three-quarters ounces, the six-and-a-half-foot Hendrickson of two and one-eighth ounces, and a seven-footer weighing two and three-eighths ounces. The five-weight tapers are a seven-foot rod of two and a half ounces, and a seven-and-a-half-footer that weighs three and one-quarter ounces. There are two six-weight designs, the seven-and-a-half-foot model of three and three-quarters ounces and the eight-foot taper of three and seven-eighths ounces.

The Montana series incorporates the larger full-loading tapers with a much slower casting cycle. The calibrations combine a capability for distance, as well as the delicacy to fish 5X and 6X tippets with a deliberate strike and reasonable care. Thomas & Thomas have worked out tapers for two four-weight designs, the six-and-a-half-foot rod at two and one-eighth ounces and a seven-footer of two and three-eighths ounces. The five-weight Montanas include a seven-foot design weighing two and a half ounces, and a seven-and-a-half-foot version of three and one-quarter ounces. The six-weight rod measures eight feet and weighs three and seven-eighths ounces, and a second eight-footer weighing four and one-eighth ounces takes a seven-weight taper. The biggest rod in the Montana series weighs four and three-quarters ounces and requires a weight-forward eight to function best.

The Thomas & Thomas Classic line of rods includes the Gnat series, the Classic Paralights, and the Limestoners. The Gnats include three rods for a DT4F fly line, the smallest a six-footer weighing one and a half ounces and the largest a six-and-a-half-foot taper of two and one-eighth ounces. There is also a six-and-a-half-foot Gnat weighing two and one-quarter ounces that takes a DT5F line. These are short rods with a crisp, accurate delivery on brushy, overgrown waters, but unlike similar rods made by other firms, their actions flex deep into the butt and fish a relatively fine leader point.

The craftsmen at Thomas & Thomas are particularly proud of their Limestoner rods. These tapers supply a crisp control, with a tight loop and superb accuracy, plus the length to keep a backcast high above the weedy meadows of our limestone streams. There are six Limestoners made by Thomas & Thomas, three for DT4F lines and three for five-weights. The four-weights are seven feet and two and three-eighths ounces, seven and a half feet and three and one-eighth ounces, and a full eight feet weighing three and five-eighths ounces. The tapers calibrated for five-weight lines include a seven-footer of two and three-quarters ounces, a seven-and-a-half-foot design at three and a half ounces, and a basic eight-foot rod weighing three and seven-eighths ounces. These are excellent rods where both length and relative delicacy are important.

The Cahill series consists of five models, beginning with a seven-foot, two-and-one-quarter-ounce taper for a three-weight line. Two other seven-foot rods of two and three-eighths and two and three-quarters ounces are designed for four- and five-weight lines. The seven-and-a-half-footer in the Cahill series weighs three and three-quarters ounces and takes a six-weight taper, like the eight-foot, four-ounce model. Thomas & Thomas also build a fine group of big nymph and streamer rods called the Coachman series. These rods range from a seven-foot, two-and-three-quarters-ounce rod for a five-weight line, to the nine-footer that weighs five and a half ounces and powers an eight-weight with authority.

The birth of Thomas & Thomas in recent years is a blessing, since only a decade ago conventional wisdom was predicting the death of the cane rodmaker's art. *Those two young men are a miracle*, my old friend Lawrence Banks insists. *Just when Jim Payne is on his deathbed, these two appear without warning—and with a good thirty or forty years ahead of them!*

The craftsmanship of Thomas & Thomas is perhaps a fitting conclusion for the equipment and bamboo stocks that Sewell Dunton acquired when Montague finally decided to abandon the production of split-bamboo rods.

However, the finest factory rods of split cane were probably made over the years at James Heddon & Sons in Michigan. Heddon is a name perhaps more closely identified with bass fishing, since the founder James Heddon shares the honor of inventing the surface bass plug with Anson Decker of New Jersey.

Heddon also made bamboo rods in a surprising number of models and grades, and since the plant was in Dowagiac, there were a great many Heddon rods in use on my boyhood Michigan rivers. The Heddon DeLuxe and the less expensive Black Beauty were highly prized in those days. Both were remarkably beautiful rods, particularly in the vintages manufactured before the First World War, and their traditional swelled butt tapers betrayed a possible connection between the Heddon craftsmen and the prototypes of earlier makers like Murphy and Leonard.

There were many Heddon rods made over the years, and the models priced at the top of the line were often of surprising quality. Such rods are still highly regarded by their owners. The Heddon Model 10 was moderately priced, with oxidized ferrules and skeletal reel-seat fittings over a cork filler. It was usually finished with scarlet silk windings, and the seven-and-a-half-footer at three and a half ounces was perhaps the favorite model. The Heddon Folsom was a superbly finished two-piece rod with a delicately slow action. It had oxidized ferrules and reel-seat fittings over a black walnut filler. The brown silk wrappings were tipped with yellow, and except for the swelled butt tapers typical of Heddon, the Folsom is remarkably like a Payne in appearance. The seven-and-a-half-foot Folsom was a classic rod, taking a four-weight line and weighing only three and one-eighth ounces. The Heddon Black Beauty was long a popular rod on the rivers of the Middle West. It had black silk wraps and fittings with a Bakelite screw-locking filler and a graceful half-Wells cork grip. The eight-foot Black Beauty was a three-piece rod weighing only four ounces, and with an action perfectly attuned to a four-weight line. It was highly prized among the men who fished the Michigan rivers during my boyhood summers there. The Heddon DeLuxe was an exquisitely made fly rod with black fittings over a richly burled-walnut reel filler. Its grip was a reversed half-Wells like the Granger type, and it was wrapped with brown winds tipped in black silk. The Heddon DeLuxe was made in eight-foot, eight-and-a-half-foot, and nine-foot models ranging from three and a half to five and a half ounces and was one of the finest factory rods.

But the vintage Heddon rods made before the First World War are my favorites. These rods were the prototypes of the Black Beauty and the DeLuxe models that followed, and their fittings were designed with unsurpassed sense of elegance and design. The Black Beauty already had its characteristic black silk wrappings and Bakelite reel-seat filler, although the hooded reel sleeve and slender discs of German silver at the grip checks were abandoned in the modern versions. It was the DeLuxe of this period that was perhaps the vintage Heddon, and the apogee of rodmaking in the shop of Dowagiac.

Its ties to Hiram Leonard are visible in the fully swelled butt and the relatively fat cigar-type grip, although the ornamental character of the reel seats and grip checks are unmistakably Heddon. The cork grip is rather short, and the reel-seat assembly is almost as long as the grip itself. Bakelite grip checks with German-silver spacers complete the grip, along with a Bakelite winding check that tapers into the swelled cane. The lock fittings consist of a German-silver hood and screw-nut, threaded on a Bakelite filler. The butt plate is Bakelite, with a relatively slender hooded sleeve of silver. The seat filler is burled American walnut, and the slim cork rings unquestionably date these rods to the early years of this century. During my boyhood years along the Pere Marquette, there was an old fisherman who used one of these vintage Heddons with enviable skill, and for many years I believed they were the finest rods in the world.

The South Bend Bait Company acquired the famous Cross Rod Company after the First World War, and for more than a decade the Cross-South Bend rods were excellent production work. These rods closely resemble the Leonard Tournament designs that were popular after the First World War, with their full German-silver seats and slender cigar-type grips. The rods were executed in double-built construction and pale honey-colored cane. The silk windings were English tan, and the action was a smooth semiparabolic that worked into the grip. The eight-and-a-half-foot, three-piece rod at five and one-quarter ounces took a surprisingly light five-weight line. Cross used agate butt guides and split ferrules with four spiral cuts, placed counterclockwise for a right-handed caster and clockwise for a left-handed owner. The full silver reel seats were engraved with a handsome Cross medallion. The famous Cross Sylph was a seven-foot, two-piece rod weighing only three ounces in spite of its double-built construction. Its grip and reel-seat assembly were much shorter than the conventional Cross designs. Following the Second World War, with Cross himself long dead and his protégé, the exceptionally talented Wes Jordan, at Orvis, South Bend continued to make good split-cane rods both under its own trademark and for Shakespeare. These rods used burgundy-colored reel-seat fillers with a locking butt-cap nut matching their anodized automatic fly reels. The similar Shakespeare reels were a deep forest green, and the rods built by South Bend for Shakespeare used matching anodized reel seats. Some later South Bend rods used burgundy and amber-colored reel seats of plastic, and even the fine 346 series ultimately featured plastic fittings, although the bamboo remained surprisingly good.

European rodmaking was dominated by the famous House of Hardy, after it was founded by William Hardy and his tournament-casting brother, John James Hardy, in 1872. Their influence was so great that the Hardy shop on Paikes Street soon lifted Alnwick, a small town in Northumberland, to international prominence in the fishing world. Donald Overfield made these observations in his article on the Hardy operation for *Trout and Salmon* in the spring of 1973:

> From the outset, it was their aim to produce the very best in rods, and so in some respects these two men were akin to Rolls and Royce, their philosophy being to design and produce the finest possible product. Price had a secondary nature. To succeed in business on this basis, one must be correct in the assumption that one's product is unquestionably the best.

John James Hardy and William Hardy were apparently correct in that confidence, because history tells us they were soon deluged with orders. Their success precipitated a move to larger quarters on Fenkle Street, but their reputation continued to grow, and to accommodate a landslide of orders they ultimately moved to new production facilities in Bondgate. Hardy Brothers remained at Bondgate until 1967, when they moved to a still larger plant at Willowburn. Donald Overfield again captures the spirit of Hardy in his short article for *Trout and Salmon* in England:

> Just what is it that has always linked the name of Hardy with quality? Three things: meticulous craftsmanship, inventiveness, and the exquisite finish details. These things, coupled with a family tradition of angling businessmen, reaches to the present.

Early in the history of Hardy Brothers, John James Hardy became intensely interested in tournament casting. His passion was largely rooted in the conviction that only tournament competition could improve and market their work, and the family tradition of tournament competition prevailed. John James Hardy often held the European championship in salmon- and trout-fly distance, as well as the dry-fly accuracy events. Laurence Reuben Hardy and Harold Hardy also followed that tradition and became British champions in salmon-fly distance and dry-fly accuracy. The dedication of the Hardy family to the performance of their tackle on the tournament circuit continues today.

The Alnwick shops have also been responsible for many design innovations over the years, including the spiral-lock ferrule patented in 1882, and the reverse-locking reel seat in 1911. The Casting Club de France rods were introduced that same year and are still treasured by many owners as the finest light trout models ever built. Using a slender Casting Club de France, which measured only seven feet and weighed only two and three-eighths ounces, John James Hardy set a French distance record on the French competition ponds in the Bois de Boulogne. There is still an old photograph in the Hardy offices that records that triumph with John James Hardy resplendent in Cheviot tweeds, surrounded by French casters wearing bowlers and top hats in the meadows at Tir aux Pigeons.

Hardy split-cane rods were largely produced by hand, using the planing blocks developed before Victorian times, until the introduction of a milling machine in 1925. Ten years later, Hardy began building split-cane sections with the pithy core of the bamboo removed and the inner glue faces replaced with a lighter apex of select American pine. It was a system similar to the method of construction developed about twelve years earlier by Edwin Powell in California. Hollow split-bamboo rods originated in 1933, with the separate patents granted to Edwin Powell and Lew Stoner on the Pacific Coast. But Hardy introduced a remarkably different hollow rod using modern high-stress adhesives twenty-five years later—and James Hardy quickly used the new Hollolight and Hollokona designs to break the European distance records in 1959.

The influence of the Hardy designs is obvious in many classic American rods, from the work of Payne in New York to the reverse-locking Bakelite reel seats used by Powell in California. The Hardy DeLuxe with

its sliding lock-nut reel seat first appeared in 1911, and the Hardy R. B. Marston with its reverse-locking seat, concealed band blade, and full Wells grip was introduced before the First World War. The Viscount Grey at ten and a half feet and eight and one-quarter ounces was introduced in these same years, with its heavy reverse-locking seat and rubber button. The famous Houghton Club and F. M. Halford rods ranging from nine and a half feet to ten and a half feet also appeared before the Treaty of Versailles. The Houghton Club came in three models, fitted with the locking nut and bank blade, and weighed as much as nine ounces. The Halford Special was a more modern reverse-lock seat, and its design had a wide influence in the United States. The famous J. J. Hardy model had a reverse-locking seat of the Granger type, its hood sliding over a Bakelite filler, and it was introduced in 1921. The delicate Hardy Marvel was introduced the following year, and weighed only two and three-quarters ounces at seven and a half feet. It featured a skeletal seat with a butt cap and two aluminum rings, one fixed and the other sliding. Herbert Hoover owned a later Marvel with the free screw-mounted hood still used on the modern Palakona series. There were also a few exquisite Hardy Marvels built at eight feet and three and one-quarter ounces, one of the finest tapers in Hardy history. The elegant Hardy Fairchild was introduced about 1925, and included a finely detailed butt cap and hooded sleeve, with a sliding jewel-finished reel band. It was developed before the First World War for Tappan Fairchild, using the basic tapers of the Casting Club de France and adding a nine-and-a-half-foot model weighing five ounces. Fairchild fished the classic water on the Neversink headwaters, and was one of the finest American trout fishermen of his time.

Later Hardy rods continued in the classic Hardy mold, particularly with the introduction of the Itchen and Fairy models on the threshold of the Great Depression. There was also a new version of the Hardy DeLuxe, with a lighter Halford-type locking seat and reversed half-Wells grip. It was made in models ranging from eight feet, four and three-quarters ounces to a muscular ten-footer at six and three-quarters ounces. The Hardy Itchen was an attempt to match the Leonards that Skues fished and wrote about with such enthusiasm on his Abbotts Barton water, much to the chagrin of the Hardy brothers and other British makers. The Hardy Itchen is a fine rod in its own right, with a light reverse-locking seat and full Wells-style grip. Like the famous Leonards owned by Skues, the Hardy Itchen was made in nine-and-a-half- and ten-foot lengths weighing six and a half and six and three-quarters ounces.

The Hardy Fairy is perhaps the most famous model in the minds of many American fishermen, for it is this rod that was selected by the late Ernest Hemingway in the Hardy shop at Pall Mall in London. Hemingway bought his rod after the remarkable success of *A Farewell to Arms*, and it was the eight-and-a-half-foot, five-ounce Fairy that he fished later in Wyoming and Idaho, particularly on Silver Creek near Sun Valley. The rod was purchased from the Hemingway estate by my good friend,

Prescott Tolman, and presented to the Museum of American Fly Fishing.

The familiar Hardy Phantom rods were introduced following the Second World War, with a slim cigar grip and skeletal seat of butt cap and sliding ring on a cork filler. Phantoms were made in many sizes from the four-and-a-half-footer of one and a half ounces to the nine-footer that weighed four and three-quarters ounces and took a surprisingly light DT6F line. The eight-foot Phantom at four and one-quarter ounces was probably the most popular Hardy in the United States. It balanced a five-weight line. It was in the larger Phantoms, rods between eight and nine and a half feet, that Hardy introduced the Hollolight and Hollokona construction. It is these rods that represented the Hardy line until recent years, when Harrington & Richardson acquired the exclusive rights to market the Hardy products sold throughout the United States. Several months ago I was invited by Edward Rowe, the young president of Harrington & Richardson, to meet with James Hardy over dinner in Boston.

We'd like you to see our new line of Palakona bamboo rods, Rowe explained. *You already know our Hardy reels.*

The modern Hardy line starts with the Palakona bamboo long famous in the finest British rods. The tapers are designed to produce a crisp and slightly fast dry-fly action, using six-strip construction in a two-piece design. Both grip and reel seat in the six- to seven-and-a-half-foot Palakona rods are cork, with the traditional capped butt, screw-fitted hood, and sliding band first used on the Casting Club de France in 1911. The ferrules are fine nickel silver with jewel-polished aluminum plugs; and the silk wrappings at the ferrules, grip checks, and guides are a traditional black with bright green tips. In the smaller lengths and weights, the grips are the graceful cigar type first used on the Casting Club de France and Hardy Marvel, and the Hardy fishtail grip is used with a Halford reverse-locking seat in the eight- and eight-and-a-half-foot models.

The Palakona Superlight of six feet and two ounces is designed for a five-weight line, while the seven-foot Superlight weighs three ounces and takes the same size taper. The seven-and-a-half-foot Palakona weighs three and five-eighths ounces and uses a six-weight line perfectly.

The Palakona medium action rods of eight and eight and a half feet are fine all-around tapers weighing four and five-eighths ounces and five and three-eighths ounces. The eight-foot model is designed for a seven-weight line, while the longer rod is balanced with an eight-weight. The larger sizes are now made of fiberglass, with a traditional black rubber button attached to the reverse-locking seat. The Hardy Fibatube operation began in 1968, and with the fabrication of its own glass sections, the history of Hardy began a fresh chapter. Donald Overfield concluded his essay in *Trout and Salmon* with these observations on the famous rods that came from Alnwick:

The Jet fly rods produced from these blanks have rapidly become a firm favourite with countless anglers. While the name Jet is in keeping with these modern times, it is also, in fact, a tribute to the great American tournament caster who helped develop their original design and action, J. E. Tarantino.

And so the story of the Hardy rod is brought up to date. Whenever flyfishers discuss quality rods, such famous names as the J.J.H. Triumph, L.R.H. Dry Fly, Halford Knockabout, Crown Houghton, Koh-i-Noor, and Perfection will emerge, to ensure a place in the history of flyfishing for that remote little town of Alnwick, in Northumberland, and for the two men who made it all possible, John James and William Hardy.

Although the history of British rods has unquestionably been dominated by the House of Hardy, there have been many fine rodmakers in England over the past century. Knowledgeable angling historians have admired the rods built by makers like John Forrest of Kelso-on-Tweed, Bampton of Alnwick, Westley Richards of Birmingham, Allcock and Walker Falcon of Redditch, Ingram of Glasgow, Joseph Braddell of Belfast, Farlow of London, Sharpe's of Aberdeen, Sealey's, Rogan of Donegal, and the famous British firm of Millward's. Few of these firms survive, except for the merged rodmaking efforts of Charles Farlow & Company and J. S. Sharpe of Aberdeen, Davenport and Fordham at Poole, and the relatively new workshop of Clifford Constable in Bromley.

The Farlow Featherweights are two-piece construction in four models. These rods are fitted with a hooded butt cap and sliding band over a cork filler. The seven-footer weighs three and one-quarter ounces and takes a five-weight line taper, like the seven-and-a-half-foot Featherweight of four ounces. The eight-foot designed for a six-weight line weighs four and one-quarter ounces, and the eight-and-a-half-footer of four and three-quarters ounces takes the same fly-line tapers. There are four rods of the Ritz staggered-ferrule type. The Farlow Eighty-eight measures eight feet eight inches in length, weighs five ounces, and takes a six-weight. The Eighty-three is five inches shorter, takes a five-weight line, and weighs four and a half ounces. The staggered ferrule places the German-silver joints well below the nodal point in the rod tapers. Farlow also manufactures a version of the famous Ritz Fario Club, named for the small circle of internationally known anglers that meets each fall at the Hotel Ritz in Paris. The Fario Club measures eight feet five inches and takes a five-weight line. These three rods have locking reel seats on a cork filler.

Dermot Wilson collaborated with Alan Sharpe to produce the Wilson-Sharpe, which uses a hooded butt cap and sliding reel band on a cork filler, with a tapered Ritz-style grip. It measures eight feet three inches, weighs four and one-quarter ounces, and takes a five-weight taper. It is a fine British version of the Ritz Parabolic theories.

It's a rod with an international pedigree, Dermot Wilson explains enthusiastically at Nether Wallop. *It's tapers combine the result of testing among friends from Normandy to New Zealand.*

The Farlow Elf is a small two-piece rod designed for small streams and relatively light tackle. It measures six feet ten inches and weighs three and three-quarters ounces, taking a five-weight line. The Wulff-Farlow Midge and Ultimate are familiar rods to Americans who know the similar rods that Lee Wulff designed for Orvis after the Second World War. The Ultimate is a five-foot ten-inch rod built as a single stick without a ferrule. It weighs only one and a half ounces but takes a six-weight line, like the six-foot Midge, which adds a ferrule and weighs two ounces.

The fine J. S. Sharpe rods include the three-piece Aberdeen and two-piece Scottie series. The Aberdeen trout rods include a nine-footer of six and one-quarter ounces designed for a six-weight line and a nine-and-a-half-foot, six-and-three-quarters-ounce taper for a seven-weight. The Scottie series of rods is justly popular in both Europe and the United States, and like the Aberdeen group, it is fitted with full metal reel seats. The eight-and-a-half-foot Scottie weighs five and a half ounces and takes a six-weight. The nine-footer weighs six ounces, and like the nine-and-a-half-foot model of six ounces, it also takes a surprisingly light six-weight line. Both the Farlow and the Sharpe's rods are milled from impregnated bamboo, which was originally developed at Orvis in the United States, and which the Sharpe's technicians call their armor-cane process.

Two rods designed and built by Davenport and Fordham are quite popular in England, although they are virtually unknown in America. The eight-foot Fordham Exclusive features a hooded butt cap and sliding reel band on a half-Wells grip. It weighs four and one-eighth ounces and takes a five-weight taper. The eight-and-a-half-foot Exclusive weighs four and three-quarters ounces and is designed for a six-weight line.

Clifford Constable of Bromley is building a moderately priced series of fine split-cane rods. The Constable R. H. Woods rods are perhaps best known in this country, with a semiparabolic action and staggered ferrules. The six-foot nine-inch model weighs two and seven-eighths ounces and matches a WF4F perfectly, while the seven-and-a-half-footer of three and a half ounces is designed for a five-weight. Dermot Wilson has also worked with Constable to produce a six-foot nine-inch model called the Wallop Brook. It weighs two and three-quarters ounces and takes a four-weight line. The seven-and-a-half-foot Wallop Brook weighs three and seven-eighths ounces and is designed for five-weight tapers. The third Wallop Brook rod measures eight feet two inches, weighs four and five-eighths ounces, and its tapers are calibrated to take a six-weight line. Clifford Constable also builds a surprisingly delicate nine-footer called the C. C. Lightweight. It weighs four and seven-eighths ounces because of its hooded cap and reel band fitted over a cork filler, and takes a six-weight perfectly. These Constable rods are enormously popular in England, since they are hand-planed bamboo, yet cost a little more than half the price of the comparable Hardy Palakona line. This past spring I had the privilege of fishing a Constable rod with Dermot Wilson on his Kimbridge beat of the lower Test. It was late during the hatches of big *Ephemera* drakes, and the

DERMOT WILSON

fish were working on both emerging sedges and the odd mayfly spinner drifting spent on the smooth currents. The seven-and-a-half-foot Wallop Brook punched out eighty-foot casts with precision, hooked two- and three-pound trout at that range without breaking off .005 tippets, and played the fish in the weedy channels with a mixture of delicacy and control. Their qualities were surprisingly good considering their cost.

We're quite proud of Cliff Constable, Dermot Wilson explained happily at his Kimbridge fishing hut. *His handwork continues in the best traditions of British rodmaking.*

The only serious rival to these British rodmakers on the European continent is the famous French shop of Pezon & Michel located at Amboise. Although Pezon & Michel were a fine tackle firm before their association with the celebrated Charles Ritz, there was nothing in their earlier work that suggests the innovative thought and creative *élan* that Ritz brought to their rods.

His family long ago gave its name to the English language as a superlative and as a synonym for quality, through their operation of a hotel in Paris that many believe the finest in the world. The Hotel Ritz in the Place Vendôme offers a quality of comfort and service that has made it a legend among travellers. The Ritz was founded by Cesar Ritz in 1898—just seven years after his son Charles was born in Molshiem—and King Edward VII of England told Cesar Ritz that his hotel held a more accurate embodiment of what European royalty would appreciate than did the character of their own households. Ernest Hemingway expressed his admiration for the Ritz in another way in 1944, when he pushed through its revolving door during the liberation of Paris.

I have taken the Ritz, he proclaimed to the war-weary concierge, *because it is the finest hotel in Paris!* Hemingway then whispered, *Germans around?*

The Hotel Ritz is historically the creation of Cesar Ritz, although Charles Ritz can clearly take credit for its modern reputation and character. The hotel has a worldwide fame, yet Charles Ritz is equally famous because of his parabolic rods and his writings about fly-fishing among anglers who know nothing of his connection with the half-legendary family hostelry.

Ritz came to the United States in 1916, working briefly at a small hotel in Connecticut while his father completed negotiations for the Ritz Carlton in New York. It was to this distinguished New York hotel that young Charles Ritz was ultimately dispatched, and his obscure office in its cellars had an anteroom that was soon filled with fly rods in varying states of repair. His daily walks after lunch took him to Abercrombie & Fitch, where he lovingly examined the racks filled with the gleaming rods of artisans like Cross, Thomas, Edwards, Hawes, and Payne.

But these treasures were only for dreaming, Ritz explains with twinkling eyes and an expressive shrug. *My father was a careful man with the purse strings—and I was always kept quite penniless.*

Ritz found his rods in the secondhand stores and pawnshops along

Third Avenue, bundling the results of his foraging back to the office in the basement of the Ritz Carlton. He simply refinished the better rods, keeping the best for himself and selling the others. But some were altered experimentally, by cutting back their tip sections and modifying their actions. Ritz soon concluded that tip calibrations should be relatively stiff in the last few inches in any rod meant for distance casting, giving the casting stroke an instantaneous start and building great line speed. His convictions on tip calibrations have not changed over the past half century, and it was a visit to the workshop of Jim Payne that provided Ritz with the lifelong inspiration for his experiments.

Ritz stayed in the United States more than a decade, and it was finally his mother who persuaded him to return to Paris, making a special trip to bring him back in 1928. However, Cesar Ritz had filled the management posts at the Hotel Ritz, and his sense of loyalty to his staff was so pervasive that no place was made for his son. Charles Ritz patiently waited for a vacancy, working in the Paris offices of an American securities broker. During this period, a client suffering from financial problems asked Ritz to assume the ownership of a shoe store he operated. Ritz eventually bought the shop, and it finally became profitable again, although its back room was soon a clandestine meeting place for the knowledgeable fishermen of Paris—its stockroom space gradually dwindling under a growing accumulation of fly rods and tackle-repair benches and fly-tying tables.

Ritz became both president and chairman of the board for the storied Hotel Ritz in 1953, when the members of the London-based syndicate that actually owns the hotel elected him to those posts. Ritz owns only one percent of its stock, according to the corporate structure assembled by Cesar Ritz and his original backers in 1896. The board chairman of the Ritz Hotel in London, Sir Guy Bracewell Smith, is the largest single shareholder at five percent. The remaining shares are held by anonymous investors in both England and Europe, their identities cloaked in a mist of family trusts, inheritances, and the Byzantine overtones of Swiss-bank secrecy.

However, during these same years of his Paris apprenticeship, Charles Ritz was building a formidable reputation for his skills in fishing and fly-rod design. It was the late Roger Pujo who first suggested that Ritz meet with the technicians of Pezon & Michel, and they travelled together into the Loire Valley toward Amboise. It was an historic journey for the fly-fishing world.

Edouard Plantet was the production expert at Pezon & Michel, and Plantet quickly sensed that Ritz had acquired incredible insights into the philosophy of fly-rod actions and tapers during his years in the United States. After a series of exploratory meetings, Pezon & Michel invited Ritz to serve as their full-time technical consultant. Ritz clearly had almost intuitive perceptions into the calibrations of first-rate rods, in perhaps the same way that Cesar Ritz intuitively grasped the details of creating the world's finest hotel, or the instinct that Bugatti had for building his remarkable racing machines.

Like Laurence Robert Hardy, who converted his Alnwick shops from handcraftsmanship to modern milling machines, Ritz and Plantet soon decided that the artisans in their workrooms at Amboise could not produce identical rod actions in the demanding compound tapers proposed by Ritz. It was Edouard Plantet that finally designed the high-precision milling tables and pressure-wrapping machines, equipment so beautifully conceived that they were virtually free of vibration. It was a fruitful collaboration.

The third member of the Ritz triumverate was Pierre Creusevaut, who was at one time world fly-casting champion. These men built hundreds of experimental rods, with Ritz suggesting modifications in their tapers, Edouard Plantet executing them faithfully in split bamboo, and Creusevaut and Ritz both appraising the finished rods on the testing platforms at Amboise and at the casting ponds of Tir aux Pigeons in the Bois de Boulogne.

Plantet, Ritz, and Creusevaut performed countless shop tests too, observing bench vibrations, stress curves, stiffness profiles, and other precise measurements. Preliminary casting trials were ruthless. Any rod that would not cast twenty-five meters and extend its backcast easily was discarded. Slow-casting rhythms were also tried to check for line wave and loop collapse. Punching casts into a strong headwind was another test, driving out line with a vigorous double-haul, and accuracy casting completed the work. Finally, each prototype was given to a select circle of expert fishermen and fished through a complete season. This full spectrum of results was assembled and compared before any set of rod specifications was placed into production.

Each taper followed the credo of the parabolic action, Ritz explains with animation. *It must flex progressively from tip to butt, with its most obvious working concentrated toward the grip.*

Ritz developed his first parabolic taper in 1937, and in the next decade he concentrated on designs that might improve the supple flexing of the rod without reducing its power.

We found the Parabolique P.P.P. action in 1949, Ritz continues. *Its abbreviation stands for progressive pendulate power.*

His basic specifications for the two-piece staggered ferrule fly rod were first worked out in 1943, using a short butt and longer tip. This basic structural change drops the ferrule from a critical nodal zone, lengthening the flexing arm of the tip section and allowing a given rod to handle a line one size heavier. The heavier line weights lead to increased line speeds in the hands of the average fly-fisherman.

Better wind capability and distance, Ritz explains.

Like other first-rate manufacturers, Pezon & Michel uses select Tonkin cane from China, milling only those culms with dense fiber structures, straight graining, the distance between nodes, relatively small nodal segments, and good recovery from high bending stresses.

Eduoard Plantet is a firm disciple of heat treatment and developed

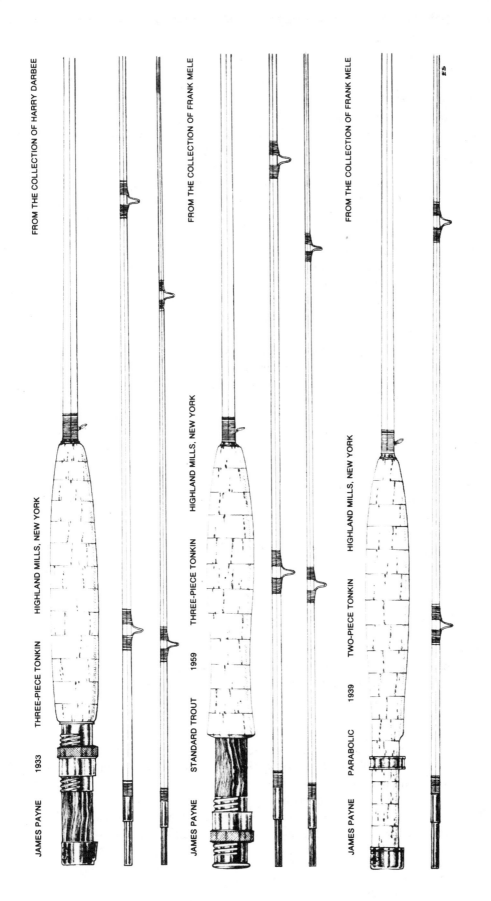

FROM THE COLLECTION OF HARRY DARBEE

JAMES PAYNE   1933   THREE-PIECE TONKIN   HIGHLAND MILLS, NEW YORK

FROM THE COLLECTION OF FRANK MELE

JAMES PAYNE   STANDARD TROUT   1959   THREE-PIECE TONKIN   HIGHLAND MILLS, NEW YORK

FROM THE COLLECTION OF FRANK MELE

JAMES PAYNE   PARABOLIC   1939   TWO-PIECE TONKIN   HIGHLAND MILLS, NEW YORK

special electrical kilns for drying and tempering the culms at Pezon & Michel. Both Plantet and Ritz argue that their kilns increase strength and stiffness, retard permanent distortion and sets in the finished cane sections, improve resistance to moisture absorption, and reduce moisture content.

Pezon & Michel makes three grades of parabolic rods. The Parabolic Speciale is the bottom of the line, the Parabolic Supreme rods are built of selected cane, and the Super Parabolic P.P.P. is the most expensive grade, using only the finest available bamboo. The Speciale and Supreme are made in two-piece construction with butt and tip sections of equal length. These grades are made in the *Normale* or medium action and relatively fast competition tapers. The Super Parabolic P.P.P. grade is made with a staggered ferrule design and the unique Ritz action except for the Midget, which has a lighter action taking a four-weight line. The ferrules are German silver, machined, and fitted by hand, with ground and split-end construction to ease the transfer of stress from metal to cane. Bronzed-steel snake guides and stripping guides are used on all three Pezon & Michel grades. Aluminum screw-locking reel seats with hooded butt caps and cork fillers are found on all Pezon & Michel rods except for the Midget and Featherlight, which use a butt cap and sliding reel band.

There are four models in the Parabolic Speciale grade, two in the Normale tapers, and two in the faster competition action. The seven-footers weigh three and a half ounces in the Normale calibrations and three and three-quarters ounces in the competition type. These rods take five- and six-weight lines. The eight-foot Speciale rods weigh four and one-eighth and five ounces in the two grades and are designed for six- and seven-weight tapers. The silk windings on the Speciale line are bright red, while the Supreme grade is wrapped in green. There are also four tapers in the Parabolic Supreme group. The seven-footers weigh four and four and three-eighths ounces, taking six- and seven-weight lines. The two eight-foot rods are four and three-quarters and five and one-eighth ounces, and are balanced by seven- and eight-weight tapers. The Super Parabolic P.P.P. series includes five models. The Midget is a six-footer weighing two and one-quarter ounces and was designed for DT4F lines. The Featherlight is a taper balanced with five-weight lines and weighs three ounces at six and a half feet. The seven-foot Supermarvel is a muscular four-ounce rod for six-weight tapers. The Ritz Colorado measures seven and a half feet and weighs four and one-quarter ounces, perfectly accommodating six weights. The Fario Club is a full eight and a half feet and weighs five ounces in the Pezon & Michel version. It also takes six-weight lines and is considered by many knowledgeable anglers to be the finest of the Ritz tapers.

Although Pezon & Michel had discontinued it, Dermot Wilson and other knowledgeable chalkstream fishermen in the south of England have insisted on the resurrection of the Sawyer Nymph. It is a superb eight-foot ten-inch rod specially designed by Charles Ritz after a session with Frank Sawyer on the Wiltshire Avon above Salisbury. Sawyer is the finest nymph fisherman in England, and his five-ounce rod is built to his specifications for

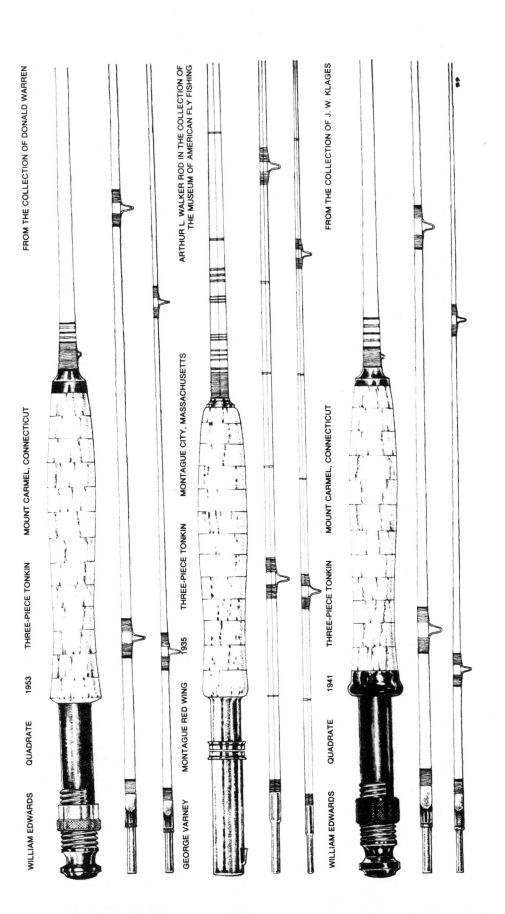

FROM THE COLLECTION OF DONALD WARREN

WILLIAM EDWARDS   QUADRATE   1953   THREE-PIECE TONKIN   MOUNT CARMEL, CONNECTICUT

GEORGE VARNEY   MONTAGUE RED WING   1935   THREE-PIECE TONKIN   MONTAGUE CITY, MASSACHUSETTS

ARTHUR L. WALKER ROD IN THE COLLECTION OF
THE MUSEUM OF AMERICAN FLY FISHING

WILLIAM EDWARDS   QUADRATE   1941   THREE-PIECE TONKIN   MOUNT CARMEL, CONNECTICUT

FROM THE COLLECTION OF J. W. KLAGES

a four-weight line and his tiny Pheasant Tail nymphs. Francois Michel is now making these exceptional nymph rods for British customers, and they are imported through Dermot Wilson at Stockbridge. It is made with a ten-inch detachable handle, its ferrule concealed in the grip. Its two-pieces are made in four-foot lengths, and its cork-filled reel seat is fitted with a butt cap and screw-locking assembly. The Sawyer Nymph is perhaps the finest slow-working action in the entire series of Ritz tapers, and it is one of the favorite rods in the collection of John Hemingway in Sun Valley.

American importers have attempted to modify the original Ritz designs for our market, changing his reverse-taper grips to the popular cigar shape and his reel seats to the locking type found on the Battenkill rods made by Orvis. It is hoped that Pezon & Michel will resist these pressures in the future, except perhaps for eliminating their purplish anodized reel fittings in favor of a simple jewel-finished aluminum. But the unique Ritz features found in the Pezon & Michel rods provide their singular Gaullic flavors, particularly in the three bright wraps above the grip check. Their delicate ornamental touch happily echoes the colors in the French flag.

Mais oui! Ritz exclaims. *It's the Tricolor!*

There are several other bamboo rodmakers in Europe, but the British and French firms unquestionably dominate the continental market. Perhaps the best known of these firms are Brunner of Austria, whose fine custom-made rods are favorites along the Traun, and the Horgård and Vangen shops in Norway.

American rodmaking has also continued to evolve, and its history is filled with some intriguing patterns. Although the influence of early artisans like Phillippe, Green, Murphy, Orvis, and Leonard is easily traced through the subsequent work of their employees and apprentices, there are also many famous American builders who developed in isolation—unique talents like Stoner, Powell, Granger, Dickerson, and Young.

The remarkable school of Pacific Coast rodmakers is perhaps the best example of this phenomenon and includes several of the finest rodmakers who ever lived. The first of these craftsmen was Edwin C. Powell, who fished the headwaters of the Sacramento, and began making fine fly rods in his shop at Marysville after the First World War. His first rod had been completed in 1912, using cane cut from the backyard of a local Chinese laundryman. Powell was thirty-six years old when he decided to build his rods full time, and the Marysville shop was already famous in 1922, when his son Walton became an apprentice. The Powell rods were all six-strip solid construction until 1933, when their patent for semihollow construction was granted.

The first Powell rods featured a relatively fat cigar-type handle, not unlike the Leonard rods made before the First World War, and a full metal German-silver reel seat with a sliding band and butt cap. Later designs clearly show the influence of the post war Hardy rods, with their Bakelite fillers and reverse-locking reel seat. Powell finally settled on a full-Wells grip about 1927, and his grips never varied until his death at midcentury.

Powell construction was always unusual, even in his solid six-strip rods. Borrowing again from Hardy, with its laminated cane and American pine sections of the period, Powell developed a similar method entirely his own. First he milled away the bamboo pith until only about an eighth of an inch of power fibers remained, and then he laminated a strip of Port Orford cedar on its inner face. Once the glue was fully set, the laminated spline was milled into a finished strip on a unique machine designed and built by the elder Powell—a remarkable technical feat considering that his education had stopped in grammar school.

Earlier in this chapter we have outlined the details of Powell's semihollow construction, which scalloped out six-inch hollows, leaving small solid sections for gluing. Powell designed and built a small saw specifically for this work, and the result was an extremely light rod with a delicate action for its length.

It was one hell of a lot of work, rodmaker Gary Howells explained one evening over dinner in San Francisco, *and I admire Powell for his exceptional talent and obvious self-discipline.*

Powell heat-tempered his culms by hand over a gas flame, and he remained loyal to the early water-soluble glues throughout his lifetime.

EDWIN POWELL

This made his hollow-built rods a little fragile, and the intermediate silk windings spaced about two inches apart were more than mere ornamentation. These wraps were actually structural, and helped to hold the splines of the semihollow butt section together. The wrappings at the grips and ferrules and guides were either brown or antique gold, and were double wrapped at the guides and ferrules. The tip guides were unusual. Their tubes were split with a fine saw, set in glue, and wrapped tightly to compress their serrated throats against the cane. The final wraps were applied in three layers, stepped like a delicate little Egyptian burial pyramid. The solid-built Powells simply held the keeper ring in a solid wrapping of silk, while the semihollow rods were always signed with delicate windings of white and black at the keeper silk. It is a maker's mark that identifies his finest work.

Powell also made his own ferrules and reel seats. His ferrules were drawn of German silver, with a swaged step on the male plugs and a hand-machined welt. Such Powell ferrules were a little brittle, and many split and broken examples have found their way into the repair shops at Winston and Leonard over the years. The reel seats were as elegant as the Hardy assemblies that Powell admired and copied, with Bakelite fillers and a reverse-locking design. The hooded cap was concealed in the cork, and Powell engraved his name and the location of his shop in a graceful ellipse on the lock nut. His name was also inked on the light brown cane ahead of the cork and protected with varnish. The grips and reel seats of the original Powell rods are so functional and classic in their beauty that many knowledgeable anglers wish that Walton Powell would resurrect them for the rods he is presently building under the original Powell patents.

Most vintage three-piece Powells are built of solid six-strip construction, and most two-piece designs use the semihollow technique that Powell patented in 1933. Powell concentrated on the longer fly rods suited to the northern California rivers. His Powell steelhead models measured nine and a half feet and weighed five and a half to six ounces, and his eight-and-a-half-foot trout tapers weighed four and a half to five ounces. The nine-footers varied from four and three-quarters to five and a half ounces, working smoothly into the butt section like most Powell actions, and taking six- and seven-weight lines. Powell built a few eight-foot rods weighing between four and four and a half ounces, and a seven-and-à-half-foot Powell is very rare. The craftsmen at Winston have refinished only two seven-and-a-half-foot, three-and-a-half-ounce Powells over the past twenty-five years.

Perhaps the finest Powell I have seen belongs to Douglas Merrick, the famous master rod builder at Winston. It was won by Merrick in a casting competition at San Francisco, and Merrick travelled north to Marysville to select the sticks personally in the Powell shop. The rod is on my work table as this is being written; its action is smooth and a little slow in true semiparabolic flexing, although Powell would have called it a regressive taper instead of a parabolic. It measures eight and a half feet and weighs four and a half ounces and is designed for a five-weight line. It is an exquisitely conceived rod, equalling any in the world.

Powell's place in the history of the art? Martin Keane observed thoughtfully at the Museum of American Fly-Fishing. *His cedar lamination and semihollow construction were not as structurally sound as the Stoner patents at Winston, but like the machinery in his Marysville shop they were entirely original—Powell was another step in the evolution of rodmaking, and a perfect example of the self-taught genius flowering in relative isolation.*

Edwin Powell died twenty-odd years ago, having lived well past eighty, and he worked with rods virtually until his death. His son Walton started working in his father's shop just after the First World War, at the fledgling age of seven years. Walton Powell is less than sixty, but already has almost a half century of experience on rodmaking, and with Tonkin cane available again Powell is building fine bamboo rods in the tradition of his father.

Walton Powell is using his father's patents and tapers, but has changed many details. His reel seats are full metal, machined from aerospace aluminum alloys, with a reverse-lock design and exposed grip slot. The handles are still the full-Wells shape, although less dramatically sculptured than the best work of his father. His wrappings are dark green on the Signature grade, and black silk on the Golden Signature series, based on the two-butt, two-tip section combination rods pioneered by Edwin Powell forty-odd years ago. Walton Powell has also adopted Swiss-type ferrules on his rods and is using an oxidized oil-and-gum finish found only on the Walton Powell product. Powell has strong ideas about rodmaking, as well as fly-fishing itself, and his combative character rises to argue over them at the slightest excuse. His temperament translated into cane has produced some excellent work, and Walton Powell already has a following of vocal partisans who insist that his rods are among the finest examples of the rodmaker's art. His father is a difficult act to follow.

I intend to carry on where my father left off, Powell insists vehemently. *His dreams and ideals shall not die, and the greatness of the Powell rod will continue to live and grow in my hands!*

It is Lewis Stoner who reigns as the acknowledged genius of the Pacific Coast rodmakers, and Stoner was the primal force behind the growth and reputation of the famed R. L. Winston Rod Company. Stoner was born in a small mining town near Walker Lake in Nevada in 1881. His father had travelled west from Kentucky during the Gold Rush, and ultimately settled at Hawthorne, where he worked as a millwright. History tells us that the elder Stoner had an exceptional reputation for making any kind of machinery, replacement part, or pithead frame needed in the Sierra Nevada mines.

The Stoner family moved briefly to California in 1893, returning to work in the mines at Reno nine years later. There was a complete woodworking shop, including a fine lathe and other machines, in a backyard garage during those Reno years. Lew Stoner continually puttered about there while his father worked, and he was a skilled woodworker before he was fifteen. Stoner tried college briefly and lasted only one half-hearted semester.

The world was too full of interesting things to do, Stoner explained to his friends, *and I finally left.*

He worked a few years in a shop that sold and maintained the Walker steam-driven automobiles and obtained one of the first chauffeur's licenses issued in California. Popular legend holds that Stoner started building rods to salvage his shares in a rod factory located in Oakland, across the bay from San Francisco, and that he began working full time in 1922.

His financial backer died a year later. Stoner returned to the tobacco business in San Francisco and spent several later years working in various machine shops. However, the bacilli of split-cane rod making had infected him, and he completed his design specifications for a power cutter that could mill the splines for bamboo rods in 1926. It was the same time that Hardy abandoned hand-milling for the accuracy of a mechanical cutter. Stoner returned to rodmaking in 1927, but the new company also dissolved in bankruptcy four years later. It seemed like the end of Stoner's dreams, but that same year Robert Winther provided a transfusion of fresh capital. With a contraction of Winther and Stoner, the famous R. L. Winston Rod Company was formed. Winston prospered in spite of the Depression, and when Robert Winther liquidated his interest in 1933, Stoner decided to leave the company name unchanged.

W. W. Loskot became a partner at the Winston shop the following year, and the partnership arrangement offers a revealing insight into the character of Lewis Stoner. Loskot was a young friend without capital and little knowledge of bamboo rodmaking and only limited experience in other business or manufacturing. However, Loskot did have a wife and children, and Stoner refused his suggestion of a half interest, although Stoner himself was Winston's primary asset.

We'll both draw a small salary to live on, Stoner insisted firmly to his fledgling partner. *Beyond that you've got a family to think about—you need extra money more than I do!*

Their partnership lasted twenty-odd years, until Loskot finally left Winston in 1953. Douglas Merrick had come into the Winston shop in 1945, shortly after his separation from the Air Corps, to purchase a new rod. Merrick had been a superb fisherman and tournament caster before the war. When the day ended, Merrick had left a better job to work at Winston, and he remains there today. Loskot sold his interest to Merrick in 1953, and the unique collaboration between Stoner and Merrick was probably the Golden Age at Winston.

These men were two of the finest artisans who ever split a culm, and with such giant talents in the shop, the fly rods that came out of the workrooms on Harrison Street in San Francisco were masterpieces. When Stoner died suddenly in 1957, Merrick became the future of the Winston Company, and that future was clearly in good hands. Winston advocates mourned the passing of Stoner, but they had come to understand that Merrick was virtually his equal in craftsmanship.

Doug was a better fly caster, Gary Howells explained, *and he has the finest instincts for selecting cane and modifying rod tapers that I have ever seen.*

That is high praise considering the fact that Howells himself has a rapidly growing reputation as a rodmaker of incomparable skills. Gary Howells started making rods in 1947, working in his cellar with a hand plane, micrometer, and planing block. His first rod took him more than a month to make and completely exhausted his supply of seasoned bamboo. Howells went to Winston for more culms and found both Stoner and Merrick unusually eager to help a beginner. With their encouragement, Howells began building a lot of rods, and the day finally came when Stoner told his young protégé that his latest effort was a rod that could stand with theirs in the Winston salesroom.

It was the proudest day in my life, Howells said.

Howells came into the Winston workshop the morning after Stoner died in 1957 and sat talking with Merrick for hours, reminiscing about Stoner over the years. The memory of the man filled the shop, and both remembered the slightly stooped figure bending over his lathes and cutters. His eyes had been bright and clear in spite of his age, and his hands were steady almost until the last. Except for his hearing aid, his skills and faculties remained almost unimpaired, and his honesty was as blunt as a granite headstone.

Lewis Stoner

Lew was one of a kind, Merrick finally said. *Why don't you come work with me now that Lew's gone?*

Howell started working the next day, performing the raw bamboo work like grading culms, splitting, sanding, node matching, gluing, and pressure wrapping. Merrick and Howells got along well together, and the younger man stayed at Winston thirteen years, finally graduating to perform the milling and fluting work itself. Many connoisseurs of fine rodmaking believe the rods they produced together after 1965 represent a second Golden Age in the exceptional workmanship at Winston.

It was a fine apprenticeship, Gary Howells remembers wistfully, *but at only forty dollars a week.*

Merrick recently sold his controlling interest in Winston to Sidney Eliason and Thomas Morgan, two well-known young western fishermen. However, Merrick remains firmly in charge of the rodmaking operations at Winston, and the quality of the workmanship remains unchanged. The quality of the Winston product begins with its supply of perfectly seasoned cane, and the Stoner patents for fluted hollow-built construction. That tradition of quality begins with Stoner himself, an artist who cared more for perfection than profit. Perhaps the best example is the unique Winston ferrules. Most manufacturers make ferrules of German silver, or even subcontract such machine work, but it was Stoner who discovered a silicon-copper and aluminum alloy called duronze. It is lighter, stronger than most steel, and highly corrosion-resistant. Winston ferrules are cut from bar-stock duronze, in spite of the fact that they are more expensive than nickel silver.

Winston rods are made from larger culms than most, giving them a denser layer of power fibers. The culms are split with a unique many-bladed wedge, its blades radiating like spokes from its striking hub. The eight-foot culms are first saw-cut to receive the multiple wedge, and then it is driven along each culm with a mallet. Eight to sixteen rough splines are formed with these Stoner wedges, depending on whether they are to be used in butts or tip sections. The raw splines are rough-milled first to approximate tapers, and then milled in the superb finish-cutter that Stoner first designed in 1926. Its maximum cutting tolerance is only .0075 of an inch, less than the thickness of the page on which this is printed. It is this Stoner milling machine that controls the taper, unique flexing behavior, action, and fine quality of every Winston split-cane rod.

After each spline is tapered properly, it is drawn through another special milling machine designed by Stoner to make the delicate U-shaped cut that removes the apex of the finished strip. Since the tips are completely structured of dense power fibers and are smaller than an average pencil lead in diameter, it is both foolish and impractical to flute them throughout their full length.

Such refinements represent an amazing evolution from the first bamboo section Stoner made to replace the middle joint of his broken Leonard in 1906, Gary Howells observes with admiration.

Each Winston ferrule is individually centered, bored, drilled, reamed, and hand-lapped for a perfect and permanent fit. It is tapered to rice-paper thinness at the transition point to the cane, and the cane itself is turned to match the exact internal dimension of the ferrule. It is driven home over a coat of special cement and pinned to secure it completely.

Winston reel seats are unique, and although many fishermen mistakenly believe they are merely a plastic unworthy of Winston rods, they are really quite expensive. The fillers are turned from a costly high-strength Bakelite that is almost totally free of expansion or corrosion. The reel fittings consist of a locking ring and hooded cap of jewel-polished aluminum. The smaller Winston rods are fitted with a slotted cork filler, lightweight butt cap, and sliding reel band. The cork grips are seated in cement, a single specie ring at each time, and lathe-turned to the Winston pattern of the popular half-Wells style.

DOUGLAS MERRICK

The ferrules, guides, and keeper rings are securely wrapped with special thread. The ferrules are completely wound in light beige silk with double wrappings at the transition to the rod. The guides are double-wrapped at the centers, and the tip guide is triple-wrapped. The silk is beige, to match the pale brown of the bamboo, and the tip windings are bright scarlet. Each wrap is coated with clear epoxy to set its color and secure it permanently before the final coats of varnish.

It was the cantankerous Peter Schwab who first badgered Winston into making its series of ultralight fly rods in 1931. *Leetle fellers,* Schwab cackled when he tried the first prototypes. *That's what these little bamboo beauties really are—they're leetle fellers!*

Lew Stoner found his term so descriptive that it is still used in the Winston catalogue today. These rods are intended only for the most skillful fishermen, and Stoner often refused to sell one to a customer whom he believed was unqualified to fish it properly. The tapers are designed for relatively short, accurate casts with great delicacy, demanding double-taper lines in three- and four-weight. There are four designs for a DT3F line: the five-and-a-half-foot Winston of one and three-quarters ounces, the six-footer of two ounces, the six-and-a-half-foot rod of two and one-eighth ounces, and the seven-foot taper weighing only two and a half ounces. The seven-foot Leetle Feller of two and five-eighths ounces and the seven-and-a-half-foot model of three and one-eighth ounces are both designed to handle a modern DT4F taper line.

Winston also makes a series of light trout rods designed for four- and five-weight lines. These rods are also remarkably delicate, but have slightly more muscle than the Schwab midge-sized tapers. Like the smaller rods, these models are assembled with a skeletal seat consisting of a butt cap and sliding ring, but the Winston screw-locking seat is available on order. It adds approximately half an ounce to the finished weight.

The light trout series includes two models designed for a four-weight taper, the five-and-a-half-footer of two ounces, and a six-foot rod weighing a quarter ounce more. The five-weight types include seven different lengths, weights, and actions: the six-foot model of two and a half ounces, the two six-and-a-half-footers of two and a half and two and three-quarters ounces, two seven-foot rods weighing two and seven-eighths and three ounces, and a brace of seven-and-a-half-foot tapers of three and one-quarter and three and a half ounces.

The Winston standard trout rods are perhaps the lightest for their length and power of any rods made, except for the similar tapers built by Gary Howells, since they use the hollow construction protected by the Stoner patent. They will fish with delicacy at relatively short ranges, yet handle surprisingly long casts with ease. These eight- to nine-foot rods are fitted with the locking Winston reel seats of black Bakelite and jewel-finished aluminum.

There is a single eight-foot Winston designed for a four-weight line, weighing three and five-eighths ounces. Three models are designed to take five-weight tapers, the eight-footers at three and three-quarters and four ounces, and an eight-and-a-half-foot rod of four and one-eighth ounces. There are two eight-and-a-half-foot Winstons for six-weight lines weighing four and one-quarter and four and a half ounces, and a third eight-and-a-half-foot, four-and-three-quarters-ounce taper for a seven-weight. The two eight-foot nine-inch rods weigh four and five-eighths and four and three-quarters ounces, and take seven- and eight-weight lines. The nine-footer is surprisingly delicate, weighing only four and seven-eighths ounces and taking a six- or seven-weight. Although they are rated as steelhead rods, the nine-foot Winstons of five, five and one-quarter, and five and a half ounces take eight- and nine-weight lines, and there are many expert anglers who like fishing them at maximum distances on big western trout rivers and reservoirs.

Winston rods are justly famous, and some remarkable visitors have come to their unpretentious little workshop in San Francisco. The late Crown Prince Axel of Denmark once appeared without previous fanfare, because he wanted to meet the people who had built his favorite sea-trout rod for fishing the Laerdal in Norway. But perhaps the best Winston story was told me last fall by a British fly-fisherman who has lived in San Francisco for many years. The displaced Englishman had always dreamed of owning a Hardy rod, savoring that dream since his boyhood in England. When he finally returned to London, he quickly travelled to the Hardy shop in Pall Mall.

What sort of fishing did you have in mind? the clerk asked.

Well, the transplanted British fisherman replied, *living in San Francisco, I've been fishing primarily for steelheads.*

And you want a steelhead rod from Hardy?

Yes, the fisherman said.

The finest steelhead rods in the world are made in San Francisco, the Hardy salesman smiled. *Winston makes them!*

Like other artists, the stature of a great rod builder is sometimes measured by the quality of his apprentices and the reputation they later achieve in their own workshops. Hiram Leonard is unquestionably the principal wellspring of such early influence on American split-cane rods, but the late Lew Stoner is also beginning to achieve some measure of fame in the work of his disciples. Douglas Merrick is one of the finest rodmakers alive, and the younger Gary Howells was strongly influenced by both men over the years. Howells left Winston to start his own small rod company in 1969, and his work has been highly successful.

Obviously, Howells explained last winter, *I wanted to build rods under my own name, but I also wanted to build rods with the lightness and power of a Winston or Powell—yet with the elegance and grace of a Payne.*

There is a rapidly growing circle of Howells' partisans willing to prove with their fly rods that he has succeeded in achieving his dream. Howells builds only two-piece rods. No better rods have ever been made, and their detailing is exquisite. His cane is tempered more than the Winston culms, giving his finished rods a slightly darker look. Since Howells is more fascinated with fishing minute flies on western spring creeks than with distance work on the steelhead rivers of Oregon and California, his delicate tapers are not carbon copies of the Winston specifications. His hollow-built butts flex smoothly and powerfully into the grips like the finest Winstons or Powells, but his tip calibrations are finer and better attuned to fishing tippets between .003 and .005. The ferrules use the same silicon-copper-aluminum alloy that Lew Stoner first used at Winston, machined by Howells himself from solid bar-stock. The males are hand-polished to tolerances of .0001, until they separate smoothly yet still pop like a bottle of fine California champagne.

Howells uses three grip styles on his rods. The tapers designed for three- and four-weight lines in the lengths under seven feet are fitted with a Payne-type fishtail grip, butt cap, and sliding reel band over a cork filler. The heavier seven- to eight-foot sizes feature the same elegant Payne-style grip with a reverse-locking reel seat. The reel cap is concealed in the grip, and although the screw-lock fittings resemble the Orvis Battenkill hardware, they are machined from slightly heavier aluminum stock and carefully jewel-polished. The hardwood fillers are turned from African zebrawood, which is richly colored and displays a darker graining than conventional walnuts. On the larger eight-and-a-half- to nine-and-a-half-foot Howells rods, the cork grips are a classic full-Wells style that echo the cork handles on the finest Powell rods.

The wrappings are exquisite, their medium brown silk and pale yellow tips a quiet homage to the work of Payne. The ferrules are completely covered in brown silk, each trimmed with a delicate wrap of yellow. Each guide is also secured with brown and yellow wraps, double-wrapped at the feet in the Winston style. The grip check consists of two delicate rings, a slim duronze band set inside an aluminum sleeve. The fly keeper is wrapped in brown, with red and yellow tips to identify its fluted hollow-butt construction. The trim wraps enclosing the Howells name, rod length, weight, and serial number echo the Winston silk windings, but the Winston wraps at the midpoint of the butt section are omitted in the Howells rods. The windings are set in clear epoxy before varnishing. Howells' finish is the equal of the Payne varnish work that most knowledgeable collectors agree is the finest rodmaking.

There's no secret about my finishes, Howells insists quietly. *Just four coats of the best varnish and a lot of work.*

Howells builds forty standard rod tapers, and because Howells insists on performing every operation himself, his production is limited to only one hundred rods a year.

The response has been beautiful, Howells continues, *and I'm always behind in my orders—like most rodmakers!*

There are three six-foot Howells rods. The one-and-three-quarters-ounce model and two-ounce tapers are designed for three-weight lines, and the two-and-a-quarter-ounce Howells takes a four-weight. There is a

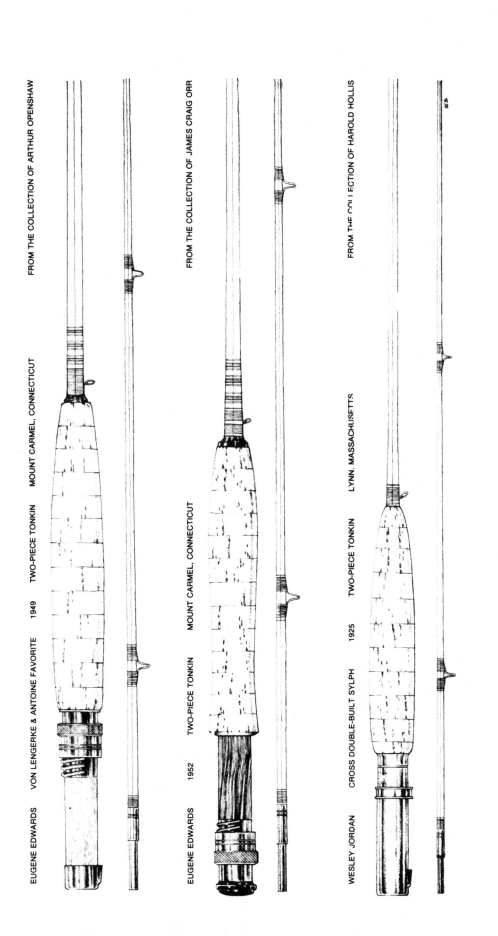

EUGENE EDWARDS   VON LENGERKE & ANTOINE FAVORITE   1949   TWO-PIECE TONKIN   MOUNT CARMEL, CONNECTICUT   FROM THE COLLECTION OF ARTHUR OPENSHAW

EUGENE EDWARDS   1952   TWO-PIECE TONKIN   MOUNT CARMEL, CONNECTICUT   FROM THE COLLECTION OF JAMES CRAIG ORR

WESLEY JORDAN   CROSS DOUBLE-BUILT SYLPH   1925   TWO-PIECE TONKIN   LYNN, MASSACHUSETTS   FROM THE COLLECTION OF HAROLD HOLLIS

delicate six-foot three-inch design, like the famous Young Midge, but the Howells version at two ounces is designed for a three-weight line. The six-and-a-half-foot rods weigh two and one-eighth and two and three-eighths ounces and are balanced by three- and four-weight tapers. There are five seven-foot models. The two-and-one-quarter-ounce taper takes a three-weight, while the two-and-a-half-ounce rod is a four-weight model of surprising versatility. The seven-footer at two and five-eighths ounces is designed for five-weight lines, like the slightly more powerful two-and-three-quarters-ounce Howells. The seven-foot, three-ounce taper takes a full six-weight line and has an action totally unlike the seven-foot three-inch, two-and-three-eighths-ounce rod for a DT3F. Howells makes six seven-and-a-half-foot models. The two-and-a-half-ounce version takes a three-weight too, and the three-ounce taper is a remarkable little fly rod designed for a DT4F. There are two versions for five-weight lines, excellent rods of three and one-eighth and three and one-quarter ounces, and the two seven-and-a-half-foot rods for six-weight lines are surprisingly powerful sticks of three and three-eighths and three and five-eighths ounces.

The eight-foot Howells rods are masterpieces of delicacy and versatility, starting with the three-and-a-half-ounce model for three-weight lines. The three-and-five-eighths-ounce rod is a delicate rod designed for a four-weight. There are two designed for five-weight lines, weighing three and three-quarters and three and seven-eighths ounces. There are also two eight-footers for six-weight lines, fine all-around tapers weighing four and one-eighth and four and one-quarter ounces. There is also an eight-foot three-inch model of three and three-quarters ounces for a four-weight line.

Howells makes seven eight-and-a-half-foot rods. The four-ounce model takes a four-weight line, while the four-and-one-quarter-ounce taper takes a five-weight. There is a second eight-and-a-half-foot rod of four and one-quarter ounces for a six-weight line, and the four-and-three-eighths-ounce rod takes the same line size. Both the eight-and-a-half-foot, four-and-a-half-ounce Howells and the four-and-five-eighths-ounce model take seven-weight lines. Howells adds an eight-and-a-half-foot, four-and-three-quarters-ounce rod designed for WF8F and WF8S fly lines, completing his eight-and-a-half-foot series of trout rods.

His big-water models include three rods of eight feet nine inches, weighing four and five-eighths to five ounces and designed for seven- to nine-weight lines. There are four nine-footers weighing from four and three-quarters to five and a half ounces which are balanced by seven- to ten-weight tapers. Howells also makes a powerful nine-foot three-inch rod weighing five and five-eighths ounces, designed for heavy-duty work.

Last year, Gary Howells built me a superb seven-and-a-half-foot, three-ounce rod with unique calibrations that is a joy in both fishing and casting. It is fitted with an exquisite African zebrawood filler and reverse-locking reel seat, and a slender Payne-style grip. It fishes beautifully, handling small streamers or sinking lines, as well as tiny flies on fragile .003 nylon. It has a supple poetry, and I have fished it happily from

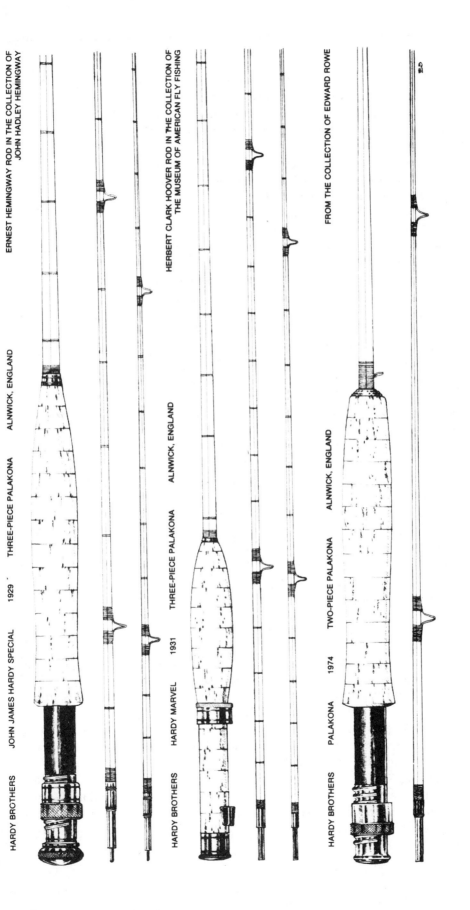

ERNEST HEMINGWAY ROD IN THE COLLECTION OF
JOHN HADLEY HEMINGWAY

HARDY BROTHERS   JOHN JAMES HARDY SPECIAL   1929   THREE-PIECE PALAKONA   ALNWICK, ENGLAND

HERBERT CLARK HOOVER ROD IN THE COLLECTION OF
THE MUSEUM OF AMERICAN FLY FISHING

HARDY BROTHERS   HARDY MARVEL   1931   THREE-PIECE PALAKONA   ALNWICK, ENGLAND

FROM THE COLLECTION OF EDWARD ROWE

HARDY BROTHERS   PALAKONA   1974   TWO-PIECE PALAKONA   ALNWICK, ENGLAND

the flats of Silver Creek in Idaho to the Longparish beats of the British Test, where it subdued a nymphing fish of almost five pounds.

It fished so beautifully that I called Howells after a particularly successful afternoon on the Brodheads, when our selective browns forced us to fish .003 and tiny flies.

It's incredibly lovely, I said. *It's so fine I've got to have the others.*

Well, Howells laughed, *we can make forty types.*

Yes! I groaned. *That's expensive!*

Like Powell and Stoner developing in isolation on the Pacific Coast, Goodwin Granger was a superb craftsman who designed and produced a series of fine split-cane rods in Denver. Granger began making his rods after the First World War, and these swelled-butt three-piece rod designs are still highly prized among both fishermen and collectors.

The first Goodwin Granger models were usually made with full-metal reel seats of German silver, with a reel hood soldered to the barrel and a sliding band. The Granger Champion had red silk wrappings tipped in black, and I have seen eight-footers weighing four and one-quarter ounces, eight-and-a-half-foot rods of four and three-quarters ounces, and powerful nine-foot rods of five and a half ounces. Granger probably also made a fine nine-and-a-half-foot Champion of six and a half ounces during these early years of his career. The Goodwin was a similar Granger assembled with a sliding-band seat of nickel silver, and jasper winds tipped in yellow silk, and was made in similar eight- to nine-and-a-half-foot tapers.

The Goodwin Granger Special had yellow silk windings, and introduced the German-silver screw-in locking seat typical of later Granger workmanship. It also introduced seven-and-a-half-foot calibrations weighing three and three-quarters ounces, and the early Granger Aristocrat with tan silk wrappings tipped in chocolate introduced an even lighter model of seven feet weighing only three and a half ounces. Later Aristocrats were simply wrapped in brown silk and changed the seven-foot model to a delicate two and three-quarters ounce design for four-weight lines. The early Granger De Luxe rods featured jasper windings tipped in yellow and embraced the full spectrum of Granger tapers from the seven-foot, two-and-three-quarters-ounce model to the nine-and-a-half-footer of six and a half ounces. These vintage Grangers have a smooth action typical of the later rods produced in his Denver workshop, and are exceptionally fine split-cane rods. Their character echoes both the Colorado climate with its low humidity perfectly suited to seasoning cane and building rods, and the exceptional craftsmanship of Goodwin Granger.

Granger was acquired by the Wright & McGill Company of Denver after the Second World War, and like the production work of Heddon and South Bend, their volume of split-bamboo rods continued to flow with surprising average quality. These Wright & McGill Grangers are clearly among the finest factory rods ever made. The production Grangers included six models at midcentury; and in these years the shop foreman was already William Phillipson.

The least expensive was the Granger Victory, with its orange and black variegated wraps tipped in black. It sold for only twenty-five dollars when I visited the Denver shop of Granger after the Second World War, and such rods are now worth four times that price on the secondhand market. The Granger Special was slightly more expensive, and was finished with wrappings of lime-colored silk. The Granger Aristocrat was next, its wrappings of tan silk tipped in chocolate. The Favorite was more expensive and had jasper winds tipped with pale yellow, plus yellow ornamental windings. The Granger De Luxe was still higher in price, and featured black and silver variegated windings tipped in bright yellow. It was the Granger Premier with its intricate yellow wrappings that held the top of the line, its price an astronomical seventy-five dollars in my boyhood years. These little Grangers were remarkable rods.

The first really good rod I owned was a fine eight-foot Granger Special with handsome lime green wrappings and a locking German-silver reel seat. It was the birthday rod my father gave me when I was seven years old. My recent book *Nymphs* includes these observations on that treasured boyhood companion:

> Granger built three-piece rods in those years, precisely wrapped in olive silk under a perfect finish of hand-rubbed varnish. The ferrules were exquisitely machined with elegant angular welts, and it had the hooded German-silver reel seat that ultimately became the Granger trademark. Its action was slow and smooth, perfectly matched with an HDH King Eider. It was years later that I came to appreciate fully its ability to fish a nymph, on the Grundbach in southern Germany.
>
> It is a pastoral reach of water. Mists shroud the mountains of the Allgäu in the mornings, and there are fine hatches. The little Grundbach is man-made, gathering several Alpine brooks into a half-mile millpond at Fischen-im-Allgäu. Its entire length measures about two miles from those duckpond beginnings to the bigger glacier-melt river below Oberstdorf.
>
> We fished it regularly after the war, finding good hatches of dark claret-bodied *Leptophlebias* almost every morning. Overcast mornings were best, with a light misting rain that hung in the valley. The trout rose steadily to these little mayflies, but one rainy weekend in September the fly hatches were unusually abundant.
>
> Good browns porpoised softly in the rain, working steadily in the weedy channels. The current was covered with mayflies, but we fished dry-fly imitations for several hours without results. Finally I tried a small nymph imitation, and took a fish promptly on the first cast.
>
> *They're nymphing!* I called to my father.
>
> Like most fly-fishermen these past few years, we were

intrigued with ultrasmall tackle, and I was fishing a two-ounce rod of six feet. It worked reasonably well on the trout working close along the bank, and those swirling to emerging nymphs along the weeds from forty to sixty feet out.

We took fish after fish that morning on nymphs, until I located a really large brown working in midchannel below the town. It was a cast of almost ninety feet, virtually beyond the little rod when I was waist-deep in the trailing weeds. There were conflicting currents between us that required mending the fly swing both up and down. It was a difficult problem.

Cast after cast worked out into the rain, and either fell short or dragged slightly just under the surface. The fish ignored me, porpoising every few seconds.

Finally I walked back to the car and put up the eight-foot Granger, stringing its undressed silk and selecting a ten-foot leader tapered to about .005. The worn little nymph that had taken fish steadily that morning was added to the tippet, and I waded back toward the trout.

The fish was still working. *Let it soak,* I thought, pressing the coiled leader into a layered bed of silt.

Finally, I was ready and the leader sank readily in the current. The nymph worked out and settled above the trout. The rod delivered the cast smoothly, without drying the fly, and it sank cleanly into a swing across the slow current above the fish. Raising the tip, I mended line and held the rod high as the fly reached its feeding station.

It porpoised lazily and I tightened. *He took it!* I shouted, *He took it and he's on!*

The trout finally surrendered, weighing almost five pounds and measuring twenty-four inches. The rod was perfect for reaching the bigger fish, and I continued to fish it when they were nymphing. Its length worked the fly swing perfectly in the cross currents among the weeds, its smooth action kept my nymphs wet and sinking, and its power was sufficient to reach fish beyond eighty feet easily.

The little Granger was a superb rod, and although it was stolen a year after our return from Europe, there are times when I still fish it happily in my mind.

It is interesting that a number of fine fly rods bearing the Granger De Luxe trademark were made after Wright & McGill decided to abandon split-cane rods for fiberglass. These rods use the standard Granger tapers and fittings, with some singular modifications to the reel seats, and adding the elliptical full-Wells grips that would later become the signature of a Phillipson rod.

The light seven- and seven-and-a-half-foot models were made with a skeletal cork grip, flaring slightly at the butt plate and holding the reel with a knurled sliding band and a fixed hood soldered to the grip check. These modifications reduced the seven-foot models to only three ounces and the seven-and-a-half-footers to three and one-quarter ounces. The larger De Luxe tapers were fitted with a skeletal locking seat, using the fixed and locking hoods with a walnut filler. These fittings also reduce the weight of the original Grangers. The eight-foot rod weighed three and three-quarters ounces, the eight-and-a-half-footer became four and a half ounces, and the nine-foot De Luxe weighed five and a half ounces. These rods were finished with bright scarlet windings, and in spite of their Granger markings, they are unmistakably early Phillipson products.

The most common is perhaps the Phillipson Peerless series, made with walnut screw-locking seats. Several lengths and weights were produced, starting with the seven-and-a-half-foot, four-ounce taper. The eight-foot Peerless weighed four and one-quarter ounces, the eight-and-a-half-foot model at five and one-quarter ounces was in great demand on my boyhood rivers in Colorado, and the nine-foot rod went a full six ounces. These rods were later made with full metal seats, in slightly heavier assembled weights. The functional and ornamental windings were black silk tipped with white. There were also a few rods made that paralleled the standard Peerless tapers. These models were called Peerless Specials, and their calibrations were designed to take a heavier line size in each corresponding weight and length in the Phillipson line.

The Phillipson Pacemakers were moderately priced bamboo rods incorporating these same tapers, ranging from seven and a half feet and four ounces to nine-foot, six-ounce models. These rods were fitted with brown and black anodized reel and lime winds tipped in yellow.

Perhaps the finest split-cane work was found in the Phillipson Paramount 51 series. These rods were made with both walnut and full-metal reel seat fittings and featured slightly more delicate tapers than the less expensive Phillipson grades. The seven-and-a-half-foot model weighed only three and a half ounces, the popular eight-footer weighed four ounces, the eight-and-a-half-foot Paramount was four and three-quarters ounces, and the nine-foot tapers weighed only five and a half ounces. These rods featured jasper winds tipped with yellow and black and had exquisitely smooth actions.

Phillipson also made several special models. The Phillipson Grand Teton was an eight-and-a-half-footer of five and a half ounces, designed to handle a seven-weight forward taper according to the specifications of the late Bob Carmichael. It had red silk windings and was made of impregnated cane. The Phillipson E. M. Hunter was named for the famous outdoor writer featured in the *Denver Post* during my boyhood years. His special Phillipson was a delicate eight-and-a-half-footer of only five and one-eighth ounces; it was designed for a six-weight double taper and had austere black-silk windings. Hunter once wrote a column about the fine sport that Frank Klune and I enjoyed on the Frying Pan in Colorado.

Phillipson also made a few two-piece rods. The best-known was probably the Phillipson Preferred; it was made in a seven-foot, three-and-one-quarter-ounce taper for four-weight lines and in a seven-and-a-half-foot version of three and three-quarters ounces for the same double taper in a four-weight. The Phillipson Preferred had functional wraps of chocolate silk and was a fine production fly rod of first quality bamboo.

It is intriguing that two exceptionally talented rodmakers also developed in Michigan before the Second World War. These men were Lyle Dickerson and the late Paul Young, two of the finest craftsmen ever to mill a strip of delicate Chinese cane.

Lyle Dickerson was born in Michigan in 1892, and grew up in his birthplace of Bellaire. He graduated from the local high school in 1909, and completed his degree from Hillsdale College on the eve of the First World War. During his high school years, Dickerson built a few bait rods from materials like ironwood and white cedar, but his fishing and rodmaking were interrupted by service with the fledgling Air Corps in France.

After the Treaty of Versailles, Dickerson returned to Detroit and started selling trucks and real estate. His interest in trout fishing was ultimately rekindled, and he spent a lot of time on the Au Sable, Pere Marquette, and Manistee. His work went fairly well until the Great Depression when everything collapsed and, like many others, Dickerson found himself without work. His frugal background had caused him to save enough cash to survive, and although there was almost too much time for fishing, Dickerson lacked decent tackle.

During the next few years, Dickerson found several months of work in Grand Rapids, and his association with the highly skilled furniture makers there ultimately led him into rod building. These artisans often spoke little English, having carried their guildlike skills from Europe, and Dickerson himself believes that it was their passion for quality that influenced his later craftsmanship. His Grand Rapids years also placed Dickerson in contact with furniture manufacturers like the late Ralph Widdicomb, who had a fishing cottage on the Pere Marquette. Combined with the automobile manufacturers and timber-cutting families from Bay City and Saginaw, these furniture makers formed the elite of the trout-fishing fraternity in Michigan. Dickerson did not know it, but these men would later become his principal customers.

When I finally decided to build bamboo rods, Dickerson explains, *I started searching the libraries for books that would tell me how they were made—and found absolutely nothing of help!*

Such books on rod building existed, but not in the jack-pine towns of northern Michigan, and the secrets of split-bamboo craftsmanship were closely guarded. The few men in Michigan who knew those mysteries worked for companies like Heddon, and their workshops were closed to outsiders. Rodmaking equipment was also unknown, although Dickerson did purchase a few culms of bamboo from Heddon, and he dismantled a few unserviceable rods to study their construction. Since they were

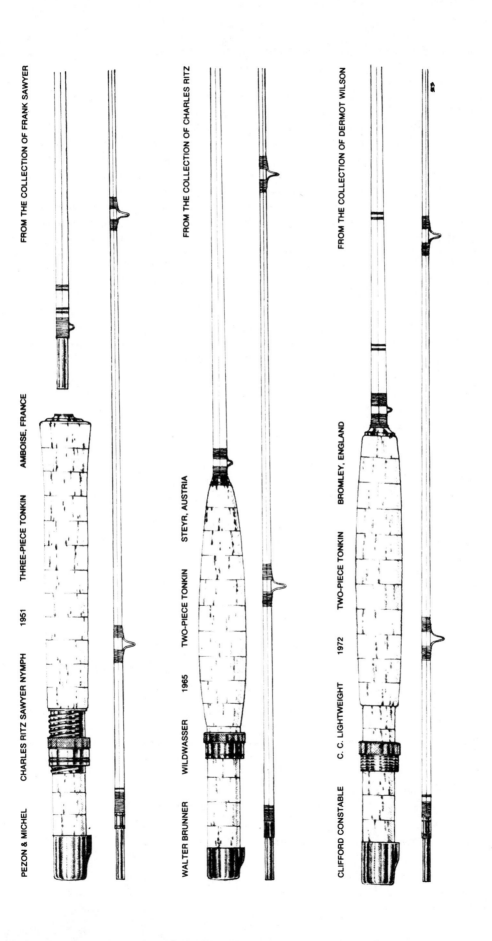

PEZON & MICHEL   CHARLES RITZ SAWYER NYMPH   1951   THREE-PIECE TONKIN   AMBOISE, FRANCE   FROM THE COLLECTION OF FRANK SAWYER

WALTER BRUNNER   WILDWASSER   1965   TWO-PIECE TONKIN   STEYR, AUSTRIA   FROM THE COLLECTION OF CHARLES RITZ

CLIFFORD CONSTABLE   C. C. LIGHTWEIGHT   1972   TWO-PIECE TONKIN   BROMLEY, ENGLAND   FROM THE COLLECTION OF DERMOT WILSON

laminated with fish-bladder glue, the strips could be separated by soaking them in water. Dickerson then borrowed some fine split-cane rods and took their calibrations, attempting to duplicate their tapers with homemade planing blocks and tools. Subsequent fishing on the Michigan rivers around Bellaire resulted in extensive modification of his tapers, and ultimately led to the unique performance associated with Dickerson rods.

Dickerson finally moved back to Detroit, and started building rods there in 1933. It was difficult work and there were few buyers of rods from a relatively unknown craftsman, even at the modest price of thirty-five dollars. It is surprising how few anglers could afford that cost, although the quality of the Dickerson rods rapidly became known in Michigan.

However, it was the late Ray Bergman who really launched Dickerson and his reputation for quality. Bergman travelled to Michigan to fish the Au Sable with his old friend Charles Merrill, and met Dickerson in Detroit. Before the success of *Trout*, Bergman had once been a tackle salesman for William Mills & Sons, and his favorite rod was a seven-and-a-half-foot Leonard of a relatively fast tournament-type action. Dickerson offered to match its action for Bergman, and took notes on its calibrations before the author travelled north.

Fast tapers were my meat, Dickerson explains.

Bergman was immensely pleased with his new Dickerson and expressed that pleasure in print, giving its maker his first taste of a national reputation. Dickerson rods later accounted for national dry-fly accuracy championships on two successive years; then the Second World War ended the shipments of bamboo. Dickerson soon exhausted his inventory of seasoned cane, and he stopped making rods until 1946.

Although solid fiberglass rods had just been introduced at Shakespeare, Dickerson was quickly swamped with back orders far beyond the capacity of a one-man shop, and his prices had climbed to sixty-five dollars. The Dickerson line included seven three-piece rods. His seven-and-a-half-foot, three-and-three-quarters-ounce and eight-foot, four-and-one-quarter-ounce rods were immensely popular, and his eight-and-a-half-footer of four and three-quarters ounces is one of the best all-around rods ever made. There were two nine-footers, weighing five and a half and six ounces, as well as a pair of nine-and-a-half-foot models of six and six and a half ounces. Two-piece Dickersons were made in five tapers. The beautiful seven-and-a-half-footer weighed three and a half ounces, and there were eight rod models of four and four and one-quarter ounces. The eight-and-a-half-foot rod weighed four and a half ounces and the nine-foot Dickerson in two-piece construction was a five-and-a-half-ounce rod for a seven-weight line. Dickerson used extremely large culms with extra heavy wall density, and his tapers magnified the quality of the cane into remarkably fast actions. The rods were fitted with the gun-blued ferrules typical of all Dickerson work and screw-locking seats with select American walnut fillers. His silk windings were chocolate with black ornamental tips.

Dickerson rods were unusually stiff and fast, with blue ferrules and a glass-perfect

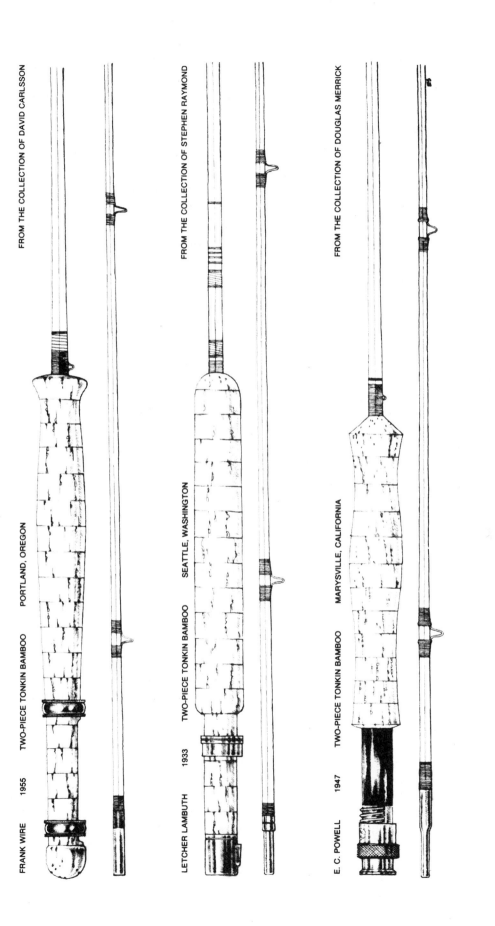

FRANK WIRE   1955   TWO-PIECE TONKIN BAMBOO   PORTLAND, OREGON

FROM THE COLLECTION OF DAVID CARLSSON

LETCHER LAMBUTH   1933   TWO-PIECE TONKIN BAMBOO   SEATTLE, WASHINGTON

FROM THE COLLECTION OF STEPHEN RAYMOND

E. C. POWELL   1947   TWO-PIECE TONKIN BAMBOO   MARYSVILLE, CALIFORNIA

FROM THE COLLECTION OF DOUGLAS MERRICK

finish, Martin Keane observed at his home in Connecticut, *and old masters like Lyle Dickerson never built anything that wasn't perfect inside or out!*

Dickerson tried to retire about fifteen years ago, but his customers continually badgered him into making repairs or replacing a broken tip section. Many loyal customers insisted that another Dickerson rod was absolutely critical to their future happiness, and Lyle Dickerson found old friends difficult to refuse. Finally he left Detroit, returning to his birthplace at Bellaire to escape his customers, and in his eighties, Dickerson is no longer working with bamboo. His lifetime production was slightly more than 2,000 rods and the three-piece specifications follow:

7½	761510	3¾ ounces	3 piece	HEH
8	801510	4¼ ounces	3 piece	HDH
8	801611	4½ ounces	3 piece	HDH
8½	861711	4¾ ounces	3 piece	HDH
8½	861812	5 ounces	3 piece	HCH
9	901711	5¼ ounces	3 piece	HDH
9	901812	5½ ounces	3 piece	HCH
9½	961812	5¾ ounces	3 piece	HDH
9½	961913	6 ounces	3 piece	HCH
10	102013	6¾ ounces	3 piece	HCH

Dickerson made the following two-piece rods:

7	7011	3¼ ounces	2 piece	HEH
7½	7312	3¾ ounces	2 piece	HDH
8	8013	4 ounces	2 piece	HDH
8	8014	4¼ ounces	2 piece	HCH
8½	8614	4½ ounces	2 piece	HDH
9	9015	5 ounces	2 piece	HCH

However, his knowledge and philosophy of rod building are still being translated into fine split-cane work. Dickerson has two disciples who have recently started building rods under their own trademarks. Perhaps the best known is Thomas Bedford, who was production manager for Kaiser automobiles and an ardent Dickerson fan almost thirty years ago. When Kaiser abandoned Detroit, moving its automotive operations to Argentina, Bedford was transferred to California in the Kaiser construction organization. Bedford himself finally retired near San Francisco and convinced Dickerson that his rodmaking equipment should continue making rods. Dickerson finally agreed, sold his tools and machinery and remaining stocks of bamboo to Bedford, and spent a month in California setting up a new rod-building shop there. The Bedford rods are painstakingly faithful to the

Dickerson specifications and quality, except that his work has added richly-patterned reel seat fillers of exotic hardwoods. His other disciple is Robert Summers, who learned his rodmaking skills from Paul Young, and now lives only forty miles from Dickerson at Traverse City. Summers has always admired both Dickerson and Young, and since Young died in 1960, his mentor these past years has increasingly become Lyle Dickerson.

Although I have never owned one of his rods, I once fished one of a matched pair of Dickersons that belonged to the late Gerry Queen of Detroit. It was fitted with a beautiful little Hardy St. George and a King Eider double taper, and I will never forget its ability to punch out big dry flies into a brisk headwind along a poetic reach of the Little South Pere Marquette in Michigan.

Arnold Gingrich has observed that Lyle Dickerson was the Guarnieri of the crisp dry-fly action, and if that analogy is accurate, it should be added that Paul Young was the self-taught Stradivari of the semiparabolic rod tapers—since like the legendary Italian violinmakers, both craftsmen lived and worked in the same city.

Paul Young was born in Arkansas in 1890, just forty miles west of Memphis. It was a curious beginning for one of the finest craftsmen in the history of American fly-fishing. Young was fishing at an early age, working set-lines for catfish in the Mississippi and fishing crayfish and minnows for smallmouth bass in the winding limestone valley of the White. Young hunted ducks in the bottoms too and was a skilled taxidermist long before he entered the University of Arkansas in 1908.

Following his graduation at Fayetteville in 1912, Young decided to travel extensively through Canada and the United States, sampling the fishing and shooting. His interest in taxidermy ultimately led to fly tying, and Young settled briefly in Minnesota in 1914, where he sold fishing tackle at Duluth and fished the nearby Brule and Namekagon in Wisconsin. After his marriage in 1921 to Martha Young, whose name graces one of his most popular rods, the couple moved to Detroit. His first job there was working as the principal taxidermist in the famous sporting goods store operated by Louis Eppinger.

Young opened his own tackle store on Grand River Avenue in Detroit only three years later, and his knowledge of trout fishing in both Michigan and Wisconsin soon made his shop a mecca for serious fly-fishermen throughout the Middle West.

Fishermen were always coming into the store, Martha Young explained last spring at her cottage on the Au Sable, *asking his opinion on their fly rods and other tackle problems.*

Young demonstrated his intuitive knowledge of actions and rod tapers quite early, and he soon began experimenting with eight and eight-and-a-half-foot lengths, modifying the fashionable wet-fly actions that still dominated American trout-fishing practice. Young built his first rods about 1923, using bamboo culms purchased from Cross in South Bend, and his experimental compound tapers first appeared in 1927.

Paul didn't know what to call those rods until John Alden Knight wrote about parabolic actions a dozen years later, Art Neumann told me along the North Branch last spring. *He called his first parabolics experimental actions—but he was playing with parabolic-type actions years before the famous bicycle accident in Paris that led to the Ritz Parabolics.*

The first rods made for sale were the Young Special series in both two- and three-piece designs. These were usually fast and medium-fast tapers. Four Young Specials existed as early as 1933, when Young himself published *Making and Using the Fly and Leader.* They ranged from a seven-and-a-half-foot, three-and-three-eighths-ounce dry-fly rod to an eight-and-a-half-foot, four-and-three-quarters-ounce model for a seven-weight line. There were two eight-foot Specials, weighing four and four and one-quarter ounces, and later Young added nine-foot tapers of five and one-quarter and six and a half ounces. The nine-foot Special 17 weighing five and one-quarter ounces was surprisingly delicate, taking a seven-weight double taper. The Special 18 weighing six and a half ounces was a three-piece powerhouse capable of handling big flies on a nine-weight line.

Later Young rods were all special designs, with each model made in a single length and taper. His little handbook lists seven experimental models, and it is possible to see future Young tapers in their prototypical specifications. One can anticipate the seven-foot, two-inch Driggs Special in the experimental seven-foot, two-and-three-quarters-ounce design listed in *Making and Using the Fly and Leader.* The popular Martha Marie of seven and a half feet, three ounces had its prelude in the experimental seven-and-a-half-foot, three-and-one-eight-ounce taper also listed in 1933. The versatile Parabolic 15 measuring eight feet and weighing three and three-quarters ounces has its unmistakable ancestry in an experimental design of eight feet, three and seven-eighths ounces that took a six-weight line. Its larger cousin, the powerful Parabolic 17 of eight and a half feet and five and a half ounces is clearly anticipated by the experimental nine-foot, five-and-a-half-ounce slow-action rod Young developed just before the Second World War. Most of his final tapers were fully worked out just after midcentury, along with his fittings and singular grip designs.

Young was a bit of a crank, Arnold Gingrich observes affectionately. *He was never interested in how his rods looked—only in the weight and taper and performance of their cane.*

Young was obviously a fanatic about weight. His specifications searched continually for new fittings and grips designed to shave mere fractions of ounces from their assembled weight, yet he always listed the weight of their bamboo separately. His fittings included a pair of free-sliding reel bands long before the Orvis Superfine made them popular, and he also developed a series of remarkable black-anodized aluminum ferrules. Although aluminum alloys lack the durability of German-silver fittings, these Young ferrules were surprisingly long-lived. Both the sliding-band and screw-locking reel seats on all Young rods are assembled with cork fillers. Young even experimented with unique skeletal grips in which a small gap existed between each cork ring to reduce weight beyond normal limits.

Young built few three-piece rods after 1952, and his midcentury bamboo work echoed the spiral-node construction pioneered by James Payne, a master craftsman Young greatly admired. His culms were flame-treated in a gas-jet ring devised by Young himself, tempering them to the threshold of brittleness to achieve exceptional power-to-weight ratios. The fingerprint of his aggressive flame tempering lies in the dark half-carbonized surfaces of the bamboo. His self-designed milling machine surpassed the tolerances that Young originally achieved with a hand plane and a skillfully worked Vixen file.

Young also developed a unique method of laminating and waterproofing the joints of his cane, using immersion in a secret process that involved synthetic resins. The exact resin formulas are still a closely guarded secret in the Young workshop at Traverse City. The bamboo sections laminated with this process are virtually as impervious to casting stress and water absorption as the fully impregnated rods made in the workrooms of Orvis and Sharpe's.

The Young pressure-wrap machine that laminated the freshly milled splines of bamboo was a surplus aircraft bomb hoist capable of achieving remarkable tensile forces. Young rods were so well bonded that their butt sections defied boiling, freezing in a block of ice, and multiple twisting without failure in their laminations. It is typical of Young rods that the heat-tempered cane itself fractures long before the glue faces fail.

Young is perhaps most famous for his Midge, an ultralight rod that has never been surpassed in its performance. It measures six-feet three-inches, weighs one and three-quarters ounces, takes a four-weight line, and its compound tapers make it radically different from any other rod of similar length and weight. Its calibrations are so unusual that its butt diameters are smaller, its ferrule is a size or two larger, and its tip guides are two or three sizes smaller than the specifications of comparable bamboo rods. The resulting performance is remarkable. The other so-called Midge rods are little power plants, capable of handling casts of eighty to ninety feet in highly skilled hands, but the Young Midge is utterly different. Most ultralight rods cannot handle fine tippets and often take surprisingly heavy lines in weight-forward tapers, but the Young version was designed for an honest DT4F combined with .005 and .006 tippets. Paul Young liked fishing tiny dry flies on the Au Sable in late summer, and his Midge was designed both for that delicate work and the highly specialized problems of the sophisticated fishermen on the limestone streams of Pennsylvania. The Midge made its debut as the lightest model in the Young line of a dozen different rods, and Young was greatly surprised to find his Midge commonly used for all-around trout-fishing problems. There were even light-tackle cranks like Arnold Gingrich who fished the Midge on salmon, and in his recent book *The Joys of Trout* he includes the following observations on Young and his remarkable Midge:

He rather grudgingly acknowledged its best-seller status in his line of rods, although for his own use he greatly preferred the Parabolic 15, an all-purpose rod of eight feet and three-and-three-quarters ounces weight, and regarded the use of a toothpick like his Midge for long casts and large fish as something of a perversion of its natural purpose. He testily refused either to claim, or even acknowledge, that he had pioneered the small rod craze, pointing out that the Leonard line had featured a Baby Catskill rod, at six feet and fifteen-sixteenths of an ounce, several years before he made his first Midge, and that William Mills & Son had even advertised it as the world's smallest fly rod.

Admitting that his Midge was clearly out of the baby rod class, which he considered about as practical as a wet noodle, he still contended that it was being put to uses for which he neither intended it nor considered it suitable, and he was both amused and puzzled when he saw the term "Midge Rod" come into generic use, categorizing all split-cane rods with light mountings, measuring under seven feet and weighing two ounces or less, and thus outgrow its original application to a specific model in his line of rods.

The Driggs Special is a seven-foot, two-inch rod weighing two and seven-eighths ounces and designed as a powerful little compound taper for fishing the brushy little river in northern Michigan for which it was named. Paul Young conceived it as a relatively short rod, with both the delicacy to fish 5X tippets and the power to turn a heavy fish away from logjams and brushpiles. It was a beautiful little Driggs that I found Martha Young using on the Au Sable above Stephan's Bridge this past season in Michigan, casting a long and skillful line in the April sunshine.

The Perfectionist is a superb seven-and-a-half-foot, two-and-five-eighths-ounce rod Young designed for general fishing with relatively fine tippets, its slender tip calibrations taking a four sixty-fourths of an inch tip guide. It has become the favorite rod of the celebrated Charles Fox in recent years, ever since he spent an evening with a Perfectionist of mine along Letort Spring Run. It is difficult to find a rod that will reach out ninety feet and fish a .004 tippet, but a man like Charles Fox can utilize its full spectrum of qualities, and its status as his favorite rod is a fine vote of confidence. The Perfectionist takes a DT4F in perfect equilibrium, and is one of the finest fly-rod tapers ever designed in bamboo.

Paul Young was a restless artisan, and his lifetime production of rods was relatively small. His work was never entirely limited to his standard tapers, so unusual variations on his basic themes are relatively common. Perhaps the finest of these special tapers was a variation of the Perfectionist called the Princess. It was a Perfectionist with a radically regressive taper, working in almost flat calibrations from the stripping guide into the grip assembly. Six of these Princess rods were built, measuring seven feet,

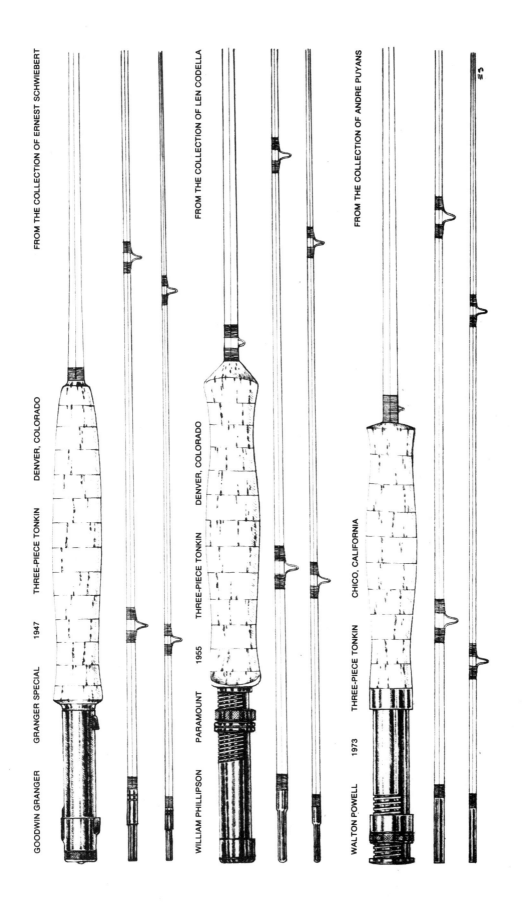

FROM THE COLLECTION OF ERNEST SCHWIEBERT

GOODWIN GRANGER   GRANGER SPECIAL   1947   THREE-PIECE TONKIN   DENVER, COLORADO

FROM THE COLLECTION OF LEN CODELLA

WILLIAM PHILLIPSON   PARAMOUNT   1955   THREE-PIECE TONKIN   DENVER, COLORADO

FROM THE COLLECTION OF ANDRE PUYANS

WALTON POWELL   1973   THREE-PIECE TONKIN   CHICO, CALIFORNIA

weighing two and three-quarters ounces, and taking a four-weight line. The rods were fitted with skeletal reel seats and wrapped in black silk, and were milled and assembled in 1958. These six rods have become highly prized collectors' items.

During the same production run, there was a single set of exceptional sticks that Young assembled into a unique seven-and-a-half-foot Princess for his own battery of rods. It was assembled with different tips, a standard feature with the larger Parabolic 15. The delicate tip had a four sixty-fourths of an inch top, making the rod weigh two and a half ounces, and the four and a half sixty-fourths of an inch tip added an eighth ounce to that assembled weight. Fitted with the light tip, it will readily handle .003 tippets and tiny flies. The heavier tip will easily punch a small streamer eighty feet if that kind of power is necessary. With its slow butt tapers and different tip sections, it is an extremely versatile rod for small streams and shy trout. This unique seven-and-a-half-foot Princess found its way into my hands after Young's death, and it is a treasure fitted with a reverse sliding-band reel seat assembly of my own design, along with a slender cigar-type handle. John Waller Hills observed that once in his life each fly-fisher encounters a rod so perfectly suited to his personality and temperament and physical skills that it becomes a part of him. Thus far in my fishing odyssey, the seven-and-a-half-foot Princess passed on to me from the collection of its maker is that rod—it is that exquisitely poetic balance of delicacy and power that comes alive in the hands.

Young designed another seven-and-a-half-foot standard model called the Martha Marie, named for the girl he married in 1921. It is a brisk three-ounce rod designed for dry-fly work on relatively large rivers, its butt power capable of handling bucktails while its tip calibrations are subtle enough to accommodate .005 and .006 tippets.

Paul Young himself loved the Parabolic 15. It is a remarkable eight-foot design, made with separate dry-fly and distance tips. The fine tip is fitted with a four and a half sixty-fourths of an inch top, while the heavier tip takes a five sixty-fourths top guide. The Parabolic 15 weighs three and three-quarters ounces with its dry-fly tip and a full four ounces with the distance taper. Most of the production models were made with a parabolic taper of surprising power, although many were also assembled with a slow-action butt in a rod called the K. T. Keller, honoring a past board chairman of the Chrysler Corporation. My own collection includes rods of both specifications, and I prefer the radical tapers of the Keller variation. It is probably the finest all-around trout rod in my collection, fishing both 6X tippets and handling big 1/0 Muddlers on western rivers at ranges beyond ninety feet. It has fished such large flies at such distances on rivers like the Big Hole and Yellowstone and Snake. It also once took a magnificent eight-and-a-half-pound rainbow on a small spring creek in Jackson Hole, fishing an ant imitation in the surface film with a tippet of .005. It is a superb fly-fishing tool.

Many partisans of the Young split-cane rods believe that the Parabolic

PAUL YOUNG

17 is the finest big-water trout rod ever built, and like the smaller Parabolic 15, it was made in two radically different variations. The standard model is eight and a half feet and five and a half ounces, taking an eight-weight line, and I have another experimental parabolic of this type that once belonged to Young himself. It has three separate tip sections. The dry-fly tip has calibrations taking a five sixty-fourths of an inch top, the delicate wet-fly tip has a four and a half sixty-fourths top, and the powerful distance tip takes a six sixty-fourths tip fitting. This rod also has an extra-slow butt taper, with little difference between the calibrations at the stripping guide and the grip. Its compound tapers are quite radical, displaying rather complex rhythms under stress. Its timing combines an ability to handle long casts easily, as well as sufficient tip delicacy to protect a 5X tippet. The distance tip will load and deliver a WF9S forward taper more than a hundred feet.

Most customers found this experimental Parabolic 17 too radical in its timing, but Paul Young loved its difficult character. It had been fished with commitment and care since its birth in 1952, and he had planned to use it during our meeting on the South Branch of the Au Sable the week he suffered his final heart seizure. His widow subsequently sent this unique Parabolic 17 to me on the eve of my first odyssey to Argentina.

Paul always wanted to fish Patagonia, Martha Young explained in the brief note that accompanied the rod. *You should fish it for him on those rivers down there—like he always dreamed!*

Young also made a number of bigger parabolics, remarkable rods almost too powerful for trout fishing. The Texan was an eight-and-a-half-foot, five-and-seven-eighths-ounce rod primarily designed for big poppers and hair frogs. The Bobby Doerr was a nine-foot, six-ounce parabolic named for the famous Boston second baseman at midcentury, who was a highly skilled fisherman on both steelhead rivers and bonefish flats. The Parabolic 18 was a similar rod of nine-feet, six and a half ounces designed for a nine-weight line. Young also made a number of Parabolic 19 models, nine-footers of six and a half ounces designed for ten-weight lines. The Powerhouse was a nine-and-a-half-foot, six-and-three-quarters-ounce rod balanced by eleven-weight tapers and was originally designed for tarpon, and I have used mine on the heavy salmon rivers of arctic Norway.

Paul Young was perhaps the most experimental craftsman in the history of the split-cane rod, and his tapers were much more radical than the compound tapers of Garrison or Ritz. Arnold Gingrich—who perhaps owns more Young rods than anyone—observed in his *Joys of Trout* that Paul Young was venerated in the last ten years of his life as the ultimate master of the Midge-size rod, and that he was a near-legendary cult figure at his death. After Young died in 1960, his rods were made by his son John Young and Robert Summers, who had worked closely with Young during the last four years of his life. John Young had displayed exceptional talent for split-cane work at an early age.

Jack will carry on, Paul Young always said thoughtfully in his workshop. *Jack is the one who was born with bamboo in his blood.*

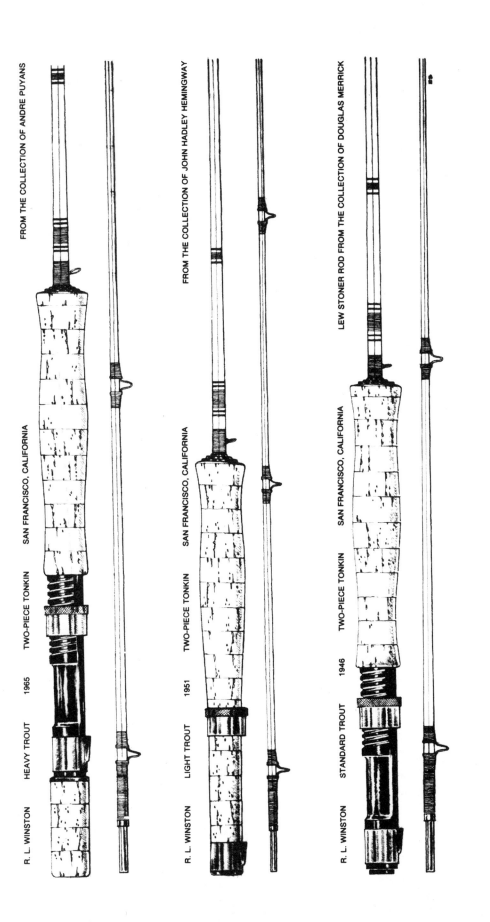

FROM THE COLLECTION OF ANDRE PUYANS

R. L. WINSTON   HEAVY TROUT   1965   TWO-PIECE TONKIN   SAN FRANCISCO, CALIFORNIA

FROM THE COLLECTION OF JOHN HADLEY HEMINGWAY

R. L. WINSTON   LIGHT TROUT   1951   TWO-PIECE TONKIN   SAN FRANCISCO, CALIFORNIA

LEW STONER ROD FROM THE COLLECTION OF DOUGLAS MERRICK

R. L. WINSTON   STANDARD TROUT   1946   TWO-PIECE TONKIN   SAN FRANCISCO, CALIFORNIA

Martha Young retired from active participation in the Young Company in 1969, and when the Southfield store was sold for the right-of-way new turnpike, John Young and Robert Summers moved the firm north to Traverse City. Young rods are still made there under the supervision of John Young, Robert Summers having since left to build bamboo rods under his own name. Just as Hiram Leonard and Lewis Stoner can be judged in terms of the craftsmen they groomed, Paul Young has left his legacy in the skilled hands of John Young and Robert Summers. Michigan has not had such a pair of artisans since both Paul Young and Lyle Dickerson were actively building rods at midcentury.

Summers started his apprenticeship with Paul Young in 1956, filing nodes and stripping the pressure wraps from freshly glued rod sections. Later he graduated to hand-scraping and filing the sticks under Young's watchful eye. It was routine work, but it was exacting and important. His work passed muster, since Summers received a pay raise after a few weeks.

Those years with Paul Young were happy, Summers told me at the Priest cottage on the Au Sable. *There were always fish stories and I was learning something I already loved, and sometimes a famous fisherman visited the shop.*

Summers left the Young workrooms briefly to work in a toolmaking shop in Detroit, attracted by the higher wages available there. It was interesting work, but Summers was already hopelessly infected with bamboo fever, and he soon rejoined Young in his rodmaking shop.

People love rods! he explains. *Not machine parts!*

When the Young rod-building shop moved north to Traverse City, Summers moved with it, and he soon became friends with Lyle Dickerson in Bellaire. Summers travelled regularly to visit Dickerson, talking about split-cane construction and examining his rods. Summers decided to start his own company in 1972, when he acquired the rodmaking machinery that had belonged to the late Morris Kushner, one of the finest amateur rod builders in the United States. Kushner was a retired mechanical engineer who had founded his own tool company and later built bamboo rods as a hobby. His stock of seasoned cane was sizable, and after adding new carbide cutters to the Kushner milling equipment, Summers started building bamboo rods of his own.

His first rods looked predictably like the Young designs, but in recent months the Summers rods have begun to evolve a character and quality of their own. His tapers are compound formulas that echo the work of his patron and principal tutor, but Summers has come to prefer the delicate tips and deliberate casting rhythms of the slower actions. His fittings still have echoes of Young, but his rods now use the reverse-locking seats found in the work of builders like Powell, Gillum, and Payne. His skeletal seats echo my own designs with a single reel band exposed and a second band concealed in the grip. It is simple and functional in its conception. The sliding band is below the reel. The system is self-tightening with the weight of the reel working down into the sliding ring, much as the head of an axe is seated with its own inertia.

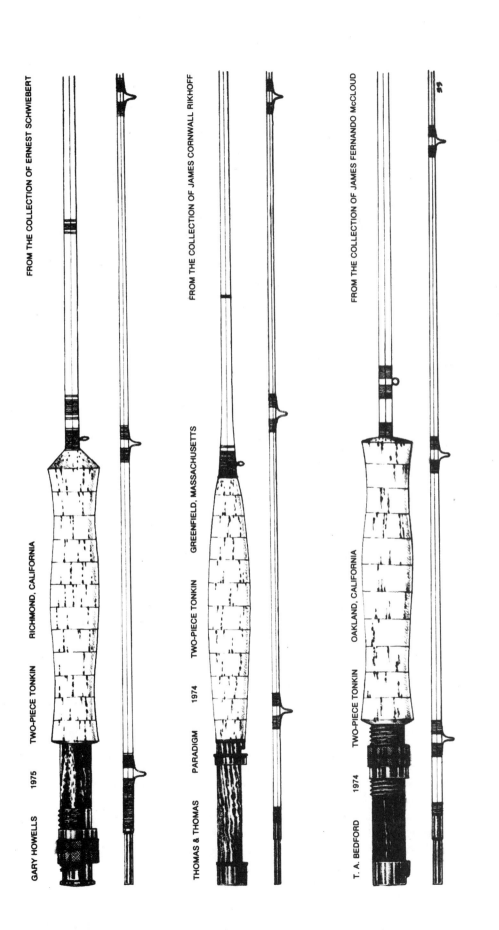

FROM THE COLLECTION OF ERNEST SCHWIEBERT

FROM THE COLLECTION OF JAMES CORNWALL RIKHOFF

FROM THE COLLECTION OF JAMES FERNANDO McCLOUD

GARY HOWELLS   1975   TWO-PIECE TONKIN   RICHMOND, CALIFORNIA

THOMAS & THOMAS   PARADIGM   1974   TWO-PIECE TONKIN   GREENFIELD, MASSACHUSETTS

T. A. BEDFORD   1974   TWO-PIECE TONKIN   OAKLAND, CALIFORNIA

The Little Manistee rods measure six and six and a half feet and weigh one and three-quarters and two ounces. They are assembled with cork reel seats and tiny grips and are slightly less powerful than the Young Midge or Driggs Special, ideally suited to small rivers and fine tippets. The Ontanagon series includes two seven-foot rods of two and one-quarter and two and five-eighths ounces, and seven-and-a-half-footers of two and a half and two and three-quarters ounces. The Pere Marquette series is fitted with a reel-seat filler of rosewood or Macassar ebony, using a single reel band of jewel-finished aluminum. It includes rods of seven and a half feet, two and three-quarters ounces and three and one-eighth ounces, eight-foot rods of four and four and one-quarter ounces, and an eight-and-a-half-foot design weighing four and three-quarters ounces. The Au Sable series is fitted with reverse-locking seats in brightly polished aluminum over fillers of exotic hardwoods. It includes a seven-foot rod of three ounces, two seven-and-a-half-foot models of three and one-quarter and three and five-eighths ounces, plus two eight-foot designs of four and one-quarter and four and a half ounces, and an eight-and-a-half-footer of five and one-quarter ounces. The Summers Big Manistee rods include an eight-and-a-half-foot, five-and-three-quarters-ounce model and a smooth nine-foot, six-ounce rod of surprising delicacy and power. The grip designs are modeled after the functional handles developed by Everett Garrison, and although there are traditional echoes in his work, the Summers rods have unmistakably evolved a unique character of their own.

Although most anglers are familiar with the work of famous eastern craftsmen like Gillum and Garrison, there are a number of other artisans who have built superb rods over the years. The roster includes familiar names like Uslan and Halstead, as well as much younger men like Baird Foster, Charles Jenkins, Walter Carpenter, Samuel Carlsson, and Minert Hull. These less famous craftsmen are artisans of remarkable skills and exceptional promise.

Nathaniel Uslan remains the principal disciple of Robert Crompton and his theories of five-strip construction, although Uslan no longer has his shop just outside New York at Spring Valley. Uslan was one of the first craftsmen to suffer from the shortages of first-quality Chinese cane that began in 1939. Uslan stopped making rods altogether in 1958, and moved to the outskirts of Miami, where he has been assembling fiberglass rods for salt-water fishing and machining German-silver ferrules and fittings for other makers. With the improving supplies of Tonkin cane, Uslan has resumed building his unusual five-strip bamboo rods in two-piece designs of seven to eight and a half feet.

The careers of Halstead and Gillum were curiously intertwined after Halstead left Leonard, where he had worked making reel seats and ferrules. George Halstead had little or no experience at milling cane, while Gillum was a genius at carpentry and precision metalworking and cabinetmaking, who had learned to build split-cane rods through a friendship with Eustis Edwards, one of the original Leonard apprentices at Bangor.

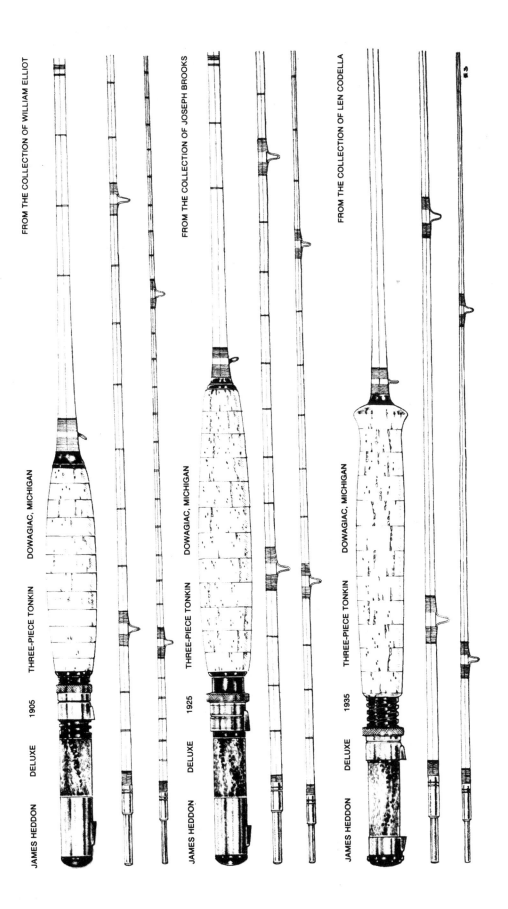

FROM THE COLLECTION OF WILLIAM ELLIOT

JAMES HEDDON   DELUXE   1905   THREE-PIECE TONKIN   DOWAGIAC, MICHIGAN

FROM THE COLLECTION OF JOSEPH BROOKS

JAMES HEDDON   DELUXE   1925   THREE-PIECE TONKIN   DOWAGIAC, MICHIGAN

FROM THE COLLECTION OF LEN CODELLA

JAMES HEDDON   DELUXE   1935   THREE-PIECE TONKIN   DOWAGIAC, MICHIGAN

Halstead once entertained the hope of a rodmaking partnership with Gillum, machining the ferrules and fittings, while Gillum made the rod sections. The partnership actually started at one point, but Halstead was late in delivering the ferrules, and when they finally arrived, Gillum was furious to find the ferrules were not completed. The welts, water stops and plugs were shipped loose, mixed in with the nickel-silver tubing for the male and female ferrules.

Gillum never forgave George, Harry Darbee told me one night along the Willowemoc. *It was the end of the partnership!*

George Halstead lived at Brewster, almost fifty miles above New York, with Gillum working nearby in Connecticut. Halstead made a few rods of surprisingly good parabolic action in his own shop, with his own ferrules and fittings. The bamboo workmanship was good, and the Halstead actions were similar to several Leonard tapers, although Halstead failed to assemble his rods with first-rate adhesives. Many of his rods separated along their glue faces, both in fishing and exposure to excessive moisture, and few survive today. Halstead died at a relatively young age, and his skills and rod specifications never reached their full potential.

Harold Steele Gillum had learned the rudiments of split-cane construction from Eustis Edwards, but his relatively close friendship with James Payne had a considerable influence on his later work. Some of his fly rods even include modified Payne ferrules and other fittings, and the character of a typical Gillum betrays an unmistakable admiration for the example of Payne.

Gillum was born at Ridgefield, just across the Connecticut line from Halstead's workshop in New York, at the turn of the century. His interest in fly-fishing came from his friendship with the older Edwards, but his later rods came closer to the dry-fly tapers developed in the Highland Mills shop of James Payne. Although the design and fittings of the Gillum rods varied extensively with his moods, his total production approached a thousand rods, with about eighty to ninety milled and assembled in his best years. Gillum began laminating his cane strips with an adhesive formula supplied by George Halstead, and when several of his first rods failed, he took a sample of the Halstead glue for precise analysis to a friend who was a chemical engineer.

It turned out to be pretty cheap stuff, Harry Darbee laughs about their glue-formula quarrels. *It was a hide glue without all of the animal fats taken out, and Pinky was furious—Pinky admitted there were a lot of things you could use for gluing rods, but never forgave Halstead for a glue that was part lard.*

Gillum never quite standardized his tapers or fittings, although the heavy locking nut that was engraved with his name and simply identified him as the maker, was pretty much a trademark. His early rods were often fitted with ferrules made by George Halstead, and after Halstead died he made a large number of rods using the old Super-Z ferrules. Some Gillum rods even have Payne ferrules, and finally Gillum turned to making his ferrules himself. Two-piece Gillums of seven feet, three ounces are the

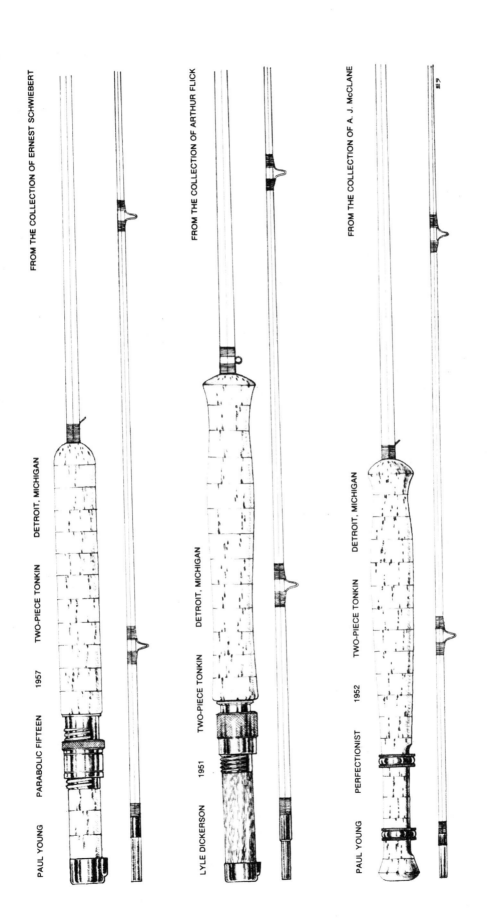

FROM THE COLLECTION OF ERNEST SCHWIEBERT

PAUL YOUNG   PARABOLIC FIFTEEN   1957   TWO-PIECE TONKIN   DETROIT, MICHIGAN

FROM THE COLLECTION OF ARTHUR FLICK

LYLE DICKERSON   1951   TWO-PIECE TONKIN   DETROIT, MICHIGAN

FROM THE COLLECTION OF A. J. McCLANE

PAUL YOUNG   PERFECTIONIST   1952   TWO-PIECE TONKIN   DETROIT, MICHIGAN

smallest examples I have seen, except for two or three exhibition rods made for Ellis Newman, and there are many two-piece Gillums of seven and a half, eight, and eight and a half feet in the collections of men like Harry Darbee and Arthur Walker. These are probably the vintage lengths for the two-piece Gillums, although there are also nine- and nine-and-a-half-foot tapers as heavy as seven and a half ounces. Gillum also made a few rods that were sold under the trademark of the Daly Shotgun Company, although these were largely big two-piece rods designed for salt-water work. There were also a number of three-piece Gillums made, mostly rods of eight and a half, nine, and nine and a half feet. Most Gillum rods were assembled with the reverse-locking seats of the style perfected by James Payne, although Gillum made his wood fillers of both walnut and mahogany, arguing that his mahogany fillers were lighter than cork. Gillum also made a few rods with a conventional butt cap and locking-seat hardware.

Gillum refused to heat-temper his bamboo except to straighten the culms or milled sections, giving the cane a slightly slower action that he compensated for in his unusual tapers. His rod actions tended toward a relatively stiff butt, its flexing node a few inches above the grip check, and a fast tip that combined delicacy with surprising power. The late John Atherton, whose slim book *The Fly and the Fish* is an American classic, had two exceptionally fine Gillums that he loved on his Battenkill between Shushan and Arlington. The first was a seven-footer of only two and three-quarters ounces that Gillum had designed for a DT4F and late summer work. Atherton's favorite Gillum was an eight-footer, weighing three and seven-eighths ounces and balancing five-weights.

After his sorry experience with natural adhesives, Gillum turned to his friend Everett Garrison for advice. Garrison had the technical background to understand that a rod heats slightly in casting, as its molecular structure is flexed, and that during very hot weather the conventional fish and hide adhesives could reach temperatures that softened their laminations and reached the threshold of failure. Such adhesives are heated approximately 130 to 150 degrees during rod-assembly, and in casting during 100-degree weather, a rod can gradually become soupy and suffer permanent damage. Synthetic adhesives can withstand more than 300 degrees without structural denigration, a temperature range well beyond any thermal problems encountered in fishing. Garrison was the first to employ the modern synthetics for bonding his rods, preferring a black adhesive that is clearly visible as a razor-slim line in the finished sections, and Gillum quickly became a convert to his theories. Although his bamboo was darker, approaching the rich patina of a Payne, Gillum rods display the same cobweb-fine seam of black glue found in the pale sections of a Garrison. These synthetic glues are slightly less flexible than the conventional fish and hide adhesives, but they retain their exceptional strength and resilience for many years, and they are virtually impervious to moisture or heat.

Although the Gillum rod was not the equal of the comparable Paynes in their overall quality of fittings and workmanship, and his cork grips are

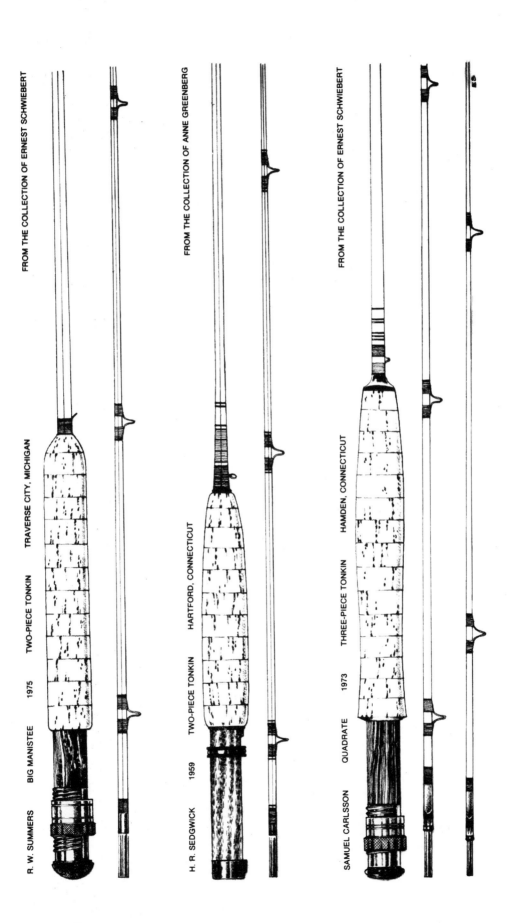

FROM THE COLLECTION OF ERNEST SCHWIEBERT

R. W. SUMMERS   BIG MANISTEE   1975   TWO-PIECE TONKIN   TRAVERSE CITY, MICHIGAN

FROM THE COLLECTION OF ANNE GREENBERG

H. R. SEDGWICK   1959   TWO-PIECE TONKIN   HARTFORD, CONNECTICUT

FROM THE COLLECTION OF ERNEST SCHWIEBERT

SAMUEL CARLSSON   QUADRATE   1973   THREE-PIECE TONKIN   HAMDEN, CONNECTICUT

often somewhat poorly finished, Gillum was probably more willing to experiment with his tapers than many of his contemporaries. Gillum partisans as well known as Harry Darbee, Arthur Walker, and John Atherton form an impressive jury of men who believe their Gillum rods are matchless weapons. Atherton praised Gillum highly in *The Fly and the Fish*:

> Every angler has his own favorites and he will undoubtedly find, at some time in his career, which is best for him. Whether or not we agree with the English anglers in their choice of rods, we must admit that with their fishing, the winds so constantly present on their streams, and the necessity of casting from the bank rather than from the water, an entirely different type of weapon is clearly called for.
>
> Rather than condemn it all as useless in America, we should profit by some of their discoveries. There are occasions here when the longer, softer rods might be an advantage. Wherever the delivery should be very delicate, or where a long, light cast is essential, our short powerful rods are sometimes unable to give us what we want. And particularly if one fishes where wind is a governing factor, it can be very discouraging to try to achieve the proper results with a rod inadequate for the job.
>
> Of course, for the man who can afford a large battery of rods of every length, weight and description, it is not difficult to find something to take care of the unusual condition. But for the one- or two-rod man, it is something else again. If I could only have a single rod for trout, it would be either eight feet, three inches or eight and one-half feet, of medium rather than stiff action, to handle a line not over size D in silk or nylon. This would enable one to fish delicately if desired, cover large water and handle a wind, or fish a short line. And I would ask my friend Pinky Gillum to make it for me.

Harold Steele Gillum was a moody, insular craftsman who did not marry until he was almost fifty, and his character had a cantankerous side that triggered quarrels with everyone, including close friends like Harry Darbee. Yet when Gillum died in 1969, men like Darbee mourned him deeply, and one of our finest craftsmen had passed into history.

Since the deaths of Lewis Stoner, Paul Young, and James Payne, Everett Garrison is unquestionably the Dean Emeritus of American rodmaking. His skills are so unique and his craftsmanship is so exacting that his stature on the threshold of eighty is richly deserved, and those skills have happily been passed on to protégés like Baird Foster and Charles Jenkins. Edmund Everett Garrison was born in Yonkers, a sprawling suburb of New York that lies along the Hudson, in the winter of 1893. He attended school in Yonkers, and later received a degree in electrical engineering at Union College in 1916.

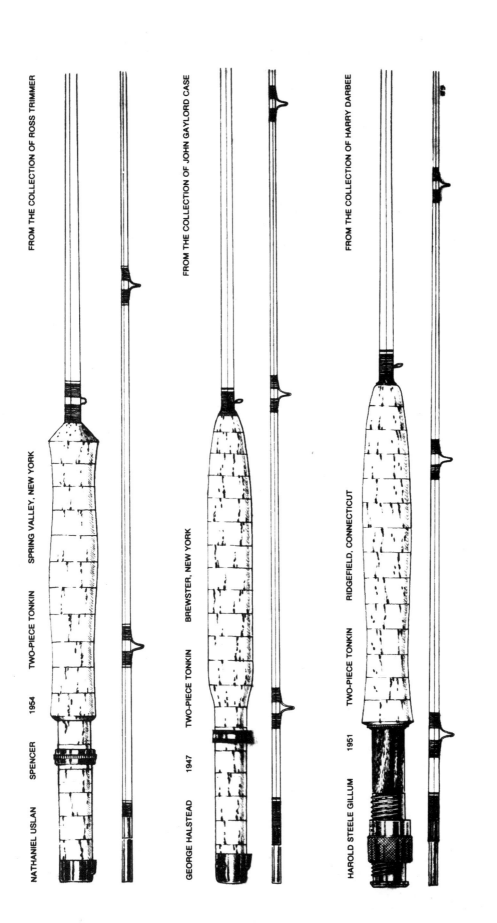

NATHANIEL USLAN   SPENCER   1954   TWO-PIECE TONKIN   SPRING VALLEY, NEW YORK   FROM THE COLLECTION OF ROSS TRIMMER

GEORGE HALSTEAD   1947   TWO-PIECE TONKIN   BREWSTER, NEW YORK   FROM THE COLLECTION OF JOHN GAYLORD CASE

HAROLD STEELE GILLUM   1951   TWO-PIECE TONKIN   RIDGEFIELD, CONNECTICUT   FROM THE COLLECTION OF HARRY DARBEE

His first work was with Curtiss-Wright, testing the metallurgical quality of the steels intended for their aircraft engines. Technology was obviously in his blood, since his father held two degrees in engineering from Columbia University. With the outbreak of American involvement in the First World War, Garrison tried to enlist in the Signal Corps, for flight training in its observation planes. There were continuous postponements of his enlistment that puzzled Garrison, until he discovered that officials at Curtiss-Wright had been quietly interfering in his plans to keep him in their plant. Garrison quit in anger and entered flight school in the summer of 1918, although his dreams of aerial combat ended six months later with the Armistice in France.

After the war, Garrison became involved in the design and construction of railroad trackage and structures, and he spent an increasing amount of time on Catskill rivers like the Neversink and the Rondout. The Rondout was his favorite, and when it was ruined with the construction of a reservoir for the New York water system in 1930, Garrison felt as though a member of his family had died.

Hiram Leonard had many apprentices who later made rods professionally, but there were also amateurs who regularly flocked to his shop at Central Valley. The most famous was perhaps George Parker Holden, who also made bamboo rods as a hobby at his house in Yonkers. Holden published his book *The Idyll of the Split-Bamboo* in 1920, and a mutual friend introduced him to Garrison two years later. Garrison was also a skilled amateur golfer who was building shafts of ash and hickory for his own clubs, and he was intrigued with the idea of club shafts made of split bamboo. Both men soon shared their love for trout fishing, and Garrison became fascinated with both the bamboo rods and the culms of seasoned cane in Holden's garage.

Garrison built his first rods using Holden's stock of cane, borrowing his first tapers from a two-piece Payne that belonged to a fishing friend. The results were unsatisfactory, according to Garrison himself, but he continued to build more rods with increasing success. It was a prelude to the most disciplined, painstaking approach to rodmaking in the entire history of split bamboo.

Other rodmakers were intuitive craftsmen who worked out their actions and tapers empirically, but it was Garrison who actually focused his background in stress analysis on the dynamics of casting behavior. His test rod in this analysis was a two-piece Payne of eight feet, four and a half ounces. Garrison calculated the working stresses at five-inch intervals under maximum deflection in bending. His studies indicated that bending stresses often reach 15,000 pounds per square inch and that maximum loading in the Payne occurred five inches from the tip. His search for a theoretical basis in predicting and designing rod actions evolved into a rich tapestry of mathematics, using a mixture of conventional calculus and moment-force diagrams and the progressive stresses found in the complexities of wave-linear dynamics. Although his rods are both hand-split and hand-planed,

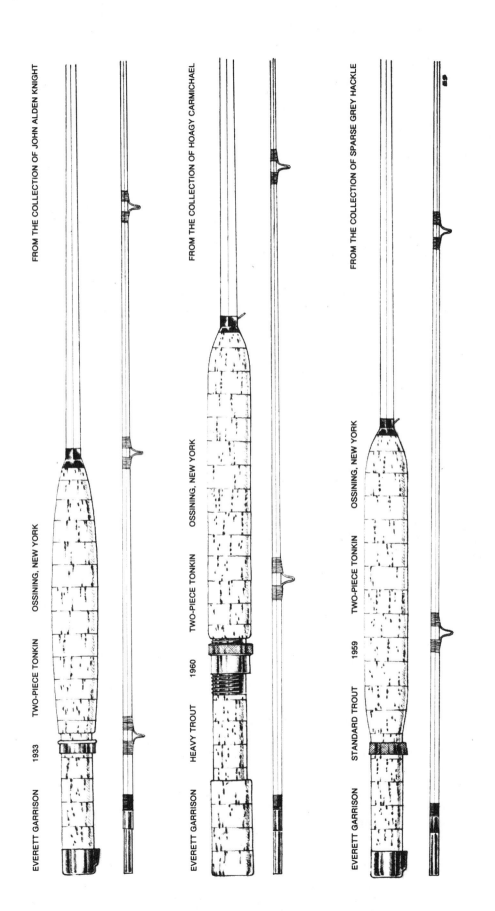

EVERETT GARRISON   1933   TWO-PIECE TONKIN   OSSINING, NEW YORK   FROM THE COLLECTION OF JOHN ALDEN KNIGHT

EVERETT GARRISON   1960   HEAVY TROUT   TWO-PIECE TONKIN   OSSINING, NEW YORK   FROM THE COLLECTION OF HOAGY CARMICHAEL

EVERETT GARRISON   1959   STANDARD TROUT   TWO-PIECE TONKIN   OSSINING, NEW YORK   FROM THE COLLECTION OF SPARSE GREY HACKLE

there is nothing empirical about his approach to rod tapers and actions. Garrison also designed his own planing blocks and tools and other equipment.

Tolerances are everything, Garrison explained one evening at the Anglers' Club of New York, *and I soon realized that Holden's hardwood planing forms were not precise enough.*

Garrison conceived an adjustable planing form of cold-rolled steel, and had it built by William Mallott at his machine shop on Seventy-second Street in Manhattan. Unlike the Holden blocks, which could only hold tolerances of between one thirty-second and one sixty-fourth of an inch, these Garrison forms used differential setscrews to control the tapers with exceptional precision.

They're quite good. Garrison adjusts his forms with quiet pride. *Each full turn of the screws opens or closes the planing forms exactly .008 inch—just what I needed in my work.*

The pressure-winding machine, used after the dark synthetic adhesive is applied to the splines, is typical of most rodmakers, although Garrison's design is capable of achieving a section almost uniquely free of torque or twisting stresses.

Garrison also developed other unique features in the assembly of his sections. Inspection of two Garrison tips laid side by side will reveal that the same nodes in each section were adjacent splines in the original culm, a Garrison refinement designed to make both rod tips as identical as possible. Perhaps more remarkable is the Garrison method of staggering his node patterns. Payne and Young employed a famous spiral-type pattern, while Leonard pioneered an alternating method in placing his bamboo nodes. Garrison took these principles another step, restlessly searching for absolute perfection, and has worked out a unique nodal system. It is so perfect that each bamboo node exists in complete isolation. Not only are there no other nodes in the adjacent strips of cane, one can also spin a Garrison section in vain, searching for other nodes anywhere at that point in the tapers. The result is split-cane sections so perfect that one rolls them in vain to find the bamboo face that bends the most, the low side of the section that usually receives the guides.

But without a high side, I once asked Garrison at a meeting of the Theodore Gordon Flyfishers in Manhattan, *it's impossible to pick a face for the guides—how do you select it?*

There's still room for intuition, he smiled.

Garrison even winds his guides in opposite directions to equalize the twisting forces in his sections. His restlessly inventive mind developed a highly sophisticated method of finishing his rods, using tall cylindrical tanks filled with warm polyurethane of carefully controlled viscosity. His rod sections are dipped with the ferrules plugged and wrapped with tape, and are withdrawn by a motor-driven system that exposes a freshly dipped rod at a speed synchronized with the exact drying rate of the finish.

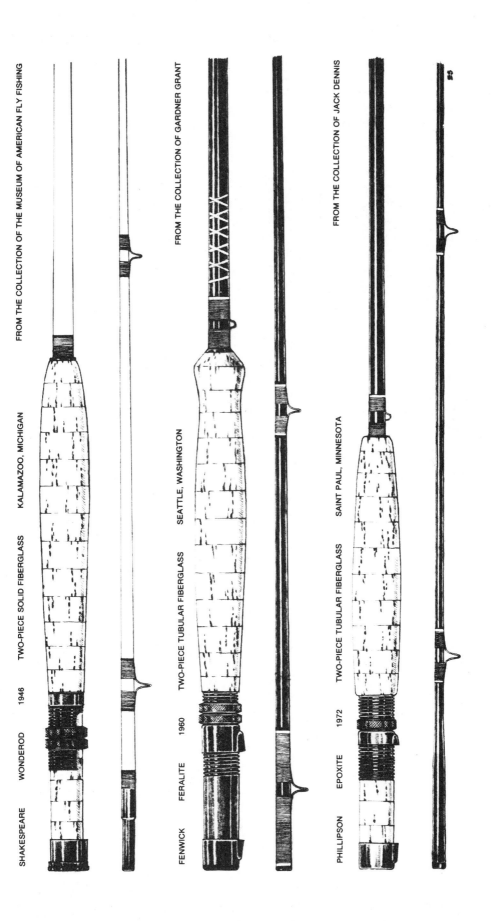

FROM THE COLLECTION OF THE MUSEUM OF AMERICAN FLY FISHING

SHAKESPEARE   WONDEROD   1946   TWO-PIECE SOLID FIBERGLASS   KALAMAZOO, MICHIGAN

FROM THE COLLECTION OF GARDNER GRANT

FENWICK   FERALITE   1960   TWO-PIECE TUBULAR FIBERGLASS   SEATTLE, WASHINGTON

FROM THE COLLECTION OF JACK DENNIS

PHILLIPSON   EPOXITE   1972   TWO-PIECE TUBULAR FIBERGLASS   SAINT PAUL, MINNESOTA

The tolerances in his rods are measured in terms of .001 or less, tolerances that give Garrison considerable pride.

Sparse Grey Hackle refused to believe that I could hold such tolerances with a hand planing-block, Garrison laughed with pleasure, *until he checked several sticks with a micrometer!*

The first rod that Garrison felt satisfied with was given to the late John Alden Knight, and it appears in his book *The Modern Angler* in a plate that demonstrates the open grip that Knight preferred in casting. It was fitted with the butt cap that Garrison still used, and a simple sliding ring machined with a knurled welt. His modern rods use a tapering band of knurled aluminum, a refinement that Garrison worked out so the ring would seat firmly on the reel and remain ninety degrees to the cork filler. It is typical of his concern for detail. The chocolate wrappings that replace the conventional grip check found on most rods are still found on Garrison rods forty years later, along with a circular fly keeper of unique design. Chocolate winding also secures the ferrules. The guides are wound in functional wraps of white silk that seem to vanish when the rod is finished. The Garrison grip is smoothly tapered to meet the bamboo, and its shape has changed from the cigar type of his first rods to a seemingly straight handle. The grips actually taper about one thirty-second of an inch from the reel seat to the thumb position, echoing the theories of Charles Ritz about grip design.

John Alden Knight did not mention Garrison specifically in *The Modern Angler*, but his chapter on rods contains these paragraphs about Garrison and his work in 1936:

> Until a few years ago, I was under the impression that rods vary in their personalities just as the men who use them and, for that reason, to copy the action of one rod when building another was not possible. Today I do not believe this is entirely true. A skilled workman, who knows bamboo and who has the mechanical ability to work accurately and consistently in thousandths of an inch, can so nearly duplicate rod action that the most sensitive hand could not possibly tell the difference between the original and the copy. I fully realize that this is heresy—a stone hurled at one of the ancient and accepted beliefs of angling.
>
> A rod has always been regarded by its owner as non-replaceable and therefore to be guarded with life itself. And then I saw the impossible accomplished. This particular rodmaker, an amateur who has recently turned professional, duplicated a rod perfectly for me.
>
> I sat in his workshop and watched him make it, noting the meticulous care with which he set his steel forms. His micrometer readings and measurements where made with the aid of a powerful magnifying glass, and checked and rechecked before the final cutting of the strips.
>
> When he had finished I tried both rods under actual fishing conditions and could not, I am positive, have been sure which was

mine had not the silk wrappings on one differed from those on the original.

An accident, you say? Not at all. This man does not depend on accidents in doing his work. Before starting work on a new rod, he takes the old one and calibrates it at short intervals throughout its entire length, taking three readings at each interval so as to include variations in all six sides of each section in his measurements. Next, using a method best known to himself, he charts the stresses in the rod and shows them graphically in a stress-curve or power-curve. Seeing such a stress-curve of your pet rod is much like looking at an x-ray picture of your interior workings—and, to the layman, such a stress-curve means about as much.

However, with this record to check against as he does his work, there is little chance for error. Variations in bamboo strength are allowed for in the cutting and corrected later. In some cases, it is necessary to rebuild some sections. But the main point is that the job can be done—not just once in a while but as often as desired.

Garrison gave his second rod to his friend Vernon Heiney, who had lost his job during the Depression, and was planning to spend the summer on the Beaverkill. Heiney was a skilled caster and fisherman who used Payne rods of more conventional tapers, and he was critical of the casting rhythms in his first Garrison. But later Heiney learned to appreciate his Garrison so much that he revised his entire philosophy of casting to suit its singular rhythms.

Perhaps the most unusual Garrison is a rod with all of its nodes removed horizontally with almost surgical precision, completely eliminating the weak points in its cane.

It took forever, Garrison admitted. *I wanted to see if I could really do it!*

But the ordinary Garrison rods are instruments of such beauty and perfection that any angler who appreciates fine workmanship cannot help but revere them. Most anglers are looking for his seven- and seven-and-a-half-foot rods today, avoiding the eight- and eight-and-a-half-foot designs that were popular when he began building rods professionally in 1933. It is unusual that Garrison even makes his own rod cases of aluminum tubing, machining their end caps of hard yellow brass, and sewing the poplin rod sacks himself. His lifetime production of less than a thousand rods might have been larger had he not insisted on making everything himself, from the reel fittings to those poplin bags. Perhaps the final touch on the typical Garrison rod is the accent of bright silk on one tip section, an identifying mark of his work. The winding is intended to permit the disciplined rotation of each tip.

Every time a man fishes a rod he should alternate its tips, Garrison believed. *That way each tip section ages and deforms equally over the years—and a rod will have the same feel with either tip.*

Garrison rods are based on the same compound-taper theory, although the tip calibrations of rods intended for sinking lines and big-water tactics are proportionately heavier. Some use heavy-wall cane and are stiffer. His long three-piece designs are unusually slow but powerful. Garrison actions work deeply into their butt tapers, bend less in their middle and upper calibrations, and conclude with a delicate tip.

Garrison has fierce partisans, and each has favorite Garrison designs. The most popular rods in his series included the following models:

MODEL	LENGTH (FEET)	WEIGHT (OUNCES)	LINE WEIGHT
193	$6^3/_4$	2	4
201	7	$2^1/_8$	4
201E	7	$2^1/_4$	4
202E	7	$2^1/_2$	5
204E	$7^1/_4$	$2^5/_8$	5
206	$7^1/_2$	$2^3/_4$	5
209	$7^1/_2$	3	6
209E	$7^3/_4$	$3^1/_8$	6
212	8	$3^1/_2$	5
212E	8	$3^3/_4$	6
212	$8^1/_2$	4	6
212E	$8^1/_2$	$4^1/_4$	7
215	$8^1/_2$	$4^3/_4$	8

Many fishermen dream of owning the delicate seven-foot, two-and-one-quarter-ounce design for a four-weight. Other disciples prefer the stiffer seven-foot taper designed for a DT5F. Garrison particularly liked the seven-foot three-inch rod weighing two and five eighths ounces. It cast beautifully with a DT5F the afternoon he let me fish his 204E at Henryville.

The seven-and-a-half-foot Garrisons usually weigh between two and three-quarters and three ounces, and like the odd seven-foot nine-inch design, they take DT5F and DT6F tapers. The eight-foot Garrisons weighing four ounces, and fishing six-weight lines, are the original 212E rods that essentially made Garrison's reputation shortly before the Second World War.

Before I acquired one of these smaller Garrisons, I had cast and fished several, including a handful of his own rods.

Others included the 212E that Philip Nash let me fish at the old Haase farm water on the Brodheads, on a pretty April afternoon with barn swallows taking *Ephemerella* flies under the footbridge. Other exquisite examples included the 212 that Martin Bovey let me fish on the headwaters of the Ruby in Montana, and the 206 he offered on the Firehole a few months before his death. Such rods are worth twenty-five and thirty times their original cost today, and I salute those anglers who possess such masterpieces.

My collection of Garrison's work has grown since *Trout* was first published in 1978.

The smallest is a Garrison 201E, measuring seven and a half feet. It weighs two and a half ounces and takes a DT4E. The lovely 206 is a seven-and-a-half-footer that also takes a four-weight line, although it probably took a DT5F when it was new. The 212 in my collection is a poetic eight-foot rod. It weighs three and a half ounces and takes a DT5F, and was perhaps the most popular Garrison in his later years. The smooth 212E at eight and a half feet was my first Garrison trout rod. It weighs four and one-eighth ounces and has the quality of a fine violin. It was originally rated for a DT7F, but it is one of the early Garrisons, and casts better with a six-weight today. These four Garrisons are virtually a matched set between seven and eight and a half feet, and they are a source of great pleasure.

With the approach of eighty, Garrison was still building a dozen rods each year. His clients included a circle of anglers like Otto von Kienbusch and the late Sparse Grey Hackle.

During recent months, I have seen mint Garrisons sold and auctioned at startling prices. Some have gone for thousands of dollars. Such prices are a tribute to the quality of Garrison's work, and the relatively small number of rods he made during his life. Garrison produced his rods at a trickle after 1973, lacking the vigor and intensity of his early years. His time was spent puttering, modifying, and perfecting his equipment and tools, perhaps reluctant to leave artifacts behind that did not meet his yardstick of absolute perfection. Our sporadic conversations suggested that he lamented a growing scarcity of proper fittings, first-quality specie cork, and select culms of the Chinese bamboo.

Garrison drove himself unsparingly, unwilling to accept anything less than his dream. His standards were so austere that he refused to work with bamboo during the humid summers along the Hudson. His loyal partisans are grateful for each rod that met his standards and left his basement workshop.

Everett Garrison died on February 8, 1975.

He was a genius, a rare mixture of technician and poet who made six-strip rods of yellow cane so perfectly that his sticks lacked a high side. The most experienced hands have rolled them in vain to determine their stiff and soft planes of bending. His skeletal reel seats and cork grips are almost ascetic, utterly lacking affectation or artifice. The dark chocolate silk at the ferrules and cork are a functional counterpoint for the transparent silk that secures the guides. The tapered reel band, its outer surfaces tightly knurled and finished, is a simple accent on a fly rod whose visual character is eloquent testimony to its simple craftsmanship.

Like other great artisans, Garrison insisted on almost monastic under-statement in his work, refusing extra weight or the embellishment of bright silk wrappings. It is simple and sure-handed. His rods speak eloquently through their functional perfection and performance, archetypes of their craft, and a Garrison has become the ultimate iconography.

Other makers are in his footsteps.

Hoagy Carmichael made a documentary film about Garrison and his work, and unwittingly became a disciple and apprentice. Garrison and Carmichael were collaborating on a book when the master craftsman died. The apprentice lovingly pulled together a half-completed manuscript and a tangle of notebooks, cassette recordings, and photographs. Carmichael plunged into completing the book, forgetting his filmmaking business entirely. It finally became *A Master's Guide to Building a Bamboo Fly Rod,* which Carmichael published in 1977.

The Garrison story does not end there.

Like many disciples, Carmichael had become so completely involved with his patron that he has started building the Garrison tapers himself. The perfectly seasoned bamboo culms and technical data and Garrison's tools are all in Carmichael's shop today.

The first rods are superbly executed, and Carmichael is still building the full Garrison list. It is exciting to think that the classic Garrison tapers still live, and that the following designs are still split and hand milled on his original planing blocks:

MODEL	LENGTH (FEET)	WEIGHT (OUNCES)	LINE WEIGHT
193	$6^3/_4$	2	4
201	7	$2^1/_8$	4
201E	7	$2^1/_4$	4
202E	7	$2^1/_2$	5
204E	$7^1/_4$	$2^5/_8$	5
206	$7^1/_2$	$2^3/_4$	5
209	$7^1/_2$	3	6
209E	$7^3/_4$	$3^1/_8$	6
212	8	$3^1/_2$	5
212E	8	$3^3/_4$	6
212	$8^1/_2$	4	6
212E	$8^1/_2$	$4^1/_4$	7
215	$8^1/_2$	$4^3/_4$	8

The Carmichael rods are excellent, and the Garrison book has created a full circle of other disciples. Leon Hansen is building Garrison tapers full time at his Plymouth shop in Michigan. His rods are entirely hand tempered, lovingly split and planed, and use Garrison-style fittings. Hansen rods are made in the following models with walnut seats:

MODEL	LENGTH (FEET)	WEIGHT (OUNCES)	LINE WEIGHT
91-3	$6^{1/2}$	2	3
91-4	$6^{1/2}$	$2^{1/4}$	4
92-4	7	$2^{1/2}$	4
93-4	$7^{1/2}$	$2^{3/4}$	4
93-5	$7^{1/2}$	3	5
$93^{1/2}$-4	$7^{3/4}$	$3^{1/8}$	4
$93^{1/2}$-5	$7^{3/4}$	$3^{1/4}$	5
94-5	8	$3^{1/2}$	5
94-6	8	$3^{5/8}$	6
$94^{1/2}$-4	$8^{1/4}$	$3^{1/2}$	4
$94^{1/2}$-7	$8^{1/4}$	$4^{1/4}$	7
95-8	$8^{1/2}$	$4^{3/4}$	8

Gary Souffker is another Garrison disciple, and I first cast samples of his rods at an exposition in Seattle. His early work echoed classic tapers like the 212 and 212E, in eight and eight and a half feet. Souffker lacked the old dense-wall cane in the Garrison stocks, so those first prototypes were a little slower than the original Garrison designs. His rods are now being split and planed at Klamath Falls, in southern Oregon.

Edwin Hartzell builds his Garrison tapers farther north at Portland, and I have seen a number at meetings of the Flyfishers of Oregon. His workmanship is excellent, befitting the discipline of a retired teacher who drives a beautifully restored MG roadster and wears rumpled Cheviot herringbones.

I'm obviously entranced by old things of solid worth, Hartzell confesses. *Helplessly!*

Hartzell first introduced himself at the Kaufman store in Tigard, on the southern periphery of Portland, and we talked almost an hour before he showed me his work. It was a raw winter day, mixing cold rain and wet snow, and when it softened slightly we walked outside to cast the rods. His craftsmanship was obvious, and his variations on the Garrison 212 and 212E tapers easily cast an entire double-taper line. Later I was asked about his work. *Anybody who loves antique cars and herringbone tweeds,* I laughed, *can't be all bad!*

Several rod builders have recently started to mill split-cane tapers in New England and the Catskills, where our American tradition flowered.

Maine has disciples of its pioneers, craftsmen like Leonard and Thomas and Crocker. William Taylor is both artist and rodmaker, with old roots in the brook-trout tradition.

Connecticut has E. F. Roberts, whose little shop at East Granby carries on in the tradition of Gillum and Sedgwick and the entire Edwards family. Marc Aroner is working in fine Tonkin cane at Conway, farther north in the mountains of New Hampshire.

Ron Kusse once operated the Leonard fishing store at Central Valley, an hour north from Times Square, at the threshold of the Catskills. Kusse started the Leonard shop when the company was still owned by the family of the old William Mills & Sons store in lower Manhattan. Ted Simroe was its foreman, and old Tom Bailey still crouched over his lathe, turning German-silver tubing and billets into ferrules and reel-seat fittings. Central Valley has been the home for H. L. Leonard & Company for more than a century, and famous rodmakers like Payne, Edwards, Thomas, Hawes, and Varney all passed their apprenticeships in that little Catskill town. Payne returned to build his own shop in nearby Highland Mills, and when Leonard closed its tackle store in 1979, Kusse started his own rodmaking in Washingtonville.

Kusse had long been moonlighting at the Leonard shop, building and restoring rods for himself. His apprenticeship was obviously both diligent and attentive, for his split-cane work is excellent. The following models are currently available:

MODEL	LENGTH (FEET)	WEIGHT (OUNCES)	LINE WEIGHT
KSC-260	6	$1\frac{1}{8}$	2
KSC-360	6	$1\frac{1}{4}$	3
KSC-366	$6\frac{1}{2}$	$1\frac{1}{2}$	3
KSC-466	$6\frac{1}{2}$	$1\frac{3}{4}$	4
KSC-370	7	$2\frac{1}{4}$	3
KSC-470	7	$2\frac{1}{2}$	4
KSC-570	7	$2\frac{3}{4}$	5
KSC-476	$7\frac{1}{2}$	3	4
KSC-576	$7\frac{1}{2}$	$3\frac{1}{4}$	5
KSC-676	$7\frac{1}{2}$	$3\frac{1}{2}$	6
KSC-580	8	$3\frac{3}{4}$	5
KSC-680	8	4	6

His own collecting of antique Leonards and Paynes has led Kusse to ferrules and fittings machined from German silver. Ferrule plugs are included too. The rod cases have brass caps that are polished and knurled, like the Thomas cases from Bangor fifty years ago. Kusse offers butter-yellow bamboo, brownstone finishes like the old Hunt pattern at Leonard, and a strongly flame-toned cane that echoes the work of Paul Young. Special grips are available, including smooth and gunstock-checkered hardwoods, along with special rod tapers. The reel-seat fillers are elegantly finished, with richly grained walnut and cherry and tiger maple.

It's the little things, Kusse insists, *that made the old makers memorable.*

John Weir leads a family rodmaking firm with a history reaching back across the continent, from Los Gatos in northern California to our gentle

Appalachians. Its craftsmen still produce hand-planed tapers, although most of its rods are milled on a unique machine that can mill six strips simultaneously. Weir rods echo the early Leonards, exquisitely crafted and pale, and the following models are available:

MODEL	LENGTH (FEET)	WEIGHT (OUNCES)	LINE WEIGHT
LM603	6	$1\frac{1}{4}$	2
D603	6	$1\frac{3}{4}$	3
D661	$6\frac{1}{2}$	$2\frac{3}{8}$	3
D701	7	3	4
HW701	7	$3\frac{3}{4}$	5
LM763	$7\frac{1}{2}$	$2\frac{1}{2}$	4
M601	$7\frac{1}{2}$	$3\frac{3}{4}$	5
D761	$7\frac{1}{2}$	$3\frac{7}{8}$	5
HM761	$7\frac{1}{2}$	$4\frac{1}{8}$	6
LM803	8	$3\frac{3}{4}$	4
M801	8	4	5
D801	8	$4\frac{1}{8}$	6
D861	$8\frac{1}{2}$	$4\frac{1}{2}$	7

Gus Nevros is a rare artisan who still works in both five- and six-strip cane. His honey-colored sticks are slightly tempered. Both skeletal and down-locking hardware are available, with beautifully grained rosewood fillers. Nevros makes these five-strip rods:

MODEL	LENGTH (FEET)	WEIGHT (OUNCES)	LINE WEIGHT
N714-5	$7\frac{1}{4}$	3	3
N823-5	$8\frac{3}{4}$	4	4

The following six-strip bamboo designs are also available from Nevros:

MODEL	LENGTH (FEET)	WEIGHT (OUNCES)	LINE WEIGHT
N612-6	$6\frac{1}{2}$	$2\frac{1}{4}$	4
N712-6	$7\frac{1}{2}$	$3\frac{1}{4}$	5
N800-6	8	$3\frac{3}{4}$	6
N814-6	$8\frac{1}{4}$	$3\frac{3}{4}$	5
N823-6	$8\frac{2}{3}$	5	8

Michael Montagne is another young rodmaker with a sense of probity and great skill. His work has obvious roots in the four-strip theories of construction found in the Quadrate rods built by William Edwards in eastern Connecticut. His cork is a mixture of the Ritz and Garrison theories of grip design, but his silk wrappings are utterly transparent, in obvious homage to Garrison alone. The dark chocolate wraps at the ferrules and cork are echoes of Garrison too.

But Montagne is a craftsman of startling originality, and not all of his creativity is obvious. Edwards built symmetrical four-strip rods. Montagne builds his sticks at irregular angles to create their widest flats, and the primary power fibers, perpendicular to the planes of casting.

His four-strip design offers twice the density of cane power fibers found in six-strip construction of the same section thickness.

Such four-strip sections offer more than mere power fibers. Montagne rods resist bending across the corners, concentrating deflection in the casting plane. Such performance tends to correct casting faults that twist other rods. Better distance and accuracy are also improved. Wave-linear behavior is crisp and clean. The ratio of power fibers to inert cane along the neutral bending axis is multiplied, even slightly higher than power fibers in the earlier Edwards Quadrates.

Montagne oven-tempers his Tonkin culms and splits them by hand. The nodes are hand dressed and polished with pressure and heat. The lateral strips are triangular, and the strips in the bending plane are trapezoids. Both rind and waste pith are removed by meticulous hand-work, using files and perfectly sharpened planes. The asymmetrical strips are unusual, but the ascetic dedication is typical of our most meticulous craftsmen in rodmakers like Howells and Dorsey.

The Montagne rods part sharply with tradition in their reel-seat designs. The rod shaft is neither cut nor modified in any way. Its structural integrity is not affected. The seat fittings are a reverse-locking type, but they are utterly unlike other reverse-locking designs. Montagne's concept is almost defiantly creative, and still more monastic than the work of Garrison. There is no reel-seat filler, and the locking device is a truncated cone that places the reel foot in flexure, levering it firmly in position. It is lighter than conventional designs, both original and austere.

This past September I was fishing with Kirk Gay at Six-Mile Lake in Alaska. Although I had seen a few Montagne rods, I had never cast or fished one until another angler offered me his nine-foot steelhead model for a weight-forward eight line. Its smooth power and control in the Tularik winds were surprising, and its elegance was obvious. Its visual character was startling to other anglers, but its creativity and probity were unmistakable.

Montagne is building fourteen models. His series includes the following designs:

MODEL	LENGTH (FEET)	WEIGHT (OUNCES)	LINE WEIGHT
MM-763	7½	2¼	3
MM-764	7½	2½	4
MM-765	7½	2¾	5
MM-804	8	3	4
MM-805	8	3¼	5
MM-806	8	3½	6
MM-866	8½	3¾	6
MM-867	8½	4¼	7
MM-868	8½	4¾	8
MM-869	8½	5½	9
MM-906	9	5	6
MM-907	9	5¾	7
MM-908	9	6	8
MM-909	9	6¼	9

Orvis continues its innovations too, and its new bamboo models include the C. F. Orvis 125 series. It is intended to celebrate Charles Orvis and the tackle company he founded 125 years earlier.

Orvis 125 rods are exquisitely crafted and finished. Standard cigar, full Wells, reversed half Wells, and tapered cigar grips are available. All fittings are machined from German silver. Silver ferrule plugs are included. Reel seats available include a butt cap and sliding-ring design, reverse-locking type, and a down-locking design with a butt cap. The reel-seat fillers are beautiful bird's-eye maple. The C. F. Orvis 125 series includes the following rods, in cases intended for engraving and presentation:

MODEL	LENGTH (FEET)	WEIGHT (OUNCES)	LINE WEIGHT
JM9657-62	6½	2⅛	4
JM9353-62	7	2½	3
JM9705-62	7	2¾	4
JM9701-62	7	3½	6
JM9759-62	7½	3¾	5
JM9751-62	7½	4⅛	6
JM9809-62	8	4	6
JM9808-62	8	4½	6
JM9801-62	8	4½	7

MICHAEL MONTAGNE   TROUT   1983   TWO-PIECE TONKIN   OLEMA, CALIFORNIA   FROM THE COLLECTION OF BARRY MOORE

HOWARD STEERE   C. F. ORVIS 125   1983   TWO-PIECE TONKIN   MANCHESTER, VERMONT   FROM THE COLLECTION OF LEIGH PERKINS

THOMAS DORSEY   PARADIGM   1983   TWO-PIECE TONKIN   TURNER'S FALLS, MASSACHUSETTS   FROM THE COLLECTION OF ERNEST SCHWIEBERT

Twenty-five years ago, the angling world was filled with omens and gloomy predictions of the death of bamboo rods. Such predictions were a little premature. American artisans are not only building rods that match the best work of history, but there are also more first-rate rodmakers than ever before.

Like our decoy carvers, the most celebrated American rodmakers are finally receiving just recognition for the eloquence of their skills.

Thomas & Thomas was recently honored by the White House when a specially fitted Sans Pareil was selected as a gift of state for Prime Minister John Malcolm Fraser of Australia. The White House also chose my two-volume *Trout* as a gift of state, with a hand-tipped frontispiece and presentation vellum page. Both gifts were given to the prime minister in a brief protocol ceremony at the White House.

The rod posed some interesting problems. Protocol officials at the White House had become aware that the Australian leader was an avid trout fisherman. It was determined after a series of telephone calls that only his government could help us specify a correct rod for his sport, and a comedy of errors resulted.

Thomas Dorsey told me the story. *We asked the Australians to tell us where the prime minister liked to fish,* he said. *It could tell us exactly what to build.*

The Australian diplomatic service supplied our protocol officers with a list of favorite rivers, and it was ultimately decided to build a nine-footer for eight-weights. Dorsey had started to work when something curious happened.

My telephone rang early.

It was a young protocol officer attached to the White House, and the call had a comic desperation. The teletypes at the Australian embassy had received a strange message over the weekend, and it had puzzled the duty officers. It was obviously concerned with the gift of state intended for the prime minister.

It was in some kind of code, the young official explained. *But the cryptographers didn't have a clue about its meaning—their people or ours.*

What was the message? I asked.

Pretty strange stuff, the protocol officer continued. *Something about DT6F or WF8F.*

I started to laugh and stopped.

What's funny? she asked.

Line sizes! I was chuckling now. *Those are line-weight and taper codes!*

Line weights and tapers?

That's right, I said. *The prime minister knows about your little project—and he's telling us exactly what rod he wants—the WF8F line will fit the rod you've already got in the works.*

No wonder it wasn't in the code books!

The Sans Pareil was elegantly conceived and finished. It was flawlessly milled with a satin finish and a swelled butt taper. Both its ferrules and its reel-seat hardware were German silver, and the reverse-locking system is a precisely mortised design. It is quite simply the most beautiful locking hardware in rodmaking today, and its fillers are a richly polished pigeon-grade walnut. It had both a butt plug and a beautifully made extension butt. There were chocolate wraps at the ferrules, with clear silk at its other fittings. Silver ferrule plugs were included. The rod case was of highly polished ebony, and capped at both ends with brass. The smaller chamber housed the fighting butt in its own poplin sack. The polished caps were delicately knurled, but the crowning touch was a gold seal from Tiffany's, like a freshly minted coin: the blue-and-gold seal of the president of the United States.

It was a great success! The White House reported. *The prime minister loved it—and the book was perfect too!*

EVERETT GARRISON

My collection now includes a matching nine-foot rod for eight-weight tapers. It lacks the delicate inscription from the president to the prime minister and the gold seal from Tiffany's.

Thomas Dorsey is building remarkable artifacts at his little shop in northern Massachusetts. His work combines the grace of a concert violin, with the utility and beauty of a fine British double gun. There is an exquisite two-piece Paradigm in my collection too, a slender eight-footer for a DT4F. Its poetry rivals the delicate Young Princess that I have treasured for many years. It is a richly beautiful thing.

But his skills refused to accept its perfection, and my most recent prize is a three-piece Sans Pareil that Dorsey built me for fishing the Henry's Fork.

It is eight and a half feet and weighs four and a half ounces. Its delicacy is poetry itself. It is fitted like the White House rod, although its calibrations are designed for a DT5F line. Its reverse-locking hardware is German silver, mortised into beautifully grained walnut. Its brass-capped case is slipped into a sailcloth sack, along with a tip case that is also fitted with brass hardware. It carries a delicate surprise: two matching tip sections for a DT4F, giving the Sans Pareil remarkable versatility.

The torch has clearly passed. Other generations of craftsmen are telling us unmistakably that our skills have not atrophied. Our best modern work has never been surpassed, in spite of our stories and sentimentality.

The iconography of the split-cane rod still has the magic to capture our hearts, with its unique mixture of poetry and power.

It is the spirit of bamboo.

2. The Evolution of the Fiberglass Rod

Istory tells us that it was the restless mind of Edward Ringwood Hewitt that started the evolution of the modern synthetic rod. His role is not surprising to anyone who remembers his tenacity and his constant experiments with the problems of trout fishing. Hewitt was cantankerous and aggressively unwilling to stop puttering in the workshop of his mind, and he always displayed a Menckenlike suspicion of past dogma. His habitual inconoclasm inexorably led Hewitt toward new developments and fresh ground, and the technology evolving on the threshold of the century soon flooded the world with a cornucopia of synthetic materials.

It was the Belgian chemist Hendrik Baekkelund who opened the floodgates with the first synthetic resin in 1909. His Bakelite was quickly utilized in a number of industrial products, including the fittings of rods and reels, and it is still found in the impregnating process used to temper and moisture-proof bamboo at both Orvis and Sharpe's.

More synthetics evolved in the decade following the First World War, including many resins, polyesters, and a remarkable new fiber called nylon. It was nylon that fascinated Hewitt, and he experimented in several ways with its elasticity and tensile strength. Since the molecular structure of bamboo is linear, Hewitt soon tried to utilize nylon strands in a fly rod. Hundreds of fine nylon strands were stretched around a tapered wooden core to simulate the linear anatomy of split cane. Hewitt bonded the fibers together with a plastic resin, wrapping its entire length with a continuous nylon filament. Hewitt apparently built several prototypes just before the Second World War, using a uniformly tapered mandrel.

Hewitt soon abandoned his theories. The nylon proved far too elastic under the wave-linear stresses of fly casting; its fibers stretched too readily and failed to recover from major dynamic loads, and its flexing tended to fight with the resin bonds. The resins fractured and the rods failed quickly. However, Hewitt remained convinced that the remarkable new synthetic fibers and resins would ultimately provide fishermen with several exotic new rod materials.

History is still proving him right.

Fiberglass was the first synthetic fiber to provide the casting performance Hewitt had predicted. It was woven into a fabric of glass with remarkable properties, and many corporations and small manufacturers were soon experimenting with its potential.

It was Doctor Arthur Howald who built the first fiberglass fly rod in 1944. Howald was engaged in fiberglass research, and when he smashed the tip section of a favorite cane rod on a Michigan trout stream it was logical to attempt a replacement in glass. Split bamboo was virtually impossible to obtain during the war years. Howald was thoroughly versed in both plastics and fiberglass manufacturing processes, and he constructed a mold matching the size and taper of his broken tip. Howald shaped a wooden core and layered it with fiberglass, bonding both the fibers and the mandrel core together. Although his tip did not match the performance of his split-cane rod, and it looked milk-colored and strange in its casting oscillations, Howald happily fished it during the war years.

Shakespeare became interested in fiberglass rod construction the following year, and started a series of experiments with the new material. The first rods were introduced at the Chicago Coliseum in 1946, and the white Shakespeare Wonder rods were a sensation in a country that had wet-nursed its aging bamboo rods through the entire Second World War. The fiberglass butts were too stiff and the tips were mushy, although glass unmistakably offered some unique properties and the manufacturer was eager to exploit them. The material was both light and remarkably strong. It was capable of absorbing abuse and neglect that would ruin a bamboo rod, and fiberglass rods required virtually no maintenance. Fiberglass rods seldom take a twist or set, and moisture and temperature that could irreparably damage cane have almost no effect on the new rods. Oxidation and mildew were no longer a problem. Stress fatigue and denigration from exposure to light will gradually take its toll of fiberglass construction, but structural fatigue is more serious in both metal and bamboo. Glass is both more resilient and stronger than cane, measured ounce for ounce, but it can also fracture under a sharp blow or extreme casting load. Once I saw one smashed when an angler lost a big rainbow, struck the water in a mixture of anger and despair, and broke the tip section of his fiberglass rod.

Shakespeare soon abandoned the Howald wooden-core construction, and its first production rods were solid fiberglass designs. Shakespeare still controls many basic patents on fiberglass construction methods, for both tubular and solid blanks. Although modern fiberglass rods cost far less than fine split-cane rods even in the custom-modified designs made by superb fiberglass artisans like Neumann and Cummings and Peak, it should be remembered that the first Shakespeare fly rods were just as expensive as a vintage Leonard or Payne when they were introduced.

Conolon first developed the tubular fiberglass designs that now dominate modern rod production, forming the fiberglass cloth around a steel mandrel that is removed after curing. Shakespeare and Heddon soon adopted tubular construction. The fiberglass revolution quickly gathered momentum, and as the manufacturers worked out the details of production, their costs plummeted until glass dominated the tackle market. Workable glass rods are available at less than ten percent of the price a handmade Garrison commands, and even the most expensive fiberglass makers charge half the price of the Orvis Battenkill. More than three million rods are sold annually in the United States, employing more than half a million pounds of fiberglass, and less than two percent of total sales are bamboo.

The physical properties and character of any rod section are rooted in the fishing for which it is intended, the size of both the fish and the flies required, the character of the water, and the personal skills and philosophy of the fisherman. All blanks must provide an equilibrium between strength and resilience under the stresses of bending. Such performance must also spring from a relatively light tubular blank, with elastic properties that provide a rapid recovery from dynamic loads. The material should also have a pleasing visual character. Fiberglass offers these several properties to a remarkable degree, and provides them at relatively low cost.

Fiberglass construction aligns the fibers in optimal relationship to the longitudinal axis of the blank. Such alignment provides the performance under flexing stress. Blank diameters and wall densities provide recovery from bending, while the lateral fibers resist deformation of the tubular cross section. Fiberglass cloth and the plastic resins used to form it into finished rod blanks can provide relatively light weight, durability and strength, controlled calibrations and action, and reasonable esthetic character.

Solid fiberglass blanks were the first type that became available after the Second World War. Such blanks are drawn through a resin bath and then formed in a die and curing tube. The solid blanks are trimmed to length and ground to the required tapers. All the fiberglass strands lie parallel to the axis of the rod, providing good bending behavior, crush resistance, and strength. However, the most rudimentary knowledge of materials under bending stresses tells us that the core fibers add little or nothing to casting performance. Such production techniques are surprisingly simple, the materials and equipment are relatively inexpensive, and low-priced rods are possible. Performance is generally sluggish and poor, and such rods are seldom suitable for fly-rod-casting dynamics.

The Howell process is a technique in which fiberglass yarn is saturated with a polyester resin. The saturated fibers are then formed over a removable mandrel, with a spiral of cellophane tape to shape and control the wall thickness. The tape is stripped free once the resins have hardened and cured. The optimal performance of such blanks depends on the use of polyester resins that have been specially developed for rods. Color is mixed into the resin, too. The core fibers are wrapped in a controlled spiral, providing tubular resistance to deformation under bending stresses. The surface cloth is applied to align its fibers longitudinally where optimal flexing performance is needed. Fine tip sections are not possible with tubular construction, since the inside diameters are too small for the mandrel method of construction. Such tips are usually of compound design, with solid tip calibrations and tubular construction in the middle and butt diameters. Rod sections fabricated with the Howell patent method are relatively durable and perform well in most fishing situations. Although considerably lighter than comparable solid blanks, tubular rods of this type are heavier than the tubular designs used in most fiberglass fly rods. However, since production of blanks with the Howell patent utilizes relatively inexpensive fiberglass and resins, and mass production techniques with little handwork are possible, such construction results in relatively inexpensive rods.

The best fiberglass rods are built using a specially woven cloth designed for fishing-rod performance. The rod fabric is a crow-foot weave with semi-unidirectional glass fibers. Such a weave is intended to maintain a large proportion of fiberglass filaments in the axial alignment, and these longitudinal fibers are positioned and held relatively straight along the axis of the rod section, with widely spaced cross weaves. Two cloth weights are commonly employed. The heavier type has ten axial fibers for each cross weave, and the lighter fabric is woven with a six-to-one ratio. These cloth layers are cut in trapezoidal patterns precisely worked out to control wall thickness and provide the desired casting performance.

When the fabric is patterned and cut for a rod section, the fiber direction is laid parallel to its axis, providing the longitudinal alignment of the fiberglass. The cross weaves lie circumferentially around the mandrel, aligning the axial fibers properly and providing lateral tube strength, and resisting the elliptical deformation of the glass under heavy casting loads. The stabilizing effects of these cross fibers are critical to the proper strength and casting power and action of any rod taper.

Several techniques of thermal curing have evolved. Primitive fiberglass rods were made with plasticized nylon phenolic resins. Its performance was excellent, but its coloring caused problems. Such phenolics darken with age, and these problems have been solved with newer epoxy and polyester resins that have replaced the phenolics. Some rods are finished with other colors, and still use the older phenolics. However, most modern fiberglass blanks have their color pigments mixed into their resins. Both polyester and epoxy resins are remarkably durable, and their coloring is relatively stable. The fabric method of tubular rod construction will permit an unlimited spectrum of rod tapers, depending on the cloth patterns and wall densities used, and their ultimate costs are a function of design complexity and metal fittings.

The early glass rods were relatively poor, since the manufacturers had not learned to handle the new material and shape it into workable fibers. Most early tapers were also the prisoners of the Hewitt influence that had advocated rather fast actions that could handle the rapier flick-flick rhythms Hewitt insisted were necessary to dry the hackles of the dry fly. Hewitt himself abandoned such fast-action tapers in his middle years, but his influence had a persuasive inertia. Basic fiberglass rod actions have evolved in terms of four primary designs, although the rigidity of a thin-walled tube of relatively large diameter is ideally suited to the Hewitt fast-butt theology. Extra-fast rods display their most dramatic curvature in the upper quarter of the rod tapers. Their quick rhythms are suited to a series of brisk false casts and are easily mastered by fishermen with marginal casting skills, which made them popular with both rodmakers and a large percentage of their customers. However, they will not fish ultrafine tippets well or accommodate extremely long casts except in the hands of a skilled power caster, and they are tiring to use. Fast-action rods do most of their bending in the upper third, and with maximum curvature confined to the upper two-thirds of the taper, a fly rod has a moderate fiberglass action. Slow-action rods that bend progressively from the tip into the handle are most desirable for trout fishing, since delicacy is more important than the raw butt power needed to break a tarpon. Such actions have long been the hallmark of the finest modern split-cane rods, particularly in the radical tapers of American builders like Garrison and Young—and in the Pezon & Michel parabolics worked out by the remarkable Charles Ritz.

Such refinements have been slow in coming in most fiberglass production rods, although considerable improvement has occurred in the past dozen years. The compound tapers found in the best modern bamboo, with their extremely fine tips and steep calibrations to a relatively muscular midsection and a flat taper flexing well into the handle from the butt guide, were first explored by craftsmen like Young and Garrison. Perhaps the most radical experiments came from the cane-littered workshop of Young, although some of the finest unquestionably were split and hand-planed by Garrison. Such compound tapers will fish a finer tippet and cast longer with greater delicacy and less effort, ounce for ounce, than any other fly rods ever built. Fiberglass production rods are much lighter than comparable bamboo tapers, but ultralight tippets and distance with both delicacy and precision are still a little beyond their technology. Perhaps the fiberglass rods of artisans like Neumann, Cummings, and Peak, who modify the wall thicknesses by hand after culling through first-grade blanks carefully, are the best examples of glass construction approaching the unique qualities present in a really fine bamboo rod. Most knowledgeable fiberglass partisans admit that glass has yet to equal the violinlike excellence of superb split-cane rods, and some major fiberglass manufacturers even admit they are still trying.

Bamboo is a pretty remarkable material, Jim Green of Fenwick observed at Sun Valley last summer, *and trying to match its unique qualities in glass can only increase your respect for cane.*

Fly-rod tapers are largely determined in the problems associated with the stresses and considerations of casting. Trout-fishing considerations seldom equal the fish-playing loads encountered in salt water, where the raw strength of billfish and tarpon becomes as important as the dynamics of fly casting. Few fiberglass rods are now manufactured with anything but medium actions, and the clublike tapers that were common in the early years have mercifully disappeared. The better fiberglass rods are approaching the smooth, progressive tapers that work well down the butt sections and into the grip itself. Such semiparabolic actions have some demanding rhythms, and the choice between them and more conventional tapers really depends on the skills and preferences of each fisherman.

The full spectrum of these factors is involved in the calibrations and design tapers of modern fiberglass rods. The skilled rod designer who knows fiberglass understands that the amount of filaments at any particular calibration in a blank will determine the casting performance and character of the finished rod. The density of glass fibers is controlled by varying the cloth pattern that is cut from a roll of fiberglass at the genesis of each fly rod. The fabric pattern itself is tapered, although it does not resemble a finished rod. Typical patterns are trapezoidal in shape, looking more like a classic leg-of-mutton gun case. The butt dimension of the cloth pattern is typically much wider than the tip fabric, and the diagonal between the two varies widely. Variations in casting performance are achieved by increasing or decreasing the width of the cloth taper along its diagonal chord.

Since increasing the fiber count at any point will stiffen the rod action there, and decreasing the number of glass fibers results in increased flexibility under stress, an almost infinite number of rod actions are possible with minor changes in the cloth pattern.

Hollow blanks are fabricated by rolling the cloth pattern around a tapered mandrel. Design of the mandrel is important, and when a slender mandrel is used the wall thickness of the blank is relatively heavy. Using the same cloth pattern and a larger mandrel will obviously produce a larger diameter blank with slightly thinner wall thicknesses. However, when identical patterns are used, both blanks will have identical weights, but the thinner wall rod will have much greater power. The reason is the increased distance from the axis of the blank to its outer walls. Therefore both mandrel and cloth pattern are primary factors in the action of a fiberglass fly rod, and an equilibrium between mandrel diameter and pattern design is necessary to produce an optimal fiberglass rod.

Such thin-walled blanks are superior to a thick-walled section of equal weight and a smaller diameter, although there are limits to their advantages. Too much butt diameter is clumsy-looking and offers unacceptable wind resistance in casting. Large thin-walled blanks are also difficult and expensive to manufacture.

Once a new taper has been successfully field-tested, it is placed in production. Its woven fiberglass fabric is impregnated with resin and passed through rollers to remove the excess. The glass cloth is then oven-dried to evaporate the solvents and dry the resins until they are slightly tacky. The impregnated fabric is then rolled again with a sheet of polyethylene to separate the layers. Most manufacturers unroll the impregnated cloth later, cut sections slightly larger than the patterns, and stack them in layers on a pattern-cutting table with the longitudinal fibers aligned with the axis of the blank. The size of the stack is determined by the number required in an economical production run. Heavy metal templates are laid on the stacked sheets and a single pattern-cut prepares a number of rods simultaneously. Metal templates are necessary both because scoring the cloth along their contours is easier and because their weight holds the several layers firmly, duplicating the pattern with precision.

Heat attaches the straight edge of the prepared pattern to its tapered mandrel, and it is tightly rolled into a tapered tube. Many industrial methods are used, but perhaps the best is rolling the prepared mandrel between two heated platens under controlled pressures. The precision of this process is absolutely critical in the production of a high-quality glass rod. The machinery must be quite precise to maintain uniform pressure and control along the entire length of the mandrel while the pattern is being rolled. The laminating material is important, too, and its wall density is the key to a quality glass blank. Really dense glass walls are almost totally free of porosity, and such integrity of lamination is critical in both lightness and strength. Making a dense laminate is impossible without inside and outside molding pressures. Obviously, the internal mold is provided by the mandrel, while the external molding pressures are accomplished by several methods. Cellophane film wrapped under tension is commonly used, but a tightly wrapped polyester or fleuroplastic film is also employed by some manufacturers. Silicone rubber tubing molded around the freshly wrapped fiberglass cloth is a third method. Whatever the method, the external pressures working on the laminates must be applied with a precisely controlled uniform tension. The quality of the laminate depends on the uniformity of the tensile wrapping, and its pressures accomplish two things: its primary effect is compression of the laminates during its original spiralling application, and its secondary effect is the increased pressure applied when it shrinks in the curing cycle.

Once the laminate is pressure-wrapped in cellophane or some other synthetic film, it is ready for the final curing of its resins. Final curing of the wrapped mandrel occurs when it is hung in a vertical oven and subjected to from 300 to 350 degrees, depending on the specific resin used, for thirty minutes to an hour. The thermal stresses force the resins to flow with a lowered viscosity, while the cellophane film simultaneously shrinks and applies great pressure to the laminate of fiberglass cloth and resins. During the proper curing period the gelatinous resin hardens and cures.

When curing is complete, the mandrel core is extracted from the freshly hardened fiberglass blank. Extraction is usually accomplished with a power ram and metal-plate die. The die consists of a hole precisely drilled

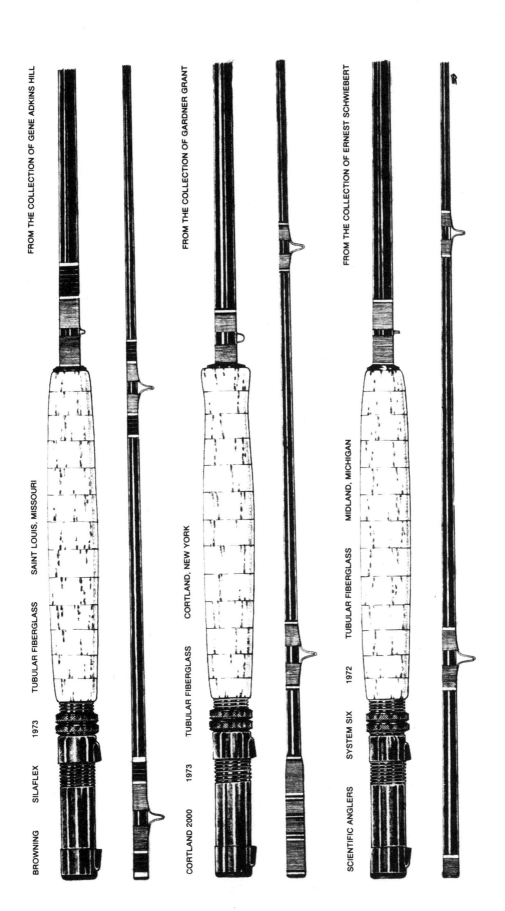

BROWNING   SILAFLEX   1973   TUBULAR FIBERGLASS   SAINT LOUIS, MISSOURI   FROM THE COLLECTION OF GENE ADKINS HILL

CORTLAND 2000   1973   TUBULAR FIBERGLASS   CORTLAND, NEW YORK   FROM THE COLLECTION OF GARDNER GRANT

SCIENTIFIC ANGLERS   SYSTEM SIX   1972   TUBULAR FIBERGLASS   MIDLAND, MICHIGAN   FROM THE COLLECTION OF ERNEST SCHWIEBERT

to receive the mandrel butt, but not large enough to accept the freshly cured blank. The power ram strips the mandrel from the tubular blank, and it is cleaned and prepared to receive another cloth pattern.

The freshly cured blank is complete at this stage of fabrication, except for stripping the cellophane and finishing. The cellophane wrappings are removed with abrasive brushes, tumbling, conventional cutting and stripping, and high-pressure steam. With the film stripped and removed, the resin still carries the fingerprints of its spiral wraps. Some rodmakers leave these spiral wrapping patterns in the resin surfaces of the blank, perhaps liking their appearance, although they play no role in the performance of the finished rod. Other manufacturers polish their blanks to a satin finish, and a final finish will be applied later. Custom builders often polish the blanks at this point, not only to remove the resin spirals, but also to modify wall thickness and action.

The finish coating applied when the blank is completed is intended to protect the rod. It is usually a modern synthetic finish that improves both the durability and appearance of the fiberglass. Tough synthetics like epoxy, acrylics, and polyurethanes protect the glass from moisture, scratches, mars, solvents, and structural denigration from the ultraviolet components of sunlight. Such finishes also protect the material from temperature extremes, and must be applied in a series of thin coatings that will not dampen the rod's action and make it feel sluggish. The several coats are separately applied and buffed until the finish is hard and glasslike. The fiberglass blank is then finished and ready for assembly.

Mounting the ferrules that join the rod sections together is usually the first step of assembly, and most fiberglass rods were originally fitted with conventional metal ferrules. Chrome-plated brass is common because it is easily worked and relatively inexpensive. Anodized aluminum ferrules are also used extensively, because they are also easily fabricated and much lighter than the conventional chrome-plated brass. However, both aluminum and brass wear easily and their factory fit is short-lived. Some manufacturers have added a rubber or nylon gasket to their male ferrules to extend the life span of brass and aluminum stock. The custom builders use nickel-silver ferrules, like the traditional makers of fine split-cane rods, because they work and machine beautifully. The material is relatively expensive, but it holds its tolerances for many years, popping melodically like a bottle of fine wine.

However, several manufacturers have introduced variations of fiberglass ferrules in recent years. These ferrules have the advantage of a more flexible transfer of power than a metal ferrule can supply. The sleeve-type ferrule is fabricated by seating a larger sleeve of fiberglass over the rod tip and fitting the butt section inside that sleeve. Browning has added the wrinkle of a sleeve-type ferrule designed to wear continually into a deeper fit across the life of the rod. The spigot-type glass ferrule involves a solid fiberglass plug permanently seated into the butt section, and the hollow tip section is fitted tightly down over the plug. It provides the most secure fit of any fiberglass ferrule type, and it is more flexible than any metal design, although it is a little heavier than the sleeve-type joint. Perhaps the most unusual fiberglass ferrule is the Feralite design patented by Fenwick in 1962, in which the hollow tip section slides down over the butt. The female tubular fit is reinforced with a guide position directly over its stress zone, and the Feralite design is unquestionably the lightest joint available on modern glass production rods.

Assembly begins with mounting the ferrules. Mass production work usually supplies the blanks with an extra tab of fiberglass at the point where the ferrule will be seated. The blank is trimmed empirically in the shop and the glass is polished slightly to the proper fit. Most builders use a hot-melt cement to mount the ferrules on the blanks, permitting minor adjustments to achieve a straight fit that perfectly aligns the rod sections.

Once the ferrules are properly mounted, the reel fittings and grips follow. Some makers use preshaped cork grips, although the best fiberglass rods use the same specie-cork rings that fine bamboo craftsmen have used since the years that Halford reigned on the Houghton water of the Test and Gordon lived like a hermit on the Neversink. These rings are seated and glued separately and are shaped on a lathe after they are mounted on the butt section.

Cheap guides too widely spaced were too often a commonplace flaw in the early fiberglass rods. The same fine carboloy and stainless guides used on first-rate cane rods are used on the better fiberglass models these days. Too many guides create shooting friction in casting, while too few guides permit the line to slap the rod and generate even greater friction. First-rate cane rods have at least one snake guide per overall foot of length, plus the butt guide, to distribute casting loads properly. Since glass is less fragile, fewer guides are needed. The guides are mounted with thread wrappings in essentially the same fashion on both bamboo and fiberglass rods, although some fiberglass rodmakers have regrettably started to use garish wrappings of gold or silver mylar tapes—and even some of the best fiberglass rods are still guilty of tastelessly excessive ornamentation of their products.

The windings are usually fixed with a color preservative and finished with a protective coat of lacquer, varnish, or synthetic material. Cummings covers only the windings of his rods, leaving the rest in the matte finish of his hand-rubbed blanks. Lacquers are commonly used because they are cheap and provide a high lustre. However, most custom fiberglass rods are fully protected with a fine spar varnish. Modern rodmakers also have many other finishes available, including epoxies, polyurethanes, and various acrylics. These materials are infinitely more waterproof and wear-resistant than the finest varnish. Polyurethanes are readily available and are remarkably durable, although they are relatively difficult to apply and dry quite slowly. Modern epoxies are also durable when mixed with components that absorb ultraviolet light. Acrylics are usually available in colors, and are not readily available in clear solutions, since their primary market lies in automobile finishes.

Many anglers are still a little uncertain about the immutable differences between split bamboo and fiberglass.

Cane is just a rich man's affectation, is a common observation on our trout water these days. *Glass is just as good for anybody!*

There is some truth in their arguments. Certainly the fiberglass revolution has virtually eliminated the cheap and moderately priced cane rods that once flooded the market, particularly the imports of poor Japanese bamboo. Such rods deserved the extinction they suffered with the perfection of fiberglass designs, and only the moderately expensive and expensive bamboo makers have survived. The best fiberglass rods are lighter, more durable, and considerably less expensive than our modern split-cane rods.

The finest glass rods are better than many moderately expensive bamboo models, although they have yet to match the poetry of the best split-cane craftsmen. There has never been a question of making a glass rod that could equal the performance of first-rate cane since fiberglass is a medium with utterly different properties. Our best fiberglass craftsmen have finally begun to forget trying for a bamboo facsimile and have started to search for topologies of wall thickness and rod tapers true to the unique character of glass itself.

My experience with fiberglass rods over the past thirty-odd years has pinpointed an intriguing mixture of virtues and faults in the casting performance of glass. Bending stresses result in virtually no dimensional distortions in split-cane rods, except for the obvious rhythms of tension and compression that occur in its cellular structure. The more casting stress imposed on a bamboo section, the more power it generates toward recovery from that stress. Bamboo will continue to accept increasing loads and gather power progressively until it reaches its stress limits and shatters. Tubular glass behaves quite differently. Bending action in any tube tends to make its cross section elliptical, and when the bending-plane axis of the oval is exaggerated enough, the tube cannot accept the load. Bending an ordinary drinking straw will demonstrate the deformation of a tube under such stress. Tubular glass starts to accumulate power as quickly as its loading begins, but when the casting loads deform it too radically, it fails to gather power and accommodate those loads. Any caster skilled enough to handle a line longer than the loading capacity of his glass rod has felt it refuse such casting stresses, although its resiliency and strength keep it from fracturing—and it will handle such distances better with slightly reduced line velocity and loading. Such variables are the behavior differences between tubular and solid construction in any material, but their differences in recovery from stress are related to the physical properties of bamboo and fiberglass themselves.

Recovery from stress is simply the speed and manner in which a bent material recovers its original shape. It is relatively easy to demonstrate with a fly rod. The rod should be held out horizontally with a rigid wrist and stressed downward with a sharp stroke. Its tip section will snap toward the floor and recover swiftly, rising slightly above the horizontal before it returns to rest. The recovery rates of bamboo and glass are different. The finest cane rods recover a little more slowly, but their recovery is precise, and their oscillations end more quickly. Their behavior stems from their longer cell fibers, while glass rods have much shorter fibers and recover from flexure more quickly.

Strangely, the resilience and recovery of fiberglass under the loads of casting is so good that it becomes a disadvantage. The problems are readily apparent with the same stress-recovery demonstration: holding the rod horizontally and stressing it sharply downward. The tip section will recover rapidly, snapping back above its original plane, and it will continue to oscillate above and below the horizontal before it stops. Such behavior under stress is simply implicit in the character of fiberglass.

Skilled casters can partially compensate for this weakness, but it unquestionably affects their performance. Casting really well is difficult with fiberglass, and it is no accident that the finest fly casters invariably prefer bamboo. This preference lies partially in the willingness of split cane to accept the loading limits of the caster's full strength and timing and skills. Some of the ability of bamboo rods to accommodate stress and deliver power lies in their sharp recovery from stress, with less vertical oscillation in the tip section. Such oscillation results in line slap against the guides and the rod itself, causing friction that can kill the precision and velocity of a really long cast. Oscillation also tends to pull the line back, short of its full distance. Accuracy and distance both suffer, and delicacy is almost impossible in the lightest glass tapers.

Although their impacts are perhaps less obvious, ordinary fishermen are clearly affected by these problems; and because of his limited fishing time and practice a less skilled caster finds it difficult to compensate for them. Timing and accuracy are just a little more difficult to master. The methods of fiberglass fabrication also result in slightly thicker tip calibrations, which mean more power is required to drive the tip through the atmospheric resistance to the completion of the cast. Such extra power does not readily lend itself to subtle delivery of either line or fly, although it will throw a stylishly tight casting loop, and heavier tip diameters in a fiberglass taper are ill-suited to cobweb-fine tippets. The radical compound tapers found in the parabolic designs of craftsmen like Young and Garrison and Payne, with their steep final calibrations to a delicate hooking tip, are almost impossible in the fabrication of glass.

Fiberglass has three disadvantages for casting and fishing in modern terms: its tubular rod sections deform and become oval-shaped under ultimate casting loads; it tends to oscillate too much in its recovery from casting stress; and its fabrication techniques are not suited to really fine-tip diameters. Obviously, there are excellent fiberglass rods of superb performance and cheap products that fish poorly. The best quality blanks and tapers minimize the marginal properties of tubular glass construction, but these inherent physical problems exist.

However, this does not mean that a modern fisherman must confine himself to split-cane rods. Their cost alone places them beyond the reach of most anglers, while the price of a fine fiberglass rod is moderate. Glass requires less pampering and care, and is ideally suited to the beginner or occasional fisherman. It can also survive excessive moisture and temperature extremes, making it a good choice in some climates. It is much lighter than a comparable bamboo rod. Its weight makes a long rod less tiring to use, which can be important to children or women, since rod length is advantageous in learning to cast. Glass rods can combine both lightness and length. Such properties are also important where distance and continual casting are important—and even an expert fisherman can appreciate a fiberglass rod after a long day, simply because it fatigues him less.

It is virtually impossible to purchase a bamboo rod of poor quality cane if it has been produced in the United States, since our best rodmakers never exhausted their seasoned stocks, although the end was in sight for some companies. However, it is possible to purchase an inferior fiberglass rod. Tubular blanks come from many manufacturers and vary surprisingly in quality. There are many factors involved. Quality of fabrication, diameter, wall thickness, fiber alignment and calibration, type of weave, and the character of the taper are equally important. Perhaps the best advice lies in purchasing a glass rod from the best manufacturers.

The angler who fishes often and fishes difficult or demanding water should probably choose bamboo. Its performance will improve both his pleasure and his sport. It will give him great pride of ownership. Since it will last many years with reasonable care, it is not really expensive. But the man who fishes seldom and merely wants a rod available from time to time does not need a really first-rate piece of equipment. Spare rods and camp rods for guests fall into this category. It is doubtful that the best fiberglass rods are really necessary for such purposes. The cost and choice of a fly rod, in either fiberglass or cane, should be based on the skills that a fisherman already has or hopes to acquire. If his aspirations include selective trout on hard-fished waters, he must find a way to afford the finest possible rod.

There are several fine manufacturers who produce good factory-built rods of fiberglass, and there are also several artisans who modify factory blanks and add more expensive reel seats and fittings than are commonly found with glass. Several manufacturers of bamboo rods also assemble first-rate glass blanks with the fittings normally found on their more expensive split-cane products.

Fenwick was founded at Seattle in 1954, and its leadership in the fiberglass field dates to the arrival of Jim Green as its technical director six year later. Green is one of the finest fly casters in the world, and his work has led to several technical innovations. Fenwick pioneered the first fiberglass ferrules in 1962, and Green kept on experimenting with the fiberglass tapers and construction methods. He has continued to refine his Feralite ferrules, until their present design is an unusual combination of lightness and strength. Most ferrule connections consist of a single rod shaft

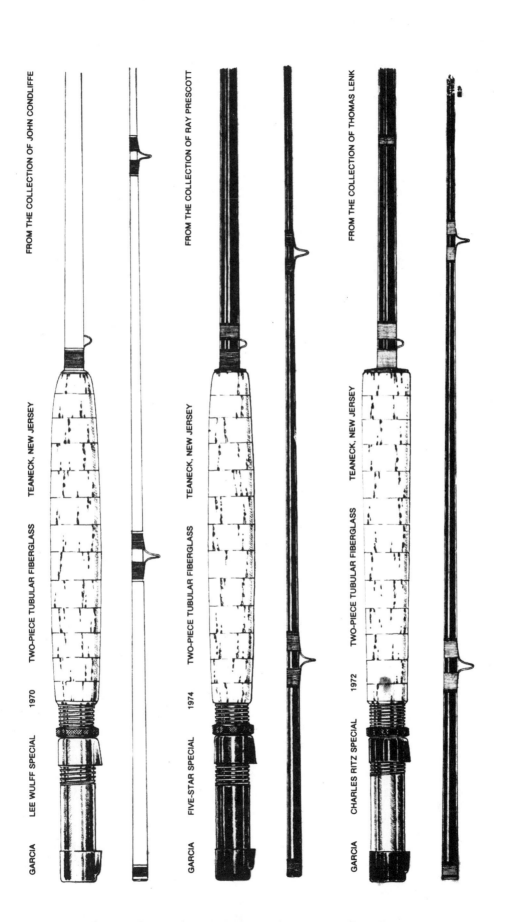

FROM THE COLLECTION OF JOHN CONDLIFFE

GARCIA   LEE WULFF SPECIAL   1970   TWO-PIECE TUBULAR FIBERGLASS   TEANECK, NEW JERSEY

FROM THE COLLECTION OF RAY PRESCOTT

GARCIA   FIVE-STAR SPECIAL   1974   TWO-PIECE TUBULAR FIBERGLASS   TEANECK, NEW JERSEY

FROM THE COLLECTION OF THOMAS LENK

GARCIA   CHARLES RITZ SPECIAL   1972   TWO-PIECE TUBULAR FIBERGLASS   TEANECK, NEW JERSEY

cut in two or three sections and joined together, but the Fenwick patent involves two separate rod blanks. The tip section has a hollow butt reinforced with a firmly seated guide, and the butt section has a tip reinforced with a solid glass plug. The design had some early problems, since it involved discontinuous rod tapers, and many expert casters felt it had some stress problems of power transfer. Fenwick clearly recognized the problem and acquired one of the major fiberglass blank manufacturers in 1969, hoping to control the discontinuous tapers by making the glass rod blanks themselves in Seattle.

High-pressure lamination and experimental mandrels have since produced fly rods that have successfully married the large hollow tip sections to the solid small-diameter butt. Although their tubular diameters are radically different, their performance under casting loads has now achieved good continuity of stress transfer. High-quality fiberglass and control of wall thicknesses have achieved this breakthrough. Fenwick achieves such high-density lamination that the glass fibers become almost homogeneous, leaving a smoothly lustrous finish that almost glows in bright sunlight and requires no opaque finish to conceal the blemishes and flaws so often found in fiberglass.

The fittings are typical of the best production glass rods. Anodized reel seats with a fixed butt cap, movable hood, and tightening rings are made of workable aluminum alloys. The guides are chromium-plated steel, and the nylon wrappings are a rich chocolate that closely matches the reddish brown translucency of the rod itself. Trim accents of black and white nylon finish the wrappings, and the rods and wrappings are protected with three hand-applied coats of clear epoxy. The understated appearance of the Fenwicks is perhaps marred slightly by the coarse nylon cross-wrappings on the lower butt and a trademark that is too large, but their performance is excellent. Their prices are in the medium range for good fiberglass production rods, and Fenwick rods have many partisans, particularly among the skilled fly casters along the Pacific Coast. There are several fine trout-size models.

Fenwick makes six fly rods for relatively delicate presentation and five-weight lines. The FF535 and FF605 weigh less than two ounces, are fitted with skeleton reel seats and sliding bands, and are five and a half and six feet, respectively. The FF705 is a delicate seven-foot taper weighing just under three ounces and is ideally suited to fishing fine with small flies on relatively small streams. It is fitted with the standard locking reel seat, like all the Fenwick rods above seven feet. The FF755 model is seven and a half feet, weighing three and one-eighth ounces, and taking a five-weight line. It is a fine all-round rod for delicate presentation on medium-size waters. The FF805 is eight feet, weighs three and three-eighths ounces, and is designed for relatively small-fly work on the larger rivers of our western mountains. The FF855 is a surprisingly delicate eight and a half feet and only three and five-eighths ounces, matched with a five-weight line, and is one of the best models in the Fenwick line. These six rods designed for five-weight lines are intended for normal casting ranges of ten to fifty feet, except for the two smallest models, which are intended for distances of ten to thirty feet in normal fishing. These small rods are capable of handling sixty-odd feet in the hands of skilled casters, while the others will punch out the entire fly line, although they are not primarily intended for distance work on big water.

There are four Fenwick rods designed for six-weight lines and more general trout-fishing problems, ranging from small dry flies to medium-size streamers, except for the FF706 model. It is seven feet long, weighs only three and one-eighth ounces, and is intended for general fishing with relatively small flies and light tippets. The FF756 is seven and a half feet, weighs three and one-quarter ounces, and is perhaps the best all-around rod of its size from Fenwick, although many knowledgeable anglers like the FF806. It measures eight feet and weighs three and a half ounces, and is also quite versatile, with the muscle to handle relatively large trout flies and streamers. FF856 is a superb long rod delicate enough for a six-weight line and weighs only three and seven-eighths ounces at a full eight and a half feet. It is a fine nymphing rod, with sufficient length to mend line and control fly speed, and it is also ideally suited to fishing the big western spring creeks, where a fisherman must false-cast in shoulder-high reeds or crawl infantry-style along the banks, with sufficient rod length to hold his backcasts high.

Fenwick makes two fly rods for the seven-weight line, which Jim Green believes is the best all-around line size for all kinds of trout fishing. The FF807 rod is his favorite design. It measures eight feet and weighs three and three-quarters ounces. Green believes his FF857 model at eight and a half feet and three and seven-eighths ounces is an ideal fly rod for general fishing on big-trout water. These rods are both designed for a normal casting range of fifteen to sixty feet, although eighty-foot casts are not beyond a good fisherman, and in the hands of a real distance man one-hundred-foot casts are possible.

The Fenwick rods designed for eight-weight lines are probably all the muscle any trout fisherman needs, except perhaps for really big steelheads. The FF858 is an eight-and-a-half-foot rod weighing four and one-eighth ounces, and will handle all the line you can throw. The FF908 is a similar taper measuring nine feet and weighing only four and a half ounces, giving the big-water fisherman the delicacy of an eight-weight with the extra length for deep wading. There are several larger fiberglass rods in the Fenwick line, but except for the FF909 for a nine-weight line, they offer more power than a trout fisherman needs—unless he fishes big water often with large bucktails and streamers.

Scientific Anglers have developed a series of fine fiberglass rods of excellent quality and design, matching them with fly lines of their own manufacture and reels of their own design that are built by Hardy in England. These matching rod systems have become quite popular in recent years, and the rods themselves are beautiful in their simplicity.

The high-density blanks are designed in a continuous slow-action taper joined together with a spigot-type glass ferrule, with a male plug in the butt section that fits into the hollow female tubing of the tip section. The tubular blanks are densely laminated out of high-quality fiberglass cloth, using phenolic resins under controlled pressures, and with a reasonably delicate tip calibration for each design. The actions are slow and work deep into the butt section under progressively longer casting loads. The ferrule system is a little heavier and less flexible than the Feralite type, but it is a little more secure, and some connoisseurs of fiberglass argue that it is better looking. The blanks are beautifully finished with multiple sandings, coatings, and bakings that result in a rich mahogany finish. Stainless snake guides and a carboloy butt guide are found with dark brown wrappings and paler trim. The reel seats are anodized a chocolate color to match the rods, although I have often thought some consideration might have been made to relating their fittings to the brightwork of their matching reels—thereby making them a visual system of fly tackle, as well as a system based upon the weight of the lines and reels alone.

Scientific Anglers offer a light rod of seven feet two inches, weighing three ounces, for a matching four-weight line. The System Four reel measures two and three-quarters inches in diameter and weighs three and a half ounces, making this the lightest fiberglass production rod from any manufacturer in terms of its matching line weight.

The System Five and System Six rods are medium-light to medium actions ideally suited to most trout-fishing problems. The Five is seven feet, seven inches long, weighs three and one-quarter ounces, and takes the matching five-weight lines. It is recommended for small- to medium-size water, while the six-weight rod is suited to slightly larger streams and fly sizes. It measures eight feet one inch and weighs three and a half ounces. The matching System Five reel is three inches in diameter and weighs three and three-quarters ounces, while the slightly larger System Six measures three and one-quarter inches and weighs four and one-quarter ounces. These are both excellent basic rods designed for knowledgeable trout fishermen, although their manufacturer does not recommend them for bucktails.

Their System Seven and System Eight tapers have the power for bucktails and bigger water. The Seven rod is eight feet five inches in length and weighs four ounces; its matching reel is three and seven-sixteenths inches in diameter and weighs four and a half ounces. The System Eight rod is eight feet eight inches and weighs four and five-eighths ounces, and its reel is three and five-eighths inches in diameter and weighs five and three-quarters ounces. These two fly rods have enough power to cast long lines and handle large fish easily, and I have taken many twenty-pound salmon on the System Eight—as well as several big bonefish on the Bahamas marl flats.

The System Nine measures eight feet eleven inches and it weighs a full five ounces. Its reel is three and three-quarters inches in diameter and weighs six and one-quarter ounces, taking a nine-weight forward taper with ample Dacron backing. Although the System Nine seems a little too powerful for most trout fishing, it has a surprising number of supporters on big western rivers like the Snake and lower Yellowstone and the swift-flowing Deschutes.

Some anglers have questioned the irregular lengths of the Scientific Anglers series of fly rods, arguing that varied wall thicknesses and tapers could have achieved the same equilibrium with line and reel weights. The quiet visual character of the rods is perhaps the best of the major manufacturers, and the four-weight model is unique among large-scale production tapers. Although their price range is among the most expensive of fiberglass rods, even from the bamboo makers who also market glass, these are superb fishing tools with first-rate workmanship and design specifications.

Although Phillipson does not make fiberglass rods for smaller lines than a five-weight taper, their products are among the finest available today. Phillipson uses the finest fiberglass cloth, cross-reinforced and having extremely high linear counts of glass fibers, and laminates it over a special inner mandrel with epoxy and unusually high pressures to achieve extremely dense tubular walls. Such epoxy laminates are demonstrably stronger than conventional tubular blanks, making smaller diameters possible throughout the length of the tapers, as well as lighter total weights. The finish is a delicate salmon-tinted brown, fashioned of smooth, durable epoxy, and concealing the seams in the sleeve-type ferrules. The ferrule sleeves are reinforced with a delicate metal band that has become a Phillipson trademark, and the guides are carboloy and stainless steel. The nylon wrappings have the simplicity found only in the work of first-rate bamboo craftsmen, as Bill Phillipson is part of the split-cane tradition, going back to his years of building bamboo at Granger. The anodized aluminum reel seats are nicely machined, and like many fine cane rods, the fillers are shaped of first-quality specie cork. Phillipson manufactures three grades of fly rods, although his Epoxite series is his finest achievement in fiberglass thus far.

There are nine tapers in the Epoxite series. Although they have not been available for long, many fishermen are extolling the virtues of the high-density laminates and their performance. The EF60 measures six feet and weighs only one and three-quarters ounces, taking either a four- or five-weight line. It is certainly one of the best midge-size rods in glass. The FF66 is a six-and-a-half-footer of two and one-eighth ounces, also rated for either four- or five-weight tapers, and it also is a fine midge-type rod. The Phillipson EF70 is a seven-footer weighing only two and a half ounces, taking the five-weight lines, and the EF76 is seven-and-a-half, weighing two and seven-eighths ounces. It also takes the five-weight tapers. The EF80 is a fine, all-around design at eight feet and three and one-quarter ounces, its six-weight tapers well suited to most American fishing with medium-size waters and flies. The EF86 is eight and a half feet and three and five-eighths ounces, taking a seven-weight taper and supplying a relatively delicate rod with a distance capability. The EF90 is a surprising rod for an eight-weight line at nine feet and only four ounces and is a superb tool for big-water problems at unusually light weight, but the most surprising design in the Epoxite series is unquestionably the EF96. It is nine and a half feet in length, but it weighs only four and one-eighth ounces and takes only a five-weight line—certainly an optimal tool for fishing fine on a big western river where distance is also needed; its delicacy and length make it a fine nymphing rod.

These Phillipson Epoxites are priced competitively with the Scientific Anglers' rods, and while I prefer the coloring of the Scientific blanks, the functional wrappings and skeletal-locking reel seat with cork fillers found on the Phillipsons should be commended for a simplicity and esthetic restraint seldom found on factory rods. It is almost impossible to convince the corporate mentality that our fishermen recognize and pay for performance and quality, and that the baroque ornamentation of mylar and variegated threads found on too many fiberglass production rods are really not important in fly-fishing sales.

Phillipson makes a second series of fiberglass rods at about half the price of his Epoxite models. These Royal Wand rods have a less expensive fiberglass ferrule of the sleeve type, and are made with less expensive glass blanks laminated with epoxy. Their finish is also epoxy, and the snake guides are still stainless steel. The stripping guide is carboloy, and there is an anodized full-locking reel seat. The smaller models in the Royal Wand line have cork reel-seat fillers, making them quite light although their matching lines are not as light as those in the expensive Epoxite.

The RWF60 is six feet and one and seven-eighths ounces, but its calibrations and action demand a six-weight line, like the RWF66, which is six and a half feet and weighs two and three-eighths ounces. The RWF70 is seven feet and two and five-eighths ounces, and like the RWF76 at seven and a half feet and three ounces, it also takes a six-weight line. The RWF80 at eight feet and three and three-eighths ounces is also designed for six-weight tapers. The RWF86 measures eight and a half feet and weighs three and five-eighths ounces, taking a relatively light seven-weight, and the RWF90 is a full nine feet. It weighs only four ounces, and its action is superbly accommodated with an eight-weight taper. Although the lighter models are a little muscular for fishing really fine tippets, taking six-weight lines in spite of their midge-size weights and dimensions, these Royal Wand rods in the lengths beyond eight feet are quite delicate. Their price lies in the Fenwick range.

Phillipson also manufactures its Master series of fiberglass fly rods, which cost about half the price of their Royal Wand line, yet many fiberglass partisans rate them the best of the inexpensive glass products. These are light brown blanks of quality glass fabric laminated in conventional phenolic resins and are—surprisingly, considering their low price—fitted with nickel-silver ferrules.

BERKELEY SPECIALIST 1971 TWO-PIECE TUBULAR FIBERGLASS SPIRIT LAKE, IOWA FROM THE COLLECTION OF DOUGLAS SWISHER

HARDY JET LIGHTWEIGHT 1973 TWO-PIECE TUBULAR FIBERGLASS ALNWICK, ENGLAND FROM THE COLLECTION OF EDWARD ROWE

R. L. WINSTON MEDIUM TROUT 1972 TWO-PIECE TUBULAR FIBERGLASS SAN FRANCISCO, CALIFORNIA FROM THE COLLECTION OF THOMAS MORGAN

The MF60 has a cork reel-seat filler, measures six feet and weighs one and seven-eighths ounces. It takes a six-weight line like the MF66, which is six and a half feet and two and seven-eighths ounces with its full locking reel seat. The MF70 is a seven-foot rod weighing three and one-eighth ounces for a six-weight line. There are two seven-and-a-half-foot rods in the Phillipson Master series. The MF76L weighs only three and one-eighth ounces, taking a five-weight double taper perfectly, and the MF76 matches a six-weight line at three and a half ounces. The MF80L is also unusually light for its length of eight feet and weight of three and three-quarters ounces, and it is also rated for a five-weight taper. The straight MF80 is eight feet in length and weighs four ounces, taking a six-weight line. The MF86 weighs four and one-quarter ounces and is a full eight and a half feet. Its seven-weight line makes a fine big-water tool, and the MF90 takes an eight-weight line at nine feet and four and a half ounces. But the most intriguing rods in this series are the seven-and-a-half foot and eight-foot tapers for five-weight lines, particularly at their moderate cost.

Cortland is producing a similarly priced series of fiberglass rods it calls the FR2000 models, and many knowledgeable anglers endorse them without regard for their bargain prices. The Cortland rods are relatively light and their tapers are well designed considering their modest prices. These rods use a strong fiberglass ferrule with a firm spigot-type plug. Stainless steel snake guides and a carboloy butt guide complete the fittings, secured with chocolate wrappings and pale brown trim. The anodized double-locking-ring reel seat has a rubber butt plate like the more expensive Fenwick and Scientific Anglers rods. The fiberglass blanks and guide wrappings are protected by epoxy finishes. The six-and-a-half-foot model weighs two and three-quarters ounces and takes a five-weight double taper line. The seven-foot Cortland weighs a full three ounces and matches a six-weight taper, like the seven-and-a-half-footer at three and a half ounces. The eight-foot design weighs four and one-quarter ounces and takes a seven-weight, while the eight-and-a-half-foot Cortland requires a full eight-weight taper at four and three-quarters ounces. There are some big-water anglers who swear by these Cortland rods, particularly considering their relatively low cost, and I know several good fishermen who like the four-and-three-quarters-ounce rod for surprisingly heavy work.

Browning manufactures five fiberglass rods of fine, high-density phenolic laminates. The rods are a rich chocolate brown and are fitted with a glass-to-glass ferrule designed to wear into a deeper fit over the years. The anodized screw-locking reel seat matches the rod color, and the price range of the Browning rods is moderate. The seven-footer weighs two and a half ounces and takes a five-weight line, while the seven-and-a-half-foot model at two and three-quarters ounces is balanced with a six-weight. The eight-foot Browning weighs three and a half ounces for a seven-weight taper. The eight-and-a-half-foot model is a full five ounces and matches weight-forward taper in eight-weight. The nine-foot Browning weighs five and one-quarter ounces and will handle a nine-weight line.

Garcia controls the Conolon manufacturing operation that first developed the tubular fiberglass construction methods that still dominate the rod industry, and in recent years Garcia has worked with celebrated anglers like Lee Wulff and Charles Ritz to design new fiberglass tapers. Conolon also pioneered the longitudinal weaves, high-density laminates, and difficult phenolic bonding methods that have made our modern fiberglass actions possible. The Wulff tapers include the familiar six-foot design for ultralight salmon fishing, which has too much tip muscle for really light trout work, but the larger models include some tapers that work well down into the butt section under casting stresses. The Wulff series is surprisingly moderate in price. The Ritz tapers are somewhat more radical, coming from perhaps the chief proponent of the compound calibrations that Ritz christened the parabolic action thirty-odd years ago. Duplicating and improving the Pezon & Michel performance that Ritz developed over the years proved so difficult that Conolon retained Russ Peak, perhaps the most celebrated of the fiberglass craftsmen, to work out the Ritz templates for preparing the glass cloth in the Ritz series. Peak also added the aluminum ferrule covering that fits inside the glass tip like a conventional spigot-type joint.

The Wulff series for Garcia is finished in a dull blue epoxy with blue anodized locking reel seats and the spigot-type ferrules. The seven-foot model weighs three ounces and takes a seven-weight line; and the seven-and-a-half-foot, for seven-weight, weighs three and a half ounces. The eight-foot Garcia Wulff weighs four ounces and also is designed for seven-weight lines. The eight-and-a-half-foot rod at four and a half ounces takes an an eight-weight Wulff long belly beautifully, and many knowledgeable western trout fishermen find it best in the Garcia Wulff series. The nine-foot model is designed for a ten-weight forward taper, weighs five ounces and has the muscle to cast big flies in high winds.

The Wulff series also has two one-piece rods fitted with skeletal sliding-band seats. The five-and-a-half-footer weighs one and a half ounces and takes a six-weight double taper. The six-footer weighs one and three-quarters ounces and is balanced with a seven-weight—the classic Wulff prescription for salmon fishing.

Charles Ritz has been fascinated with the potential of fiberglass for fly rods these past twenty years, ever since the first Harnell blanks became available in Europe. His bamboo rods were much more responsive and recovered better from stress, but even these first fiberglass sections demonstrated remarkable power-to-weight possibilities. Ritz experimented first with the tip section of a nine-foot Harnell married to the butt section of an eight-foot Pezon & Michel parabolic. It produced a remarkably powerful rod capable of handling three line tapers from eight- to ten-weight, something no split-cane rod could ever manage.

It could even cast a spoon, Ritz admits ruefully.

That's interesting, the late Cornelius Ryan replied puckishly over lunch in Manhattan, *but who would want to?*

Ritz found his first hybrids unsatisfactory. The tip section recovered too swiftly and sloppily from stress, and the butt was too stiff, but Ritz lacquered the entire rod black and embellished it with a skull and crossbones before sending it to Pezon & Michel at Amboise.

The death of cane is coming! Ritz added.

It is surprising that Ritz would not have tried a split-bamboo tip on a fiberglass butt section, since his cane parabolics were always compound tapers that felt a little top-heavy, and the brisk recovery from stress implicit in bamboo would solve the problems of most fiberglass rods. Such hybrid designs were not long in coming. The indefatigable Ritz soon married the delicacy and sharp-stress recovery of a fine bamboo tip with the lightness and power of a tubular glass butt. The production tapers of these hybrid rods were called the Variopower series, and they were manufactured at Pezon & Michel.

Variopower rods were certainly distance tools. The compound tapers and weight of their bamboo tips were magnified in combination with a tubular fiberglass butt. The glass had sufficient power to handle these tips without deforming badly under stress, and it made the Variopowers lighter than rods of comparable strength. The elasticity of the glass quickly multiplied the line velocity and casting loads of the double-haul technique, extending line length rapidly, while the bamboo presented the final cast with precision. Many steelhead fishermen still use these Variopower rods religiously, and the late Albert Godart used one to reach 150 feet in trout-fly distance competition. Ritz and Pierre Creusevaut, the former world fly-casting champion who had worked with Ritz since 1932, were elated as fiberglass improved in its loading and casting qualities. Both men became convinced that a fiberglass rod would soon be possible that flexed deeply into the butt, with the same decreasing flexure in the tip section, and almost no bending in the final twelve inches at the top guide. Ritz and Creusevaut reasoned that such a glass taper would match the superb line-lifting and high-speed-line work of their Fario Club in split cane.

But manufacturers were still closely tied to the American tradition of stiff-butt rods with free-flexing tip action. It is a tradition well suited to average casting skills, since its timing places minimal demands on the angler who fishes only a few days each season, and its casting rhythms are comparable to the driving restlessness of many American fishermen. Rod tapers that match their temperaments will never cast as long or fish as fine as the so-called parabolic tapers, but they do complement the character of their owners at leisure. Creusevaut and Ritz were both convinced that stiff-tip-action rods were the principal obstacle to really superb fiberglass rods, and that tip-action dogma made it virtually impossible to convince the glass rodmakers to change. However, both men continued to experiment with hand-modified glass blanks.

Their chance arrived in 1967, when Cornelius Ryan came to Paris and stopped a few days at the Hotel Ritz in the Place Vendôme. Ryan was the author of *The Longest Day*, the story of the Normandy invasion that was the beginning of the end in the Second World War. He was in Europe looking for film locations as well as trout and salmon, including two expeditions to arctic Norway, and Ritz engaged him in some fishing talk.

But enough talk! Ritz soon exploded.

His swift little Lancia was soon on its way toward the Bois de Boulogne, and the casting ponds of the Casting Club de France at Tir aux Pigeons. The back was filled with fly rods. Ritz bombarded Ryan with a drumfire of gestures and dialogue, punctuated with brief demonstrations of flawless high-speed, high-line casting techniques. Ritz continued his restless monologues while the Lancia careened back along the boulevards, its Michelin radials protesting shrilly in the turns. The session ended in the Ritz bar over several glasses of Chivas Regal.

Charles, Ryan finally interjected into the voluble spate of rod theory, *you are wasting your time in Europe!*

Ritz argued that his theories had already been rejected by American fiberglass rod builders with their stubborn commitment to tip-action rod tapers, and he doubted that they would be receptive. Cornelius Ryan was a close fishing companion of Thomas Lenk, who controls the Garcia Corporation and its Conolon fiberglass subsidiary, and he promised to discuss the Ritz theories with Lenk in the United States.

The following summer, Ritz was fishing salmon on the Nausta in western Norway when both Ryan and Lenk arrived to fish the Laerdal from the charming farmstead at Moldebø. Ryan arranged a meeting and Ritz travelled south into the Sognefjord to discuss building glass rods on the Ritz parabolic tapers. He subsequently arrived at the Conolon factory late in 1968, and in spite of the tip-action dogmatics among the technicians there, several prototype rods were soon produced for Pierre Creusevaut and the testing ponds. Two superb rods were among these first experimental tapers, and Thomas Lenk was surprised when they soon lengthened his casting distances as much as ten to fifteen feet.

The Ritz Garcia fly rods soon followed. Their performance specifications are not designed for delicacy and fine tippets, but their casting dynamics are superb. Conolon high-density blanks are laminated with phenolic resins, and their long-flex behavior in the Ritz tapers ensures a surprising capability to lift line from the water. Their flexing under casting loads keeps the rod in touch with the working line both behind and ahead of the angler. Such smooth control and transmission of power mean that excessive glass vibration during recovery from stress is largely a thing of the past, and line oscillation and flutter are easily mastered. Modern high-density fiberglass has overcome most of the casting faults found in earlier production rods and is increasingly able to accept casting stress without deformation. The increased flexing power, strength and weight ratios, and recovery from stress without excessive vibration of these rods are readily apparent. Casting distances are easily increased. High-speed performance under casting loads keeps the backcast amazingly high and reduces line drop and flutter. The ability to lift fifteen percent more line off the water reduces false-casting efforts, keeping the fly on the water where it belongs, and the rods throw a surprisingly tight loop.

The smallest rod in the Ritz Garcia series is six and a half feet in length, weighs three and a half ounces, and takes a six-weight line. The second rod is slightly longer than seven feet, and takes a six-weight line at only three and three-quarters ounces. The third model is slightly under eight feet, weights four ounces, and balances a seven-weight line. The taper that measures just over eight feet weighs four and one-quarter ounces and is designed for an eight-weight. It will lift and load more than fifty feet in the hands of a skilled fly caster. The eight-and-a-half-foot Ritz Garcia weighs four and three-quarters ounces and requires a nine-weight line. Its loading capacity is a surprising sixty to sixty-five feet of lift and casting stress. The largest model is just under nine feet, weighs five and a half ounces, and perfectly casts an eleven-weight forward taper. Its line ceiling is almost seventy feet, lifting it cleanly from the water and carrying it while false casting. Such performance is not found in other fiberglass rod tapers. Ritz tapers are designed for optimal distance-to-weight ratios, rather than for fishing cobweb-size tippets, and his seven-weight and nine-weight designs have proved the most popular.

Ritz is experimenting with synthetics like boron and carbon graphite fibers and has abandoned his earlier passion for split bamboo. His new infatuation with high-density phenolic glass is obvious in these lines from *A Fly Fisher's Life*:

> Given blanks of high quality and tapers of the correct design, glass is not only ideal, it is also the only material from which fly rods should now be made. This does not mean that other materials, lighter and with still more flex-power, will not be used eventually for rods. I am already experimenting with such materials, and have reason to hope that I shall be one of the first to perfect a fly rod of this type. But that is looking to the future: for the present there can be no question that glass reigns supreme.

Garcia makes a series of surprisingly inexpensive glass rods, starting with its seven-footer weighing three and a half ounces. There are also a fine seven-and-a-half-footer of three and a half ounces and an eight-foot model weighing four ounces. The eight-and-a-half-foot rod in the Garcia 5-Star line weighs four and a half ounces, and the nine-footer of five ounces has the muscle to handle ten-weight.

Berkeley is another large tackle manufacturer that is now experimenting with parabolic fiberglass actions, and although their Parametric series has the flaw of overembellishment so typical of production rods, their new Specialist designs promise both fine casting performance and great esthetic character. Their fittings and visual qualities and unique touches are the work of Douglas Swisher, the author of *Selective Trout* and the new technical director at Berkeley. His new Specialist series of rods are an optimal combination of casting power, delicacy, and appearance.

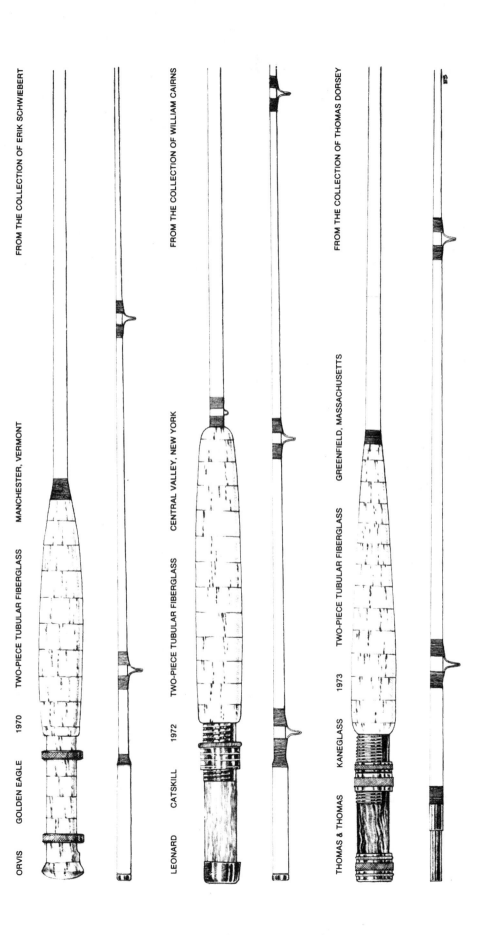

ORVIS   GOLDEN EAGLE   1970   TWO-PIECE TUBULAR FIBERGLASS   MANCHESTER, VERMONT   FROM THE COLLECTION OF ERIK SCHWIEBERT

LEONARD   CATSKILL   1972   TWO-PIECE TUBULAR FIBERGLASS   CENTRAL VALLEY, NEW YORK   FROM THE COLLECTION OF WILLIAM CAIRNS

THOMAS & THOMAS   KANEGLASS   1973   TWO-PIECE TUBULAR FIBERGLASS   GREENFIELD, MASSACHUSETTS   FROM THE COLLECTION OF THOMAS DORSEY

These Berkeley rods are built with hand-culled fiberglass blanks using high-density phenolic laminates, and are finished in a rich chocolate-colored epoxy. The functional wrappings are black and the carboloy butt guides are complemented with snake guides of stainless steel. The ferrules in these Berkeley rods are the glass-spigot type and are aligned with positioning dots. The specie-cork grip is a modified cigar shape, and the reel seat has two unusual features: its solid walnut filler has a hand-sanded cork inlay to seat the reel firmly, and is fitted with black anodized ring and butt cap. The butt is fitted with a slotted hard-rubber cushion, designed to protect the rod from abrasion and impacts and to prevent leader crimping when a nylon taper longer than the rod is necessary.

The six-and-a-half-foot Specialist weighs only one and three-quarters ounces and takes a four-weight line. The seven-foot model weighs two and a half ounces and is balanced with a five-weight taper, while the seven-and-a-half-foot taper weighs three ounces and uses a recommended six-weight line. These three fiberglass rods are excellent fishing tools, flexing well into the grip and fishing relatively light tippets. The seven-foot Specialist is a remarkably subtle rod, and these rods are the most impressive of the production fiberglass types. This past season, Doug Swisher and I fished the seven-footers extensively on the Au Sable in Michigan, and I found them a first-rate product in both appearance and performance.

Hardy Brothers have long been a bastion of split-bamboo tradition, but in recent years Hardy has turned to fiberglass, too. The Hardy glass series has been named its Jet line, which is perhaps appropriate to our age of turbines and sophisticated technology, although it lacks the romantic overtones of its traditional Palakona trademark.

The Hardy fiberglass rods are assembled from quality high-density blanks of a continuous slow-action taper. The ferrules are the solid plug-spigot type, which give fine glass-to-glass transfer of power in casting. High-quality fiberglass cloth is made into densely laminated blanks with phenolic resins, and like the Scientific Anglers line, the Hardy Jet series offers relatively fine tip performance for production fiberglass work. The blanks have a rich brown color, and their behavior under casting stress works deep into the butt calibrations under increasing line loads. The fittings are excellent and the polyurethane finishes are tough and mirror-bright. The reel seats are the typical Hardy hardware. The screw-locking seats are the aluminum reverse type, with a hooded ring concealed in the cork grip and a butt cap and filler of hard rubber. The lighter models have skeletal butt caps and sliding rings on a specie-cork filler, and except for the unfortunate trademark decal, the Hardy fiberglass rods are perhaps the most handsome production rods anywhere, with an elegance of fittings and understated wrappings worthy of split cane and beautifully matched to their handsome reels.

The seven-foot Hardy weighs two and three-quarters ounces and takes a four-weight line, while the seven-and-a-half-foot model at three ounces is designed for five-weight tapers. The eight-foot Jet matched with a six-weight line weighs three and a half ounces. The eight-and-a-half-footer at three and three-quarters ounces also takes six-weight line tapers, while a second design of the same length and four and one-quarter ounces works beautifully with an eight-weight line. Hardy offers three nine-foot models. The lightest weighs four and a half ounces and takes a seven-weight line, and the medium design is for eight-weight lines at four and three-quarters ounces. The largest of the three Hardy nine-footers weighs five and one-quarter ounces and takes a nine-weight, making it as muscular a stick as any trout fisherman needs. These Hardy rods are essentially American high-density blanks and cost a little more in this country because of import duties, but their fittings may satisfy a fisherman who cares about the visual character of his rods.

Dermot Wilson is the designer of the famous Silver Creek series of fiberglass rods, along with Jack Hemingway in Sun Valley. Hemingway took Wilson fishing on the famous Idaho spring creek in the bottoms at Picabo, and he soon discovered that Silver Creek had much in common with the chalkstreams at home in Hampshire. Its selective rainbows demanded fine tippets, delicate casting, lightness, and the ability to handle a long line in the wind.

It took a special type of glass taper, Wilson explains, *and we both felt the Hardy blanks might work best on Silver Creek.*

Hardy agreed to provide the blanks, and Wilson worked closely with Tony Fordham to perfect the final tapers. The production versions are handsome rods of typical British design and moderate price. The blanks are medium brown and joined with spigot-type ferrules.

The eight-foot Silver Creek weighs three and a half ounces and takes a five-weight line, while the eight-and-a-half-footer is a four-ounce rod designed for six-weight tapers. The nine-foot Silver Creek weighs only four and one-quarter ounces and also takes a six-weight forward-taper line, and there is a surprisingly delicate nine-and-a-half-foot model of five and three-quarters ounces designed for a seven-weight. All of these rods have reverse-locking reel hardware except for the butt cap and sliding band on the eight-foot design. These rods are wound with tan wraps tipped in pale orange, and the guides are all stainless steel. Their popularity in both Europe and the United States is well known, and testimony to the skills of their several designers.

Several of the famous American split-cane manufacturers have also added high-density fiberglass rods to their lines, using the same fittings found on their bamboo work. Such firms as Powell, Winston, Leonard, and Orvis all make fine fiberglass fly rods.

Walton Powell is carrying on the tradition started by his father E. C. Powell on the rivers of northern California just after the First World War. Powell was one of the great innovative pioneers of hollow split-cane construction, along with the late Lew Stoner of San Francisco, and his son Walton is equally skilled in both cane and fiberglass construction. His fiberglass rods are fashioned of high-quality glass fabric laminated with maximum linear fiber-counts and phenolic resins, with a lovely pale brown color protected with a clear epoxy finish. The guides are fine tungsten steel with simple olive wrappings. The ferrules are the Swiss-type machined by Walton Powell from fine nickel silver, giving a precise and long-wearing fit, and the reel seats are the same heavy aluminum locking type designed and machined for the Walton Powell bamboo rods. Powell fiberglass rods range from seven-and-a-half- to eight-and-a-half-foot two-piece designs, taking five- to seven-weight lines, and three-piece glass rods from eight to nine feet. The three-piece designs are perfectly matched for six- to nine-weight tapers. Since the Powell reel seats are designed for strength and security, total rod weights are heavier than most glass rods of comparable length, and Powell argues that assembled weights are rather meaningless. The Powell actions are smooth and relatively slow, working well down into the butt section, and they have many ardent admirers among skilled distance casters on the Pacific Coast.

Winston is perhaps the best-known American rod company on the Pacific Coast, long famous for their Stoner patent hollow-butt bamboo work, and now producing first-rate glass rods, too. The introduction of fiberglass rods with the Winston fittings and name did not happen overnight, just as Hardy waited in England before it adopted glass. The artisans at Winston began experimenting with fiberglass blanks twenty-five years ago, but they quickly concluded that the tapers were bad. The rods were too stiff and unresponsive in their butt calibrations and too soft toward their tips, and Lew Stoner and Douglas Merrick soon decided that glass would have to wait until better fabrics and laminating resins were available, and they could work out their own mandrel tapers.

Fiberglass technology had evolved to that point about ten years ago, and Winston started working out its own rod designs and forming mandrels. It is interesting that like the technicians at both Scientific Anglers and Hardy, Stoner and Merrick chose phenolic resins instead of epoxies or polyesters in laminating fiberglass cloth specially woven for fly rods. Finally, Winston had worked out tapers and forming cores and curing techniques that provided them with a fiberglass blank that approached the superb slow-butt tapers in their bamboo work. The blanks are finished with an oven-baked polyurethane applied in five separate coats that results in a rich color not unlike flame-darkened cane. The guides are first-quality stainless steel and the butt guides are carboloy. Winston has also developed its version of the spigot-type fiberglass ferrule, giving its rods a superb load-transfer in casting. The wrappings are maroon nylon with white trim, and secured in a clear epoxy coating. The grips are select specie-cut cork, and either a full-locking aluminum reel seat or a skeletal cork seat with a butt cap and sliding ring is available on the trout rods. The Winston glass rods are unquestionably among the finest.

Winston makes six ultralight models in its fiberglass series, each with a skeletal sliding ring and butt cap. The five-and-a-half-foot rod weighs only one and five-eighths ounces and takes a four-weight line. The six-footer weighs barely one and three-quarters ounces and is also designed for four-weight tapers, like the six-and-a-half-foot model that weighs two ounces. Both the seven-foot rod at two and one-eighth ounces and the seven-and-a-half-foot design at two and one-quarter ounces are designed to function with five-weight fly lines. These are perhaps the finest lightweight fiberglass rods made anywhere. Doug Merrick is adamant about the unfishability of short, lightweight rods that take relatively heavy lines and cannot accommodate really fine tippet diameters.

Any little rod that needs a six- or seven-weight line to make it cast decently is an abomination, he grumbles testily. *It's certainly no trout rod!*

The ultralight fiberglass rods are also available with a full-locking aluminum reel seat, and many anglers prefer them on the seven- and seven-and-a-half-foot models. However, they increase the weight of these exquisite lightweight glass rods approximately three-eighths of an ounce, which seems a little like forcing a fine gaited mare to pull a plow. Fishermen who want the security of a fully locking reel seat should probably fish the larger fiberglass rods from Winston.

Like their fine split-cane rods, these fiberglass Winstons are hand-culled from blanks that have already been inspected at the factory and are rigorously checked again before assembly. Only the finest workmanship and fittings are used. The wrappings are deep maroon with clear white trim, protected with a fine epoxy finish, and the specie-cork grip is shaped with the Winston half-Wells style. The guides are the same stainless and carboloy quality found on the Winston split-cane rods, and these beautiful fiberglass rods are also available with a butt cap and sliding ring over a cork filler. This skeletal reel seat reduces the finished weights three-eighths of an ounce.

The seven-and-a-half-foot rod weighs two and three-quarters ounces, with its locking reel seat, and takes a six-weight line. There are two eight-foot models in the standard glass series. The first is a surprisingly delicate three-and-one-eighth-ounce design that weighs only two and three-quarters ounces with a sliding-band seat and is matched with a five-weight taper. The second eight-foot rod weighs three and a half ounces and takes a six-weight. The three-and-a-half-ounce, eight-and-a-half-footer is an amazingly delicate rod that takes only five-weight lines, and the six-weight taper in the same length weighs only three and seven-eighths ounces. Both of these rods are quite smooth and subtle, considering their length and potential power. The eight-and-a-half-foot rods at four ounces take a seven-weight line and are more typical of most production fiberglass tackle. The nine-foot rods weigh four and one-quarter ounces and take seven-weight tapers, and it is interesting that the Winston rod builders think a heavier stick is not suited to fishing river trout—their fiberglass designs for eight- and nine-weight lines are recommended as steelhead tackle, and are fitted with a detachable three-inch butt.

The first nine-foot Winston weighs four and one-quarter ounces and takes an eight-weight forward-taper line, and the second nine-footer takes a nine-weight and weighs four and a half ounces. There are also nine-foot rods for ten- and eleven-weight lines and still larger designs for tarpon and king salmon and billfish on flies, but these rods have more muscle than any trout fisherman needs. The larger Winston fiberglass rods have radical compound tapers derived from the unusual tapers of their famous hollow-butt bamboo rods and are superb tools for effortless distance work. These superb Winston rods are more expensive than the comparable Fenwick models and slightly less expensive than the series of rods from Scientific Anglers and Phillipson.

Leonard is the oldest rodmaker in the history of American fishing tackle and still builds its split-cane jewels, but it has also made some first-rate fiberglass rods. The Leonard Spring Creek and Catskill series are fitted with the same elegant Leonard hardware found on their superb bamboo fly rods. The smaller rods are available with the standard skeleton seat, with the sliding ring and butternut filler and elegantly engraved butt cap typical of Leonard for a century. The two-piece rods are joined with the Leonard patent ferrules, hand-machined, and welted of German silver. The fiberglass models beyond seven and a half feet are fitted with the hand-machined Leonard reel seats and butternut fillers associated with the classic Leonard rods—like the beautiful 50L in my collection, which takes a five-weight line at eight feet, or the 50DF taper originally designed by Edward Ringwood Hewitt.

The six-and-a-half-foot Spring Creek rod weighs two ounces and takes a four-weight line, and the seven-foot Leonard weighs two and one-quarter ounces, taking a five-weight taper. These rods have either locking or skeletal seats with either cork or butternut fillers. The six-foot Catskill rod weighs two and seven-eighths ounces with its locking reel seat and takes a six-weight line. The seven-and-a-half-foot, two-and-three-quarters-ounce model also takes a six-weight taper, while the eight-foot, three-and-one-quarter-ounce rod takes a seven-weight. The eight-and-a-half-foot rods are designed for eight-weight lines and weigh three and a half ounces. Like the Winston series, these Leonard fiberglass rods are more expensive than the Fenwicks, being roughly competitive with the Scientific Anglers and Phillipson Epoxite rods.

Leonard is not the only tradition-minded eastern firm to enter the fiberglass lists, since the Orvis Company is making two separate grades of glass fly rods. The Orvis blanks are a gleaming pale olive fiberglass, rolled under extreme pressures and laminated with epoxy, like the Phillipson rods. Orvis builds its trout-size glass rods with two reel seats typical of their older bamboo designs. The guides are stainless steel with a carboloy stripping guide and are seated with functional wraps in variegated olive. The nylon wrappings are wisely limited to the ferrules, guides, grip, and tip winds, with admirable esthetic restraint. No garish trademark flaws the appearance of these rods, which are simply identified with ink script under a clear epoxy finish. The Orvis Golden Eagle rods employ a sleeve-type glass ferrule reinforced with an aluminum welt, and a solid glass plug reinforcing

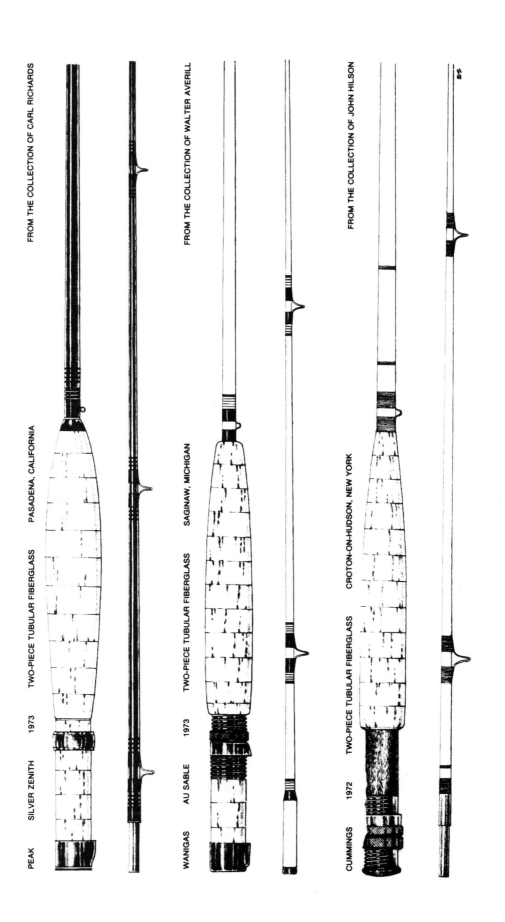

PEAK   SILVER ZENITH   1973   TWO-PIECE TUBULAR FIBERGLASS   PASADENA, CALIFORNIA   FROM THE COLLECTION OF CARL RICHARDS

WANIGAS   AU SABLE   1973   TWO-PIECE TUBULAR FIBERGLASS   SAGINAW, MICHIGAN   FROM THE COLLECTION OF WALTER AVERILL

CUMMINGS   1972   TWO-PIECE TUBULAR FIBERGLASS   CROTON-ON-HUDSON, NEW YORK   FROM THE COLLECTION OF JOHN HILSON

the ferrule end of the butt. These fiberglass rods have relatively fine tip calibrations and slow actions that work well into the grip zone, with the quick canelike dampening action typical of fine epoxy laminates. Orvis Golden Eagle rods are among the most expensive glass designs from a major manufacturer, but their fine recovery from stress and delicate tip tapers make them worth the price.

Orvis has found its most popular rod in the Golden Eagle line has been the six-and-a-half-footer at one and seven-eighths ounces, designed for delicate work with a four-weight line. It is a fine fiberglass taper, honestly designed to fish a 6X tippet with finesse, and one of the few glass rods in my collection. The seven-foot Golden Eagle weighs only two ounces and takes a five-weight taper, while the seven-and-a-half-foot rod weighs two and three-eighths ounces and is designed to fish a six-weight line. These three Golden Eagles are fitted with the slim two-ring Phillipe-style grip introduced years ago on the Orvis Superfine rods, and classic in its simplicity.

The larger Golden Eagles are fitted with the traditional Jordan cigar grip and walnut-filler reel seat used for many years on the Orvis Battenkills. The eight-foot model weighs three and five-eighths ounces and takes a seven-weight line. The eight-and-a-half-foot Golden Eagle weighs four and one-eighth ounces and is designed for an eight-weight taper, and is an excellent big-water instrument. There is also an eight-and-a-half-footer weighing four and three-eighths ounces and taking a nine-weight line, perhaps more rod than is needed for most work.

Orvis also offers its Fullflex series of fiberglass rods at about the same price as the Fenwick rods. These rods are a natural cane-yellow color, and although they are not quite as delicate as the more expensive Golden Eagle rods, their actions are the desirable slow type that flex deep into the butt section. The stainless steel snake and stripping guides are attached with bright scarlet wrappings, and the rods use the glass sleeve-type ferrules. The Jordan-type cigar grips and walnut screw-locking reel seats found on the Battenkills are also fitted on the Fullflex fiberglass series.

The seven-and-a-half-foot Fullflex, designed for a five-weight line and weighing three and one-quarter ounces, is perhaps the most delicate and popular rod in the series. The other tapers are a bit more heavy-handed, tending more toward all-around fishing than midge-type delicacy. The seven-foot rod weighs three and one-eighth ounces and takes a six-weight line, and there is a second seven-and-a-half-foot taper that weighs three and three-quarters ounces and is rated for eight-weight lines. The eight-and-a-half-foot model is also an eight-weight taper at four ounces, and is a first-rate big-water trout rod.

Thomas and Thomas are also building a line of fine fiberglass fly rods which they call their Kaneglass series. These fiberglass rods are fitted with the same fine grips, ferrules, and reel seats found on their Classic bamboo rods. Since their firm is deeply committed to craftsmanship in split bamboo, it is interesting that the modern high-density glass blanks have begun to approach their exacting standards in rod performance. Thomas Dorsey writes of their experience with earlier fiberglass rods with these candid observations:

> Glass has come closer to duplicating the qualities of cane than any material thus far encountered, but even it has fallen far short of matching cane. The nature of glass fiber, however, has offered nearly unlimited potential, as it is in many ways similar to the power fibers of bamboo. The problem has been to control the glass technologically, and to bind the fibers longitudinally after the fashion of natural cane. Modern techniques and bonding agents have been good, but not fully acceptable, for glass rod construction with these resins has had to retain a great amount of resin in the rod, and to incorporate into the structure a large percentage of fibers traversing the circumference of the rod. This has made glass rods relatively cumbersome, with as many as fifty percent of the fibers in the average glass rod wasted, contributing nothing to its performance in casting.
>
> We have a vested interest in the development of new rod materials at Thomas and Thomas, and we have observed as carefully as possible each new attempt to reproduce the properties of cane with synthetics.
>
> Nothing met our approval until the development of the new high-density glass blanks. These new blanks are truly remarkable. They overcome most of the problems in earlier glass rods which most manufacturers have attempted to avoid, or conceal by emphasizing the indestructibility of glass or substituting eye appeal for action. Epoxy and pressure are the secrets. This modern bonding agent and pressures as extreme as 2,000 pounds per square inch has led to greatly reduced resin content in the finished blanks. Less resin is required and excess resin is squeezed out during high-pressure lamination. The result is also much greater control of wall structure and internal tapers, permitting extremely fine tolerances and more flexibility in design tapers than were possible in earlier glass rods. Longitudinal alignment of virtually one hundred percent of the glass fibers is also possible with high-pressure epoxy.
>
> The result of this new technology is a line of fishing rods that actually approach the qualities of cane, and deserve assembly with first-rate fittings.

Thomas and Thomas make two tapers for relatively light fly lines, the seven-and-a-half-foot model that takes a four-weight and the eight-footer for a five-weight. There are also several designs for medium-weight lines. The six-footer of two ounces takes a six-weight line, like the six-and-a-half-footer that weighs two and a half ounces. The seven-foot, three-ounce Kaneglass also requires six-weight lines, along with the seven-and-a-half-foot model of three and one-eighth ounces and the eight-footer that weighs three and a half ounces. The eight-and-a-half-foot Kaneglass of three and three-quarters ounces is balanced with a seven-weight taper.

There are also three Thomas and Thomas Kaneglass models designed for heavier work. The eight-footer of three and three-quarters ounces has been conceived for eight-weight performance, like its companion rods of eight and a half feet and four ounces, or the nine-foot Kaneglass that weighs five ounces. These fiberglass rods are among the finest manufactured in the United States.

There are also a number of custom rodmakers who work only with hand-culled fiberglass blanks, their own grip and reel seat designs, and who modify the wall thickness of the densely laminated sections in their shops to get remarkable compound tapers of subtle delicacy and power. Perhaps the best of these craftsmen are Arthur Neumann from Michigan, Russ Peak on the Pacific Coast, and the master builder of the most delicate fiberglass rods, Vincent Cummings of New York.

Each of these makers has the standard glass-cloth templates modified to his specifications in production, and then hand-modifies their wall thicknesses after fabrication. Arthur Neumann prefers a chocolate-colored epoxy blank of high-density fiberglass and carefully manipulates the wall thickness of his tubular blanks to approximate his classic Wanigas bamboo designs. The fittings and wrappings are typical of his work. The lighter rods can be fitted with a skeletal reel seat of black anodized butt cap and sliding ring over a cork filler. The bigger rods are fitted with black locking seats and butt caps over cork. The Au Sable grade is fitted with a carboloy stripping guide and black tungsten snake guides, and there is a sleeve-type fiberglass ferrule. Neumann also makes a less expensive Pere Marquette grade and an economy grade called the Two-Hearted—after the famous Michigan river celebrated in the Hemingway story.

The six-foot Wanigas Au Sable weighs two and one-eighth ounces and is truly made for a four-weight line and reasonably delicate work. The six-and-a-half-foot model weighs two and a half ounces and is designed for a five-weight, like the seven-footer at two and three-quarters ounces. The seven-and-a-half-foot Wanigas weighs three and one-quarter ounces and takes a six-weight double taper perfectly. The eight-foot model weighs three and three-quarters ounces and takes a seven-weight, while the eight-and-a-half-foot rod takes an eight-weight at four ounces. There is also a Wanigas for a nine-weight line at nine feet and five ounces. Although Neumann modifies his blanks far less than builders like Peak and Cummings, his Wanigas rods have excellent light-tackle properties.

Russ Peak is probably the high priest of the fiberglass cult, and his rods are the equal of the finest split bamboo in their sense of craftsmanship and attention to detail. Peak has accumulated a growing circle of fierce partisans who argue that his rods equal the finest split-cane work, and his clan includes some impressive names like Charles Kerlee, Dan Holland, Carl Richards, and the celebrated Arnold Gingrich. It was Gingrich who first observed that when it came to delicate midge-size rods, Peak was the ultimate craftsman of fiberglass construction. The following observations from *The Joys of Trout* are vintage Gingrich and also tell us a lot about the workmanship of the Peak fly rods:

> With something over thirty cane fly rods in my upstairs storeroom at the time, I had thought the day would never come when I heard myself asking for a glass one, but after a day with it on the Firehole, I knew I couldn't live without a Zenith. So I took the one I'd been using, and some months later he came through with the one-piece job I'd been asking him about, that first day, finishing it in time to inscribe it with the annotation that it was a Christmas present to me from my wife Janie.
>
> Of course, nothing involving that much hard work can be cheap, in this day and age, and there's a lot of bamboo around for less than Russ Peak has to get for one of his glass rods. But this is one case where the medium is far from constituting the whole message, and the fact that Russ Peak happens to embody his ideas in fiberglass is as coincidental, say, as the circumstance that Benvenuto Cellini chose to work his artistry in a cup of gold. It would have been no less a marvel in silver or pewter or brass, or even in dull-colored lead.

Gingrich goes on to explain that he selects his fiberglass Peaks when he wants extra distance, longer casts than he can get from cane with the same expenditure of energy. Conversely, Gingrich chooses bamboo when he wants more tip delicacy than even fine artisans like Cummings and Peak can deliver.

There are no standard rods in the Peak series, although there are three basic grades. The Golden Zenith rods are the top of the line, with the most modification of wall thickness and remarkable compound tapers that flex well into the butt section. Peak Golden Zeniths are easily recognized by the delicate gold wrappings laid over the underwrap of mahogany silk. The Silver Zeniths have bright silver embellishments over the undersilk, and the Peak Zenith lacks these delicate ornamental wraps. There are white aligning dots at the ferrules, which in themselves are unique. Peak fits a delicate aluminum sleeve with a machined welt over the tip section, and the epoxy finish which conceals the ferrule is so strong that it actually becomes part of the rod structure itself. The male ferrule is a brightly polished aluminum plug which is finished with a silver ring at its fully seated position. The reel seats are all of the skeletal type, fitted with accents of copper on the Zenith series and delicate little wafer-thin stops of gold or silver on the more expensive Golden and Silver Zeniths. The reel-seat fittings are anodized a coppery color, with a butt cap and sliding ring in the ultralight models and a screw-locking assembly on the heavier rods. The grips are the relatively fat Peak cigar-style on both locking and skeletal types, although a full-Wells grip is common on his big-water rods. The fly-keeper ring is a spiral of fine copper, gold, or silver wire unique with the Peak designs, its color depending on its grade within the Zenith line. Like all custom builders, Peak supplies more guides on his rods than most, with two guides more than the rod length typical of his work.

There are no standard models in his Zenith line, since each rod is custom-made to order, although like all superb craftsmen Peak really builds each rod to suit his own standards of performance and design. The specifications listed are those of particular rods belonging to fishing companions across the entire United States and are typical of the Peak rods. There are one-piece Peaks available from five to six feet in length, weighing from one to one and a half ounces, and taking three- and four-weight double tapers. Two-piece rods in five, five and a half, and six feet are also available. The five-and-a-half-footers weigh about one and one-quarter ounces and take a four-weight taper. Arnold Gingrich owns several of these mini-Peaks, and describes the acquisition of his first in *The Joys of Trout*:

> I wondered, for instance, whether he could make me a six-foot one-piece rod like the Orvis Superfine, but a little more limber in the tip, because while I thoroughly enjoyed the Superfine for grilse I found its upper extremity a bit thick-ankled for trout.

The fact that these delicate Peaks truly balance three- and four-weight lines is eloquent testimony to their qualities. The six-and-a-half-foot two-piece Peak, weighing one and three-quarters ounces and taking a four-weight line is a joy in itself, like the four-weight rod at seven feet and a slender two ounces. There is also a seven-footer at two and one-quarter ounces for a five-weight taper. The screw-locking reel seats usually begin at seven and a half feet, weighing two and three-quarters ounces and matching a five-weight. There are several eight-foot Peaks with screw-locking seats, weighing from three and a half to four and one-quarter ounces, and taking lines ranging from a four-weight to a seven-weight forward taper. The eight-and-a-half-foot Peaks I have seen vary between three and three-quarters and four and three-quarters ounces, taking five- to eight-weight lines. Typical nine-footers weigh from four and a half to five and a half ounces and will take lines ranging from eight- to ten-weights. Generally speaking, the Peak rods represent fine craftsmanship mixed with superb power-to-weight performance ratios, and although they are relatively expensive, they are truly the zenith of fiberglass rods.

Vincent Cummings is an equally skilled custom rodmaker who chooses to work with modern high-density glass. Like Russ Peak, whose philosophy of fly-rod action is grounded in the distance casting needed on our western rivers, Cummings has his philosophical roots in the delicacy and refinement of the Catskill tradition above Manhattan. Cummings has created a superb fishing tool utterly without the embellishments of fittings or wrappings found in the work of Neumann or Peak—rods as ascetic in their simplicity as the work of Everett Garrison in split bamboo.

ARNOLD GINGRICH

His trout-size rods are fitted with skeletal reel seats using both sliding aluminum bands and full-locking designs. The locking seats are reversed in the Payne style, fitting the reel into a hooded cap concealed in the grip. Elegant walnut fillers are used in the screw-locking rods and walnut caps with the sliding-band seats. The grips are a gracefully tapered cigar shape, and the blanks are hand-rubbed to remove excess phenolic resins accumulated during lamination. Like the Orvis impregnated rods, the Cummings fiberglass receives no finish except for hand-waxing and polishing. Spar varnishing protects the functional wraps at the cork grip, guides, and ferrules. Cummings believes that the glass sleeve- and spigot-type ferrules can never provide the fit and lifespan of fine German-silver machining, and that the flexing of a sleeve-type glass connection is only a marginal benefit. There is minimal flexing in the solid fiberglass plugs used in spigot-type ferrules, and Cummings insists on using more costly German silver instead.

The Cummings rods are radically modified by handwork once the custom-designed blanks are received from the factory. Wall thickness of the densely laminated fiberglass is reduced empirically in the Cummings shop until the compound-taper feel is achieved. The typical Cummings action has a delicate hooking tip that rivals all but the finest bamboo, and the thin-walled butt section flexes dramatically into the cork grip itself, like the best of the Ritz and Garrison and Young parabolics. Cummings stubbornly resists questions about his special techniques for reducing wall thickness, and his secret heat process for straightening the tubular blanks.

Macy's doesn't tell Gimbels, Cummings concludes wryly, betraying his Manhattan beginnings. *Right?*

Like the one-piece designs of Russ Peak, Cummings makes a lovely six-foot trout rod in a single blank that weighs one and three-eighths ounces and has the delicacy to fish a four-weight line and a 6X tippet. There are two models just over six and a half feet. The lighter of these tapers weighs only one and three-quarters ounces and takes a four-weight line, while the heavier rod weighs two and a half ounces and is balanced perfectly with a five-weight. The heavier rod has a screw-locking reel seat. The seven-and-a-half-foot Cummings weighs three and a half ounces and takes a six-weight double taper. The eight-foot model is designed for a seven-weight line and weighs only three and three-quarters ounces. The eight-and-a-half-foot rod scales a full four ounces and fishes superbly with an eight-weight forward taper. The muscular nine-foot Cummings for a nine-weight line weighs four and a half ounces and is fitted with an extension butt for heavy work. My favorites in the Cummings series are the one-and-three-quarters-ounce model for a five-weight double taper, which is a superb tool for ultralight tippets and selective fish, and the eight-footer at three and three-quarters ounces is a fine all-purpose trout rod.

Cummings firmly believes that his phenolic high-density laminates demonstrate that modern fiberglass is now better than cane, and he abandoned split-bamboo construction eighteen years ago. Certainly the entire field of fiberglass rodmaking is rapidly coming to maturity in the work of craftsmen like Peak and Cummings. Even the most die-hard partisans of the bamboo tradition admit that their rods are remarkable, equalling all but the rare split-cane rods that have the qualities of an exquisite violin. The bamboo fanatics are increasingly limited to quibbling about esthetics, rod diameters, hardware, wrappings—and the fact that fiberglass rods are round.

Remember, Russ Peak chides gently in conversation, *the first split bamboo rods looked ugly to a generation raised on hickory and greenheart—and the early rodmakers had to make them round!*

Our discussion of fiberglass manufacturers would not be complete without adding three rodmakers from the Pacific Coast who have become important since the fiberglass chapter was written: the seasoned Harry Wilson at the Scott Powr-Ply Company, the energetic Ferdinand Claudio in San Francisco, and the computer-minded young technicians at Lamiglas in southern Washington.

Harry Wilson is the skilled artisan at the Scott factory who worked out the concept of using internal sleeves rather than modified wall thickness to achieve his compound actions and tapers. His blanks are a handsome medium brown, with dark brown wraps at the guides and ferrules, and simple grip and reel-seat designs. Both skeletal fittings and reverse-locking seats are available, along with fixed-extension butts of one- and two-cork designs. Like the late Paul Young, Wilson is primarily interested in the functional aspects of his rods, rather than preoccupied with problems of visual design. Scott presently builds the following trout rods in fiberglass:

MODEL	LENGTH (FEET)	WEIGHT (OUNCES)	LINE WEIGHT
F-60	6	$1^5/_8$	3
F-65	$6^1/_2$	$1^7/_8$	3
F-70	7	$2^1/_4$	3
F-71	7	$2^3/_8$	4
F-74	$7^1/_2$	$2^1/_2$	4
F-75	$7^1/_2$	$2^3/_4$	5
F-79	8	3	4
F-80	8	$3^1/_8$	5
F-81	8	$3^7/_8$	6
F-82	8	4	7
F-84	$8^1/_3$	$3^3/_8$	5
F-86	$8^1/_2$	$4^3/_8$	7
F-87B	$8^1/_2$	$4^7/_8$	8

Lamiglas has been building rod blanks of E-type fiberglass for other manufacturers for many years; it was not until development of the remarkable S-type glass that they assembled rods themselves. The surprising high-modulus performance of the new type of glass led the

Lamiglas craftsmen to become rodmakers too. S-glass rods are more sensitive, responsive to bending stresses, and twenty percent lighter than comparable equipment of conventional glass. Lamiglas has made full use of the computer technology available in the Seattle aircraft industry to design and perfect its tapers. The excitement of S-glass performance has led Lamiglas to introduce these models:

MODEL	LENGTH (FEET)	WEIGHT (OUNCES)	LINE WEIGHT
8175	$7^1/_2$	$3^5/_8$	5
8180	8	4	6
8185	$8^1/_2$	$4^1/_4$	7
8190	9	$4^5/_8$	8

Like his close friend Gary Howells, rodmaker Ferdinand Claudio is an advocate of both new technology and traditional esthetics. Howells works in split bamboo, while Claudio is a fervent admirer of modern fiberglass. Both craftsmen were also disciples of the late James Payne, perhaps the finest artisan to ever split a Tonkin culm, and their rods clearly owe their imagery to the Payne tradition.

Claudio spent his boyhood years within a half mile of the celebrated Golden Gate Casting Club in San Francisco. Its members have largely dominated tournament casting over the past fifty years, and its own tradition had its beginnings in 1893. Young fishermen all have particular heroes, and Claudio found his in skilled casters like Jack Horner and Ted Halvorsen. His apprenticeship ended long before Claudio himself became the president of the Golden Gate Casting Club.

His glass tapers are modified to produce the precise character and action that Claudio came to admire in years of competitive casting, yet his esthetic values are obvious too. Medium brown glass is combined with richly machined fittings, elegant cork-grip designs, beautiful hardwood fillers, precise golden windings and eggshell ornamental wraps, and a reverse-locking reel seat and handle clearly in the character of earlier Payne designs.

Claudio has succeeded in combining modern fiberglass tapers with the esthetic sense of the split-cane tradition, and the following models are among the most beautiful glass fly-rods made:

MODEL	LENGTH (FEET)	WEIGHT (OUNCES)	LINE WEIGHT
705B	7	$2^3/_4$	5
755B	$7^1/_2$	3	5
805B	8	$3^3/_4$	5
806B	8	4	6
855A	$8^1/_2$	$4^1/_2$	5
856A	$8^1/_2$	5	6
898A	$8^3/_4$	$5^1/_2$	8

Sage has introduced a series of fiberglass trout rods in recent years, using the finest high-modulus glass and templates. The fittings are stamped aluminum, with a pair of locking rings and cork and dark mahogany fillers. Like the Sage graphites, the glass rods are finished in a rich chocolate urethane. The fittings are serviceable, with brown wrappings and amber trim. The Sage high-modulus glass designs include the following:

MODEL	LENGTH (FEET)	WEIGHT (OUNCES)	LINE WEIGHT
SFL476	$7^{1/2}$	$3^{1/8}$	4
SFL580	8	$3^{1/2}$	5
SFL686	$8^{1/2}$	$3^{5/8}$	6
SFL789	$8^{3/4}$	$3^{7/8}$	7
SFL990	9	$4^{1/8}$	8

The Sage rods are handsomely designed and fitted, like the Claudio series, echoing the character of old Thomas and Payne bamboo. The select-cork grips, fillers, urethane finishes, wrappings, and hardware make them among the most handsome production rods in the entire fiberglass tackle industry.

Fiberglass is getting better and better.

Traditional values still die slowly in some circles, and while the fiberglass has yet to equal the finest split-cane work of artisans like Garrison, Payne and Howells, it is approaching such levels of perfection. However, there are bastions of tradition that stubbornly resist the revolution, and perhaps the most famous is the Anglers' Club of New York.

Sparse Grey Hackle was its unchallenged Dean Emeritus, a survivor of the Golden Age on the Catskill rivers and an angler so thoroughly steeped in tradition that he testily refused to fish anything but the exquisite butter-colored cane of his slender Garrisons and Leonards.

Sparse, one fellow member joked recently at the Anglers' Club, *when are you going to fish fiberglass?*

The old man took a thoughtful swallow of straight Laphroaig, a special pot-still whisky so strong it numbs the tongue.

I'll fish fiberglass, Sparse muttered behind his steel-rimmed spectacles, *the morning after some concertmaster plays a concerto at Carnegie Hall on a plastic violin!*

3. The Synthetic Fly Rods
of the Future

When do the steelhead start coming? I asked.

The first ones usually come up from the lake in October, Dave Borgeson replied. *Usually the biggest cockfish come in the fall.*

Big October run? I continued.

No, Borgeson shook his head. *The runs start coming in late winter and early spring—starting in February and March.*

How many runs come then?

The first big run enters the river in late February and in March, Borgeson explained. *The biggest spring run usually comes toward the end of March, and a third run arrives in April.*

Just about now, I said.

That's right, Borgeson nodded. *The biologists have still been netting some in the estuary at Ludington, and there should be some bright fish in the river.*

Dave Borgeson is the director of the trout and salmon programs for the state of Michigan, having played a major technical role in a highly successful introduction of steelhead and salmon. However, his first love is probably the big steelhead that enter the Pere Marquette each winter to spawn in its headwaters. Borgeson was convinced that these rainbows could be taken consistently with flies, in spite of the salmon-egg tradition that argued against fly-fishing for Michigan steelhead, and he finally worked out the basic tactics. His steady parade of big fly-caught Michigan steelhead was irrefutable evidence and finally led to legal winter fishing on the beautiful flies-only water of the upper Pere Marquette.

Look familiar? Borgeson grinned.

Sure does. I shivered in the early light. *I used to fish it regularly from Waddell's Riffle to the Forks.*

230

It's probably better now than it was then, he said.

How's that? I asked.

It's fly-only from Danaher Creek to the M-37 Bridge, he explained, *and it has a fantastic population of wild fish.*

And no more put-and-take stocking, I said.

That's right, Borgeson nodded again.

It was cold on the Clay Banks above the Deer Lick Riffle, and an April snow filtered down through the jack pines and cedars. It was just after daylight, but there already was a camper parked in the Clay Banks clearing. The sandy trail leads down the ridge through the trees, and we could see the serpentine loops of the river far below, dark through the falling snowflakes. The Whirlpool was upstream, hidden in the wintry trees beyond the swift reach of the river the steelheaders call Shapton's Run.

You sure we had to get up this early? I laughed.

Feel like you're after pickerel? Borgeson stopped on the path where it started down to the Deer Lick. *The steelhead lie in the deep holes at midday, particularly in bright weather, and they move out on the spawning riffles just before dark. They work the gravel during the night, and early morning is a good time to fish them, since they haven't been bothered for several hours.*

You mean we fish spawning steelhead? I speculated.

They seldom take the fly, although a cockfish may attack a bright streamer defending his territory, Borgeson explained, *but it's usually other fish that take a dead-drift nymph.*

Stray males and females? I added.

Exactly, Borgeson said.

It was a stretch of swift-flowing river that I had not fished since boyhood, and twenty-five years had passed since my flies had covered the Whirlpool and Green Cottage and Deer Lick stretch of the beautiful Pere Marquette in Michigan.

Boyhood seasons had been summer fishing in the whippoorwill twilight, with sulphur-colored hatches coming off in the gathering darkness and spinner flights with their bright egg-sac females in the swarm. There were morning fly hatches too, like the small *Ephemerella* and *Paraleptophlebia* flies that emerged just after breakfast, but the fish were only eight to fifteen inches and our season was closed when the steelhead were running.

It had all started in 1885, when the hatchery at Big Rapids received a shipment of steelhead fry from the Caledonia Hatchery in New York. The baby steelhead were introduced into the Pere Marquette the following spring, and many were caught that summer, but the next year the silvery California trout had vanished. Crackerbarrel opinion pronounced them worthless, and many fisheries experts agreed, not realizing the fish had migrated to Lake Michigan. Since the big lake-fattened rainbows did not return to the Pere Marquette until October, long after the regular trout season was closed, and finished spawning before it opened again, it was many years before Michigan fishermen realized they had created a superb steelhead fishery.

It was Fred Clark, the distinguished biologist who operated the Northville Hatchery in Michigan, who first became convinced that the big rainbows turning up in the meshes of the commercial netters were the result of the river stockings between 1876 and 1895. Clark began experimenting with pure steelhead strains in 1904, and the modern Michigan fisherman can thank his efforts for the big lake-run rainbows in rivers like the Au Gres, Platte, Betsie, Pere Marquette, Muskegon, Manistee, Little Manistee, and the lower Au Sable.

Steelhead fishing in Michigan improved steadily as these stockings took hold, until several of its rivers were quite famous for their lake-run rainbows. Fishermen travelled great distances to fish the steelhead runs in rivers like the Platte, Muskegon, Manistee, and Au Gres, but most of the trout were taken by fishing bait. Popular wisdom argued that nothing but spawn sacs and night crawlers and hardware would work, and most of the fish caught were probably snagged.

Many skilled fly-fishermen tried and tried to take them with little or no success. With the completion of the Welland Canal, both the alewives and the lamprey eels entered the Great Lakes, and their ecology was irrevocably changed. When the lampreys attacked and swiftly eradicated the lake trout, the invading alewives and native smelts were virtually free of predators, and their populations skyrocketed. The bright rainbows also thrived on these exploding baitfish populations, and steelhead fishing in Michigan exploded too, until the merciless lampreys turned to them. The predatory eels soon decimated the steelhead population, and fishing them seemed tragically ended until chemical control of the lampreys checked their reign of terror, and the big rainbows stubbornly replenished themselves. Each winter more and more steelhead were found ascending the Michigan rivers, spawning there in March and April.

Skilled Michigan steelheaders all rig their terminal tackle to work their flies on the bottom. Perhaps the most effective method uses a tiny triangle swivel. The nine-foot leader to about twelve-pound test is clinch-knotted to the first swivel-ring, with a twenty-five inch tippet fastened to the opposite swivel. About six inches of ten-pound nylon is knotted to the bottom swivel with a knot in its lower end. The split shot are added to this dropper nylon, adjusting the number of shot to the depth and speed of the current. When the weight is right, it is possible to walk the lead right along the bottom gravel, feeling it tick against the stones. The fly rides slightly higher, buoyed on the specific gravity of the nylon, but working right in front of the fish. The most effective quality of the lead-shot dropper is that when it fouls the bottom, the lead strips free or the dropper nylon breaks, while the tippet and fly are recovered.

It isn't the most graceful fishing, Dave Borgeson admitted while we rigged our leaders, *but it works.*

How big do these steelhead run? I asked.

Twenty to twenty-five pounds, Borgeson replied. *Simmy Nolphe took one last fall on a fly that weighed seventeen.*

You sure you want to use that derrick? I pointed to his powerful fiberglass rod. *Looks too muscular.*

Safer than your three-ounce graphite, he said.

We'll see! I laughed.

The snow was still falling when we reached the Deer Lick, and I was looking forward to field-testing one of the Fenwick graphite rods on Michigan steelhead. Muscling such fish in the brushy runs and cedar deadfalls of the Pere Marquette would test a rod to its breaking point.

We waded across the river above the Deer Lick riffle, its swift currents strong and slightly tea-colored, sucking fiercely through our waders. *Somebody's fishing the Deer Lick already*, Borgeson pointed upstream. *Looks like it might be Ron Spring.*

Did he invent the Spring's Wiggler? I asked.

That's right, Borgeson nodded.

We walked downstream through the willows, past a ten-pound steelhead hanging from a cedar deadfall, where the fisherman was working his nymph in a dark run under the trees.

Hello! Spring waded ashore and shook hands.

Looks like you scored, Borgeson said.

Took that one right after we got here, Spring explained. *My partner got another one downstream under the cedars.*

Seen a lot of fish? Borgeson asked.

Some, Spring admitted, *but this riffle is full of good fish this morning—just look at the bottom out there!*

What do you mean? I asked.

The bottom is covered with winter algae, Borgeson explained, *but out there where the steelhead are working their redds, the yellow gravel is showing.*

So you look for a riffle with pale gravel areas like those, I pointed to the shallows, *where the bottom has measles?*

Exactly, Spring laughed.

Spring explained that he had fished the run above the overhanging cedars earlier, but without any luck, although he had seen three fish before it started snowing.

I've had enough, Spring said. *You fish them.*

It's all yours. Borgeson pointed upstream.

Spring climbed a sapling above the riffle to locate the fish.

There are three out there, he pointed, *and another pair against the deadfall.*

They're big fish, Borgeson added.

It was snowing harder now, and I shivered a little wading into position, but not from the cold. The current worked swiftly against the clay banks upstream, gathering under the trees above the Deer Lick. It was smooth and silky over the pale gravel redds where earlier fish had spawned, and the steelhead were there, dark pewter-colored shadows just off the sheltering cedars.

You see them? Borgeson asked.

I nodded and rolled a cast upstream, its three-shot dropper looping high and falling clumsily into the swift current, and raised the rod to tick the lead along the bottom. It took a little practice to fish it right, feeling the lead grab slightly in a crevice, and raising the tip gently to free the dead-drift swing of the nymph.

The first two or three casts worked deep along the bottom, and I took a shuffling half step downstream between fly swings, covering the current in a series of concentric quarter circles. The two biggest fish expressed no interest in the drifting nymph.

There may be more fish in that dark run along the bank. Ron Spring pointed downstream. *Try a swing through there.*

The cast rolled out and dropped just above the cedar deadfall, and I stripped a little slack until I felt the lead start ticking along the gravel. The nymph worked deep and started into a teasing swing through the dark tea-colored water under the overhanging trees.

There was a heavy pull. *Fish!* I yelled.

The big steelhead threshed angrily, throwing spray with its spade-sized tail, and the Orvis reel screamed as it turned into the swiftest current-tongues of the Deer Lick. It held stubbornly for several seconds, keeping its head tight against the bottom, and then it cartwheeled under the cedars and was running again.

How deep is the Deer Lick Bend? I yelled. *The way he's taking line I may have to follow him through there!*

You can wade diagonally down along the bar, they said.

It could come to that! I laughed.

The steelhead threw rooster tails of spray down the shallows, about twenty yards into the backing, and I picked my way carefully down along the alders in pursuit. Deer Lick Bend is a deep reach of water above the Anderson cottage, and there is a logjam tangled with brush on the far bank, just where the riffle shelves off into the pool. There is deep water under the deadfalls there, and even deeper water in the bend itself, on my side of the river. It is a tightrope act wading diagonally downstream between these holes, particularly with the April currents tea-colored and full.

He's stopped! Borgeson yelled.

I fought to recover line, and regained all of my Dacron backing. *But he might try for the brush pile.*

You think that little rod can hold him? Spring asked.

The fish had its second wind now, and it bulldogged stubbornly along the bottom toward the tangled logjam. *Damn!* I groaned and applied butt pressure. *He's trying to get under there!*

That's some bend in that lead-pencil rod! Borgeson said.

What kind of rod? Spring asked.

Graphite, I laughed.

The slender graphite butt throbbed and held, turning the fish short of the logs, and the fight was over. There were several short half-sullen runs that were easily parried, and some panicky threshing to avoid the net, but finally Spring netted the tired steelhead and waded happily ashore.

What'll he weigh? I yelled.

He'll go nine or ten pounds easy, Spring answered. *He's a lot of fish in heavy water on a light rod like that!*

Graphite is light, I nodded, *but it's pretty strong.*

What's that rod weigh? Borgeson asked.

Three ounces. I grinned.

You can't fish three split-shot and steelheads on a three-ounce rod, Borgeson admitted. *Not bamboo or fiberglass anyway!*

It's an amazing material, I added.

Carbon graphite is one of several new synthetic fibers that have emerged from aerospace research in recent years, and its remarkable properties threaten to displace fiberglass from its supremacy in fishing rods once production costs become competitive.

Many expert fly-fishermen have never really liked fiberglass rods, except for wrestling with big chinooks or salt-water species, and it is the moderate price rather than optimal performance that causes glass to dominate the marketplace. American fishermen purchase approximately 3,000,000 rods annually, and almost ninety-seven percent of those rods are glass, fabricated from more than 500,000 pounds of specially woven fiberglass cloth. Glass rods have completely dominated the fishing tackle field since the first crude fiberglass rod section was built by Arthur Howald in 1944.

Factory-made glass rods, however, have failed to solve some of the problems in highly skilled trout fishing. Glass is unquestionably stronger and more resilient than bamboo, but its superior elasticity is strangely a disadvantage in fly-rod performance. Its resilience under casting loads is almost too lively to provide delicate tip calibrations capable of fishing modern nylons from .005 to .003 in diameter. Such 6X to 8X leader tippets are critical for success on our hard-fished modern trout streams, particularly on eastern waters.

Although fiberglass cloth is both lighter and stronger than bamboo, it is formed over a steel mandrel into tubular form. Fine split-cane rods are made in four-strip, five-strip, and six-strip sections, although ninety-nine percent are made in the hexagonal six-strip tapers. Even the partially hollow bamboo rods manufactured on the Pacific Coast do not deform under casting stresses, accepting the loads evenly and progressively, until those stresses reach the fracture point.

Fiberglass blanks become slightly oval under bending loads, since a tube deforms into an ovoid cross section in flexure, regardless of its construction. Glass tubes will accept casting stress until their cross sections deform into exaggerated ovals, and abruptly refuse to gather and release more power. It is possible to overload them far short of their breaking strength, because of their elasticity and tubular resilience, although they seldom actually break or shatter.

Fiberglass has another quality related to its mixed virtues of elasticity and strength that affects your fishing. Its modulus of elasticity is comparable to fine structural steels. It involves the ability of a flexing material to spring back from any deflection under stress to its original alignment. Engineers call this its rate of recovery, and since fiberglass has a shorter fibrous structure than bamboo, it springs back more quickly than a split-cane section. Its normal rate of recovery is exceptionally fast, but paradoxically it recovers too quickly for optimal casting performance. Its recovery is so rapid that too much inertia develops in the opposite direction, and the tip oscillates beyond its original alignment before it comes to rest again. Such sloppy dampening behavior slaps the shooting line back and forth against the rod and its guides, killing both distance and control in a really long cast. The recovery of fine split cane is sharper.

However, a really fine fiberglass rod is still a third the price of the best bamboo work, in spite of its problems. Skilled fishermen soon learn to compensate for its faults, adjusting their timing and power stroke to minimize its heavy-handed behavior with delicate tippets, its tendency to deform and saturate under casting stress, and its oscillations after final delivery.

Since fiberglass has great advantages in its price range, it quickly cornered the fishing tackle industry. Sufficient time has passed that an entire generation has grown up fishing with fiberglass only, and it seems perfectly happy with its performance. During these same years, the artisans famous for bamboo fly rods began dying off, and it looked like their art might die with them. Many expert trout fishermen gloomily looked ahead to a future without split-cane rods. It seemed virtually certain that fiberglass would triumph.

Its ultimate triumph is less certain today. Aerospace technology has developed several completely new synthetic materials for fishing rods in recent years, each with its own unique properties and character. Several tackle manufacturers have been experimenting with synthetic fly-rod prototypes of such materials as boron fibers, alumina, advanced types of high-modulus fiberglass, silicon carbide, boron carbide, high-modulus carbon graphite, and a new fiber called PRD-49, being kept secret by its developer, Du Pont. PRD-49 has slightly less stiffness and strength than these other exotic materials, and has problems with compressive bending stresses, but it costs and weighs much less than promising materials like boron and graphite.

These materials have some exotic properties. Boron is a semimetallic compound, deposited in vapor form on extremely fine tungsten wire. Its vapors take shape in a filament varying from .003 to .004 in diameter. It has twice the strength and stiffness of the finest steels, yet it weighs seventy percent less. It has produced rods closely approximating the performance of split cane, including its delicacy and feel in some exaggeratedly slender prototypes built by Don Phillips in Connecticut. These experimental boron rods achieved a twenty-percent reduction in diameter and a forty-percent reduction in weight, compared with similar rods in bamboo.

However, boron has some problems in terms of its fabrication into fly rods. Its fibers are not woven into a synthetic fabric, like carbon graphite or

CORTLAND 1975 TWO-PIECE TUBULAR CARBON GRAPHITE CORTLAND, NEW YORK FROM THE COLLECTION OF LEON CHANDLER

FENWICK H.M.G. 1973 TWO-PIECE TUBULAR CARBON GRAPHITE SEATTLE, WASHINGTON FROM THE COLLECTION OF ERNEST SCHWIEBERT

ORVIS LIMESTONE SPECIAL 1975 TWO-PIECE TUBULAR CARBON GRAPHITE MANCHESTER, VERMONT FROM THE COLLECTION OF ERNEST SCHWIEBERT

glass, and are arranged in a longitudinal alignment in a boron epoxy tape. Such tape is tightly wound and cured around a wire-forming core instead of a tubing mandrel, and early boron epoxy rods were of solid rather than tubular construction. Since there are no lateral fibers, like the spacing filaments in both fiberglass and carbon graphite fabric, to provide hoop strength, some potential structural problems exist in boron-fiber construction. However, there is also remarkable potential in the material, and some of the finest synthetic-fiber rods that I have tried in tapers for ultralight tippets have been boron epoxy prototypes. Like carbon graphite fibers, boron is still costly enough that its use is largely restricted to aerospace systems, where its strength and lightness are worth the price.

Boron and carbon fiber are perhaps the most promising synthetic fabrics for building rods in the immediate future. The basic costs and problems of fabrication involved in the other exotic fibers suggest that their full-scale introduction to the tackle industry lies well in the future. But my first field experience with the Fenwick and Orvis tubular graphite tapers, more than two years before they reached the public, clearly indicated that we were on the threshold of a fly-rod revolution—perhaps more extensive than the recent impact of fiberglass on bamboo, or the earlier impact of bamboo on hickory and greenheart more than a century ago.

Don Phillips has performed some intriguing comparative studies with the new exotic fibers. His work suggests that the modern S-type fiberglass has a clear performance advantage over earlier glass cloth. Low-modulus graphite was not yet available for his studies. High-modulus graphite and exotics like PRD-49 fibers were less adaptable to bending loads than boron filaments, although they are remarkably strong.

His calculations were based upon a theoretical rod section of tubular fabrication measuring one foot in length, with a constant stiffness factor of 500 pound-inches squared. Constant diameter was also assumed, with the structural fibers laminated parallel to the longitudinal axis and distributed equally in a wall thickness of thirty percent fiber densities. Such densities are possible without die-molding techniques under high pressures, and Phillips points out that his test section suggested the properties typical of an eight-foot synthetic-fiber rod for a seven-weight line at its midpoint, which he proposed as average.

Phillips found that modern fiberglass weighs .056 pound per cubic inch when fabricated into his theoretical section. Boron fibers weigh .055 pound and graphite only .053 pound per cubic inch. The boron section was clearly superior in bending, sustaining loads as high as 125,000 pounds per square inch, more than 100,000 pounds stronger than structural steel. Carbon fibers can accommodate bending stresses of 115,000 pounds per square inch, while the advanced S-type fiberglass can sustain loading of approximately 112,000 pounds. Such performance is a remarkable calibration of these exotic fibers.

Working with his stress formulas, which are outlined in the chapter on split-cane construction, Phillips continued to explore the properties of such materials. He quickly discovered that bending modulus (resistance to deformation) is clearly the factor in which the exotic fibers easily excel even the finest fiberglass. The S-type glass has a modulus of elasticity of almost 4,000,000 pounds per square inch when laminated into Phillips' theoretical section. Carbon fiber in the same blank would display a modulus of more than 9,000,000 pounds per square inch—more than twice that of the finest-quality glass. Boron fibers can deliver a modulus of elasticity exceeding 19,000,000 pounds per square inch, which is approximately twice the performance of graphite in Phillips' comparative studies. Such remarkable properties are eloquent testimony to our technology.

Fully assembled into hypothetical rods, Phillips concludes, a boron-fiber prototype would be half the weight of a comparable fiberglass design. Carbon-fiber construction would be about forty percent heavier than the boron prototype.

Rod-diameter studies offer other interesting factors. Fiberglass required a section diameter of .228 inch at the midpoint of its seven-weight taper. Boron fibers in a comparable rod design measured a remarkably slender .152 inch. Carbon graphite fibers laminated into a similar rod were .183 inch in diameter, requiring a slightly larger tubular design. Boron displayed a moment of inertia roughly twice that of S-type fiberglass, while the moment of inertia in the comparable graphite section was almost twice that of boron. Both moment of inertia and rod diameter play a role in fly-rod performance and tip speed, which translate into casting.

Although several manufacturers were field-testing equipment laminated from exotic fibers, Fenwick was the first to exhibit its experimental rods in 1973. Their debut came at the annual summer conclave of the Federation of Fly Fishermen, which gathered in Sun Valley.

André Puyans, a highly skilled professional fly-dresser with a fine fishing shop near San Francisco, was out of breath when he found me having lunch at the Ore House.

You've got to try those new rods! he said excitedly.

What new rods? I asked.

Carbon graphite fibers! Puyans gestured with typical animation. *You've got to try those graphites!*

Can't I finish my lunch first? I teased.

No! Puyans insisted.

We walked back toward the casting pond after lunch to talk with Jim Green of Fenwick about his new high-modulus rods. Green is unmistakably one of the finest casters who ever lived, with a poetic stroke and great economy of style, and I was eager to have his opinion on the new carbon-fiber tapers. There were four prototypes in the rack. The smallest was seven-and-a-half feet and only two ounces.

Two ounces! I shook my head in disbelief. *Only two ounces and it's rated for a five-weight line?*

Green put the rod back in his rack. *Carbon graphite has some remarkable properties.* He smiled at my excitement. *Our eight-foot model weighs a half ounce more and takes a six line.*

Two and a half ounces! I flexed it.

It would probably weigh four ounces in glass, Puyans said, *and still more in bamboo.*

Look at the others too, Green suggested.

The slender eight-and-a-half-foot rod was rated for an eight line, and weighed only three and one-quarter ounces. Fiberglass rods taking an eight-weight forward taper usually weigh about an ounce more, and comparable cane rods can reach five ounces. The nine-foot graphite was as slender as a delicate bamboo, was rated for a ten-weight line, and weighed only four ounces.

It will even throw an eleven-weight, Green said.

You're joking! I protested.

He's serious, Puyans interrupted. *Try one!*

We took all four rods to the casting pond, and Green strung the eight-and-a-half-foot model with a floating forward-taper line. The line looked too delicate for an eight-weight.

That really an eight-weight floater? I asked.

No. Green smiled. *It's a six.*

But you said the rod was rated for an eight, I protested. *What weight line does it really take?*

Puyans laughed. *Just stop talking and cast!*

Okay, I agreed.

There was a light wind coming straight in toward our casting platform, riffling the pond. The graphite rod felt stiff until it had a line loading at about forty feet, and then its character became slower and more poetic. It possessed surprising quickness, and it was so light for its relative power that it seemed ridiculously easy to slice a tight loop into the wind.

Since casting beyond sixty-odd feet is a problem in overcoming atmospheric effects on both the rod and its working line, and in achieving optimal tip speed at the moment of delivery, both the relatively thin diameter of the rod and its incredible lightness were obvious advantages in making long casts with amazingly little effort. It was surprisingly easy to pick sixty to seventy feet of line off the water, something I had never seen done with comparable cane or glass, and the backcasts were tight and high. The tip speed effortlessly held a narrow loop, and although distance casting had not been a particular skill of mine, these casts rolled out and turned over some surprising lengths of fly line.

The little rod was so fast and light that I was stunned. *You're right!* I said. *It will really handle line!*

Green and Puyans smiled broadly. *You haven't seen anything!* they said. *That's a six-weight you're throwing.*

But it's rated for an eight! I said.

Green stripped the line from the guides and rigged it with another reel. *Try it with a ten-weight,* he suggested.

Ten-weight! I protested. *It won't throw it!*

Just try it! Puyans growled.

The little rod worked the line out with surprising ease, loading more and more distance in a tight loop. It picked seventy-five feet off the water cleanly, accepted still more in my reverse shoot into a high backcast, and laid the entire line out with a single left-hand pump. Perhaps the most remarkable aspect of its performance was the sensation that I had made only minor adjustments in my timing to accommodate a fly line two sizes larger than its rated weight. The narrow loop accelerated with a lazy double-haul, shooting the entire line and a dozen feet of pale backing.

Better than a hundred feet! I was stunned.

Wrong! Puyans laughed and took the rod. *That's thirty-five yards of tournament taper, plus some backing hanging out and your leader—and that's more like a hundred and twenty!*

But I can't cast a hundred and twenty! I said.

Puyans smiled. *You just did!*

Carbon graphite fiber is a remarkable development. It is produced in a series of heat treatments which expose polyacrylonitrile to increasing temperatures and decreasing densities of oxygen. The polyacrylonitrile fibers are first oxidized at 200 to 300 degrees centigrade. Carbonization is achieved in a second stage at 1200 to 1500 degrees C., and they literally become graphite at kiln temperatures of 2000 to 3000 degrees.

During these final kiln settings, which occur completely without oxygenation, microscopic crystals are gathered as carbon graphite fibers. These somber-looking little fibers become delicate filaments approximately .0003 inch in diameter, with ratios of stiffness and weight that closely parallel those of boron, although carbon graphite is less expensive.

Appreciating synthetic-fiber equipment involves an understanding of not only the bending stresses of a material in flexure, when a material is exposed to strong oscillations between tension and compression, but also the concepts governing modulus of elasticity. Tensile forces, found in a taut violin string, are also present in the upper fibers of a rod while playing a fish. Compressive forces, such as are exerted on a load-bearing building wall, are also found in the lower fibers of the rod under the strain of the struggling trout. During the rhythmic stresses of casting, any rod is constantly changing its power-fiber stresses from tension to compression and back again.

Modulus of elasticity is a theoretical measure of a material in terms of its resistance to deformation. Applied to rod action, modulus of elasticity calibrates an exotic-fiber tube in terms of its intrinsic stiffness and its rate of recovery from stress. The Phillips studies demonstrate that the modulus of elasticity in boron- and carbon-fiber rods displays a remarkably dramatic change over that of past materials, including S-type fiberglass. Our grasp of modulus of elasticity and its role in fly-rod action is critical in understanding exotic fibers.

Carbon graphite has rapidly become the principal synthetic fiber in modern rod construction. Raw carbon fibers have a remarkable modulus of elasticity, reaching as much as 50,000,000 pounds per square inch. Such fibers are easily woven into clothlike fabrics that can be formed around a mandrel into rod sections. The basic process is quite similar to the manufacture of most fiberglass blanks. But the astounding rigidity of carbon-fiber tubular sections makes it virtually impossible to deform them under casting loads, or exceed their capacity to accept more bending stresses, unlike earlier fiberglass tapers. Carbon-fiber rods will stress cleanly and return crisply to their original alignment, with swift rates of recovery that shame the finest bamboo.

Fenwick discovered in its first high-modulus prototypes that carbon graphite rods had half the butt diameter of glass rods of comparable performance, and were twenty-five percent lighter. Comparisons with split cane are even more striking. Fenwick found that its early graphite tapers were about thirty percent smaller than the typical butt calibrations of bamboo designs, and their weight demonstrated a surprising fifty percent reduction over split-cane construction.

When these early Fenwick prototypes were finally available, they cost almost as much as many split-cane rods. Such prices were surprising to a generation conditioned by glass, but perhaps we should remember that when the first Shakespeare fiberglass rods were introduced, after the Second World War, they cost as much as an exquisite Payne or butter-colored Leonard.

The early Fenwick prototypes had black-anodized reel fittings of both skeletal and locking designs. Chromium snake guides, and stripping guides and tops of ceramic aluminum oxide, were also standard equipment. These tapers were based upon a hybrid construction which combined both graphite power fibers and fiberglass for tubular strength in conditions of lateral stress. Both wall thickness and tip diameters were relatively overdesigned in these early models, and their relatively stiff actions were received with mixed reviews from the advocates of both glass and split bamboo, whose casting habits often failed to extract the full potential of these carbon-fiber tapers because they were used to softer actions in glass and bamboo. The following rods, built by Fenwick, were the first carbon-fiber designs in production:

MODEL	LENGTH (FEET)	WEIGHT (OUNCES)	LINE WEIGHT
GFF755	$7^1/_2$	$2^1/_2$	5
GFF806	8	$2^5/_8$	6
GFF856	$8^1/_2$	$2^7/_8$	7
GFF858	$8^1/_2$	$3^1/_4$	8
GFF901	9	4	9

My first experience with carbon graphite was with field-testing the eight-and-a-half-foot design for an eight-weight line, using a taper designed for trout fishing to fish giant chinooks in northern California. Its capacity to handle big salmon in strong currents was surprising, and its ability to make long casts with ten- and twelve-weight shooting heads was nothing less than remarkable. It was even able to accommodate experimental shooting heads fabricated of lead-core trolling line, easily throwing distances beyond a hundred and twenty-five feet, and subdued chinooks of forty to fifty pounds. However, Fenwick soon abandoned these early designs, both because they were too stiff for the average caster and because its planners had begun to understand that graphite possessed an unusual potential for rods of greater length and delicacy. The second generation of Fenwick carbon-fiber rods includes the following trout-fishing tapers:

MODEL	LENGTH (FEET)	WEIGHT (OUNCES)	LINE WEIGHT
GFF634	$6^1/_2$	$1^7/_8$	4
GFF705	7	$2^1/_4$	4
GFF755	$7^1/_2$	$2^1/_2$	5
GFF756	$7^1/_2$	$2^5/_8$	6
GFF805	8	$2^5/_8$	5
GFF806	8	$2^3/_4$	6
GFF856	$8^1/_2$	3	6
GFF857	$8^1/_2$	$3^1/_4$	7
GFF858	$8^1/_2$	$3^1/_2$	8
GFF905	9	$3^1/_8$	5
GFF908	9	$3^3/_4$	8

These later designs were fitted with sliding ring and butt cap reel fittings in the models lighter than the GFF755, and with a black-anodized reverse-locking reel seat in the bigger rods. Fenwick has steadily worked to improve its graphite rod-tapers, and these current designs include several exceptional models. My experience with the Fenwicks leads me to admire the eight-foot GFF805 for a five-weight, and the eight-and-a-half-foot GFF856 tapered for a six-weight line. My introduction to the unique nine-footer designed for a five-weight occurred in the Paulina country of Oregon, when tournament caster Steve Rajeff let me fish the GFF905 Fenwick prototype he was field-testing.

The third generation of Fenwick graphites has dropped the delicate four-weight GFF634 and GFF705 designs. It has added the GFF756 and GFF906, which are six-weight tapers. Other new models are the GFF907, which takes a seven-weight line, and the nine-and-a-half-footer for a nine-weight. The current Fenwick HMG series includes these models:

MODEL	LENGTH (FEET)	WEIGHT (OUNCES)	LINE WEIGHT
GFF755	$7^1/_2$	$2^1/_2$	5
GFF805	8	$2^3/_4$	5
GFF905	9	$3^1/_8$	5
GFF756	$7^1/_2$	$2^5/_8$	6

MODEL	LENGTH (FEET)	WEIGHT (OUNCES)	LINE WEIGHT
GFF806	8	$2^3/_4$	6
GFF856	$8^1/_2$	3	6
GFF906	9	$3^1/_4$	6
GFF857	$8^1/_2$	3	7
GFF907	9	$3^1/_8$	7
GFF858	$8^1/_2$	$3^1/_8$	8
GFF908	9	$3^1/_4$	8
GFF959	$9^1/_2$	$3^5/_8$	9

Orvis started its line of carbon-fiber rods shortly after Fenwick introduced its high-modulus designs. Leigh Perkins sent me an early experimental model completely without Orvis markings, although its Superfine grip style and delicate reel bands clearly revealed its origins. The prototype was an eight-foot trout rod weighing less than two ounces and designed for a six-weight line. Other models quickly followed the success of the first Orvis graphites, which were trout rods designed for six- and eight-weight tapers, and the initial catalog included these types:

MODEL	LENGTH (FEET)	WEIGHT (OUNCES)	LINE WEIGHT
M9270	7	$1^5/_8$	5
M9276	$7^1/_2$	$1^3/_4$	6
M9280	8	$1^7/_8$	6
M9286	$8^1/_2$	$2^7/_8$	8
M9290	9	$3^1/_8$	9

Perkins was so excited by the performance of these early graphite rods that he soon decided Orvis would build its own graphite rod plant, making it possible to control both design and quality. Each of these early prototypes remains in the Orvis line, although some modifications in taper patterns and lamination quality have occurred. Orvis fabricates its rods with the same excellent fittings originally machined for its justly famous Battenkill split-cane rods. Its carbon-fiber rod blanks are left with the curing wraps exposed, like the original Howald windings on the first fiberglass rods from Shakespeare. Leaving their graphite rods with the wraps exposed echoes the Orvis tradition of finishing the impregnated Battenkill line without varnish, and the technicians at Orvis' Vermont factory firmly believe that stripping the spiral wraps can damage the carbon fibers that will sustain maximum bending stress. Such stripping and polishing did not affect fiberglass performance, and some custom glass rodmakers often modify their actions by polishing down wall thickness intentionally, but it could prove fatal in graphite. Perkins is restlessly improving and changing his line of carbon-fiber rods; the following trout rods are in the second Orvis line:

MODEL	LENGTH (FEET)	WEIGHT (OUNCES)	LINE WEIGHT
M9250	5	$1^{1}/_{8}$	5
M9266	$6^{1}/_{2}$	$1^{3}/_{8}$	4
M9270	7	$1^{5}/_{8}$	5
M9276	$7^{1}/_{2}$	$1^{3}/_{4}$	6
M9276-2	$7^{1}/_{2}$	$2^{1}/_{8}$	6
M9280	8	$1^{7}/_{8}$	6
M9280-2	8	$2^{1}/_{4}$	6
M9287	$8^{1}/_{2}$	$2^{5}/_{8}$	6
M9286	$8^{1}/_{2}$	$2^{7}/_{8}$	7
M9286-2	$8^{1}/_{2}$	4	8
M9290	9	$3^{1}/_{8}$	9
M9297	$9^{1}/_{2}$	$3^{5}/_{8}$	8

These rods include some remarkable tapers that I have greatly enjoyed fishing in recent months. The first few hours of field-testing taught me that the more delicate Orvis designs were striving to provide actions capable of fishing nylon tippet diameters of .005 inch, and the responsive stroke and tip speed of tapers like the M9280 made roll casts as long as eighty feet possible. The more delicate M9287 design, at eight-and-a-half feet and well under three ounces, was specially conceived for fishing fine tippets and difficult spring-creek conditions. It is perhaps my favorite Orvis graphite, although steelhead and sea-bright coho salmon in Alaska have led me to appreciate the fine qualities of the nine-and-a-half-footer designed for an eight-weight forward taper. Orvis is continuing to refine and augment its carbon-fiber line, and I fully expect longer rods of surprising delicacy and performance.

Orvis is still experimenting widely, discarding some of its earlier graphite prototypes, refitting others, and adding fresh surprises. Its current catalogues include these trout-fishing models:

MODEL	LENGTH (FEET)	WEIGHT (OUNCES)	LINE WEIGHT
JM9272-1	$7^{3}/_{4}$	$1^{1}/_{2}$	2
JM9274-1	$7^{1}/_{2}$	$1^{1}/_{2}$	3
JM9277-1	$7^{1}/_{2}$	$1^{5}/_{8}$	4
JM9262-1	8	$2^{1}/_{2}$	4
JM9262-21	8	$2^{1}/_{2}$	4
JM9288-1	9	$2^{7}/_{8}$	4
JM9270-11	$7^{1}/_{2}$	$1^{5}/_{8}$	5
JM9279-1	$7^{3}/_{4}$	$2^{1}/_{8}$	5
JM9242-21	$8^{1}/_{2}$	$2^{1}/_{2}$	5

MODEL	LENGTH (FEET)	WEIGHT (OUNCES)	LINE WEIGHT
JM9293-1	$9^{1}/_{4}$	$2^{3}/_{4}$	5
JM9298-1	9	$3^{1}/_{8}$	6
JM9278-21	$7^{1}/_{4}$	3	6
JM9278-1	7	$2^{5}/_{8}$	6
JM9276-1	$7^{1}/_{2}$	$1^{3}/_{4}$	6
JM9276-11	$7^{1}/_{2}$	$2^{1}/_{8}$	6
JM9280-1	8	$1^{7}/_{8}$	6
JM9287-1	$8^{1}/_{2}$	$2^{5}/_{8}$	6
JM9292-1	$9^{1}/_{4}$	3	6
JM9291-11	$9^{1}/_{2}$	$3^{1}/_{2}$	6
JM9283-1	$8^{1}/_{4}$	$2^{1}/_{2}$	7
JM9284-1	8	3	7
JM9294-1	9	3	7
JM9294-21	$9^{1}/_{4}$	$3^{1}/_{4}$	7
JM9286-1	$8^{1}/_{2}$	$2^{7}/_{8}$	8
JM9297-1	$9^{1}/_{2}$	$3^{5}/_{8}$	8
JM9290-1	9	$3^{1}/_{8}$	9

The JM9280-1 model is still similar to the first prototype that Leigh Perkins sent me for testing in 1974, and the JM9287-1 is a current match for the earlier Limestone Special. The new JM9262-1 is an eight-and-a-half-foot rod, weighing only two and a half ounces, and is matched with a DT4F line. The JM9242-21 is designed for the Henry's Fork and its problems, and is a superb fly rod for taking large fish on light tackle. The Spring Creek design is currently listed as the JM9293-1 model, and is a favorite tool in the collection of Jack Hemingway. Although I have fished it with pleasure, with both Hemingway and Bill Mason, it is missing from my collection because its length makes travel difficult. The JM9297-1 is similar to the older M9297, which was originally christened the Presentation Special. The so-called Tippet is a delicate three-weight JM9274-1 model, which I have enjoyed on small trout streams. The most recent Orvis in my collection is the JM9272-1, which weighs $1^{1}/_{2}$ ounces and is designed for a unique DT2F line. Its delicate casting stroke is a little startling, and I cannot wait to fish it in the spring.

Leonard quickly followed with its own series of pale-gray graphite rods, but its first production runs were rather ill-fated, using carbon-fiber blanks from a manufacturer with little tacklemaking experience. The early Graftek models were fitted with standard, fully machined Leonard fittings combined with black reel-seat fillers. Bright orange wrappings were a sharp contrast to the pale-gray epoxy finish. The following prototypes were the first Leonard graphite designs:

MODEL	LENGTH (FEET)	WEIGHT (OUNCES)	LINE WEIGHT
1310	7	$1^7/_8$	4
1312	$7^1/_2$	$2^1/_4$	5
1322	8	$2^3/_4$	6
1316	$8^1/_2$	3	7
1318	$8^1/_2$	$3^1/_2$	8

The rod-blank manufacturer unquestionably had problems with quality control in these early Leonard designs, just as several other tacklemakers experienced trouble in their first production runs. Considerable breakage occurred, both at the ferrules and in the graphite blanks themselves. Leonard obviously acquired some painful experience with its first carbon-fiber rods, and its lessons were not entirely technical. Their new production line consists of some of the most beautiful graphite rods yet made, and my experience with their character and performance is a testimony to their quality. The blanks are a rich golden brown, with a braided layer of carbon fibers to provide lateral tube strength to the longitudinal filaments that accept the bending stresses of casting. Black reel-seat fittings of typical Leonard excellence are mounted on cork or hardwood fillers in the skeletal and reverse-locking designs. The dark finish makes this series perhaps the most handsome of the current carbon-fiber rods, and it has been widely praised for its elegance. The following graphite models are found in the Leonard line:

MODEL	LENGTH (FEET)	WEIGHT (OUNCES)	LINE WEIGHT
504G	5	1	4
703G	7	$1^3/_8$	3
704G	7	$1^1/_2$	4
754G	$7^1/_2$	2	4
755G	$7^1/_2$	$2^1/_4$	5
756G	$7^1/_2$	$2^3/_8$	6
804G	8	$2^1/_4$	4
805G	8	$2^3/_8$	5
806G	8	$2^1/_2$	6
807G	8	$2^5/_8$	7
855G	$8^1/_2$	$2^1/_2$	5
856G	$8^1/_2$	$2^5/_8$	6
857G	$8^1/_2$	$2^3/_4$	7
858G	$8^1/_2$	$3^1/_8$	8
906G	9	$2^7/_8$	6
908G	9	$3^1/_4$	8

Carbon fibers were first developed in Britain. Leonard has christened these new rods its Golden Shadow models, and its blanks are fabricated entirely of graphite fibers in the United Kingdom. Since experiencing such troubles with its earlier sleeve-type ferrules, Leonard has changed to a boron-reinforced ferrule incorporating a spigot-type design. The strength of the boron fibers makes it possible to grind the spigot plugs to a precise ferrule fit. The reel-seat fittings used on these Golden Shadow rods are the same elegantly tooled fittings originally specified for the split-cane Leonards. The tapers designed for three- and four-weight lines are fitted with continuous cork handles and reel-seat fillers, mounted with butt caps and sliding rings. The carbon-fiber rods for five- to seven-weight lines feature elegant reverse-locking seats and hardwood fillers, with graceful Hardy-type handles. Golden Shadow rods designed for eight-weight tapers are fitted with standard down-locking Leonard hardware and cork grips.

There are several exciting graphite rods in the Leonard line. The seven-foot model for a three-weight is unique, and the 754G is a delicate graphite designed for a four-line that displays great promise. I have fished the eight-footer of just over two ounces that is rated for the four-weight tapers, and have found it perfectly suited to delicate spring-creek tactics. The eight-and-a-half-foot design weighing only two and a half ounces and taking a five-weight line is quite unusual too, and fishes well where the difficult mixture of long casts and fine tippets is required. The nine-footer for a six-weight is also intriguing.

Scientific Anglers has followed the success of its excellent fiberglass fly rods with a line of all-graphite models. Ceramic stripping guides are standard, and the running guides and tops are chrome stainless. The carbon-fiber blanks are built entirely of graphite, and the slender ferrules are exclusive with Scientific Anglers, combining high-performance alloys with spigot-type designs. Six models are available in tapers and line weights intended for trout fishing:

MODEL	LENGTH (FEET)	WEIGHT (OUNCES)	LINE WEIGHT
System G4	8	$2^3/_4$	4
System G5	$8^1/_4$	3	5
System G6	$8^2/_3$	$3^3/_4$	6
System G7	$8^5/_8$	4	7
System G8	$8^3/_4$	$4^1/_8$	8
System G9	$9^1/_3$	$4^1/_2$	9

Cortland has joined in the competition for the carbon-fiber tackle market, and recently introduced its line of uniquely built rods. Its Diamondback series takes its trademark from a combination of axial fibers and cross-braided graphite to provide an outer layer of power laminations. These diagonal hoop-strength fibers are visible, and inspired the Diamondback name. Cortland rods also combine tubular construction with solid tip-design for unique performance and durability. Aluminum oxide stripping guides are combined with hard chromium tops and guides. Cortland has also incorporated a solid exotic-fiber spigot ferrule. Several of its Diamondback series are trout-size equipment:

MODEL	LENGTH (FEET)	WEIGHT (OUNCES)	LINE WEIGHT
7034	7	$1^7/_8$	4
7056	7	$2^1/_8$	5
7645	$7^1/_2$	$2^1/_8$	5
7667	$7^1/_2$	$2^5/_8$	6
8056	8	3	6
8078	8	$3^3/_8$	7
8656	$8^1/_2$	3	6
8689	$8^1/_2$	4	8
9056	9	$3^1/_4$	6
9910	9	$4^1/_2$	9

Harry Wilson is the alchemist at the Scott factory, and after several months of empirical work, the company has selected its basic line of carbon-fiber rods. The following models are available:

MODEL	LENGTH (FEET)	WEIGHT (OUNCES)	LINE WEIGHT
G85-4	$8^1/_2$	2	4
G85-5	$8^1/_2$	$2^1/_8$	5
G90-3	9	$2^1/_8$	3
G90-4	9	$2^1/_4$	4
G90-5	9	$2^3/_8$	5
G90-6	9	$2^1/_2$	6
G90-7	9	$3^1/_4$	7
G95-8	$9^1/_2$	$3^1/_2$	8
G95-9	$9^1/_2$	$3^7/_8$	9

Lamiglas has totally accepted computer-design methodology to leap-frog the first-generation rods of other companies. Computer work has enabled the Lamiglas technicians to develop a surprising number of first-rate rod designs in the past two years. The company is also willing to build custom tapers and actions, and it offers a number of eight- to nine-foot rods of suppleness and remarkable delicacy. The present series of graphite tapers is available from Lamiglas:

MODEL	LENGTH (FEET)	WEIGHT (OUNCES)	LINE WEIGHT
F704	7	$1^7/_8$	4
F764	$7^1/_2$	$2^1/_{16}$	4
F765	$7^1/_2$	$2^1/_8$	5

MODEL	LENGTH (FEET)	WEIGHT (OUNCES)	LINE WEIGHT
F803	8	$1^{7}/_{8}$	3
F804	8	$2^{11}/_{16}$	4
F805	8	$2^{13}/_{16}$	5
F806	8	$2^{15}/_{16}$	6
F865	$8^{1}/_{2}$	$2^{15}/_{16}$	5
F866	$8^{1}/_{2}$	$3^{1}/_{16}$	6
F867	$8^{1}/_{2}$	$3^{3}/_{8}$	7
F904	9	$2^{7}/_{8}$	4
F905	9	$3^{1}/_{16}$	5
F906	9	$3^{3}/_{16}$	6
F907	9	$3^{5}/_{16}$	7
F908	9	$3^{15}/_{16}$	8
F909	9	$4^{1}/_{16}$	9
F964	$9^{1}/_{2}$	$3^{5}/_{16}$	4
F965	$9^{1}/_{2}$	$3^{1}/_{2}$	5
F966	$9^{1}/_{2}$	$3^{7}/_{16}$	6

Winston is another famous maker of split-bamboo rods that has accepted carbon-fiber technology. Based upon its testing of rods built by other manufacturers, Winston concluded that carbon fibers were best suited to fast- and medium-action tapers, that their exotic properties were perfectly suited to making powerful rods of surprisingly little weight, and that they held the promise of delicate fly rods of unusual length and lightness.

Winston turned to the same manufacturer that built its superb fiberglass sections, Kennedy Fisher of Los Angeles, and started a program of research and development. Taper patterns and delicate mandrels were required if Winston intended to translate its famous hollow-built bamboo performance into graphite. It took considerable empirical work to develop and perfect the right combinations of taper patterns and lamination mandrels, and to select the proper carbon-fiber cloth to fabricate rods of graphite and fiberglass for lateral reinforcing. The method resulted in rods composed almost entirely of graphite, and offered the Winston designers considerable versatility in their tip calibrations and performance. Sleeve-type ferrules are mounted on the tip sections, and are fashioned of fiberglass reinforced with carbon-fiber cloth. Winston fittings are of the same quality found on their split-cane designs. The light rods offer skeletal reel seats with sliding rings and butt caps on specie-cork fillers. Their medium trout models have elegant down-locking hardware and hooded butt-cap assemblies. The hardwood fillers are available in teak, black walnut, and richly grained rosewood. The classic Winston assembly of down-locking hardware on a Bakelite filler is still available on special order. Perhaps the most surprising feature of the Winston graphite line is its rich forest-green finish, combined with matching green wrappings, and offering the typical Winston craftsmanship. The following models will be available:

LENGTH (FEET)	WEIGHT (OUNCES)	LINE WEIGHT
$7^1/_2$	$1^7/_8$	4
$7^1/_2$	$1^7/_8$	5
8	2	4
8	$2^1/_8$	5
8	$2^1/_2$	6
$8^1/_2$	$2^1/_8$	4
$8^1/_2$	$2^1/_2$	5
$8^1/_2$	$2^5/_8$	6
$8^1/_2$	3	7
9	$2^3/_4$	5
9	$2^7/_8$	6
9	$3^1/_4$	7
9	$3^1/_2$	8
9	$3^5/_8$	9

Winston has several unique combinations of rod length and delicacy and line weight in its list, and its designers obviously do not believe in rod lengths under seven and a half feet for an exotic material with the high-modulus stiffness of graphite. The series includes an eight-foot rod and an eight-and-a-half-footer designed for the light four-weight lines, and nine-footers for both five- and six-weight tapers.

Ron Kusse has started building carbon-fiber rods of excellent design, using the same elegant fittings of German silver found on his split-bamboo work. His smoothly polished graphite shafts are available with either spigot or German-silver ferrules. Walnut, cherrywood, cork, and tiger maple reel-seat fillers are available on the following rods:

MODEL	LENGTH (FEET)	WEIGHT (OUNCES)	LINE WEIGHT
KCF-603	6	1	3
KCF-664	$6^1/_2$	$1^1/_8$	4
KCF-704	7	$1^1/_4$	4
KCF-705	7	$1^1/_2$	5
KCF-763	$7^1/_2$	$1^1/_4$	3
KCF-764	$7^1/_2$	$1^5/_8$	4
KCF-765	$7^1/_2$	2	5
KCF-804	8	$2^1/_8$	4
KCF-805	8	$2^1/_4$	5
KCF-806	8	$2^1/_2$	6

MODEL	LENGTH (FEET)	WEIGHT (OUNCES)	LINE WEIGHT
KCF-865	8½	2¾	5
KCF-866	8½	3¼	6
KCF-867	8½	3½	7
KCF-868	8½	3¾	8
KCF-906	9	3½	6
KCF-908	9	4	8

Jerry Fleming is a friend building fine graphite rods in British Columbia, and I first cast with them at a boat show in Oregon. The rods are beautifully fitted and finished, and their aesthetic character had an impact on the rods built by bigger manufacturers. My experience with the Fleming rods suggests that his five- and six-weight models are excellent, particularly in the nine-foot lengths. The small Fleming designs under eight feet are fitted with cigar grips and a sliding-band seat, and the longer rods offer reverse-locking seats and full-Wells grips. The Fleming series is the following:

MODEL	LENGTH (FEET)	WEIGHT (OUNCES)	LINE WEIGHT
JFG-763	7½	1½	3
JFG-764	7½	1⅝	4
JFG-805	8	2½	5
JFG-806	8	2¾	6
JFG-865	8½	2½	5
JFG-866	8½	2¾	6
JFG-867	8½	2⅞	7
JFG-905	9	3	5
JFG-906	9	3¼	6
JFG-907	9	3½	7
JFG-908	9	3¾	8
JFG-968	9½	4	8

Sage carbon-fiber rods are relatively new, but their quality has quickly established them in the marketplace. The quality and design of the Sage blanks are no accident. The technical excellence and quality of the Sage line comes from a cadre of old Fenwick staff members, including Les Eichorn and Don Green, who played major roles in the creation of the first carbon-fiber rods.

Fittings and finishes were a major part of our thinking, Eichorn explained on the Kulik in Alaska. *We wanted graphites that looked like the finest old bamboos—the old Leonards and Paynes.*

Sage manufactures and finishes its own blanks, and their tapers, cloth

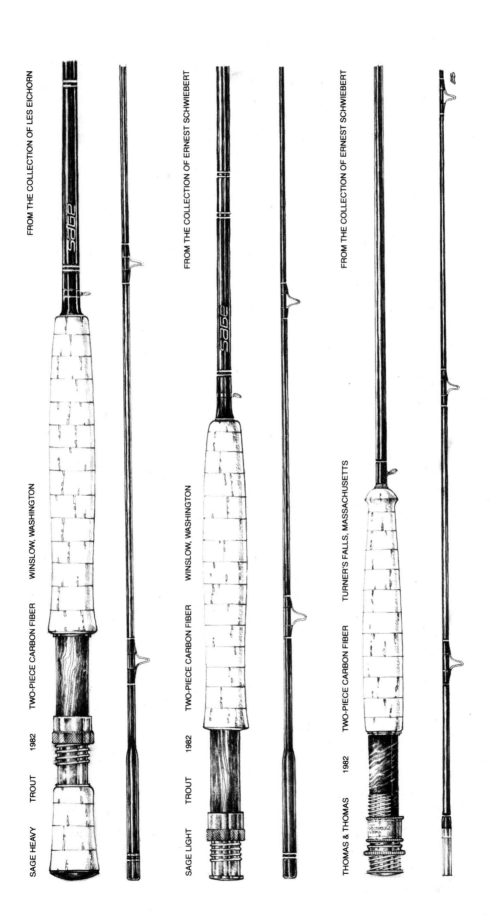

FROM THE COLLECTION OF LES EICHORN

SAGE HEAVY   TROUT   1982   TWO-PIECE CARBON FIBER   WINSLOW, WASHINGTON

FROM THE COLLECTION OF ERNEST SCHWIEBERT

SAGE LIGHT   TROUT   1982   TWO-PIECE CARBON FIBER   WINSLOW, WASHINGTON

FROM THE COLLECTION OF ERNEST SCHWIEBERT

THOMAS & THOMAS   1982   TWO-PIECE CARBON FIBER   TURNER'S FALLS, MASSACHUSETTS

patterns, and curing are exceptionally fine. Its fabrication equipment and techniques have explored fresh ground. Sage tapers have a distinct casting stroke, perhaps a little slower than some designs, but with the butt power to lift cleanly and control a tight casting loop. The Sage graphite rods are ninety-seven percent carbon fiber. The sleeve-type ferrules offer a taper-fit design, without boron or fiberglass or carbon fibers.

The rich brown finish is flawlessly cured and polished. The final epoxy coating is mirror-bright, compounded to resist abrasion, solvents, and the damaging effects of sunlight.

Sage specifications include quality most typically associated with traditional bamboo makers. The grips are select specie-cork rings cut from Spanish cork-oak trees. Shotgun-grade walnut fillers are used in Sage reel seats. Jewel-polished aluminum fittings are used in both standard and reverse-locking designs. Guides and fly-keepers are first quality. The hand wrappings are subtly keyed to the chocolate finishes of the rods: rich brown with a few ornamental turns of dull amber. The visual character of Sage rods is unique, although like most bigger manufacturers, its trademark is perhaps too large and garish. Sage produces a relatively large volume of rods, and its line is justly admired. The trout-fishing models in the Sage line include the following:

MODEL	LENGTH (FEET)	WEIGHT (OUNCES)	LINE WEIGHT
GFL470	7	$2^{1/4}$	3
GFL476	$7^{1/2}$	$2^{3/8}$	4
GFL576	$7^{1/2}$	$2^{1/2}$	5
GFL676	$7^{1/2}$	$2^{5/8}$	6
GFL580	8	$2^{5/8}$	5
GFL680	8	$2^{3/4}$	6
GFL586	$8^{1/2}$	3	5
GFL686	$8^{1/2}$	$3^{1/8}$	6
GFL786	$8^{1/2}$	$3^{1/4}$	7
GFL490	9	$3^{1/8}$	4
GFL590	9	$3^{1/4}$	5
GFL690	9	$3^{3/8}$	6
GFL790	9	$3^{1/2}$	7
GFL890	9	$3^{5/8}$	8
GFL696	$9^{1/2}$	$3^{5/8}$	6
GFL896	$9^{1/2}$	4	8
GFL996	$9^{1/2}$	$4^{3/4}$	9

My own collection includes three Sage rods, although I have either cast or fished most of its line. It is important to understand, as it was also true of Winston and Powell rods in their early years, that Sage rods almost unconsciously echo the unwritten criteria of western fishing. Most of these rods are keyed to fishing big water, wading deep, and distance work. Except for the shorter designs, which are fashionable eastern lengths and line-weight tapers, even the four- and five-weight designs offer enough length to mitigate the problems of selectivity and big fish on a daily basis. Few eastern anglers face more than selective feeding and small waters. Big fish are a rarity. Sage equipment manages a fine equilibrium between performance and aesthetics, and its line offers some unique designs. The GFL490 is nine feet and takes a four-weight. It is a favorite in both New Zealand and Alaska, on big trout in relatively small waters, and it is excellent on western spring creeks on days with little wind. The GFL690 is a nine-foot rod for a six-weight taper, and is better under windy conditions on such streams. The GFL896 is a longer eight-weight rod that easily casts an entire line under windy conditions, and has proved itself on difficult rivers from Alaska to the Antipodes.

Thomas & Thomas started working in carbon fibers about six years ago, and its first prototypes quickly rivaled the excellence of its craftsmanship in cane. Both fittings and performance were enviable.

With a growing tradition of delicate split-cane designs, Thomas Dorsey sought to transpose the best of his bamboo tapers into graphite patterns. The first models were entirely two-piece designs, with gracefully faired graphite-to-graphite ferrules, and a machined band of German silver to reinforce each ferrule throat. The rod blanks are entirely fabricated from carbon-fiber cloth. Carbide stripping guides were combined with stainless guides, tops, and flykeepers. The grips are first-grade Spanish specie cork. The early Thomas & Thomas graphites were fitted with the same elegantly machined butt caps and sliding-band hardware found on its cane rods, with shotgun-grade hardwood fillers. Models intended for fishing seven- to nine-weight lines have a Hardy-style grip and reverse-locking hardware, with both polished aluminum and wood fillers. The following rods were in the first Thomas & Thomas line:

MODEL	LENGTH (FEET)	WEIGHT (OUNCES)	LINE WEIGHT
TTGF-407	7	$1^{3/4}$	4
TTGF-467	$7^{1/2}$	2	4
TTGF-567	$7^{1/2}$	$2^{1/4}$	5
TTGF-408	8	$2^{3/8}$	4
TTGF-608	8	$2^{1/2}$	6
TTGF-668	$8^{1/2}$	$2^{5/8}$	6
TTGF-768	$8^{1/2}$	$2^{7/8}$	7
TTGF-868	$8^{1/2}$	$3^{1/8}$	8
TTGF-509	9	$2^{3/4}$	5
TTGF-809	9	$3^{7/8}$	8
TTGF-669	$9^{1/2}$	3	6
TTGF-969	$9^{1/2}$	4	9

These early Thomas & Thomas graphites were excellent rods, and I particularly enjoyed fishing the eight-foot model for a DT6F. The TTGF-509 of nine feet, and fitted with a five-weight line, was another early design of great promise.

Current Thomas & Thomas graphites have both fully machined German-silver ferrules and exquisite reverse-locking reel seats. Both pigeon-grade hardwood and polished aluminum fillers are available. Guide wrappings are ebony with silver ivory trim. The following Thomas & Thomas graphites have been added:

MODEL	LENGTH (FEET)	WEIGHT (OUNCES)	LINE WEIGHT
TTGF-568	$8^1/2$	$2^1/2$	5
TTGF-569	$9^1/2$	3	5
TTGF-909	9	$3^7/8$	9

Thomas Dorsey also introduced a series of unusually elegant carbon-fiber rods in his Special Dry Fly series. His modern template-patterns have been married to his sense of tradition in these designs. The Spanish specie-cork grips have been shaped into modified Hawes-style handles, both slightly old-fashioned and unique. The Special Dry Fly rods have quickly become best-sellers at Thomas & Thomas.

The tapers combine a slightly faster action with unusually sensitive tip calibrations. The first rod in the series was an eight-foot design intended for a DT4F or DT4$^1/2$F taper. Thomas & Thomas owners soon asked for a slightly bigger dry-fly rod, intended for five- and six-weight performance. My experience with the SDF-408 suggests that it is a remarkably conceived piece of equipment, and I have fished mine widely. It has proved itself on difficult trout waters and even in bug-fishing on big bluegills, with Bob Buckmaster in Wisconsin. It has been such a pleasure that I bought a matching SDF-408 for my son, when he finished preparatory school in 1982. The Special Dry Fly series includes two superb trout rods:

MODEL	LENGTH (FEET)	WEIGHT (OUNCES)	LINE WEIGHT
SDF-408	8	$2^3/8$	4
SDF-538	$8^1/4$	$2^1/2$	5

Several other manufacturers are studying the potential of carbon-fiber technology, along with the justly famous custom builders who have worked extensively in glass. There are seemingly an infinite number of cloth patterns and mandrel tapers and hybrid laminations of fiberglass and graphite to explore.

Carbon-fiber rods have perhaps generated more short-term excitement among serious anglers than any other single bench mark in the history of fly-fishing equipment.

Some advocates have hailed the exotic new fiber as the ultimate material for rod construction, while others have expressed some nagging doubts. Considered solely in terms of its casting properties, graphite construction is quite remarkable. Its physical properties of stiffness and recovery from stress offer singular power-to-weight ratios, as well as tight casting loops combined with high line speed. Such qualities mean less fatigue, better casting performance on windy days, and more distance with less casting effort.

There is also a lot of crackerbarrel talk about greater tip sensitivity, which seems misplaced. Sensitivity seems to imply delicacy in fishing, and the delicacy of fine split-cane craftsmanship is relatively absent in most graphite rods. There is a relatively swift transmission of vibrations through a carbon-fiber structure, but that quality stems from its quickness rather than its sensitivity. Carbon graphite has remarkable speed in its recovery from stress, and that quality is rooted in its modulus of elasticity, yet its sharp response to stress and its brisk recovery from that stress cannot be considered sensitivity. Such properties are superb in casting, but in fishing they can also shear a fine tippet or tear the fly out of a head-shaking fish, particularly when the rod dances harshly.

Too many fishermen have interpreted the tensile strength and high modulus of elasticity found in carbon fibers as raw strength in rods. It has been a painfully expensive myth. Graphite rods are much more fragile than fiberglass, although less brittle than bamboo. Fabricated into tubular blanks, graphite is amazingly strong in its casting properties, but it will fracture easily under a careless lateral impact. It is important to understand that graphite rods are easily broken, even though the exotic fibers in their tubular structures are twice as strong as fiberglass, six times as strong as steel. Modulus of elasticity is the secret of both weakness and strength in graphite: while fiberglass will display as much as four percent deformation without failure, carbon graphite can accept less than one percent before fracturing. Graphite must be given the respect offered to bamboo.

Since fiberglass will deform without breaking, its followers have often developed some bad habits. Glass will often accept excessive casting loads before fracture, while graphite will continue to absorb stress until it literally explodes. I have broken two graphites in field-testing. The first sustained a spiral fracture while I was attempting to pick up exaggerated lengths of line from the casting pond. The second literally exploded in my hand. It was an eight-and-a-half-footer designed for a six-weight line, and we were double-hauling unusual distance casts. I had just picked up more than sixty feet, accelerating it high into the backcast, and was allowing line to shoot in to my forward false-cast. When I closed my fingers to check the forward shoot and started back into the second left-hand haul, the graphite exploded like a pistol shot under my casting hand and completely shattered the grip. Like any other fine piece of equipment, graphite rods must not be carelessly abused.

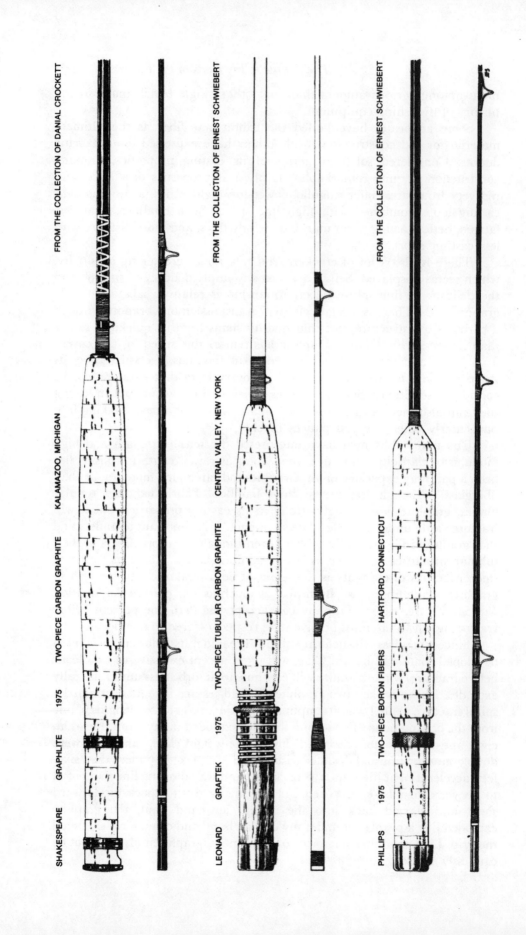

SHAKESPEARE   GRAPHLITE   1975   TWO-PIECE CARBON GRAPHITE   KALAMAZOO, MICHIGAN

FROM THE COLLECTION OF DANIAL CROCKETT

LEONARD   GRAFTEK   1975   TWO-PIECE TUBULAR CARBON GRAPHITE   CENTRAL VALLEY, NEW YORK

FROM THE COLLECTION OF ERNEST SCHWIEBERT

PHILLIPS   1975   TWO-PIECE BORON FIBERS   HARTFORD, CONNECTICUT

FROM THE COLLECTION OF ERNEST SCHWIEBERT

Fishermen have responded quite emotionally to graphite. The advocates of split-cane tend to dislike its somber appearance, its roots in a technology that utterly abandons the violin-building aspects of rodmaking, and a lack of delicate poetry in its action.

The fiberglass generation has embraced these exotic fibers as enthusiastically as their parents accepted the first Howald-patent glass rods after the Second World War. In those years the pot-belly stoves of trout-country bars and tackle shops across the country witnessed many sermons predicting the swift demise of bamboo. Similar talk is alive again, with a new generation, infatuated with exotic fibers, expecting the extinction of both fiberglass and cane.

It is important to understand that graphite rods have already experienced a surprisingly swift evolution in their brief history. The present carbon-fiber products vary widely, and are not as alike as many knowledgeable anglers seem to believe. There are striking variations in actions and specifications and tapers. Such differences reflect the understandable preoccupation of each rodmaker with either particular fishing problems or the preferences of its customers.

Since graphite tackle in several price ranges is starting to appear in the marketplace, there is some confusion among fishermen about carbon-fiber quality and costs. The quality of carbon-fiber cloth is relatively constant. Variables obviously exist in the technology of taper patterns, mandrel specifications, lamination, adhesives, and curing techniques. Price variables also relate to the percentage of graphite cloth used in a particular rod blank. Fiberglass-and-graphite laminates are common. Delicate layers of glass fabric are used both to reinforce the lateral strength of the tubular rod blanks and to soften a harsh graphite action. Some rods are fabricated with pure graphite fibers, while others are more than ninety percent carbon-fiber construction. Still others are sold as graphite equipment when in reality they are fiberglass blanks with a veneer of graphite cloth so thin it scarcely affects the action. It is wise to purchase these exotic-fiber rods from well-known manufacturers with a fine reputation to protect—and to expect to pay their prices.

Graphite and its sister synthetic fibers have both triggered a revolution in rodmaking and created a storm of controversy. The new rods have proved themselves quite popular, yet many experienced fishermen still seem a little baffled by their properties and character. Many anglers have sampled graphite rods only in the confines of tackle shops, and most carbon-fiber rods seem stiff without a line working.

Forget everything you think you know about rods when you wiggle a graphite without actually casting it, Jim Green observes wryly, having watched such meaningless rituals for many years. *You can't tell anything about graphite without a line in the air—because graphites are the first rods with insufficient density to flex themselves!*

Working with these fibers gives you a fresh respect for cane, Leigh Perkins argues. *They're more like bamboo than bamboo.*

4. The Story of Borontrichloride

The day was cold and raw.

It was a strange time to test an exotic new fishing rod. The hotel doorman was busily hailing taxis from the traffic that filled Fifty-ninth Street, and a brittle winter sun tried to warm the bare trees in Central Park.

The Theodore Gordon Flyfishers were having their annual March banquet in Manhattan. The membership was gathering before lunch to explore the tackle manufacturers' booths and to attend the films and lectures scheduled in the ballroom of the Essex House.

Later I was sitting in the bar with Charles De Feo and Everett Garrison, enjoying a mixture of whisky and winter twilight among the leather and mahogany millwork and mirrors. It was early in 1973.

Can you spend fifteen minutes? It was Don Phillips, an aeronautical engineer from Hartford. Phillips held a slim six-foot tube in his hands. *I've got something here that might surprise you.*

Fly rod? I asked.

Heard you express some doubts about building really delicate rods with aerospace fibers, Phillips explained. *So I built you a surprise.*

Graphite, I asked, *or something else?*

Boron, Phillips said quietly.

We walked to the main ballroom, which stood empty after the last fishing program. We moved along the center aisle below glittering chandeliers, and through acres of folding chairs that had witnessed years of weddings, bar mitzvahs, and cotillions.

Phillips drew a frail-looking rod from its six-foot case. Its calibrations were startling, the butt was scarcely the diameter of a soda straw, and its tip section was as delicate as a pencil lead. Such diameters were a revelation after years of fishing the fat fiberglass tapers that evolved just after the Second World War.

Even the first tubular carbon-fiber prototypes, which I had field-tested before Fenwick introduced them, seemed fat in comparison.

It's pretty delicate, I said.

It's an exaggeration to make my point, Phillips admitted. *But I decided to copy the Leonard one-piece Baby Catskill in boron—because you thought it was impossible.*

Can we try casting it?

That's why I brought you in here, he said.

Phillips produced a Hardy Flyweight fitted with a two-weight British silk. It seemed strange in the empty ballroom, casting a half-ounce rod and its antique line, and watching it deliver casts on the faded carpets.

Well, I said sheepishly after a dozen casts, *I've been wrong before.*

Graphite and boron are hardly new.

As a young air force officer, I had first seen both materials in the aircraft testing laboratories at Wright Field, just after the Korean War.

Ten years later, working in test facilities planning, I saw these exotic filaments used in experiments with propellers and helicopter rotors and engines. It was startling to find such exotic technology being used in fishing rods.

Carbon graphite was the first aerospace material to emerge in the tackle industry. It was woven into a strong fabric like webbing that could be cut easily into patterns, and adapted to the tubular fabrication methods of fiberglass production at acceptable costs.

Although graphite and boron have similar properties, it is impossible to weave boron into a cloth, Phillips explained. *Boron is more difficult to make, and building it into rods takes some handiwork—so boron rods are more expensive.*

Boron is surprisingly common.

The element is widely distributed in nature. Its character includes a unique mix of strength, hardness exceeding the carbides, low density, a remarkable capacity to withstand distortion under both compression and tensile stress, and the ability to perform under extreme temperatures. Such properties have obvious attractions for aircraft technology.

Boron is most commonly found in borax. Armchair television historians will remember it was mined and transported by twenty-mule teams in early California.

Commercial deposits of borax are typically found in the sedimentary beds of desiccated seas. Its original commercial uses included antiseptic solutions, preservatives, soldering and welding fluxes, Pyrex glassware, shellacs, enamel finishes, ceramic colors and glazes, and cleaning compounds before detergents were widely introduced. Other remarkable uses have evolved in recent years. The ability of boron to resist abrasion and thermal stress, and its poor conductivity and inert chemistry, have led to sophisticated applications ranging from fuel additives to control rods in nuclear reactors.

It is curious that Sir Humphrey Davy, who is better known to fishing bibliophiles for his charming book *Salmonia,* discovered boron in his laboratory in 1808.

Davy would be fascinated by the sophistication of our boron technology today. Its fabrication at the Avco Laboratories near Boston has obvious overtones of science fiction. It has the tight security associated with other secret projects. Guards and security badges and checkpoints control access to its commonplace buildings, but its boron chambers themselves are firmly rooted in the future. Boron filaments are made in partially darkened chambers filled with glowing tubes. The corridorlike rooms are bathed in their eerie orange light resembling settings in books by Fleming or Deighton or LeCarré.

The boron-making process takes place in these glowing tubes. The tubes are filled with a secret mixture of gases that includes borontrichloride.

The entire process is monitored in each tube by its own fluttering meters and gauges. There is a thin tungsten wire at the axis of each tube, and it is fed through its chamber at a precisely controlled rate. The mixture of gases is held at exact temperature. The tungsten wire and gases are given opposite electrical charges, extracting boron crystals from the borontrichloride gas, and precipitating them on the slowly moving wire. Each boron filament is a crystalline structure on a tungsten core, and measures .004-inch in diameter. Avco scientists believe a similar process might be developed to precipitate boron crystals on a spiderweb filament of graphite, making still lighter and stronger boron fibers possible.

Each tungsten-core filament is collimated in quarter-inch Mylar tapes. Boron crystals are so abrasive that such parallel filaments cannot be permitted to cross or touch, since they would quickly cut or abrade one another. After quality-control testing, Avco uses a complex stagger-frame system that feeds the individual boron filaments into their final tape alignment through a fifty-three die plate. The fifty-three fibers are fixed to the Mylar tape with epoxy resins, and the quarter-inch tapes are assembled on fiberglass backing in twelve-tape increments, to a maximum width of forty-eight inches. Fully collimated and cured sheets are rolled between polyethylene to protect the boron filaments from themselves, and are shipped in Styrofoam containers.

The abrasive properties of boron crystals suggest that weaving their filaments into clothlike fabrics is unlikely, and that sandwiching them into fishing rods will remain a costly process.

Don Phillips was the first to understand the potential of boron filaments in fly-rod design.

It was a series of happy accidents, Phillips explains. *We were working on propeller and rotor applications of carbon fibers and boron at Hamilton Standard in 1966—and the stress analysis in propellers and helicopter rotors is surprisingly close to describing the oscillations of working stress in fishing rods.*

What about the bad rumors? I asked.

What rumors?

The stories about boron's being dangerous in a thunderstorm, I explained, *or that it can explode into needles when it fractures.*

Both things are myths, he said.

What happens?

Boron is such a poor conductor that it is used in lightning arresters and insulators, Phillips replied. *It fractures pretty much like bamboo—shattering across its linear fibers when it goes.*

Phillips built his first boron prototypes late in 1971, and took his first trout with one that following spring on the Battenkill. His first rods were adaptations of the early Howald patents in fiberglass construction, and their boron tapes were shaped around a balsawood armature. Phillips was excited about his first experiments, but admits they were relatively fragile. Other concepts were tried later, and he finally settled on a solid boron design formed around a .03-inch diameter tungsten core held in tension. It is a hundred percent boron construction, with its permanent tungsten armature. Phillips has filled more than 350 orders since 1972, and owns the pioneering patents on solid-boron fabrication and several boron-hybrid composite designs.

I took an eight-foot Phillips boron to the Yellowstone country in 1973, and its baptism took place on free-rising cutthroats at Buffalo Ford.

It was fitted with conventional guides and a sliding-band reel seat. Its solid construction on a tungsten core made both sleeve- and spigot-ferrule designs unworkable. Phillips decided on German-silver ferrules, like those still used on expensive cane rods, and his boron rods are still fitted with them today.

The action of the eight-foot Phillips was slow and smooth, designed for a DT4F line. Its slightly top-heavy feel demanded precise timing and patience. Its stroke could not be forced, or fished with a left-hand haul. Hard casts simply caused it to flutter, throwing a wavy line or unwanted hooks, but it cast cleanly with a slower casting rhythm. It was perhaps a bit too spaghettilike in its middle calibrations. Refusing the line loads of casts beyond seventy-five feet, it also had a tendency to bounce out-of-plane under the impact stresses of big head-shaking fish. Other synthetic rods have displayed similar problems. Erratic oscillation while playing large trout or forcing long casts has been troublesome in many light rods, in virtually all light, tubular fiberglass and carbon-fiber and boron designs. Yet the Phillips eight-foot rod offered exciting promise, fishing 6X tippets on big trout.

It was late September on the Yellowstone at Buffalo Ford, and on the winding flats at Slough Creek. The fish were taking minute *Tricorythodes* spinners in the late mornings, and hung just under the surface after lunch, sipping tiny midge pupae in the film. It took imitations of these insects, dressed on size twenty hooks and fished on fragile .005 nylon, to take the steadily rising trout. The rod fished the delicate tippets and tiny hooks flawlessly, its subtlety unmatched by the other synthetic rods of its time.

Although such prototypes were still flawed, the Phillips design was a revelation. It was completely unlike the stiff power-tapers of the first carbon prototypes I had tested on big chinooks in 1971. Boron was an exciting prospect.

The first graphites were casting cannons. I reported to Phillips when I returned from the Yellowstone. *Perfect for shooting heads and distance casting—but your boron rod has a lovely stroke, soft and a little like bamboo.*

We're still trying things, he said.

Five years ago, another Phillips prototype arrived for testing. It was a second eight-foot model that specified a three-weight line, and it had corrected the earlier problems. Three-weight rods are not designed for long casts, but the new rod delivered forty to sixty feet with both delicacy and crisp control. It was a delight to fish when I first tried it on the Brodheads.

Later that season, I fished the rod in northern Colorado, on a pretty river called the Little Snake. It winds lazily along the Wyoming border, its course circling under limestone bluffs and cottonwoods. It lies well off the paved roads, across a low pass between Saddle Pocket and Steamboat Springs. It is not a large river, even below its junction with Battle Creek, but it offers pleasant fishing and a surprising sense of history.

Its battle involved a party of fur trappers, including famous frontiersmen like Bridger and Meek, and a large force of Indians. The trappers were surrounded on a brushy island, but their weapons included Sharps buffalo guns mixed with a few Hawken and Creedmore rifles. Although they were surrounded, it was hardly a fair fight, given the marksmanship of the fur trappers.

Indian warriors were shot at extremely long ranges, and when their chief was literally exploded by a heavy-caliber buffalo round at several hundred yards, the war party stopped fighting.

Jeremiah Johnson wintered with his Indian wife along the Little Snake, building a comfortable dugout that looked south toward the river and its junction with Battle Creek. There is a still pool above its mouth today, at Saddle Pocket Ranch, where the fish rise greedily on late summer mornings to the swarms of *Tricorythodes* flies.

There is colorful outlaw history too. Butch Cassidy and his Wild Bunch often wintered at Brown's Hole on the Green. Their wanderings took them through most of these valleys in western Colorado and Wyoming; and across the Wyoming line, the explosive party held by the Wild Bunch in its old hotel was the high-water mark in the history of Baggs.

The first times I fished the Little Snake, I was on the Saddle Pocket water with Frank Meek, who operates a fishing shop at Steamboat Springs. Meek teaches courses on things as esoteric as *Finnegan's Wake* and *Ulysses* during the winters, although his family tree includes Joe Meek, the celebrated frontier trapper.

The river winds through the ranch in a series of small flats and pools. We never fished it together in the spring, with more water and better hatches. It was always difficult sport in late summer, with a hot sun on its arid September hills, and tiny flies hatching. But it still held a lot of fish, and a few good ones. The morning *Tricorythodes* swarms were dependable, but seldom produced large trout. Cloudy weather often triggered good hatches of little *Baetis* flies, and in the big flats above the ranch itself I took several sixteen- to eighteen-inch fish. The Big Bend downstream, its currents circling past large boulders and reflecting its high limestone bluffs, held such fish too. These trout were all selective, and it took tiny polywing spinners and duns and terrestrials to fool them, fishing 6 X and 7 X polyamide tippets. The experimental Phillips boron performed well, cushioning the fine tippets against setting the book and playing the fish. The boron performed better than the graphites I had fished at that point, in striking and playing trout on light gear, although the crisp stroke of the carbon-fiber rods makes them superb casting tools. The Phillips rod was a happy surprise.

I really like it, I told Phillips later. *It fishes like bamboo—I really like it.*

Congressman Pete McCloskey was in our party the third time I fished the Little Snake. We flew over from Steamboat Springs and landed at the Lidstone ranch, upstream from Saddle Pocket. It was pocket water, colder and with a steeper profile than the cottonwood pools downstream. It held few brown trout, mixing rainbows with some surprisingly large cutthroats. The day was hot and windy. The fish came greedily to a big Carpenter Ant fished wet, casting upstream into the pockets. The trees cast longer shadows across the river when I finally reached a bigger pocket under a fallen cottonwood.

It looked promising and I stopped fishing to study its problems. The best slick eddied tight against the roots. It was slipping into a late afternoon shadow, and I watched it several minutes.

There was a soft rise. *Looks like a good fish,* I thought. *Mark him down.* It rose again.

Several dark caddisflies were hopscotching over the water, mating and laying eggs. I changed the Ant to a dark sedge pattern, the slate-colored Hemingway Special. The fish sipped again, tight against the roots, and then porpoised almost lazily.

Good fish! I was getting excited.

The trout settled into steady feeding, and I made a tentative cast. Its line of drift circled too far from the roots. The second cast flirted with the shadows, bobbing under the roots, and the fly vanished. I tightened into a trout that bolted upstream and jumped.

Twenty inches! I guessed.

My guess was right, and the big cutthroat tested the three-weight Phillips to its limits. It bolted wildly again, probing stubbornly under the roots, and ran into the pockets downstream. The rod cushioned the delicate nylon, and it controlled the fish surprisingly well for a three-weight. Finally I netted the fish and released it, regretting that I carried no camera. It was a handsome native.

Pete McCloskey was sitting upstream, under a big cottonwood tree. The long flat there was completely in shadow, and a good fish rose steadily.

I'm dogging it, McCloskey explained. *Saved that rising fish for you.*

You try him, I suggested.

Already tried him, McCloskey laughed ruefully from the shade. *Show me what he'll take.*

I'll try, I said.

The trout was not as large as the fish I had just released downstream, but it was close. Its rises came steadily, too soft to suggest caddis activity unless it was on spent egg-laying sedges. Drowned *Baetis* spinners travel under the water to lay their eggs, creating a subsurface drift instead of a spinner fall, and were possible too.

The fish refused the sedge imitation that had worked before. Its rises were tiny bulges that came steadily. I tried a spent sedge pattern and the fish tipped up, inspecting it carefully. The fly drifted past its position untouched, and I retrieved it to try another.

Gary Borger sent me some small olive-bodied flies dressed with dun hen hackles several years ago, telling me they worked on such smutting fish. The pattern had worked for me during *Baetis* activity on many western streams, and I decided to try one. It was lightly dressed with dry-fly ointment, touching its hackles to get it to float slightly awash. The delicate tippet was free of casting knots, and finally I was ready again.

What're you trying now? McCloskey asked.

Junk pitches, I said.

The little nondescript fly fell gently into the right line of drift, and I lost it momentarily in the reflected light. The fish dimpled quietly, where I thought the fly might be, and I tightened.

The quiet pool erupted as the two-pound cutthroat threshed angrily, and bolted swiftly upstream. It had taken the Borger pattern.

Nice work! McCloskey called.

The delicate tactics that broke the code that September afternoon were methods that I had usually associated with expensive cane tapers specifically designed for such work. The Phillips three-weight boron had proved itself, and it is currently found in a fourteen-rod series:

MODEL	LENGTH (FEET)	WEIGHT (OUNCES)	LINE WEIGHT
SBP-160	6	$^3/_4$	2
SBP-260	6	1	4
SBP-370	7	$1^1/_4$	3
SBP-470	7	$1^1/_2$	4
SBP-575	$7^1/_2$	$1^3/_4$	3
SBP-675	$7^1/_2$	2	4
SBP-775	$7^1/_2$	$2^1/_4$	5
SBP-875	$7^1/_2$	$2^1/_2$	6
SBP-980	8	$2^3/_4$	3
SBP-1080	8	3	4

MODEL	LENGTH (FEET)	WEIGHT (OUNCES)	LINE WEIGHT
SBP-1180	8	3¼	5
SBP-1280	8	3½	6
SBP-1390	9	3¼	4
SBP-1490	9	3½	5

The Phillips rods are not tubular designs, but solid boron fabricated over a wire mandrel, which makes them much thinner than other manufacturers' rods, but also heavier, due to their density. The method has its obvious advantages; it also makes big rods for seven- and eight-weight lines impractical. Don Phillips understands his medium perfectly, and his excellent designs concentrate on slender rods for relatively light fly-lines.

Boron filaments are still costly and exotic.

The fabrication of such materials occurs at only two factories in the United States. Avco manufactures more than seventy percent of the total of American boron filament at its Lowell plant near Boston. Composite Technology Corporation produces virtually all of our other boron fibers at its Broad Brook facilities outside Hartford.

Few anglers understand the technology of materials behavior, and talk of such things as modulus of elasticity is familiar in strength-of-materials engineering but it baffles the fishing world.

The confusion has led many fishermen to assume that boron is substantially lighter than graphite, and that it is stronger and more sensitive. Boron is neither significantly stronger nor lighter than carbon fibers. Its alleged sensitivity is highly subjective. It is seemingly the result of connotations, rather than technical facts. Reams of copy have been written about the so-called sensitivity of both graphite and boron rods, but sensitivity is a term used to describe their quick response to stress. Both materials respond swiftly to stress, and their recovery is equally swift. But such character cannot be described in terms of sensitivity.

Poisson's ratio is familiar to all students who survive to reach the courses in mechanics, subjects usually taught in the sophomore year of any engineering curriculum. Statics, dynamics, and strength of materials are the subjects, and they teach a fledgling architect or engineer to employ mathematics in simulating the structural performance of their designs.

Modulus of elasticity lies at the root of Poisson's ratio. The stress performance of both graphite and boron are based on their singular modulus of elasticity. The modulus of any material is a measure of its ability to resist deformation, and its rate of recovery once deformed.

Modulus of elasticity in fishing rods has been slightly distorted in its meanings. It has come to describe their stiffness-to-weight ratios, their quickness, and their rate of recovery from stress.

Carbon fibers display a remarkable modulus of elasticity, offering as much as 50,000,000 pounds per square inch. Such performance is approx-imately seventeen times the modulus of fiberglass. Boron filaments offer a modulus of elasticity that is thirty percent higher still. But it is critical to understand that modulus of elasticity is relatively meaningless in fishing tackle until a material is translated into specific calibrations.

The important thing to know about boron filaments, explains Paul Goffman of the Avco Corporation, *is that they deliver more strength than our finest aircraft alloys at considerably less weight—and boron can take temperatures that could melt aluminum right off the air frame of high-performance aircraft.*

What about the boron stories? I asked.

You mean the horror stories?

That's right, I said.

The stories about exploding into microscopic particles? Goffman laughed and stared out across the old factories of Lowell. *And particles so toxic that we are forced to include a six-page warning pamphlet in every shipment we make?*

You've heard them too, I smiled.

It's difficult to know how such stories get started, Goffman said, *but it's just not true.*

What is true?

The myth of exploding comes from stories of its stiffness, he explained, *but boron is only thirty percent less elastic than graphite—and you've seen that we manufacture both at Lowell.*

What about toxicity?

Boron is mildly toxic, Goffman continued. *That's why it's used in some antiseptics, eyewashes, and astringents—but its toxicity is displayed only in large doses, extremely large doses.*

Boron fibers are not toxic?

Their chemistry is virtually inert, he said, *and the resins used in all tubular fishing rods—fiberglass and carbon fiber and boron alike—are more toxic than the rod materials themselves.*

Rodon Corporation uses the boron-filament tapes and fibers pro-duced at Avco, and it introduced a hybrid design that combined boron fibers over a carbon-fiber armature. Its designs include a surprising range of tapers, from smutting trout to muscular salt-water rods. There have been many opportunities to fish their rods in recent months, and the full inventory of two-piece trout models is the following:

MODEL	LENGTH (FEET)	WEIGHT (OUNCES)	LINE WEIGHT
T-2704	7	$1^{3}/_{4}$	3
T-2753	$7^{1}/_{2}$	$1^{7}/_{8}$	3
T-2804	8	2	4
T-2755	$7^{1}/_{2}$	$2^{5}/_{8}$	5
T-2806	8	$2^{7}/_{8}$	5
T-2855	$8^{1}/_{2}$	3	6

MODEL	LENGTH (FEET)	WEIGHT (OUNCES)	LINE WEIGHT
T-2906	9	$3^{1/4}$	6
T-2807	8	$3^{1/8}$	7
T-2857	$8^{1/2}$	$3^{1/2}$	6
T-2908	9	$3^{5/8}$	8
T-2957	$9^{1/2}$	$3^{3/4}$	8

Rodon has also introduced a series of three-piece trout models, which are intended to pack and travel conveniently:

MODEL	LENGTH (FEET)	WEIGHT (OUNCES)	LINE WEIGHT
T-3856	$8^{1/2}$	$3^{1/8}$	6
T-3906	9	$3^{1/2}$	7
T-3857	$8^{1/2}$	$3^{1/8}$	7
T-3908	9	$3^{3/4}$	8
T-3957	$9^{1/2}$	$3^{7/8}$	8

Travel also dictated the introduction of four-piece trout rods at Rodon:

MODEL	LENGTH (FEET)	WEIGHT (OUNCES)	LINE WEIGHT
T-4806	8	3	6
T-4857	$8^{1/2}$	$3^{3/4}$	7
T-4908	9	$4^{1/8}$	8

The first Rodon model that I field-tested was a prototype of their T-2804, with a cork-filler reverse-locking seat. It was eight feet long and weighed $1^{7/8}$ ounces, and I fished it with a four-weight double taper. It was relatively soft and slow, and it shocked easily when I forced a cast, sending a fluttering oscillation along the line. But it was not intended for tight-loop work. It was designed to work close and fine, and it performed its function perfectly.

Its baptism came on the upper Firehole, where it took several decent fish on small nymphs and dry flies, but it really proved its worth when I was fishing with Mike Lawson at Last Chance, on the Henry's Fork of the Snake.

You want to test a four-weight boron? Lawson asked. *You're in the right place tonight.*

We drove to the river and waited, studying the banks for particularly good fish. Clouds of egg-laying caddisflies gathered along the grassy

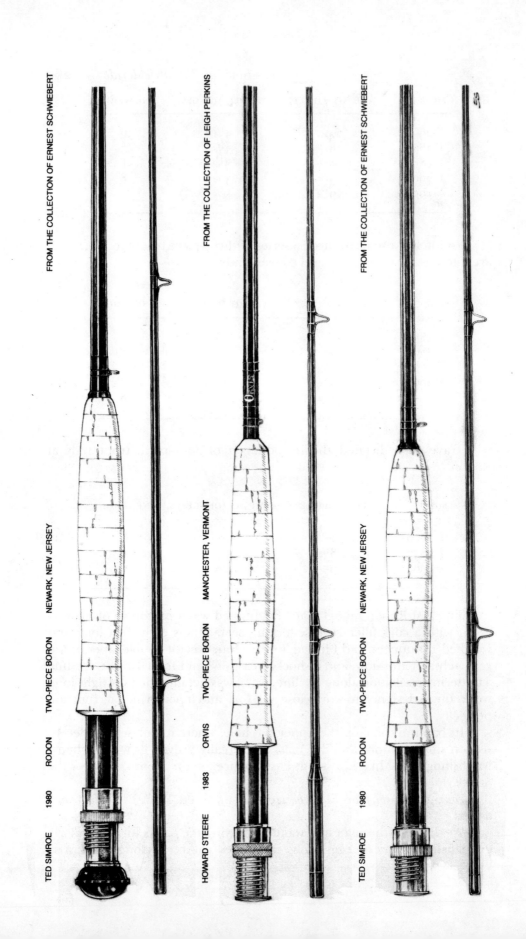

TED SIMROE   1980   RODON   TWO-PIECE BORON   NEWARK, NEW JERSEY   FROM THE COLLECTION OF ERNEST SCHWIEBERT

HOWARD STEERE   1983   ORVIS   TWO-PIECE BORON   MANCHESTER, VERMONT   FROM THE COLLECTION OF LEIGH PERKINS

TED SIMROE   1980   RODON   TWO-PIECE BORON   NEWARK, NEW JERSEY   FROM THE COLLECTION OF ERNEST SCHWIEBERT

margins of the stream, and the small fish were already working as we arrived. We leaned against the truck and waited.

There! Lawson breathed.

He pointed to a smooth current that flowed tight against the grass. Seconds passed before the big rainbow came softly again. Its rise was only a sucking bulge, but its disturbance sent small waves undulating downstream.

Good fish! I nodded.

Let's wait, Lawson suggested. *We should let him settle into a steady rhythm. And others might start working.*

Like that one?

Lawson chuckled when a bigger trout rose softly, fifteen feet upstream. Its rises were subtle. It rose in a lazy steeplechase roll, showing its dorsal fin and tail. It was a big trout, and it was soon rising steadily.

He's really a good fish! Lawson said excitedly. *But you'll have to try the little one first.*

Little one! I laughed.

He'll go four pounds, Lawson admitted, *but the other one's bigger—and you'll have to fish the lower guy first.*

It won't be easy, I said.

Try it.

I circled well below both fish and slipped carefully into the water. Sometimes careless wading can spook a fish at surprising distances. I worked very slowly upstream until I was about fifteen feet behind the lower fish. Both trout were rising steadily. The rises were so quiet that most fishermen would assume they were small fish. Getting close was critical. The undulating weeds and grassy banks spawn a nightmare of half-seen currents, and too much line will quickly drag the fly. The first cast fell short. The tiny spent sedge pattern dropped perfectly a few false casts later, and the big rainbow inhaled it softly.

He took it? I was surprised.

The big fish shook itself momentarily, and bolted past me into open water. *Would I give you the wrong fly?* Lawson chuckled. *And the other guy's still working.*

The little four-weight boron parried its stubborn fight until it finally surrendered. It went twenty-one inches. I unhooked the tiny sedge from its jaw and slipped it back into the current. The fragile 7X tippet was a tangle, its elasticity all spent from the fight, and I replaced it. Lawson had given me a half-dozen spent sedges with partridge wings, and I knotted a fresh fly to the tippet.

The other fish was still rising. *He won't be so easy,* Lawson observed quietly. *He's moving around a lot between rises—settling and moving again.*

Rainbows are like that.

The fish was obviously bigger. It was working a beat, rising steadily in a feeding zone about the size of a bathtub. It was covering several lines of drift. *You'll just have to keep casting until he sees it,* Lawson chuckled, *but don't line him!*

Casting as softly as possible, I kept dropping the tiny fly in the feeding zone. The fish was still working quietly. Once it brushed the drifting leader, and there was a sudden, nervous swirl.

Scared him, I thought unhappily.

But the big trout settled back quickly into its feeding rhythm. It was a piece of luck. I lost count of the casts it took, with hundreds of spent caddis in the film and the fish working back and forth. It was a matter of timing. The trout had a steady rhythm, and I kept trying to introduce the fly just ahead of its rise patterns.

And finally it took.

Its dark head pushed above the film and intercepted the tiny fly, and I tightened. The shallows erupted. The big rainbow bolted and wallowed up the narrow channel between the bank and the weeds. It circled back into open water and jumped, running my shrill Princess deep into its backing.

Bigger than we thought, Lawson said.

It fought hard, forcing us to follow it downstream. It measured twenty-three inches, and the boron rod cushioned its struggles perfectly, protecting the fragile leader. Lawson got his camera while I unhooked the fly to hold the fish high, head down in my net.

He's pretty fat, Lawson said excitedly. *Could go six pounds on the Henry's Fork—he's a lot bigger than his rises looked.*

But I hooked a bigger fish at nightfall. It was holding in a silken current downstream that still reflected the failing light. It was a short check-cast into the bright water, but it was impossible to see the fly. It was too small and floating away. It was guesswork, and I tightened gently each time the fish rose.

We were both surprised when I hooked it, feeling its weight. Its response was unsettling. It simply drifted downstream and sulked in the shallows, until I followed it and applied a steady pressure, with the twilight gathering swiftly. I was fishing a 5 X tippet and felt more secure. It rolled lazily, and catching the sunset sky it showed a dorsal and tail that made us both gasp.

That's some fish! Lawson laughed wryly, *but unless he feels some pressure, he might lie there all night—he might even swim back upstream and start feeding again!*

He's pretty big, I agreed.

It was getting darker, and the big rainbow just held there until some drifting weed collected on the leader. It seemed to annoy the fish. More weed touched the leader and caught. The trout started slowly downstream.

He's the biggest fish I've seen hooked on this river, Lawson was almost giggling.

The fish swam lazily with the river. My light reel was steadily emptied, just a step or two faster than we could follow in the waist-deep current.

You're in trouble, Lawson said.

We stumbled along for three hundred yards, with the boron rod straining and my backing nearly gone. The fish threshed on the surface far downstream. We crossed the main flow to follow. Lawson made it without trouble, but I stumbled and shipped a little water. The big fish circled back across the river. The entire line bellied and throbbed. The strain was finally too much, and the tippet parted. We stood laughing quietly in the darkness.

He was bored, I said.

Rodon first became involved in fishing tackle with its quality rod fittings. The company subsequently hired Ted Simroe, the master rodmaker at Leonard, to help expand its activities. Simroe has obviously made the transition from subtle split-bamboo construction to carbon fibers and boron-composite rods.

Working with Composite Development Corporation in California, which already had extensive experience with boron-composite shafts for golf clubs, Simroe experimented with rod specifications and construction. His solution was a composite design that placed longitudinal boron fibers on the surface of a light carbon-fiber armature.

We knew bamboo worked like that. Simroe recalls, *with its dense power fibers outside, and the pithy inside fibers only providing its gluing surfaces. We thought we might have something once we solved the problems of bonding the carbon fibers to the boron.*

The theory anticipated that moderate casting loads could be accommodated by the graphite core. Gradually increasing stresses would involve both the core and its boron shell. Maximum casting loads would be absorbed by the high-performance boron filaments.

Boron filaments have too much stiffness and memory to provide hoop strength in a tubular blank, Simroe explains, *and hoop-strength problems gave us trouble.*

What did you try? I asked.

The solution was both sophisticated and simple. Boron could not provide lateral hoop strength. Its fibers were too stiff to form around rod diameters, and could not cross or touch without damaging each other. Spiral boron wraps developed too much torque and twisting stress. Simroe ultimately decided to try forty-five-degree helical wraps of half-inch graphite tape around a mandrel in both directions. Boron filaments were laid longitudinally over the helical armature, and sandwiched in place with a longitudinal layer of carbon-fiber cloth and epoxy resins. Like other manufacturers, Rodon finally wrapped the freshly rolled blanks in a spirally wound shrink tape, and cured them in its ovens. The mandrel is later stripped free. The rod blanks are trimmed, the shrink tape is cut away, and the surface is polished. The Rodon composites use only ten to twenty percent boron in its sections, depending on the size of specific patterns and blanks.

Since tip diameters are too slender for the boron-fiber tapes, Simroe found that single boron filaments could be added by hand. However, their alignment must be symmetrical and precise, since the slightest error can result in eccentric bending and casting. Simroe also worked out a slim spigot-type ferrule, using a boron filament plug, and it has echoed Orvis in committing itself to high-quality machined fittings.

The finishes and aesthetic character of the Simroe rods are excellent, perhaps the most handsome of the boron designs yet made, owing a debt to the reverse-locking Hardy rods built just after the First World War. Such factors are more important to fly fishermen than many manufacturers seem to understand.

The Rodon T-3906 is a nine-foot rod designed for a six-weight line, and I have fished it extensively on both trout and salmon.

My first experience with a T-3906 came at a fishing exposition in New York. It seemed so smooth that I was eager to fish it later that year. Its first tests came in floats on the Madison and Yellowstone, throwing big salmon fly patterns in hours of lifting and casting. It is demanding work, more demanding than many wading anglers know, with its quick pickups and shots at passing targets. The T-3906 worked perfectly.

But what about delicate six-weight work? I thought after a float below Varney Bridge.

Bud Lilly first introduced me to the difficult fishing at Slow Bend, perhaps the finest dry-fly water on the Madison above West Yellowstone. It was a perfect challenge.

It has excellent early summer hatches each afternoon, particularly in cloudy weather, and its browns are quite selective. The fish see a lot of anglers. The flies come steadily, but on heavily fished stretches like the Slow Bend, the good fish rise only when the sun is off the water. Few trout work in sunny weather, but even a passing cumulus cloud can trigger a brief rise of fish. Such trout are a useful yardstick. Sometimes ninety-foot casts are needed, the fly hatches are small *Ephemerella* and *Baetis* duns, and twelve-foot leaders tapered to 6X are critical too.

The Simroe T-3906 performed well, taking fish to eighteen inches at such casting ranges, and with such terminal tackle. It offered a unique mix of delicacy and power, but its full capability was tested on salmon a month later in Iceland.

The summer had been unusually dry. The salmon were running well, but the low water had shrunk the number of fishable pools on the Grimsá to a handful. The salmon were so concentrated that fishing pressure had made them as skittish as hard-fished trout. The usual methods worked fitfully, and it was time to rethink our tactics. The conventional wet-fly techniques took a few salmon, and the greased-line method was fair, but we had still not broken the code. The riffling hitch actually seemed to frighten more fish than it teased into rising, although some fish actually took it well. Tube flies produced nothing, although they rolled a few curious salmon. It was time to try a six-weight rod and tiny flies, and trout-type leaders tapered to 4X.

Bob Buckmaster was fishing with me at the place called Oddstadarfljot when I tested my new theory, fishing a tiny Emerald Silk dressed on a size-ten double. Crawling along the gravel, like a late-summer fisherman stalking trout, I cast softly across a smooth holding-lie. The fly worked into its swing and stopped almost softly.

Fish! I called upstream.

I coaxed the salmon away from its holding water, keeping low while it came grudgingly downstream. Small flies and delicate equipment were the secret that week. The Simroe T-3906 hooked the salmon without breaking off, yet had the authority to play fish between five and twenty pounds. The tactics took four other fish from Oddstadarfljot, and I found Buckmaster behind me.

I don't know what you're doing, he laughed. *But you're not going anyplace until you tell me the secret!* We had broken the code, and Buckmaster bought two nine-foot boron rods that summer.

The past winter in New Zealand, I fished the rod on more than a dozen rivers on both islands, from Te Anau to Taupo. It performed well, stalking big trout in startlingly clear waters, mostly with dry flies and nymphs. It took a six-pound rainbow in the headwaters of the Greenstone, and a bigger dry-fly fish on the Worsley. The largest rainbow was a twelve-pound henfish that took a size-ten nymph at Rangeitiki, and cartwheeled in a swift fight that almost emptied the reel. It was as brightly polished as a summer steelhead, and its fight was explosive, But the ultimate test came at the Cliff Pool on the Wilkin, with five dry-fly rainbows between four and eight pounds. The best fish was a hundred feet out, rising steadily in the still current. The Simroe T-3906 delivered a soft cast at that range, and did not break off the 6X tippet when a pale eight-pound fish took my Royal Wulff.

When I got back, I called Ted Simroe to tell him about his T-3906 and the fishing. *That's some rod,* I teased drily. *Guess your computer got lucky.*

Fenwick introduced the first carbon-fiber rods in 1973, and its principal designer is still Jim Green, who is among the finest casters alive. Its line of graphite tackle has been highly successful, and has expanded to twelve excellent trout rods, but Fenwick quickly embraced boron. Its first prototypes were unveiled four years ago, at a fishing conclave in Spokane.

Jim Green stopped me in the exhibition hall. *We're playing with boron,* he said. *Tell me what you think.*

Green had experimental prototypes of his nine-footers, designed for five- and six-weight lines. The distinctive boron action was obvious. Both rods were a little slower than comparable graphite designs, but with a patient stroke they delivered effortless casts. The final Boron-X designs were added to the Fenwick trout rods:

MODEL	LENGTH (FEET)	WEIGHT (OUNCES)	LINE WEIGHT
XF-755	$7^{1/2}$	$2^{3/4}$	5
XF-806	8	3	6
XF-856	$8^{1/2}$	$3^{1/8}$	6

MODEL	LENGTH (FEET)	WEIGHT (OUNCES)	LINE WEIGHT
XF-857	$8^1/2$	$3^1/8$	7
XF-858	$8^1/2$	$3^1/4$	8
XF-905	9	$3^1/8$	5
XF-906	9	$3^1/4$	6
XF-908	9	$3^1/2$	8

Orvis has also added a series of excellent boron rods to its lists. The trout models in its Powerflex series are composite designs, employing sixty percent boron filaments and forty percent carbon-fiber cloth. Its structure offers a higher percentage of boron filaments, giving its Powerflex designs surprising smoothness and power, although the concept is best suited to the heavier line-weight specifications. Orvis quality is obvious in these new boron rods, and these trout-fishing models are in the Powerflex line:

MODEL	LENGTH (FEET)	WEIGHT (OUNCES)	LINE WEIGHT
JM9483-1	$8^1/4$	$3^1/4$	7
JM9485-1	$8^1/2$	$3^3/8$	6
JM9486-1	$8^1/2$	$3^5/8$	8
JM9486-31	$8^1/2$	4	8
JM9489-1	$8^3/4$	$3^3/4$	8
JM9490-1	9	4	9
JM9490-31	9	$4^5/8$	9

Browning also started its development program with hybrid concepts using both boron and carbon-fiber composites. Its early rods were eighty percent boron and twenty percent graphite, like the Orvis rods for tarpon fishing. The first prototypes had problems, and were never placed in production. Browning retooled to try a one hundred percent boron structure over a thin fiberglass backing that provides lateral hoop strength. The blanks are formed on a conventional mandrel, but the Browning method of curing is unique.

Its freshly wrapped blanks are sheathed in a tightly fitted rubber sleeve, without a spiral shrink-tape covering, and pressure cured in a steam-heated autoclave. The freshly cured blanks are stripped from the rubber sleeves, polished, and finished in a handsome brown urethane. Browning builds only three rods. Its seven-and-a-half-foot model weighs two-and-a-half ounces, and is rated for a five-weight line. The eight-footer weighs three ounces and is rated for a six-weight. The Browning rods are less expensive, like the Lake King and Shakespeare series, but some fishermen have faulted their workmanship and fittings. Grip finishes are roughly worked on many rods, and their shapes vary surprisingly. The ferrules are big and clumsy and, like the anodized reel-seat fittings, seem better suited to cheaper materials. But Browning has pioneered a bold technique for fabricating blanks almost entirely of boron, and its methods offer great promise.

Ron Kusse is producing an elegantly fitted and finished line of boron-fiber rods. German-silver fittings are standard. Fully machined ferrules or spigot-type ferrules are available options, and shotgun-quality hardwood fillers are specified in reel seats. The Kusse boron rods are produced in the following models:

MODEL	LENGTH (FEET)	WEIGHT (OUNCES)	LINE WEIGHT
KBG-603	6	1	3
KBG-664	$6\frac{1}{2}$	$1\frac{1}{8}$	4
KBG-704	7	$1\frac{1}{4}$	4
KBG-705	7	$1\frac{1}{2}$	5
KBG-763	$7\frac{1}{2}$	$1\frac{1}{4}$	3
KBG-764	$7\frac{1}{2}$	$1\frac{3}{8}$	4
KBG-765	$7\frac{1}{2}$	2	5
KBG-804	8	$2\frac{1}{8}$	4
KBG-805	8	$2\frac{1}{4}$	5
KBG-806	8	$2\frac{1}{2}$	6
KBG-865	$8\frac{1}{2}$	$2\frac{3}{4}$	5
KBG-866	$8\frac{1}{2}$	$3\frac{1}{4}$	6
KBG-867	$8\frac{1}{2}$	$3\frac{1}{2}$	7
KBG-868	$8\frac{1}{2}$	$3\frac{3}{4}$	8
BKG-906	9	$3\frac{1}{2}$	6
KBG-908	9	4	8

Boron is not best for everything. Ted Simroe admits readily. *Fly-rod action is a pretty personal thing—but all things considered, we're really excited about the character of boron rods.*

Temperament and personality traits in fishermen are important factors in rod performance. Some anglers display the same restless and aggressive character they bring to their work, are probably most suited to slower tapers, and can master the more difficult timing involved in a slower casting stroke.

It's not just the material, Simroe adds. *It's tapers and calibrations and wall thickness too—it's not just the boron itself.*

Stiff rods with a fast casting stroke are perfectly designed for the tight-loop work needed in distance casting and wind. Such character is also suited to shooting-taper technique, and a sharply executed left-hand haul can flutter a softer rod. The carbon-fiber rods, and the stiff boron designs made by Orvis and Fenwick and Rodon, are outstanding in such techniques. The stiffer tapers will not flutter in tight-loop casts, with a strong double haul, and are capable of fishing distances beyond our past daydreams. Wind is less troublesome too. Such rods will increase tip-speed for all of us, no matter how skillfully we cast, and distance will improve. But neither graphite nor boron will cure our poor casting habits.

These rods won't solve our problems, Lefty Kreh wryly pinpoints the trouble with most casters. *They just make our mistakes happen faster—and farther away!*

Slow-action boron tapers have a more demanding casting stroke, in terms of their deliberate casting rhythms, but they are ideally suited to the open-loop techniques associated with long fine-tippet leaders and tiny flies. Many of the boron and boron-composite tapers I have field-tested in the past several years have been excellent examples of such slow-action boron designs.

Some of the fast-action graphites I have fished are first-rate casting tapers, but have proved a little harsh in striking and playing fish. Their fast-stroke tapers respond almost too quickly to stress. Such performance is designed for casting loads, but it can break off fine tippets in striking, particularly in average hands. Similar problems can occur with big head-shaking fish, tearing out hooks and shearing a leader.

Earlier tapers of fiberglass and bamboo tend to dampen such impact loads. Considerable fishing time with the trout-size Phillips, Fenwick, and Rodon models suggests that boron responds to impact stresses with a subtle dampening effect that rivals the finest bamboo.

Since considerable casting energy is expended in merely slicing through the atmosphere, with both a working line and the rod itself, graphite and boron offer obvious advantages.

The diameters of rods made of these fibers are much thinner than comparable actions in fiberglass and cane. The boron systems of the Browning rods are thinner than other tubular blanks, and the Phillips construction techniques produce the thinnest rods made. Less atmospheric drag is unmistakably less effort. Our casting goes better on hot days and at higher altitudes, because the atmosphere there is less dense. Since a thinner rod means less casting effort is expended in penetrating atmospheric density, higher line speeds and distance are possible with less muscle.

Sometimes we get too caught up in casting, Simroe wisely points out. *Distance casting is always more dramatic—and we forget that delicate presentation, striking fish without breaking off, and controlling the struggles of a strong fish— these things are just as important as casting.*

Boron is not cheap. Its crystalline fibers are more than eight times the price of graphite, and forty times the cost of fiberglass. The prices of finished rods vary widely, depending on the quantity of boron fibers used in their construction, and the quality of their fittings. Boron is expensive, and it deserves fittings, grip quality, designs, and finishes normally associated with the tradition of split bamboo.

Testing boron rods included a late run of bright Chinook salmon on the Pere Marquette in Michigan, where I fished a nine-and-a-half-foot Simroe fitted with a ten-weight line and a Hardy Perfect.

It was a challenge.

October squalls had stripped the hardwoods of their color, and the summer cottages on the river were boarded up for the winter. The small Michigan towns were crowded with hunters, and there was an occasional shot from the clay-bank benches above the Pere Marquette.

The river was relatively low in the fly-only water above Bowman's Bridge, with bright leaves drifting through its shoals of salmon.

It seemed like I had the river to myself. There were so many fish in the shallows at Deer Lick and Whinnery's that I hunted them visually, fishing bright-bodied Comets on a floating line. It was possible to cast to specific fish, mending the fly into their faces. Several hook-ups stripped the Perfect deep into the backing, and I stumbled downstream in pursuit. Strong fish literally burned my fingers on the line. There was a stubborn twenty-pound henfish that took me almost to Waddell's before I beached it in the shallows.

Walking back upstream, I spotted several Chinooks in a gravelly pocket along the logs. Three were dark cockfish, already purplish with spawning color, but a brace of silvery hens lay slightly upstream. Their backs were spotted and pale olive. The henfish looked fresh run, and I stripped line and cast. The yellow-hackled Comet drifted toward both fish, ticking gently against the gravel, and I was astonished when the bigger hen yawned.

It took my fly softly.

My tongue still tasted like old pennies from chasing the last salmon downstream. And my feet ached from hours of October wading. The big fish held quietly a few moments, and suddenly ran a hundred yards downstream.

I'm not sure I need another one just yet, I thought, *and this one's bigger.*

It looked thirty pounds. It bolted past me through the shallows, its back showing above the water, throwing rooster tails of spray.

It turned back and wallowed through the riffles, reaching the stronger currents under the trees. The big hen jumped twice, forty yards downstream, writhing into the sun and falling back clumsily. It thrashed wildly and stopped, and I fought to recover backing.

Finally it seemed beaten.

Circling me stubbornly with great strength, the nail knot well into the guides, it refused to surrender. It looked strong and huge. Its thick, spotted back was mostly above water, and I failed to force it on its side. There was no beach and I had to tail the big henfish in open water. Each time I forced its head upstream and circled behind it, it bolted again and stripped out line. Each time I forced it back patiently, until my arms ached into my back muscles. Its final explosion almost broke it free.

The Chinook bolted past my legs, the leader deep into the guides again, and nearly brought me to my knees. It showered me with water. Its strength literally raked the tip guide through the stones.

She's still not beaten, I thought.

But the fish was almost spent, and I tailed it and wrestled its gleaming length ashore. Its gill covers were working as I laid it along a mossy log, and pushed the brightly hackled fly free.

The tip guide was flattened and bent back at an acute angle along the rod, but the boron tip had not shattered. The stress the big Chinook had placed on the rod was fierce, particularly in the butt section, when I was pumping and reeling. The fish was still alive.

The wintry chill was settling along the river when I carried it back gently. Its gills were working strongly as I held its graceful head into the flow. The October river was alive with salmon and brightly colored leaves. Cockfish were quarreling in the shallows, churning the swift currents, and I watched the big henfish drift back into the shadows with a sense of awe.

INDEX